Cum F
of the Homestead Grays

ALSO BY JAMES E. OVERMYER

Black Ball and the Boardwalk: The Bacharach Giants of Atlantic City, 1916–1929 (McFarland, 2014)

Cum Posey
of the Homestead Grays

A Biography of the Negro Leagues Owner and Hall of Famer

JAMES E. OVERMYER

McFarland & Company, Inc., Publishers

Jefferson, North Carolina

Library of Congress Cataloguing-in-Publication Data

Names: Overmyer, James, author.
Title: Cum Posey of the Homestead Grays : a biography of the Negro
League's owner and hall of famer / James E. Overmyer.
Description: Jefferson, North Carolina : McFarland & Company, Inc.,
Publishers, 2020 | Includes bibliographical references and index.
Identifiers: LCCN 2019055236 | ISBN 9781476663944 (paperback :
acid free paper) ∞ | ISBN 9781476634845 (ebook)
Subjects: LCSH: Posey, Cum, 1890–1946. | Baseball players—United
States—Biography. | Baseball team owners—United States—Biography. |
Homestead Grays (Baseball team)—History.
Classification: LCC GV865.P677 O84 2020 | DDC 796.357092 [B]—dc23
LC record available at https://lccn.loc.gov/2019055236

British Library cataloguing data are available

ISBN (print) 978-1-4766-6394-4
ISBN (ebook) 978-1-4766-3484-5

On the cover: Portrait of Cum Posey, 18" × 13", watercolor on paper by
Dick Perez *(www.dickperez.com)*

Printed in the United States of America

McFarland & Company, Inc., Publishers
Box 611, Jefferson, North Carolina 28640
www.mcfarlandpub.com

For Ellen and Matt

Table of Contents

Preface

Given his remarkable qualifications, it took an awfully long time for Cumberland W. Posey, Jr., to make it into the National Baseball Hall of Fame. The unusual trajectory of Negro League baseball—after peaking at the end of World War II, it declined as Organized Baseball integrated in the late 1940s and 1950s, then vanished by the early 1960s—served to stifle interest in its history. Then it began to be appreciated again in the 1970s.

Proof that the Negro Leaguers had arrived, however belatedly, in mainstream baseball's consciousness was their inclusion in the Hall of Fame, beginning in 1971. But for many years after that the black baseball election process continued to focus on the large backlog of eligible players, for good reason— they are the focus of the fans who follow any sport. In the first 30 years of Negro League elections to the Hall the 18 men enshrined included only one executive. That man, Andrew "Rube" Foster, had been a team owner and the president of the first successful black league. But in his younger days he had also been a star pitcher and field manager, accomplishments that by themselves might have gotten him elected.

Few black baseball executives have made it to Cooperstown alongside Foster, and their general absence is conspicuous when compared to the number of their white counterparts already enshrined. Consider that the first three Hall of Fame classes, from 1936 through 1938, inducted 16 men (all, of course, white) among whom were five honored for their off-the-field contributions. By 2006, when the Hall asked a special committee to consider the election of more people for the bygone world of black baseball, there was a significant backlog of qualified Negro League executives. The committee, of which I was a member, elected 17, including four team owners. Cum Posey was one of the four.

Posey, a native of the Pittsburgh area, where organized sports were a dominant part of social life in the early 1900s, had team-building acumen that outstripped most of his contemporaries. In his early twenties he played outfield for a local black team, the Grays, from his hometown of Homestead,

1

becoming the driving force behind the squad as it became one of the dominant semi-professional teams in the area. Before long, he began to book the
Grays' games. Loading the team into touring cars to roam Western Pennsylvania, Eastern Ohio, and West Virginia, Posey marketed the Grays as an
opponent that could draw multitudes of fans to local ballparks.

By the early 1930s he had upgraded the Grays to one of black baseball's
elite franchises. Homestead dominated the Negro National League, one of two
black major leagues, reeling off nine straight pennant-winning years between
1937 and 1945. When he wasn't overseeing the Grays' progress, Posey spent
eight years as an officer of the Negro National League. When he wasn't doing
that, he served for 13 years as a member of the school board in Homestead, the
first black elected to that position. He also wrote a semi-regular sports column
for a major African American weekly newspaper, the *Pittsburgh Courier*.

These last accomplishments came after his prime as an athlete, when he
was regarded as one of the best, if not *the* best, black basketball players in
the East and organized a team that was the consensus national black champions for five years running. All of this earned him a rare tribute among
sports figures—10 years after his election to the baseball Hall of Fame he
became a member of the Naismith Memorial Basketball Hall of Fame, one
of only two people to enter a pair of professional sports halls.

Sports executives for black teams from the segregated era (before 1946,
essentially) deserve biographies. It was their money and entrepreneurial drive
that launched the teams, after all. But a big drawback to research is that many
of them were little heard from, at least in public. The black sportswriters,
their newspapers providing only weekly platforms for their work, tended to
use their ink on the actual sporting events and the athletes they covered. This
was not a problem for Cumberland Posey. His newspaper columns and the
additional pieces he wrote for the *Courier* on historical and contemporary
black baseball essentially stand in for interviews (albeit ones in which he fed
himself the questions). The columns, in which Posey was alternatively
informative about current events in black sports and pointed in his commentary on the state of the business, provide a depth to his views and personality unavailable to us from most of his peers.

Posey possessed a strong sense of himself, and rarely admitted he was
wrong about anything, at least in public. Among other black sports executives
of his day he was certainly respected and often admired, but he was seldom
beloved. By and large, though, players wanted to play for the Grays—except
for a few desperate years in the depths of the Great Depression, Posey had
the reputation of always paying his players on time and giving raises to the
deserving. This could not be said for all of his fellow owners.

He was an unapologetic combination of a "race man," an African American who stood up for the rights of black people, and an entrepreneur driven to be successful. After facing the prospect of financial ruin during the Depression, when he had just managed to shepherd the Grays through to better times, he had no intention of becoming a man without means again, even if his determination sometimes conflicted a little with his racial beliefs. Overall, though, the ascendancy of his Homestead Grays from hometown team to national power spoke volumes about Posey's ability and determination.

In researching Posey's life, I began with the work of Rob Ruck, a professor of history at the University of Pittsburgh. In 1987 he published a comprehensive study of African American sport in Pittsburgh, *Sandlot Seasons*, a book anyone interested in the subject ought to use as a starting point. In addition, his interviews for the book are available through the University of Pittsburgh library system's Archives and Special Collections office. Ruck, another member of the special Hall of Fame committee that elected Posey and 16 other black baseball figures, was also generous with his time and knowledge as I sent him many queries during my work.

As a group, Negro League historians and researchers are always glad to help a colleague with work. As I have done so many times, I turned to Larry Lester, the chair of the Society for American Baseball Research's Negro Leagues Committee, and he provided both research assistance and access to photographs for the book. The Negro Leagues did not maintain the sort of detailed statistical services to which followers of Major League Baseball are accustomed, and work goes on even today to mine old newspaper game accounts and box scores to recreate player stats. The work of Gary Ashwill and others for the Seamheads.com Negro Leagues Database lent important statistical context to the story of the Grays nine-year pennant run. Another writer and researcher, Doron "Duke" Goldman, was of great help when it came to Posey's relationships with fellow Negro League owners.

Pittsburgh has many repositories of historical material, and I was aided greatly by the staffs at the Detre Library and Archives at the John Heinz History Center, the Carnegie Library of Pittsburgh, the Carnegie Library of Homestead, and the Department of Court Records of the Allegheny County court system. In tracking the higher education records of members of the Poseys, a family that prized education, there was help from registrar and archives offices at Duquesne University, the University of Pittsburgh, and the California University of Pennsylvania. And, as ever, staff at the National Baseball Hall of Fame's library stepped up to assist me.

Tracking the daily fortunes of Negro League teams through historical files of daily newspapers can often be frustrating, as the white dailies in some cities did little, if any, reporting on black teams playing in their circulation areas. This, thankfully, was not the case in Pittsburgh, where the local papers— the *Daily Post*, the *Press*, and the *Post-Gazette*—covered Posey's sports ventures, especially the Grays, thoroughly.

Chapter One

A Son of Old Pittsburgh,
with a New Idea

As businessmen, educators, craftsmen, teamsters and laborers, generations of blacks helped to establish the city of Pittsburgh and its surrounding communities. But none of them made a mark like Cumberland W. Posey, Jr., did with his sports dynasties. He came along in the early twentieth century, when organized sports, particularly for African Americans, were mostly an informal affair, one in which even the best players might earn no more than a few dollars a game and often played just for the fun of it. Posey helped change that. His teams were designed for fame and, as time went on, for fortune. Playing for Posey gave athletes a shot at being well known on a national stage. It did the same for Posey, too, eventually making him one of only two people ever elected to two professional sports halls of fame.

African Americans have lived in Pittsburgh since Europeans settled the place as a frontier village in the eighteenth century. Four free blacks were among 742 signers of a petition in 1788 to have the area including what became the city organized as its own county, to be named Allegheny. In the hundred years that followed the signing of the petition the wealth of natural resources in this area located on excellent water routes (the Allegheny and Monongahela Rivers meet and form the Ohio there) had made it and its surrounding area a major manufacturing center. Coal mined in the region fired hearths that burned around the clock and iron, brass, tin, and glass were produced by the tons. Then a native Scot, Andrew Carnegie, commissioned a giant mill on the Monongahela that used the Bessemer process to make steel that was not only superior in quality but could be made more cheaply and in larger batches. Pittsburgh's reign as an Iron City was over. It was now a Steel City. It was also in the process of becoming a big city, thanks to the influx of immigrants needed to work in the big mills. Allegheny County's population of 355,000 in 1880 had more than doubled when the new century rolled around.

The African American population, swelled by blacks from the South, also grew as the city became a major manufacturing center. As in the case of the immigrants from other countries, the mills were responsible for this growth, since many blacks from the South were familiar with metal production from work in foundry cities such as Richmond, Virginia, and Birmingham, Alabama. African Americans, though, remained a small portion of the county's residents, their share reaching only 2.4 percent, or 13,501 persons, by 1890. (The black population, consistent with the rest of the growth in the county, had more than doubled by 1900.)[1] The immigrant black worker could expect to make more money than in the place he or she had come from. A 1915 study of 500 black migrants showed that many of them had, relatively speaking, substantially increased their income: 62 percent made from two to three dollars a day in Pittsburgh, while 56 percent of them had made less than two dollars at home.[2] They would likely earn their pay doing common labor, often in the mills. Another study, in 1900, showed nearly 60 percent of Southern-born blacks worked as unskilled laborers (although the percentage of European immigrants doing that level of work was even greater).[3]

The newcomers were overlaid on the existing black population, which had been creating its own culture for 100 years, working in the seams of a larger culture permeated by white privilege. Pittsburgh is only 50 miles north of the Mason-Dixon Line, the famous boundary separating pre–Civil War slave and free states. While slavery had been phased out in Pennsylvania in the early 1800s, the black community experienced ingrained discrimination, including at work in the era before the big steel mills. "Racial discrimination excluded its men from the industrial and commercial mainstream of the city's economy," writes Laurence Glasco. "Barbering was the most prestigious occupation open to blacks.... Most, however, could find work only as day laborers, whitewashers, janitors, porters, coachmen, waiters, and stewards."[4]

The hilly topography of Pittsburgh and its adjacent boroughs worked against the formation of a concentrated black community such as in Harlem in New York or Bronzeville in Chicago. The black population, like many white ethnic groups, tended to cluster together in scattered pockets, although the Wylie Avenue area in Pittsburgh, part of which was early on known as Little Hayti, was primarily, although not exclusively, African American. This cost the black population dearly in terms of political influence, since they could not dominate the voting in any of the city's political wards. It was said that white politicians always attended to the needs of their black constituents for electoral purposes, although the promised improvements in their life never seemed to materialize. Black pupils were excluded from the city's schools, for example, except for a second-rate institution that was closed in favor of integrated schooling only after parents refused to send their children there in 1875.[5]

This showed that the African American community wasn't without influence, despite the inability of blacks to attain power at city hall. A later observer, writing on behalf of the Federal Writers' Project, noted that "Negro life in Pittsburgh as elsewhere is highly organized, in the church, fraternal and secret societies, civic and social clubs ... a people, unable to participate sufficiently in the general political and social structure, through these organizations can exert among themselves those powers denied elsewhere." The families who had lived in the city from before the Civil War represented "what is now called Old Pittsburgh ... an aristocracy based on decency, honesty and clean living."[6] Old Pittsburgh members cherished the social status granted by their longevity and relatively comfortable economic situation, as compared to that of the increasing number of black migrants arriving to work in the steel mills and other manufacturing plants as the twentieth century dawned.

In *The Pittsburgh Survey*, educator and social worker Helen A. Tucker, assigned to report on the African American community, focused on an upper-class businessman, notable for his long string of successes, whom she described in detail but did not name:

> One of the most successful Negro business men lives in Homestead [a borough south of Pittsburgh proper]. As a small boy he moved from Virginia to Ohio, and came to Homestead in 1879. Up to 1890 he was an engineer on the river, the only Negro to hold a chief engineer's license. Then he went into boat building and built twenty-one river steamboats. Five years ago he organized the Diamond Coke and Coal Company in which he is now master of transportation. There are ten men in this company, the others are white. They own a mine, docks, and steamboats, and employ about a thousand men. This colored man owns considerable property. He lives in a large comfortable house and owns one on either side which he rents.... His younger son was captain of the Homestead High School football team.[7]

The unnamed businessman was Cumberland W. Posey, a major figure in the mining and riverboat businesses that fed the giant steel mills. Posey, the businessman, crossed into the white-dominated Pittsburgh business world, which valued the ability to make money over the color of a man's skin, at least if the man could make enough of it for himself and his Caucasian associates. That crossing over was impossible in the city's social world, but Posey was a well-known leader in the African American "Old Pittsburgh" community, and his name is still locally prominent.

The football-playing son, Cumberland, Jr., was a halfback and scoring star of that Homestead High team. After taking only a little time to figure out his future he made sports, particularly baseball and basketball, his life.

Residence of Captain C. W. Posey.

Posey grew up in this spacious, two-story Victorian home built by his parents around the turn of the twentieth century, when his father was well established in the boat and coal businesses and the Poseys were upwardly mobile (Pennsylvania Negro Business Directory).

Unlike his strictly locally famous father, the son became known throughout the professional sports world. But on the national stage professional sports were rigidly segregated, and there was no opportunity for ability to trump race. So Posey Junior would play, manage, and own teams in the Negro section of the sports world, the one outside the center ring. He was a superb athlete and an even better organizer and businessman, and in the end he got his due.

Born June 20, 1890, when the family had settled in Homestead but hadn't yet moved into that large, comfortable home that Helen Tucker described, the younger Posey was talented across the board. He was a natural athlete, playing baseball and basketball at the schoolboy, college, and professional levels and starring in football in high school and as a semi-professional. By the time he was in his mid–20s he was showing an aptitude for organization that put him in charge of black basketball and baseball teams in Pittsburgh that he then built into nationally known powerhouses. By his early 40s he had become a local elected official and a national figure in the African American wing of the Elks fraternal organization. As an elected Homestead officer his specialties were education and looking out for the welfare of his fellow black residents. He could write, too. From 1925 through 1945 he wrote a periodic sports column for the *Pittsburgh Courier*, the major African American weekly, in a straightforward style that allowed him to express one of his most notable personal characteristics, which was that he had great confidence in his views no matter the issue, and had no qualms about expressing his certitude. The guy with the authoritatively jutting jaw he saw in the mirror when he shaved each morning may have been the only person with whom he always publicly agreed.

The traits of a successful individual can't always be traced to parents and family upbringing, but in Posey's case all of the qualities that made him exceptional, other than, so far as is known, his athletic ability, were parental traits, too.

Cumberland Willis Posey, Sr., was born in 1858 outside Port Tobacco, Maryland (not Virginia, as Tucker had stated), at the time a small but active Chesapeake Bay port community. His parents were Alexander and Elizabeth Willis Posey.[8] Elizabeth died a few years later and Alexander, who had become a minister in the African Methodist Episcopal Church, reportedly moved to the town of Belpre on the Ohio River in southeast Ohio, before relocating to Winchester, Virginia, in 1870 with a new wife, Margaret.[9] By the time Cumberland was a man he was making his living on the Ohio River. The 980-mile waterway had served as the main transportation route from its source in Pittsburgh to the Mississippi at Cairo, Illinois, for much of the nineteenth century and was still a major freight thoroughfare after the rise of the railroads.

There are alternative versions of Posey's first job as a riverman. One is that he was a deck sweeper and laborer on a ferry providing local transportation in the area around Belpre and its cross-river

Cumberland W. Posey, Sr., rose from deckhand on the Ohio River to head of his own boat-building company and a partner in companies that mined and delivered coal to the major steel mills in Pittsburgh (Pennsylvania Negro Business Directory).

neighbor, Parkersburg, West Virginia.[10] The other has him working on a large riverboat, the Magnolia, out of Belpre.[11] Alexander, in addition to preaching, is said to have worked as a household helper for a large riverboat owner, which could have given Cumberland entrée to that world. He could have held both of the jobs, on both the ferry shuttle and big boat, in one order or the other. In any case, he soon became fascinated with the boats' engines. His 1925 front page obituary in the *Courier* says that while a deckhand on the ferry "he took an interest in the machinery of the small vessel and began to study engineering," more than likely mostly on his own.[12] He moved up to become the hands-on crew member in charge of the steam engine on a boat based downriver out of Cincinnati, and then took steps to leave the deckhand ranks and become a licensed steamboat engineer. He was licensed as a second engineer and then as a chief engineer, the latter entitling Posey to be called "Captain"

Anna Stevens Posey, Cum's mother, was one of the social leaders among Pittsburgh African American women, and proved to be a good hand with a pistol when thieves attacked her husband (Pennsylvania Negro Business Directory).

among the rivermen, and he was referred to by his title as much as by his Christian name as he rose in the area's business community. He achieved this high rank despite "much opposition on account of his color"; it was one of the last times that a racial barrier would stand in the way of his considerable success.[13] As a chief engineer he worked for 14 years for Seward Hayes, a Pittsburgh-based captain who owned several boats. The relationship was clearly a good one for Posey: He named his first son, born in 1887, after his boss.

The details of the elder Posey's courtship of Angeline (Anna) Stevens have been lost to history, but his presence in Belpre put him not too far from her family's home outside Athens, the home of Ohio University, 35 miles inland from the river. Although the area surrounding Athens was still primarily agricultural, Anna's father Acquillah worked as a railroad laborer and a stone-cutter. The neighborhood in which the Stevenses lived was predominantly white, as was the whole town. The Stevenses were very light-complexioned Negroes, which might have allowed them to fit in more easily, although it appears that race was not as limiting an issue in the Athens community as elsewhere. It certainly was not a bar in education, as the small minority of black children attended the public schools along with the white youngsters. Anna may have been the first black graduate of the local high school, but thorough research in Ohio has debunked the later claim that she was the first black graduate of Ohio State University.[14]

Anna's race was no issue in 1879, either, when at age 18 she became a licensed teacher in the local schools. A local newspaper reporter in 1882 noted that her employment to teach white students marked "progress in the march of events." What's more, the writer added, "As a teacher she possesses rare tact and efficiency and her services in this line have been in wide demand."[15] But Anna was not to be a school teacher for long. She married Posey in May 1883 before a magistrate at the Athens County courthouse.

By 1885, when their first child, Beatrice, was born, the Poseys had moved to the Pittsburgh area. An 1890 city directory found them in Homestead, where the family lived for decades. Prior to 1880 Homestead lived up to its bucolic name by being a prosperous, primarily farming community. But a glassworks opened then, and farmland along the Monongahela gave way to industry. In 1883 the steel tycoon Carnegie bought out the struggling owners of a modern steel mill, a deal that changed the place forever. "In less than a decade," writes William Serrin, "Carnegie would transform the Homestead Works into the most advanced, versatile mill in the nation, and one of the most profitable mills as well. By 1890, it would be known around the world and looked upon with awe by steelmen."[16] But in 1892 the Works became infamous as the site of a steelworkers' strike that turned violent and remains one of the bloodiest labor actions in U.S. labor history. Although the need for millworkers brought in immigrants of many racial and ethnic groups, when Cumberland, Jr., was born in 1890 Homestead was almost entirely white. The 134 blacks found in the 1890 Census were less than two percent of the population.[17]

The Posey family's first residence was in the eastern part of the borough (a Pennsylvania municipality that elsewhere would be called a town), at Harden Station on the Pittsburgh, Virginia and Charleston Railroad (PV&C), a part of the Pennsylvania Railroad system. The PV&C was a key industrial link for the coal fields to the east, the growing industrial behemoths along the Monongahela River, and Pittsburgh itself. The railroad ran close to the river at Harden Station, and the Posey's next home, on Second Street, was also near the water. Cumberland, Sr., was still primarily a riverman, and he could dock his boat at the foot of McClure Street, a major thoroughfare that ended at the river, and walk home after work.[18]

Soon, however, the Poseys rose in Homestead, not just figuratively, because of the Captain's business success and Anna's leadership in the black social world. The topography of Homestead, on the south bank of the Monongahela River across from the Brown's Hill section of Pittsburgh, elevates steadily to the south for more than a mile inland. At the turn of the twentieth century the Homestead Steel Works sprawled at the bottom of the slope, along the river. Closest to the river past the Works was lower-rent housing where newcomers, including the Poseys at first, tended to congregate, and where, since Homestead was something of a rough and tumble industrial

The Homestead Steel Works shortly after the turn of the twentieth century, when it dominated the landscape and the economy of Homestead. Part of the "Lower Wards" area where most mill workers lived is in the foreground. The Monongahela River is barely visible in the background behind the ever-present smoke (Library of Congress).

town, the town had "one of the greatest, gaudiest sin strips in America."[19] The east-west streets were numbered, going uphill from the river. Eighth Street, just above the railroad, was the main commercial street. Residential streets climbed the steep slopes from there, dominated by single-family homes, parks, schools, churches, and the big brick town library, an early gift of Carnegie's enormous program that built 2,500 community libraries around the world.

Just before the turn of the century the Captain and Anna and their three children had moved up to this neighborhood, into a spacious, decorative, two-story Victorian home at 320 East 13th Avenue, well above the downtown fray by the river. Thomas Ewell, a black journalist profiling the Old Pittsburgh upper crust in 1900, described the house as "what the home of a successful man should be." Clearly, much of the credit for this successful domesticity was due to Anna: the "parlors are tastefully, but not extravagantly, furnished. Upon the walls one's eye is attracted by some very lovely paintings; but these become all the more interesting when the fact is learned that they were painted by his wife." According to the couple's great-nephew, Evan Posey Baker, Jr., the house had engraved brass door sill plates.[20]

Since the average African American in Pittsburgh held a plant laborer's job or perhaps handled a horse-drawn freighter and couldn't afford 13th Avenue-type real estate, the move propelled the Poseys into a white neighborhood. Thirteenth Avenue was not an upper-class neighborhood, although the Poseys were in that strata within the less-well-off Pittsburgh black community. The breadwinners among their neighbors were mostly men in relatively well-paying construction trades—steelworkers, bricklayers, and miners.[21]

The family's move away from the downtown bustle coincided with the Captain's rise from "merely" piloting river towboats to owning and building those craft, which pulled barges of cargo up and down the rivers. His obituary gave him credit for launching 41 craft during his career. The primary cargo carried on the river was coal, which fueled the giant steelworks in the area (creating a continual soot and smoke problem that led to the city's reputation as "the blackest and grimiest city in the United States."[22]). Before the turn of the twentieth century the elder Posey, usually operating with white business partners, had formed a series of companies to deliver coal, starting with the Delta Coal Company in 1890, where he was the general manager. The federal government, always interested in keeping the Ohio clear for shipping, awarded contracts to rivermen to dredge accumulated sand and gravel from the river bottom, which the entrepreneurs were then free to sell. Posey was in that business, too, with the Independent Sand Company. The Captain reached the zenith of his business career after 1900 as a partner with several white businessmen in the Diamond Coal and Coke Company. His role as chief transportation officer was clearly a nod to his knowledge of river shipping, and his ability to supply towboats. The company was said to have employed 1,000 workers, making Posey a rarity as a black businessman with at least some control over hundreds of working men. Diamond Coal also owned some of its own coal mines, increasing the power of its business by vertically integrating its operations: it mined its own coal and delivered it under contract with its own boats to steel and other plants.[23]

Newspapers in big cities with seaports regularly carried shipping news of embarking and disembarking ocean craft. The Pittsburgh papers had similar columns of news about the Ohio, and Capt. C.W. Posey was frequently mentioned, usually without the descriptive adjective "Negro" or "colored." When a journalist noted his race, it was included in passing, as when *The Black Diamond*, a coal industry magazine, in 1900 referred to him as "that hustling 'colored individual.'" According to the *Colored American* reporter, "The question of color never enters his business: he is a boat builder, and master of his profession. Pittsburg needs boats; Posey supplies them; hence his success."[24]

Entrepreneurship on the Ohio appears to have been a rough and tumble experience—at least as practiced by Captain Posey. He was frequently in the

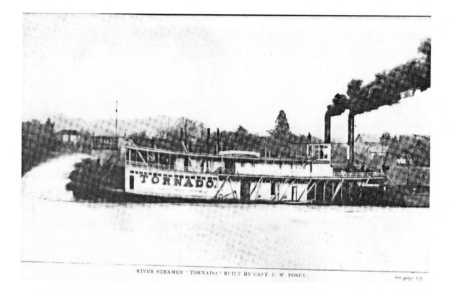

RIVER STEAMER "TORNADO" BUILT BY CAPT. C. W. POSEY.

see page 135

The steamer *Tornado*, one of 41 riverboats Captain Posey was said to have built during his long career on the Ohio River (*The Colored American*).

courts, suing and being sued. In 1903 he brought a $20,000 slander suit against a business rival who allegedly had accused him of fraud and called him a "nigger" in the process. Posey seemed more concerned with the fraud allegation than the racial slur, however: the *Pittsburgh Daily Post* reported that the Captain's suit emphasized that the fraud allegation "injured him in his business and is still injuring him."[25]

While Posey's civil court ventures sometimes went his way and sometimes didn't, a criminal conviction in 1898 landed him in jail—although in the end it only emphasized the clout he had in the local business and political community. What had begun as a civil dispute over whether or not the coal company in which Posey was a partner in 1897 had delivered inferior grades of coal to the Schoenberger Steel Company, turned into a criminal complaint against Posey, his white partner Max Seybolt, another towboat captain, and two of their employees. Seybolt beat the charge, but Posey and the employees were convicted and the Captain was sentenced the following April to 15 months in the Allegheny County workhouse. But in less than two weeks Sheriff Harvey Lowry was summoned before a criminal court judge to explain why Posey had been seen on the streets of Pittsburgh, going to his office. Lowry explained that this temporary freedom (in the company of a deputy) for inmates with important business matters was not unusual at his institution. The court told the sheriff to stop this rather informal method of imprisonment, and Posey went to the workhouse, where he was put in charge of the institution's pump house. By October, though, the Pennsylvania Board of Pardons had recommended a pardon and Posey was back in Pittsburgh, hard at work.[26]

The Captain invested heavily in real estate, and was a director of the Modern Savings & Trust Company, one of a handful of black-run banks in Pittsburgh catering to the African American populace. He was aided in his successes by Anna, who provided much more than a spouse's moral support. She often was the property owner of record in land investments, and held a contract with the U.S. government in 1900 to provide towboats for its sand dredges (with the captain as her agent). In general she was believed to have been "a guiding hand and safe counselor in the business success of her husband."[27] Her business abilities unfortunately remain mostly undocumented, since the accepted view of breadwinning in a two-parent family 100 or more years ago was that it was something the husband did. But it's clear that Anna Posey had a strong presence in the community, especially when a firearm was handy.

In July 1894, when the family was still living down by the river, a passerby came to her door to warn of suspicious characters lurking about the neighborhood. As the *Pittsburgh Press* reported, "Mrs. Posey procured a revolver, and after extinguishing the lights took a position at the open window to watch." Eventually she saw her husband, home from his day's labors, walking up McClure Street from the river. Then she witnessed an attempt by two men to rob him at gunpoint: "At this juncture Mrs. Posey fired two shots in rapid succession and the assailants fled."[28]

The pinpointing of Captain Posey as a robbery victim in 1894 may have meant he was already known as a man of means in Homestead. The armed robbery of the family home in 1907, when only a 14-year-old girl working as a domestic servant was present, clearly happened because Posey was "supposed to keep considerable money at his home." Fortunately for the family, he had banked a considerable sum only a few days before, and "only a few dollars were there." The poor girl, however, having had a gun thrust into her face and then tied up by the robber, "was found in a semi-conscious condition."[29]

Although the family was powerless to prevent that holdup, Anna Posey had been credited with "clever detective work" three years earlier when she solved the theft of $100 worth of goods at 320 Thirteenth. "Yesterday," the *Pittsburgh Weekly Gazette* reported, "she rounded up the gang, who are sons of prominent families in Homestead." The lads admitted the thefts from the Poseys, as well as from several stores. "The stolen articles were sold in Pittsburgh, they say, and the proceeds used to purchase uniforms for a football team. The families of the accused boys have promised to make good the losses."[30]

In what was probably a self-reported figure, the Captain was said in 1900 to have had a $3,000 annual salary—roughly equivalent to $600,000 today[31]—from managing his coal company. Yet while Posey was able to do well for himself on the river and in coal, and Anna was able to teach at an all-white public school in rural Ohio and act like a one-woman police department, Pittsburgh society was still quite segregated.

The African American community had its own set of social organizations, and the Poseys belonged to, and frequently led, many of them. Anna Posey's literary interests led to her to become one of the six founders in 1894 of the Aurora Reading Club. The mythological Aurora was the Roman goddess of dawn, and the club's intellectual light still shines on the Pittsburgh community some 125 years later. The artistic qualities that enhanced the Posey home were also known in the community. A March 1913 article in the *Pittsburgh Press* notes of Anna that she "has devoted a good deal of study to the fine arts, and has made a specialty of China decoration, her work along that line having won merited commendation from some of the most critical experts wherever she has exhibited her handiwork."[32]

The Aurora Reading Club sent her many times as its delegate to the National Association of Colored Women's Clubs national convention. A few months after the 1901 gathering she wrote a letter to the editor of the mainstream, white-owned and operated *Pittsburgh Daily Post* standing up for the African American women's clubs of the Pittsburgh area and taking their white counterparts down a peg for their racial discrimination: "The question of the day in Pittsburg woman's clubs seems to be, 'Shall colored women's clubs be admitted to the State Federation of Clubs?' It seems that the majority of Pittsburg women have only been brought in contact with the servant class of Pittsburg colored people, and not with the business and professional class. Can the standing of the white clubs be judged by persons that have only come in contact with the ignorant servants of the white race?"

Anna went on to describe the several educational and other achievements of leading black women's club members around the city, and then enumerated the good works of those clubs. "Can any Christian lady in proud old Pennsylvania throw one stone in the way of good, earnest, intelligent colored women that are spending their lives in the work that the Father of us all has given us to do? … We do not ask for favors but as the children of 'One Father' only for 'Justice'" she concludes.[33]

The Poseys clearly made what was a conscious decision to remain in Homestead after they started to accumulate wealth instead of moving across the river to the city, where most of the Old Pittsburgh group lived. Staying in Homestead had its advantages. For one thing, the children could attend the integrated borough schools, receiving a superior education to the one they might have received under the de facto segregation of Pittsburgh's schools. The parents' social activities, however, were centered in the Hill District of Pittsburgh, the predominant black area of the city. There they were prominent members of the influential Warren Methodist Episcopal Church and active fundraisers for a YMCA branch to serve the city's black residents. The Captain was a ranking member of the Loendi Club, the pre-eminent men's social club for Pittsburgh's African Americans. The club, named after a river and lake in Africa that had been mentioned in the journals of the explorer David Livingstone, was founded in 1897. In addition to its role as a social club for the powers that were in the black community, it regularly hosted not only local but nationally known speakers. Booker T. Washington once spoke there, as did comedian Bert Williams. Captain Posey was an early member of the board of directors and club president in 1916.[34]

He made his biggest contribution, however, when he became one of the financial saviors of the *Pittsburgh Courier*, a struggling four-page weekly begun in 1910. The mainstream white *Pittsburgh Press* had a long, regular

Sunday column, "Afro-American Notes," that covered black business, social, religious, and even sports events in Pittsburgh. But the city lacked a black-owned newspaper that could focus entirely on the community. The *Courier* strove to do just that, but in its early years it ran on a financial shoestring that soon was in danger of terminally fraying. A young Pittsburgh lawyer, Robert L. Vann, helped to find four financially solid investors to bail the paper out. Captain Posey was one of them and the *Courier*, soon to have Vann as its editor, became one of the leading black newspapers in America, with the largest circulation. Posey was president of the *Courier* corporation for a few years in the 1910s, and the Posey family owned shares of the newspaper's stock for many years.

Cumberland and Anna had three children. Beatrice, the oldest, was born in 1884. A second child, Seward was born in 1887. Although his namesake, riverman Hayes, probably pronounced his first name "Soo-ward," like the last name of Civil War–like statesman William Seward, the Posey family pronounced it "See-ward," the diminutive as simply "See." Cumberland, Jr., was born in 1890.

Seward was the first in the family to participate in organized athletics as a football and baseball player at Homestead High. He was a member of the school's first varsity football team in 1902, and possibly its only African American member—at least he was the only black among the eight former players at a 1933 reunion of the squad.[35] See was the quarterback, which at the time, just before legalization of the forward pass, generally involved taking the snap from center, initiating a play and blocking if he didn't run with the ball himself. In baseball he was the high school team's shortstop, and also pitched. And while his younger brother became famous for taking his baseball team on the road far and wide for games, See was the first to play far from home.

In May 1905, on the eve of his high school graduation, angered by "chastisement" from his parents, See ran away from home in the company of a visiting youth who was returning to his home in Richmond. He was found on a baseball diamond there, "and it was said he was putting up a pretty good game when an officer took him out of the game and placed him under arrest." The *Homestead Daily Messenger* noted that his return to his hometown was urgently awaited, "as the hill boys need his services on the home grounds in the amateur class.... Incidentally, his parents would like to see him again."[36] Cum followed in his older brother's footsteps as a Homestead athlete. He later reminisced that he had been the visiting team water boy at the local baseball park as a youngster, and had nailed a basketball hoop to a utility pole on 13th Avenue in 1906, when he was 15 years old.[37] He played through all the sports seasons, a halfback in football, a forward in basketball, and an outfielder in baseball.

Although they had not attended college themselves, Captain and Anna Posey appreciated the value of upward mobility and seemed determined that their children would get the higher education their financial success could afford. All of them completed high school, and Beatrice was the first to go on to college. She graduated in the spring of 1905 with a two-year teaching degree from the California State Normal School (now California University of Pennsylvania in the town of the same name right outside Pittsburgh). In 1908 she married a post office employee, Evan E. Baker. California University

Cum Posey as a member of the Homestead High School basketball team in 1909. He excelled at this sport, as well as baseball and football (*Pittsburgh Post-Gazette*).

alumni records show that, in addition to being a homemaker, she sometimes was a school teacher. In 1933, the *Courier* published a very favorable mention of her tea shop, the Cozy Corner, on Glenn Street not far from the Posey homes.[38] While not an athlete of the ability of his two brothers in law, Beatrice's husband Evan lent his administrative abilities several times to Posey basketball and baseball teams. His grandson, Evan P. Baker, Jr., said it was his grandfather's job during the Grays era to "take care of the money [from gate receipts]—put it under the mattress until Cum came."[39]

Seward, although eligible for Homestead High sports, had actually received his high school diploma from the Charles M. Schwab Manual Training School. Schwab, who had worked his way up through the ranks of the steel industry to become one of its titans and who at the time was head of Bethlehem Steel, had founded the trade school in 1903 in Homestead to help give the Pittsburgh industries a well-trained work force. See Posey, however, tried a different tack, enrolling in 1907 in medical school at the Western University of Pennsylvania. The university, soon to be rechristened the University of Pittsburgh, offered a four-year course for aspiring doctors and pharmacists. See left after only a year there, however, and pursued occupations as varied as foreman in a coal processing plant, low-level white collar work, and running a billiard room and some restaurants until joining what his younger brother had turned into the new family business—the Homestead Grays baseball team. His early duties included driving one of the touring cars that carried the Grays to out-of-town games, but in time he became well known as a booking agent—an arranger of games—and a base-ball talent scout.

Cum's college career lasted longer than his brother's, although in the end he, too, left without a degree. He often flashed his considerable athletic abilities, though, playing for three different schools. He actually attended classes at two of them, although perhaps he should have shown up in the classroom more often. In the fall after his spring 1909 graduation from Home-stead High he took the route available to many of his white upper-middle-class contemporaries and enrolled at Pennsylvania State College, a large state-funded school on its way to becoming the well-known Pennsylvania State University, and already referred to in the sports pages as Penn State.

Posey was one of 444 freshmen that fall in a class that was mostly all male and white. But as was the case with other African Americans in college, he ranked in what W.E.B. DuBois had labeled the "Talented Tenth," the upper echelon of American blacks who would provide the race's leadership. As a freshman he played basketball and baseball in the school's "interclass," or intramural program. His Class of 1913 included several good athletes, and its basketball squad rang up a 6–4 record in the Interclass League. A particularly satisfying victory came on March 18, 1910, in a 31–10 walloping of the soph-omores in the traditional rivalry among the underclassmen. It's clear from the game account in the college yearbook that Cum had been making some-thing of a name for himself in the league. The yearbook's jejune sports cor-respondent described the game's opening in this way: "'Bonehead' Hartz [the freshman center] made an agile leap, spun the ball on his forefinger and handed it to Posy[sic]. The flower of the Freshman team tripped coyly down the floor until requested to relinquish the ball which was tiring him." In April Posey was playing left field for a decent frosh baseball team, which had a 4–4 interclass record.[40]

The following winter Posey was captain of the sophomore interclass bas-ketball team and scored eight points at forward as his class beat the Penn State seniors, 26–11, on December 3. That game must have come at about the end of his time in the Interclass League. Besides offering physical fitness and entertainment opportunities for the students, the intramural program also served as a feeder system for the varsity teams, and a week later Posey was a substitute forward for Penn State, scoring eight points in its 41–9 slaughter of Susquehanna College. He had played his way into the starting lineup by

February 4, when he got six points in another lopsided win, a 50–9 thrashing of Albright College. Penn State went on to an admirable 9–4 record in 1910–11, winning five of its last six games after demolishing Albright. But Posey wasn't part of that strong finish. He was out of the lineup for the next game, on February 9 against Gettysburg College, apparently because he was academically ineligible, since it was reported in late February that the promising young player "has left school since the recent examinations."[41]

Even though his stay at Penn State was short, Posey had scored the first major racial breakthrough for his generation of the family, succeeding at basketball at a major school, with his race seemingly not a factor, just as his father had moved toward the top of the river industries around Pittsburgh. The son was one of the first—possibly the first—black athlete at the college, and research has him as one of a small number of blacks (not more than 10 or so) known to have played for otherwise white college basketball teams between 1900, when the sport became widespread on campuses, and the beginning of World War I.[42]

Back home in the fall of 1911, Posey enrolled in the University of Pittsburgh's pharmacy school. But according to the school's Registrar's Office, he spent only a total of four months there in the fall months of the 1911–12 and 1912–13 school years, without graduating. He didn't play collegiate sports there, although it was not for the lack of trying. And in his opinion, his failure to be allowed on the basketball court was all about the racial discrimination rampant in the Pitt athletic program. "We recall the day," he wrote in a 1942 newspaper column, "Dr. Flint, coach of the Pitt basketball team, asked this writer not to put on a uniform because the writer had participated in [a non-college game between two Pittsburgh black amateur teams]. His reason lacked weight, however, because another player, Frishman, a [white] guard on the Pitt team, had played the same night for an amateur team known as Zion council [and was permitted to play]." Posey decried the expenditure of public money on the university, which in 1942 still lacked black athletes: "The prejudiced athletic policy at Pitt is but an outgrowth of the prejudiced seed planted years ago by that regime [of the period of his youth]."[43]

His extra-curricular playing wasn't an issue at his next school, however, because even when he suited up for a game, in at least one sense he wasn't there. Duquesne University, located on the bluffs above the Monongahela, had been founded in Pittsburgh in 1878 as a Catholic college primarily for the children of working class immigrants. Posey's parents were Methodists and his only known religious affiliation was with the Clark Memorial Baptist Church in Homestead, a stone's throw from the Posey family home. Still, the school had a full sports program, and that suited Cum fine. He played some baseball but excelled in basketball, starting for three straight years from 1916 to 1918. The athletic department today considers Posey the first African American to have played on any of its teams.

The college's registrar's office, however, doesn't consider Cum to have been a Duquesne student at all. It has no record of his enrollment under either his name or the pseudonym Charles Cumbert, under which he achieved his stardom. It appears Posey, while leading the basketball squad, was never actually a student. This was not particularly unusual in the developing world of college athletics in the early twentieth century, and, apparently, it was fairly common at Duquesne. A biography of football great Art Rooney, owner of the Pittsburgh Steelers football team, who attended the college (and played for another school while also suiting up for the Dukes as a prep school student), noted simply that "eligibility rules were often ignored." The football

Top row, from left to right—Leo J. McIntyre, scorer; Michael J. Wolak, guard; Cumberland W. Cumbert, forward; Leo J. Zitsman, guard; Walter J. McMath, forward; John J. McLean, guard; Matthew B. Haley, forward; bottom row, Michael A. Obruba, center and student manager; Dr. P. M. Seixas, Columbia, referee; Rev. C. F. Hannigan, graduate manager; Captain Michael K. Morrissey, guard; below, William L. Allen, mascot.

Posey played under an assumed name, "Charles Cumbert," for the Duquesne University basketball team from 1916–18, even though he was already well-known as a professional in local athletic circles. This 1916 team photograph in a local newspaper nearly "blows his cover" by identifying him (third from left in back row) as "Cumberland W. Cumbert." Posey's friend and later political mentor, John J. McLean, is second from right in back row (*Pittsburgh Daily Post*).

team, especially, was known for recruiting "tramp athletes" who floated from school to school, playing ball but rarely, if ever, enrolling: "My dad played on the Bluff [the local name for Duquesne], recalled the Rev. Jack O'Malley: "I have pictures of him in his uniform, but I don't know how often he went to school." Father O'Malley said his father, Pat O'Malley, and his brothers hired themselves out on weekends, and "would go everywhere."[44]

Posey was already a developing sports promoter, and Rooney, who learned a few things from him, was bound for fame in that line of work also. It is likely they knew several of these "tramp athletes" and saw no reason not to enhance their own experience and reputation in the same way. Whether Posey got paid or not for his play for the Dukes is unknown (although why he would have played for nothing is hard to fathom), but he certainly didn't receive a college education in return for his sports exploits on the school's behalf.

It wasn't as if Posey had gone to school far from home and attempted to pass himself off as an unknown amateur. The Duquesne campus was only five miles from the family residence in Homestead, and at age 25, when he first began playing for the Dukes, he had been performing steadily for baseball and basketball teams that distributed part of the gate receipts to their players, making them semi-professional athletes. Duquesne opponents from outside the Pittsburgh area may not have picked up on what was going on, but local fans could hardly have been fooled, since Cum was at the time the leading player on the top African American semi-pro basketball team in the city. Rob Ruck, a Pittsburgh sports historian and an author of the Rooney biography, points out that even if Posey had adopted an alias just to conceal his local professional connections, "Given Posey's prominence as an athlete, it was a ruse that fooled few but was accepted by all."[45]

In February 1917, Posey starred for Duquesne with 14 points against the Coffey Club, a leading local white semi-pro squad. Every one of the Coffey Clubbers (and many of their fans) must have known who "Cumbert" was. Posey's paper-thin cover was even partially blown in March 1916, at the end of his first basketball season, when the *Pittsburgh Daily Post* ran a team picture that identified the young forward as "Cumberland W. Cumbert." A little passage of time didn't much obscure his real identity, either. In 1923 the university's *Duquesne Monthly*, boosting the chances of that year's hoop varsity, reported that "prospects are the most favorable, since before the days before the war, when…. Posey Cumbert thrilled the crowds." Posey himself owned up in 1935 to having played at the college.[46]

But Duquesne at the time wasn't a member of a collegiate athletic conference that might have overseen eligibility, and the National Collegiate Athletic Association, only 10 years old, was far from being able to tackle the gigantic issue of illegal recruiting. Although, the local Amateur Athletic Union committee responsible for overseeing amateur athletics in Western Pennsylvania could have provided some clarity if it had been asked. In December 1914 the AAU had revoked membership cards for both Cum and See Posey and the other members of their Monticello Athletic Association basketball team for having turned pro.[47]

There's an assumption in some quarters that Posey, light-skinned like his mother, played under an assumed name to pass himself off as white in a collegiate sports atmosphere that had little racial integration. While being regarded as a white ballplayer may have helped establish his cover identity, it was most likely that Posey became Cumbert primarily to hide the fact that he was Posey, the up-and-coming pro. Black athletes don't appear to have been generally banned in Pennsylvania college sports in the 1910 era—Cum Posey was Cum Posey at Penn State without any problem.

Duquesne, although with only one returning starter, had a 7–2 record in 1915–16, and the eagle-eye shooting of Posey/Cumbert, the new man, was a main reason for this success. In some of the victories he was good for about half the team's points, as when he scored 14 in a 33–19 win over the University of Buffalo on January 15, and 18 to help beat Waynesburg College 34–15 on February 9. In that game the *Duquesne Monthly* dubbed him the "shooting star" of the contest, as he outscored the entire opponent team.[48] In the six games for which box scores can be discovered, Posey averaged 13 points per game, a third of Dukes' 39-point average.

He did this in part because, as basketball rules continued to evolve only 24 years after physical education professor James Naismith had drawn up its first written set, teams were allowed to name a designated free-throw shooter for all of their foul shots. Posey sank 30 of 52 in the six games with box scores, a .577 percentage. This figure is nothing to rave about today, but in 1916 it was good. Among the innovations yet to come to basketball was the truly round ball. The one in use when Posey played was made of stitched leather panels surrounding an inflated bladder. Robert Peterson likened it to "a leather-encased pumpkin somewhat larger than today's molded ball, with laces along one side creating a bulge that made shooting and dribbling an adventure." As a game went on, this sphere, loosely assembled by today's standards, would often become less spherical through repeated pounding on the floor, making shooting accuracy even worse.[49]

In the pre-season write-up in the college magazine the 1916–17 Dukes were described as "a little green and ungainly," with only four returning veterans.[50] Posey, as Cumbert, was one of them, though. Described in the same article as a "dead sure shot," he demonstrated that ability by sinking seven baskets in the season opener and totaling 16 points, almost half the team's total, in a 33–25 win over Juniata College. The Dukes won eight of 11 games, defeating all seven of their actual college opponents and losing three of four to local semi-pro teams. Cum played in the first 10 games, missing the season finale against the semi-pro Pittsburgh Scholastics with a sprained ankle, and averaged 12.5 points per game. His scoring totals were depressed a little by his being shifted occasionally from the scoring position of forward to guard to improve the Dukes' defense. The 16 he scored against Juniata was only the third best game he had that season. He nailed 22 in a February 12 win over Salem College and 19 against the local St. Mary's Lyceum team, another Duquesne victory, on March 8. Again shooting most of the free throws, he accounted for about 30 percent of the Duke's total scoring before his late-season injury.

The onset of U.S. involvement in World War I loomed heavily over the Duquesne sports program, as it did at other colleges during the 1917–18 school year. The varsity football season was cancelled that fall and the varsity baseball season would likewise be scrubbed the following spring because of the number of athletes who had entered the military. But the basketball team played on, although hampered by the loss of several players. It was noted that the number of men trying out for the varsity was the smallest in the team's history.[51] Duquesne played only eight games, three scheduled contests being cancelled, one because of a blizzard, and settled for a 4–4 record. Posey wasn't always in the lineup, for reasons unexplained in the Pittsburgh newspapers or the *Duquesne Monthly*, but he had two stellar games to lead the Dukes to wins. He scored 20 against St. Ignatius on January 11 without even stepping to the free throw line. He notched 22 against Muskingum College on February 14 in a game that was tied seven times before Duquesne moved ahead. He didn't play in Pittsburgh against the semi-pro Westinghouse Club on March 2, and missed a road trip to Niagara and Buffalo colleges on March 8 and 9. He may well have been otherwise occupied—the Monticello semi-pro team on which he starred had a big contest scheduled March 8 against a black team from Cincinnati. Playing as Cum Posey, he had already fit a Monticello game in New York City on February 1 in between two Duquesne contests.[52]

Posey, as Cumbert, played on the baseball varsity in the spring of 1916, on a team that won nine straight games and suffered only two losses. He generally started in center field, although he was moved to second base for a time when the original second sacker became injured. This was Posey's first season of college baseball since the freshman interclass team at Penn State in 1909, and it was his last. He may have become discouraged by his .214 batting average.[53] More than likely, he was too busy. By then he was regular left fielder and captain of the Homestead Grays, the local black team he would soon transform into a regional semi-pro powerhouse, and then into one of the best Negro League teams ever. One has only to look at the events of June 3, 1916, to see where his baseball interests lay. At 7:25 a.m. the Duquesne baseball squad set off on the 60-mile jaunt to New Wilmington, Pennsylvania, for a game with Westminster College. Cumbert, the Dukes' center fielder, was reported, with no further explanation, as "unable to make the trip." That afternoon, as Posey, he was out in left for the Grays, snaring eight fly balls and chalking up an assist.[54]

Nineteen eighteen was the year that Cumbert finally "graduated," or at least played no more, for Duquesne, except for an appearance on the alumni basketball team in a game against the varsity in March 1919. The player by that name vanished into history—but made a comeback under his real name 69 years later. Posey was inducted posthumously into the Duquesne University Sports Hall of Fame on November 18, 1988. In 2014 his memory was further honored when the school created a $1 million endowment fund in his name to meet the financial needs of minority students.[55]

In addition to giving Posey a chance to sharpen his basketball game, his time at Duquesne led to a personal relationship with Art Rooney. Rooney, the son of a saloonkeeper from Pittsburgh's North Side, was, like Posey, an all-sports whiz as a young man, playing some minor league baseball (he was white, hence no color bar) before concentrating on football. He founded a professional football team in the city in 1933 that became the Pittsburgh Steelers of the National Football League. Like Posey, Rooney received the ultimate honor available in his chosen sport, election to the Pro Football Hall of Fame.

Posey was 10 years older than Rooney, who was a prep school student at Duquesne while Cumbert starred for the varsity basketball team. But Rooney knew Posey well from their sandlot baseball competition, and also knew that Posey had something going for him that Rooney greatly admired, his semi-professional sports teams. Rooney, as Posey had as a young outfielder with the baseball Grays, parlayed his exceptional ability as a running back for local teams into management, and then ownership, in semi-pro football and finally in the NFL. Posey mentored Rooney in the 1920s in what was in those early days the difficult business of making money off of professional sports. Rooney's biographers describe Posey as Rooney's "athletic model." What Cum modeled, they said, was "resilience, entrepreneurial talent, and a knack for organizing.... Cum taught him how to make his way in sport."[56]

Rooney, who gave help as easily as he took it, became a Posey supporter, in both large things and small. When football wasn't in season, Rooney would form semi-pro baseball teams and go barnstorming in Western Pennsylvania and the surrounding area, the stomping grounds of Posey's early Grays. Once, while Rooney's team was playing in the same West Virginia region as the all-black Grays, Posey was short a player and called Rooney to ask for his aid. "I sent him a kid, a red-haired Irish fellow," Art recalled. "Cum called me on the phone and said, 'Didn't you have something darker?'"[57] As time went on, the Steelers became a profitable NFL franchise. The Grays, as did most black baseball teams bucking the Great Depression from their disadvantaged position outside the mainstream American economy, went through some rough times. Rooney provided some funds to keep the Grays afloat, although he took no public credit for his acts. According to Posey's grandnephew, Evan P. Baker, Jr., Rooney was always ready to tide Cum over with a loan before the baseball season's gate revenues began to come in, so the Grays could go to spring training. Baker doubts that the loans were ever repaid, but that didn't seem to matter to Rooney. Baker once asked Rooney about the loans when Art was at the Posey house for lunch, but "Mr. Rooney acted like he never heard what I said. He started talking about the carrots instead."[58]

Posey's Duquesne years also allowed him to strengthen an existing relationship. Cum had coached John J. McLean on the Homestead High basketball team after leaving Penn State, and McLean, a guard, was a teammate on the 1915–16 Dukes (although, like Posey, he may not have been enrolled).[59] McLean, the son of a plumber, enlisted in the Army in May 1917, became a second lieutenant, a pilot, and a flight instructor stateside until the end of the war. When he came home he enrolled at the University of Pittsburgh, graduating with a dental degree. He captained the basketball team at Pitt, but really excelled at football. A guard, McLean played for nothing but winning teams under legendary coach Glenn "Pop" Warner, and he made the 1920 All-American team picked by *Boston Post* football editor Neal R. O'Hara.

McLean opened a dental practice in his hometown but was heavily into local politics even before graduating from Pitt. He was elected borough controller (financial officer) in 1921 and served in that office for 16 years before successfully challenging and defeating his erstwhile political partner, John J. Cavanaugh, to become burgess (mayor) of Homestead in 1938. Continuing to hold the borough's leadership, McLean also served as Allegheny County treasurer and was the county clerk of courts when he died in 1951. Posey was first elected to the borough's school board in 1931. For most of his career as a borough official he was on McLean's powerful Democratic team, helping the doctor oust Cavanaugh's discredited Republican administration in the mid–1930s. Cum's close relationship with his former player and teammate was another instance of his ability to reach across the color line and find common cause.

Posey had duly registered for the draft in June 1917 but was never called into the service, probably because he was granted a dependency deferment that put him far back on the draft list in Homestead. These deferments were available to men who were the sole support of their families and Cum, still passing as a college student on the Bluff, had a wife and two daughters, with another daughter on the way.

In June 1913 he had married 20-year-old Ethel Florence Truman, a Pittsburgh native. They had been keeping company for a while, apparently; the Homestead social news column in the *Courier* noted in the fall of 1911 that "Cumberland Posey and Miss Ethel Truman attended the Alvin theater on Monday evening," accompanied (or perhaps chaperoned) by his older sister Beatrice and her husband Evan Baker. The two of them also show up in May 1912 at the Poseys' Warren Methodist Episcopal Church in Pittsburgh as two members of a cast of 30 young people ("ably coached" by Cum's mother Anna and others) performing the play *Fifty Years of Freedom, or From Cabin to Congress*. Written by black author Katherine Chapman Davis Tillman in 1910, the play was a popular, uplifting work celebrating black progress in the country since the Civil War. Cum had the supporting role of Arthur Norton, son of a college president, while Ethel played a Quaker teacher appropriately named Ruth Penn. The 20 men in the cast were the members of the Chevaliers, a recently established social group of "well known and socially popular young men" prominent in the Pittsburgh's black community. Cum Posey was the group's president. The 10 young women in the play were the Chevaliers' "lady friends."[60]

Cum and Ethel's first daughter, also named Ethel, was born April 11, 1914. Their second daughter, Mary, was born in 1915, with Ann following in 1917 and Beatrice in 1921, following the stillbirth of another daughter the year before. True to the family's emphasis on education, three of the daughters—Mary, Ann, and Beatrice—attended college, and daughter Ethel went to nursing school but got married before finishing. After they married, Cumberland, Jr., and Ethel lived in rented apartments near what became a virtual compound of Posey homes, the big house at number 320 that the Captain and Anna had built for the family and flanking houses at 312 and 324. When everyone had moved in, the Bakers lived at 312 and Cum's family at 324.

They were the main occupants, anyway, at 324. Summer was likely to bring an influx of ballplaying boarders from the Grays. Daughter Beatrice remembered Hall of Fame pitcher Ray Brown and Wilmer Fields, another star hurler boarding with her family, and Oscar Charleston, regarded as one of the best Negro Leaguers ever, rooming next door with the Bakers. "I remember Smokey Joe Williams," she added; "He was so tall—he used to pick me up and throw me up in the air when I was a little girl." Her nephew, Evan Baker, Jr., recalled playing catch in the back yard with yet another Hall of Famer, Jud Wilson.[61]

Cum Posey is listed in early Homestead city directories as a "laborer," a label commonly used for someone not tied to a particular employer or profession. But by 1917 he, like his brother-in-law Evan, had a postal job. Cum's position was with the Railway Mail Service, which for decades transported inter-city mail. By 1925, though, he had given that up to become a fulltime sports entrepreneur, specializing in baseball and basketball but also involved in football for a few years.

Each fall after coming home from Penn State Posey made himself available to the top black gridiron squads in the Pittsburgh area, usually starting at quarterback. He was "the hero of the day," according to the *Pittsburgh Post-Gazette*, when he uncorked a long punt return and a sizeable run from scrimmage to set up two fourth-quarter touchdowns and lead the Delaney Rifles to a 12–6 win over Wilberforce University on Thanksgiving Day, 1912. The next Thanksgiving that rolled around, Posey quarterbacked the well-known Collins Tigers squad. By 1914 he had added what seems to have been an integrated Homestead team to his work with the Delaneys and in 1917, he was a co-organizer and a player on "a fast aggregation of colored college stars." By the early 1920s he was running a football version of his Homestead Grays baseball team, which lasted a few years.[62] But the football and basketball teams fell by the wayside—baseball was the sport in which Posey really dominated. As his daughter Beatrice put it, "he made his living from baseball." Life at the Posey residence pretty much revolved around the sport.[63]

As a baseball owner who was also in charge of most day-to-day team business and, in the 1930s and '40s, was a Negro League officer to boot, Posey was on the road a lot. But according to his daughter, "When he was home, he was the head of the household. He had a lot of self-confidence." Evan Baker, Cum's great-nephew, recounted that when he was eight or nine years old Posey, by then a member of the Homestead borough political organization, took him to the city jail and had him locked in a cell for a couple of minutes as a "scared straight" lesson. "Cum was that way," Baker said. "Cum got his point across. If he said something to you, that was that."[64]

Chapter Two

Shooting Baskets, Throwing Elbows, Winning It All

Posey's qualifications for the National Baseball Hall of Fame consist of his organization and operation of the Negro Leagues powerhouse Homestead Grays and his leadership positions in the Negro National League. He began with the Grays as its left fielder, but had ceased playing regularly by 1921, when he was 31 years old. He was fast, a ball hawk who on offense could get on base often enough to be a good leadoff man. But perusal of Grays box scores make it clear he wasn't a superior hitter. By the 1920s his management skills enabled him to recruit better and better players, including his own replacement.

His case for the Naismith Memorial Basketball Hall of Fame is very different. He was still a great organizer of teams and a successful promoter of early professional basketball, but his hoop bona fides are also based on his being recognized as one of the superb black players of his day. In fact, he was better known in the early 1920s as the star of his own championship hoop squad than for any of his baseball achievements to that point.

At five feet, nine inches tall, weighing only about 140 pounds, he would have hardly dominated had his teams' games been contests of size. But this was early basketball, only in its third decade since the promulgation of formal rules. Team formation strategy had advanced to the point that it was good to have a big center, since there was a repetitive center jump after every basket, not just at the beginning of periods and after tie-ups in which a player from each team shared possession, as was the case by 1938. A dominating center on the average court, which was much shorter than today's hardwoods, could win the tap and actually start plays for his team if he could propel the ball with distance and accuracy. Speed on defense and the ability to hoist up a successful outside shot were of utmost importance, and Cum excelled at both. Will Anthony Madden, himself in the thick of early black basketball in New York City as what amounted to a team general manager, picked an annual "all-star" squad each year for the *New York Age* newspaper. In 1916 he put Posey on his dream team: "There can be no all-star aggregation mentioned without the name of Cumberland Posey enrolled on the list. His great speed, together with his remarkable ability to shoot both from the field and foul line, stamps his quality."[1]

In addition to coaching the Homestead High basketball team in the fall of 1911, after having left Penn State, Posey was one of the organizers of a basketball team at the black YMCA in Pittsburgh (the one for which his father did fundraising). Posey was the team captain. The team was good—too good, in fact, for the competition a newly formed Y team would ordinarily face. It slaughtered both Sunday school teams such as United Friendship (final score: 51–17), for instance, and breezed past white amateurs that included the Homestead Independents (a 64–24 beat-down). Posey, who reportedly "made several circus shots," had 12 baskets in the Homestead game. Shortly thereafter, though, Cum, other local black basketball players, and some more established men in the black community took over the Monticello Athletic Association, a black social and athletic club that had held a fundraiser in May to launch a basketball team.[2]

The Monticello A.A. got a basketball squad, all right. It was composed mostly of the powerhouse Y team, and Posey was again the captain. By the end of the 1911–12 season the Monticellos could lay plausible claim to the title of black national champions. The team had about 10 members, but the starters were Cum Posey and Walter Clark at forward, Sellers Hall at center, and See Posey and Jim Dorsey at guard. Dorsey, a well-known African American athlete in the city (particularly as a football player), contributed something else of value, a place to practice. Just beginning a long career on the city's parks and recreation staff, he worked at the fieldhouse in the city-owned Washington Park, and opened the doors again after closing time so the Monticellos could have uninterrupted practices without having to share the floor with "every colored boy in Allegheny County who owned a pair of rubber shoes."[3]

The Monticellos were a mix of young men from upper-class and blue-collar backgrounds. The Posey brothers might have been able to claim the most prosperous father from among the group, if they had been inclined to. But Sell Hall's father George, whose occupation as a barber was a good example of the steady, although not lucrative, work available to Old Pittsburgh men before the steel mill employment boom, could lay claim to an even more august position in Pittsburgh's Negro community. He was the founder of the prestigious Loendi club, of which Captain Posey was also a director.

Sellers Hall never achieved the fame of his contemporary Cum Posey, but his accomplishments were of a similar type. He was an outstanding

The 1911–12 Monticello Athletic Association basketball team, which Cum Posey led to the consensus black national championship. He is second from the left in the front row. His brother See, also a starter, is in the middle of the second row. His brother-in-law, Evan Baker, who provided support for several Posey sports ventures, is on the right in the back row (Dorsey-Turfley Family Photographs Collection, Detre Library and Archives, Heinz History Center).

four-sport athlete at Central High School in Pittsburgh, track being perhaps the one at which he was best. Hall went to work for the post office in Pittsburgh, but played semi-pro baseball and basketball for years, often pitching on teams for which Posey played the outfield. He then ran some baseball teams, most notably the Pittsburgh Colored Collegians, rivals of Posey's early Grays. Hall's biggest achievements as a promoter, though, came in a different entertainment field. Regarded by local music historians as Pittsburgh's first African American music promoter, Sell booked big bands for dances that drew up to 2,000 people at the city's prominent venues, and he is given credit for bringing the likes of Duke Ellington, Count Basie, and Cab Calloway to the Steel City.[4] Although Hall and Posey sometimes feuded as competing baseball entrepreneurs, and once wound up opposing each other in civil court, Cum admired Sell, graciously referring to him later in his *Pittsburgh Courier* sports column as "the Alpha and Omega of Negro baseball for many years in Pittsburgh. Sell did so many things in his unorthodox manner and did them so effectively that many anecdotes concerning his long career will appear in this column from time to time." Once, Hall appeared at the Homestead borough offices to get a permit to hold a dance and was surprised when the clerks there didn't recognize him. "I am the fellow who put Homestead on the map," he informed them. "There is more than a grain of truth in what 'Sell' said," graciously wrote Posey, who in the end did even more to put Homestead on the map.[5]

Outside of the University of Pittsburgh varsity, which began play in 1906, and the teams from Pittsburgh, Homestead, and some other communities in the region that were part of the professional Central and Western Pennsylvania Basketball leagues, basketball in Pittsburgh around 1910 was more or less a local affair. Black basketball was an amateur sport, the province of the colored YMCA and a few athletic clubs for youngsters. The teams, including the Monticellos, needed to raise funds to support their play, and dances, often held after the games, became a popular addition to an evening's basketball. The team even had a "ladies' auxiliary," the Monticello Girls, who helped plan and carry out the non-basketball festivities. They appeared to be the players' sisters or girlfriends. Ethel Truman was one of them.

The Monticellos of early 1912 seem to have followed the usual athletic association template—raise some money, hold a dance, then challenge some local teams—and they found on-court success by doing it. Game accounts are few, but the team is known to have defeated the white Southside team, 24–13, in mid–February.[6] The routine changed quickly, though, when the Monticellos announced that they would play the Howard University squad on March 8. Howard, in Washington, D.C., was founded right after the Civil

War and although it was always integrated, its alumni include a number of famous black figures, including Supreme Court Justice Thurgood Marshall, New York City Mayor David Dinkins, civil rights leader Stokely Carmichael, and author Toni Morrison.

From the sporting point of view in 1912, the big man on campus was Edwin B. Henderson, a Harvard-educated physical education instructor who was a leading figure in the introduction of basketball to African American communities. (In recognition of those efforts, he was enshrined in the Basketball Hall of Fame in 2013, three years ahead of Posey.) Henderson had been running a crack team at Washington's Twelfth Street YMCA, which like other black Ys of the time provided athletic opportunities to youngsters whose access to organized sport was often limited under segregation. As such, they were crucial to the early development of African American basketball, as their best players went on to star in college or play for amateur, and then professional, club teams.

In 1910 Henderson persuaded the best players from the Twelfth Street Y to enroll at Howard, thus giving the university not only its first basketball squad, but one of the best black teams in the nation. The participants and fans in organized sports demand there be a champion, some team or individual deemed by whatever standards are available to be the best. In the 1910s there were no professional leagues or collegiate athletic conferences for black basketball. Much in the same way that black baseball teams in the late nineteenth century had, black basketball squads in the 1910s promoted themselves as champs and challenged other squads doing the same. The outcomes of the games, filtered through the judgment of the black press's sportswriters who covered the contests, produced consensus title holders. Henderson's Twelfth Street team was the consensus "world's champion" (this particular world lying between Chicago and the Eastern Seaboard, where the top black teams were located) in 1909–10. The same guys, now wearing Howard jerseys, took the honor in 1910–11.

So the Monticellos, with only the 1911–12 season together as the YMCA and the club team, had somehow gotten the black national champions to play them, and on their own court, at that. It was clear that the Monticellos, both the team and the athletic association, did not take this game lightly. Tickets for the contest, to be played in the Washington Park fieldhouse, had to be purchased in advance from Monticello supporters (including the Poseys' brother-in-law, Evan Baker, in another instance of his support for their athletic ventures). Invitations to the game and the dance to follow were mailed to selected members of the Pittsburgh black community, the Monticellos hoping to make the night "the social event of the season.... It is a fact that quite a number of Pittsburgh's best people have never witnessed a basketball game. Now is the time for them to come out and see a strenuous and pleasing game."[7]

The game was strenuous, all right, and for Pittsburgh fans, very pleasing, too. The relatively unknown squad from the Steel City beat the university team, 24–19. The fans saw fine playing and a consistently close game that included players on both sides whose reputations would outlast their actual careers. In addition to Cum Posey, there was Hudson "Huddy" Oliver, a Howard guard, who was on the Hall of Fame's list of African American nominees the year Posey was picked from it in 2016. And true to the unregulated way independent ball was played in those early days, there was negotiation over the game's rules, which turned out to significantly help the Monticellos.

They held a one-point lead, 9–8, at the end of the first half, which had been played under intercollegiate rules. Then with the second-half tipoff, the rules changed to those used by amateur club teams. The main difference was in dribbling. College rules allowed a two-handed dribble (illegal today), and a player could shoot off the dribble (a primary offensive tactic, even now). Amateur rules favored a passing game: A one-handed dribble, made difficult by the laces on the ball, was legal, but shooting off the dribble wasn't. The amateur rules seem to favor an outside shooting game, which the Monticellos certainly had. Cum Posey and Sell Hall each hit long set shots at key moments in the second half to set the pace, and the hometown *Courier* reported that "Howard seemed shot to pieces." Cum Posey led all scorers with 15 points, nearly two-thirds of Monticello's total. See Posey had a pair of baskets—his four points were the second most for the winners. George Gilmore, the Howard center, who would later play for Posey on one of his professional champions, was second high scorer with 11, although the *Courier* gave Hall credit for keeping Gilmore in check.[8]

Unsurprisingly, the Monticello players and the *Courier*, naturally, immediately claimed that beating the incumbent (albeit informally designated, black national champions indisputably gave Pittsburgh's team the crown. But others went nearly as far in praising them. By the time the edition of the *Courier* anointing the Monticellos had made it off the press, the *New York Age* had already noted that "the colored basketball world will be forced to recognize Monticello as one of the fastest of colored quints." Cum Posey acknowledged 30 years later that the change from collegiate to club rules at halftime gave his team a real advantage, since Monticello "was able to bewilder the opposition by this style of play." Posey recounted that insisting on at least one half of play under the rules his team was most used to was a standard tactic for a few years until opponents began refusing to give in. "Basketball, like baseball in Pittsburgh, had its ups and downs and petty jealousies," wrote the man who was frequently on board, and often driving the train, when those ups and downs and jealousies occurred.[9]

A rematch with Howard was on everyone's mind for the 1912–13 season, but negotiations for a game in Washington fell through. Recriminations on both sides included complaints on Howard's part about the previous season's loss. The assistant managers of both teams, Clarence W. Richardson for Howard and J.A.A. Norris for Monticello, traded charges in a series of letters to the *Age*. Richardson charged that the Pittsburgh team had orally agreed to a game in Washington in February, then backed out shortly before the scheduled date over complaints about the court in True Reformers Hall, a popular cultural center in the DC African American community. He also stated that the referee in Pittsburgh the previous March had admitted to the Howard team that he really didn't know all the rules of basketball. Norris fired back that Monticello officials had said, early and often, that True Reformers Hall was an unacceptable place to play a game and that the referee, Carroll, was a veteran official from the region's professional Central Basketball League.

Since even Richardson admitted that True Reformers was "by no means an ideal court, but it is the best we can procure," and since the switch from college to club amateur rules at halftime might well have confused a referee from a pro league, both sides of the argument may have had some justification. But each of the dueling assistant managers went hammer and tongs after his opponent. The Monticellos, Richardson averred, represented the problem of playing a non-college club team: There was no overarching organization such as a college administration to keep things on the up and up. That charge, according to Norris, tarred the reputation of the many black club teams involved in high-level basketball. Richardson responded by clarifying that he hadn't meant all clubs—just Monticello. Both Richardson and Norris were masters of acerbic rhetoric. Norris observed that "some men are made none the better by hiding behind a college name." Richardson said Norris "resorts to the trick of the infidel who goes to the Bible and picks out certain disconnected passages of Scripture to help him in substantiating his argument against Christianity."[10]

But after all the acrimony the two teams agreed to a rematch on March 13 at a neutral site, the Manhattan Casino, a large dancehall in New York City's Harlem. The Casino had become a favored place for basketball, which was drawing more fans in New York and outgrowing the church gymnasiums in which it first began there. Howard was more than ready this time, crushing Monticello, 33–17. This university team jumped well ahead in the first half and led for the rest of the game. The *Age* sportswriter gave Howard credit for "its great team work, outplaying Monticello in every department of the game." He had little to say about the Monticello players, except for one: "The burden of the work was put up to 'Cum' Posey, who is the strongest individual colored basketball player in the game to-day. But it takes more than one man, no matter how sensational his work, to win in a contest."[11]

Despite the blowout loss to Howard, which extinguished any chance Monticello would have had at the 1913 consensus championship, the team had a good season. The highlight was clearly a Christmas week road trip to New York City where, in the words of the *Age*, the Monticellos "came, played and conquered ... two of Greater New York's strongest teams."[12] The team from the Alpha Physical Culture Club, an African American athletic club that provided its own gymnasium and several sports teams, and the Smart Set team, from the upper-class black club of the same name in Brooklyn, had been playing since the middle of the previous decade. The Smart Set team had been world champions twice, and the Alphas would be so designated, along with Howard, in the current season. Nonetheless, the Monticellos beat them both, topping Alpha, 40–24 on Christmas Day and the Smart Set, 27–14, on December 27.

The defeat of Alpha set the stage for a return challenge in Pittsburgh on February 21 at the South Side Market Hall. It was showcased, as had been the Howard game the previous season, as a premier social as well as athletic event. The *Pittsburgh Press*'s "Afro-American News" column reported that the game "drew a large and brilliant assemblage of men and women of the race.... They came in crowds, the pennants of their favorite team boldly displayed and equipped with many noise-making devices. There was a brass band there also to help disturb the atmosphere, and noise reigned supreme." The crowd apparently would have gotten a bit more into the game, noted the *Press*, except for the netting that surrounded the playing area, which "kept the fans of both teams from encroaching on the players, when things became exciting."

Games played in places not designed for basketball in those early days often included netting around the periphery of the court, for the precise reason of separating fans and players in close quarters. Separating the players from each other was a chore for the referee, too. The game was rough, and "while a number on both teams was [*sic*] temporarily disabled, none were seriously injured." The preliminary game, between the Monticello second team and the Washington Athletic Association, was even rowdier: it "broke up in a near-riot, as both teams began slugging. Nobody paid any attention to the score they made."[13] This night had about everything a Pittsburgh basketball fan could wish for, except for a Pittsburgh victory. The score was tied three different times, including at 19-all late in the game, but Alpha netted the last five points, and won, 24–19. Nonetheless, Cum Posey, at his usual position at forward, led all scorers with 13 points.

For the 1913–14 basketball season the Posey brothers split off from the Monticellos, forming their own team under the sponsorship of the prestigious Loendi men's social club. Monticello was said to "regret" the parting of the ways, although Loendi players were quoted later in the season as saying that "Monticello will not agree to play Loendi under any conditions," so the parting may not have been amicable.[14] Up until now Cum Posey, while usually floor captain of any team he played on, hadn't been named as an off-the-court basketball leader. The Monticellos, for example, had Dick Garrison, a steel company clerk and a former professional baseball pitcher, in charge of booking games. The new team seems to have been the creation of Cum and See, though, and while it only lasted a year, it set a precedent for later Loendi sponsorship of an even better hoop team, one of the best in the country.

The split divided the Monticello roster. Sell Hall joined the Poseys on Loendi, while Jim Dorsey became captain of the remaining Monticellos, who promoted some second-stringers to starting jobs. With its talent thus diluted, neither team was considered for the mythical championship, which the annual consensus awarded mostly to New York City teams until Cum Posey's second incarnation of the Loendis came roaring back on the national scene in 1920.

Although the two Pittsburgh teams didn't play each other, they had a common opponent that first season, the ever-powerful Howard University quintet. Howard beat the Monticellos badly, 38–12, at the Manhattan Casino in New York in February. They had already soundly defeated Loendi, 27–14, in January in a Howard home game. One reason to suspect that Cum was in full charge of the Loendis was the string of excuses that came from the team after the loss. For all his admirable qualities as a sports team executive, Posey was always ready with reasons about how things were not his fault when they didn't go his way. The *Age* noted that the Loendi team was tired, having "travelled all night and had been held up for some time on account of a wreck." The previously maligned True Reformers Hall, Howard's home court, also came in for renewed criticism from Pittsburgh sources, who claimed the floor "is surrounded by a balcony, and has a chandelier directly in front of one of the baskets, which completely handicaps a visiting team."[15]

But for all the complaints about True Reformers' Hall in Washington, the Loendis seem to have picked a venue for a return back in Pittsburgh February 6 that combined the most interesting elements of a basketball game and a trip to Bedlam, the storied lunatic asylum. About 500 people squeezed into St. Peter's Lyceum on Pittsburgh's north side, the large attendance shrinking the size of the court. A *Press* reporter wrote, "The space for play was very limited and the players were often badly handicapped by the ball going into the crowd." He noted with tongue in cheek that "almost every time the ball went sailing through the air at the beginning of the game it seemed to land on a woman's hat, while derbies and male shins sustained more damage in the last half." The combination of two combative teams with much to prove and spectators breathing down their necks kept the game official very busy. Perhaps because of the limited space to develop plays or the constant contact on the floor, very few field goals were scored and the game hinged on foul shooting, at which Cum Posey was an ace. He hit eight of nine in the second half and Loendi won by a point. Or two, or three. Three newspapers that reported on the game and the season summary in the Howard yearbook record four different game scores: 17–16, 17–15, 17–14, and 15–14. All agreed, however, that Loendi had the bigger number.[16]

There were promises before the 1914–15 season of a grand consolidation of the Monticellos and Loendi under the aegis of the Delaney Rifles. The Delaneys had been started in 1908 as a quasi-military African American social club. Despite the fact that athletics were considered a sideline for the Delaneys, its football team, on which Cum Posey and Sell Hall sometimes played, was a powerhouse among Pittsburgh's club teams. The organization was named after Martin Delany (but with a misspelling of his last name), a black physician in Pittsburgh in the mid–1800s who worked with Frederick Douglass's abolitionist movement. Posey was present at the organizational meeting for the potential new powerhouse team, and acted as the meeting's secretary. But when sneakers began to squeak across basketball floors, most of Pittsburgh's best black basketball players were on the Delaney team, led by Jim Dorsey, while the Poseys and some of their oldest compatriots remained on the Monticellos.

The separation may have resulted from the local Amateur Athletic Union (AAU) committee's coming down on the entire Monticello starting five—the Posey brothers, Howard Hall (Sell's equally talented brother), Walter Clark, and Frank Bell—for violating its amateur standards, presumably by collecting money for their play. This happened in late December 1914, about two weeks after the big organizational meeting. The line between amateurism and semi-professionalism was often a vague one as American team sports developed; it was difficult to determine from outside a team organization whether players were pocketing gate receipts or money from "passing the hat" among spectators. In the case of the Monticellos, the AAU found the evidence of payment compelling enough to call for cancellation of the five men's amateur membership cards. As during the previous season, the dilution of talent kept either Pittsburgh team from breaking into Eastern black basketball's top ranks.[17]

By the fall of 1915 the teams had finally merged, becoming the Monticello-Delaneys. Dorsey and Cum Posey were the core of the team, which played together successfully for three seasons. There were some lineup changes as new blood came along to push out some original team members, including See Posey, who dropped out during the 1915–16 season. The Monticello-Delaneys prospered. Will Anthony Madden included them among the top seven East Coast black teams in his April 1917 post-season summary, as the Pittsburgh team began again to regularly play (and often defeat) other teams on Madden's list such as the Alphas and Lincoln University, a black college in Philadelphia.[18]

The world of black basketball was growing wider, as evidenced by the team's invitation to the Wabash YMCA team from Chicago in March 1917 for a game Monticello-Delaney won, 37–21, Posey leading the scoring with 16 points. It was also getting deeper, as interest in the game and the growth of more youth and club second teams started to produce more good players. Shortly before dispatching the Chicago team, Monticello defeated the Pittsburgh Independents, 33–22, in what was recognized as the city's black championship game.[19]

That 1916–17 season was the one in which Posey-led teams found an answer to a long-standing need, a suitable and reliably available home court. The Shriners social and benevolent organization had built its Syria Temple headquarters in 1902 at Washington and Webster streets in downtown Pittsburgh. The four-story building had a large ballroom that was the scene of parties and concerts. The Shriners soon outgrew the building and sold it to a consortium of 30 labor unions in 1910, using the proceeds to build a much bigger headquarters elsewhere in the city. The Union Labor Temple, as the building was now called, still had the ballroom, which could be converted to a court, as large indoor spaces often were in basketball's early days. The Labor Temple could hold 1,500 spectators in its basketball mode, and Posey's teams used it as a home court until 1925.

The 1917–18 season featured a couple of more signs that the times were changing in top-level basketball, right before the eyes of Pittsburgh fans. The changes, in retrospect, had the ambitions of Cum Posey plainly written all over them. On February 21, 1918, at the Labor Temple, the black team took on one of the elite Pittsburgh semi-pro squads, the Coffey Club. The Coffeys had been formed as a youth team in 1910 by John Coffey, a local newspaper circulation department employee for the *Pittsburgh Press*, who wanted to create a recreational opportunity for youth at a Jewish settlement house. Jewish players were almost as segregated ethnically as black players were racially, and were just as good at basketball. By 1920 or so big city basketball in the East featured several top-flight Jewish teams, and Coffey Club was one of them.[20] Playing the Coffeys was a big step up for the black team that had proven itself the city's best, and Monticello-Delaney's 32–31 victory (with Posey scoring 24 points, 10 as the designated foul shooter) raised the squad to a higher level. This elevated status was almost immediately made clear by a challenge from another of the city's best white teams, the Ray Pryel All-Stars.

Pryel, a white Homestead professional boxer and sports promoter, had a team that had given Coffey Club one of its rare defeats earlier in the season. The informal rules that determined the consensus national black champion also applied to this situation: If both the Pryels and the Monticello-Delaneys had beaten Coffey Club, then there had to be a match between them to determine which of the three teams was the best. Despite Posey's 19 points (15 of 20 from the foul line), the Pryels beat his team, 40–31, on March 27. Nevertheless, the very fact that one of the best white basketball teams in the area would unblinkingly challenge the Monticello-Delaneys on equal terms showed that the African American squad had risen to new heights in the Pittsburgh sports community. In baseball, Posey's Homestead Grays were already entrenched in the mostly white mix of semi-pro and amateur teams that, vaster than the Steel City's hoop world, blanketed the area. This was where his basketball ventures were going, too.

Another forward-looking feature of these two games was the importing of new talent to bulk up the team as it met tougher opponents. The all-Pittsburgh makeup of the squad was significantly changed for the Coffey Club and Pryel All-Stars games. George Gilmore, the Howard University center who had given the old Monticellos tough games just a few years ago, arrived to anchor the middle of the lineup. Posey was joined at forward by Clarence "Fats" Jenkins, most recently playing in New York City. It is very unlikely that Gilmore and Jenkins travelled to Pittsburgh without a promise of payments for their efforts beyond an informal share of gate receipts. From now on, Posey's teams would no longer seek glory just within the Steel City's niche of black basketball, and they would no longer depend only on local talent for their success.

As the 1918–19 season opened, Gilmore was again at center, with Posey and other star Pittsburgh black players arrayed around him, and a number of white teams from the area, including the arch-rival Coffeys, on the schedule. But the black team's name, which had been gaining fame throughout Northeast basketball, was gone. The squad had found a sponsor in the esteemed Loendi men's club. The Posey brothers' team that had split from the Monticellos in 1913–14 had used that name for one only fairly successful season. But now it became identified with one of the dominant black basketball teams in the country for eight years with Cum Posey in charge, his reputation for scoring, hard playing, and equally hard-headed team management growing all the time.

The newly minted, but familiar-looking, Loendis won their inaugural "tryout" game on November 30 by eight points, 36–28, over the Akron Quakers. A crowd of 1,400 (nearly capacity) packed the Labor Temple's second floor to watch "some of the best local material and notably one out of town star [Gilmore]."[21] The first Loendi season produced a successful pattern with which Monticello-Delaney rooters would have been familiar. Run-of-the-mill local teams went down to predictable defeats while the best Pittsburgh squads, particularly Coffey Club, proved hard to beat. There was the obligatory road trip to New York (required if a team was to be considered an upper-class five), resulting in a 45–21 whipping of Will Madden's Incorporators, who could plausibly be said to be defenders of the previous season's somewhat ephemeral black championship. This season was only setting the table for a multi-year Pittsburgh basketball feast. While New York's St. Christopher Club was declared the black national champion for 1918–19, the Black Fives Foundation, a group dedicated to early black basketball history, has researched the consensus champs through 1925 and found that the Loendis got the honor in four straight seasons, 1919–20 through 1922–23.[22]

Throughout the team's run, three Pittsburgh players were, barring injury, always in the starting lineup. Cum Posey was one of them, usually at forward, although more frequently at guard as he got older. Joining him were William S. "Pimp" Young, and Charles "Greasy" Betts, usually the guards. Like Posey, they had organizational skills, and became known for much more than just being good ballplayers.

Young, 17 years old in the inaugural Loendi season, was a native of Orange, New Jersey, and a graduate of Lincoln University near Philadelphia. Like his older brother Ulysses, who was an occasional Loendi when his coaching schedule permitted, he was a multi-sport athletic star. But W.S. Young had an impact on the Pittsburgh community that far exceeded his long career as a basketball star. Valedictorian of his Lincoln graduating class, he worked for a steel mill in its personnel department, wrote for and edited a local black newspaper, still on the board of the black YMCA and joined the Loendi Club. Long involved in local politics, Young was Pennsylvania's secretary of labor and industry in the 1960s. As one of a little group of 43 African American delegates to the 1964 Republican National Convention, he helped organize a demonstration against the "anti-Negro" politics of nominee Barry Goldwater. As he progressed upwards in politics and society, his nickname evolved into "Pep."[23]

Betts, who had moved to Pittsburgh with his family in 1910, was also only 17 years old when the Loendis got their start. He worked as a machinist in the Westinghouse Electric Corporation plant but became the assistant director of welfare there, with the duty, among other things, to organize company sports leagues for the workers. Betts lost his job with Westinghouse during the Depression, but he got a new one fighting the Depression, in a sense. Hired by the Works Progress Administration to help turn an abandoned Homestead building into the McClure Community Center, he wound up being its director and spent decades working on behalf of youth athletics.[24]

As Negro baseball had been before the establishment of the Negro Leagues (and still was when league controls were lax), top-level black basketball was a more or less uncontrolled free market when it came to recruiting players. As the Monticellos had added Gilmore from Howard University in the 1910s, Posey, while now and again touting the all-Pittsburgh base of his team, was ever on the hunt for stars to complement his core. Capitalizing on his team's reputation, as well as his own, and bolstered by the money to adequately compensate recruits, he at one time or another added some of the biggest names in Eastern black basketball to the Loendi lineup. Among them were James "Pappy" Ricks, James "Legs" Sessoms, George Fiall, and Specs Moton, all of whom started for Leondi during its big years, having been lured from other teams—and sometimes lured back again, such being the fluid world of independent sports.

Loendi won two-thirds or more of its games every season. Its schedule could be broken down into three categories—the average amateur and semi-pro teams in the Tri-State region of Western Pennsylvania, Eastern Ohio, and Western Virginia; the handful of best Pittsburgh pro teams: and the top black teams in the East and Midwest, from whom the consensus colored champion was selected. Posey's teams could usually defeat the run-of-the-mill area teams, sometimes even without the out-of-town stars in the lineup. But it was "all hands on deck" when playing for the Pittsburgh and black championships. The local championship contests gave Pittsburgh some of its best basketball in the 1920s, and the games were only occasionally accompanied by controversy. The black championship games were another matter. The inter-city competition was spiced by disputes among the various team managements, which were fed by black sportswriters upholding the honor of their cities. As a player, Cum Posey could usually be found in the midst of the fray on the hardwood. As a team executive, he was also at controversy's epicenter.

Posey and Loendi supporters correctly claimed for the first few years of the team's existence that it had never lost to a black opponent, although there was one peculiar outcome in 1920 when a possible Loendi win was turned into a no-decision because of the sort of hi-jinks that make the early days of many sports funny and memorable. While Loendi did beat Madden's Incorporators in 1918–19, it did not play any other teams that might have been eligible for the black national title, which went to the St. Christopher Club. The next season, though, brought a home-and-home series with St. Christopher's "Red and Black Machine," and Loendi won both games decisively, 40–27 at home in the Labor Temple and 32–15 at the Manhattan Casino, the Harlem ballroom that hosted the big New York games. The Labor Temple was packed for the first win on December 26, with the line of fans waiting to get through the turnstiles reported to be 50 yards long. Posey assumed free throw duties for the team and led it in scoring with 14 points. George Fiall of the Red and Black, who would in two seasons be enticed by Posey to become a professional Loendi, led everyone with 17. St. Christopher had jumped off to a dominating 13–2 lead, but Loendi was up a point by halftime and controlled the second half, holding the New York team to just five points. The *Chicago Defender*'s man on the scene, probably William White, its New York correspondent, claimed without providing too much detail that the St. Christopher players were roughed up (suffering a "series of accidents").[25]

The rematch on January 29 brought 5,000 fans to the cavernous Manhattan Casino, some of them arriving three hours early to make sure they got seats. Posey, according to White, "hadn't lost any of his old speed," and he led all scorers with 16 points. In White's opinion, the home team had been "outgeneraled, outplayed from every angle of the game." The Pittsburgh victory was one of pre-game tactics as well as hoop skill. Posey and his team insisted that only one referee be used in the game (there were two available), and refused to take the court for 45 minutes until St. Christopher, no doubt seeing 5,000 impatient faces in the seats, gave in. One-referee games, the standard in those days, generally allowed for more rough play away from the ball, where the ref's attention would be focused, and it might be presumed that Loendi wanted less scrutiny in order to push the Red and Black players around again. But the *New York Age*'s Ted Hooks put the blame on the ensuing roughness squarely on St. Christopher: "Fat Jenkins deliberately punched, tripped and fell upon Posey whenever opportunity permitted and Paul Robeson [the acclaimed singer and actor was a well-known multi-sport athlete in his youth] seemed to think he was back on Rutgers' football team."[26]

The next big Loendi move, still before the opening jump ball, was the team's warm-up. Posey had his men sprint to half court and take their practice shots from there. This would only be intimidating if they hit them, of course, but they did. This was not as daring as it might appear to the modern hoop fan, used to the current standard 94-foot-long court for professional and college games. The ballrooms, armories, and church recreation halls in which teams usually played in the early days had been designed for other purposes. The basketball court had to be fitted into what was already there. One comprehensive review of black hoop in that era puts the average court size at 60 by 40 feet. The entire dimensions of the floor of the Labor Temple where the Loendis played were only about 100 by 75 feet, a space that had to accommodate all the things that went inside a public building, including a stage and, of course, seating for about 1,500 fans. Posey's warm-up theatrics that night were nothing new. When the Monticellos first came to New York to play the Alphas in 1912, they "warmed up like farmers; none of them pretended to know anything about handling the ball." It turned out the "farmer" act "was only one of Cum's favorite tricks."[27]

The Loendi wins settled who would be the champ. But the victories, as clear cut as they were, only added fuel to a growing duel between the black basketball teams and the black sporting press in Pittsburgh and New York, for with a few exceptions the best African American squads in the next several years would be Loendi and whoever was on top in Harlem.

In 1920–21 Posey's team beat potential championship challengers the Forty Club of Chicago, the Athenians from Baltimore, and the Vandals of Atlantic City. Only the Vandals game was close, Pittsburgh squeaking by 31–28. According to one account, the Vandals were ahead when, with about two minutes left, "Posey went in and saved the game."[28] But the big challenge was to defeat New York's Spartan Braves, until recently an unsung team. The Braves had been playing since 1914 and had garnered respect, but few would have predicted that it would achieve the consensus championship in 1918–19, even if it came via a forfeit victory over St. Christopher. In that game, the Red and Black Machine refused to acknowledge a technical foul awarded when one of its club officials walked onto the floor, in violation of the rules, during an argument over a playing foul that had just been called.

The Spartans organizer and coach was Bob Douglas, a native of St. Kitts in the Caribbean who was known for his good nature and indefatigable efforts to put together the best black basketball team in New York. As good as the Spartans were, in the long run they were not that team. His next venture, the New York Renaissance, began play in 1923 and continued to dominate African American ball not only in the city, but everywhere, for years. Douglas would succeed Posey, much as Posey had Howard University's Edwin Henderson, as the black-hoops organizer whose efforts transcended the season's grind toward a championship, educating fans and sportswriters all over the nation to the glory of black basketball. As of Posey's induction in 2016, all three men are in the Basketball Hall of Fame.

Since the Spartans were wearing the championship crown, there was nothing for Posey and the Loendis to do but to try to knock it off their head, so he challenged Douglas to a home-and-away series that would probably decide the 1920–21 winner. The series actually went three games, the first on January 7 being declared a "no contest" due to an audacious Loendi stunt in the waning minutes. Even without the services of Cum, who had been injured in the previous game in Orange, New Jersey, Loendi clung to a 27–26 lead with a little less than a minute and a half remaining. Then a Loendi official, Posey's older brother See, grabbed the watches being used by the official timers and raced onto the floor, announcing that time had run out.

See clearly intended to stop the game while Loendi was ahead, and hopefully convince the officials that time had expired. Whatever the plan, it did not work. Loendi claimed the game was over and refused to get back on the floor. But the Braves objected vociferously, as did the big crowd at the Manhattan Casino, and another timepiece was discovered that showed a minute and 18 seconds had been remaining when play had been stopped so unconventionally. Chris Huiswood, the referee, finally just waved his arms and called the whole thing off. The ref's action was later laid to "an act of fairness to protect those who had wagered heavily on the game." It's certainly unusual for a game official to make a decision in the best interests of illegal betting. It's just as likely that the ref, eyeing all those howling fans and noting that the police riot squad was absent, decided that discretion was the better part of valor. As Cum Posey described the scene 15 years later, "Bedlam was a mild word." Back home in Pittsburgh, the local press swallowed the Loendi version of a 27–26 win. But the *Defender*, as staunch a supporter of black basketball as any of the big African American weeklies, saw the chaos as a "black eye" for the sport.[29]

With nothing officially determined by the first game (except that practically anything might happen in the heat of competition without a league authority cracking down on shenanigans), it was necessary to continue the competition. With Posey back in the lineup and without the benefit of watch-grabbing or any other skullduggery, Loendi beat the Braves in both games, thus laying claim to the national title. The first win was in Pittsburgh, by 46–29. Posey had taken Young's guard spot, with Young moving to forward and, as the designated foul shooter, sinking 12 free throws for a game-leading 22 points. Posey and Pappy Ricks were second in Loendi scoring with eight each. A game at the Manhattan Casino March 7 was closer, but Pittsburgh still won, 30–25.

Defending the title in 1921–22 primarily involved getting past Douglas's Braves again. Loendi did, although in the second win the complications of top-level black basketball's inevitable turn from amateur to professional teams forced Douglas to play more or less with one hand behind his back. The first game was at the Labor Temple on January 7, and Loendi jumped to a 16–5 lead at halftime, winning 29–16. Ulysses Young, W.S.'s older brother, who was sometimes available for home games, made his debut at center and led the team with 11 points. Twelve days later the teams met again at the Manhattan Casino. Three thousand fans attended, but the confining spirit of the Metropolitan Basketball Association hovered over the court, especially over the Braves' bench.

In New York black basketball, creeping professionalism had not been embraced by the top teams, particularly church-sponsored St. Christopher's, which led a move to form the MBA. The association was meant to enforce amateur standards and could expel teams that were using recognized pros. At the time of the second Spartans-Loendi game, Douglas's Braves and some other teams were on the MBA hot seat for using suspected professionals, and while the far-sighted Douglas could see there was no future for the sport in remaining amateur, he was in no position to buck the association in the middle of the season and have all its teams drop out of his schedule.[30]

His starting center was Legs Sessoms, quite recently the Loendi center. That fact alone strongly suggests that Sessoms was a pro. The previous season the Western Pennsylvania Amateur Athletic Union had publicly identified Loendi and other top independent teams in its area as professionals, forbidding amateur and college teams to play them at the risk of losing their own amateur status.[31] As if that weren't enough of a problem for Douglas, he also depended on Frank "Strangler" Forbes for stalwart defense. (Forbes' nickname came about when, as a basketball player, he broke up a fight on the floor by grabbing the two combatants in headlocks.) Forbes excelled in baseball and football, too, and had a long and productive career in New York as a boxing fight judge and sports promoter. But Forbes, in addition to playing basketball, had for years played baseball with top-flight black teams—who had long since gotten past any qualms about professionalism. While Forbes was not a pro hoopster, the MBA might still disqualify him for having played any professional sport recently. So Douglas sat Sessoms and Forbes at the Casino and watched as the Braves lost a 15–9 halftime lead and the game, 30–26. It had to gall the Spartans even more that Loendi's top scorer was George Fiall, whom Douglas, treading with caution to keep on the right side of the MBA, had passed on at the beginning of the season because he, like Forbes, had been a professional baseball player.

There was no question what the MBA thought of Loendi. By the end of the 1921–22 season, shocked by Posey's tendency to import paid players from places other than Pittsburgh, the association had banned its members from playing his team, which was characterized as "a menace to amateur basketball."[32] Perhaps they were, but the real danger to amateur ball resided within New York's city limits, in sports promoters Roderick "Jess" McMahon and his brother Ed. The two white promoters seem not to have had any particular equal rights agenda, but they were decidedly non-discriminatory when it came to hiring athletes who could make money for them, enhancing those players' bank accounts and reputations in the process.

The McMahons had invested in black baseball teams in the previous decade, founding the Lincoln Giants in New York in 1911, then switching to the Lincoln Stars in 1914. Fiall and Forbes had played for those teams, establishing their professional status (or tarnishing their amateur standing, depending on one's point of view). The McMahons were also boxing promoters, and unlike their colleagues downtown at Madison Square Garden, who hesitated to promote mixed-race fights, they happily signed both black and white boxers to go at it at their Commonwealth Casino and Sporting Club in Harlem. When there wasn't a fight scheduled, though, they had little to offer other than wrestling and roller skating. They were not only astute observers of what worked in the New York sports business, they had personal relationships with some of the multi-sport athletes whose baseball careers were hurting their basketball careers under the thumb of the MBA.

So before the 1922–23 season they hired Strangler Forbes as player-coach, surrounded him with Fiall, baseball and basketball star Fats Jenkins and his talented brother Harold, and others who had run afoul of the MBA. The team played at the McMahons' casino, and so was called the Commonwealth Big Five. The McMahons didn't dabble in amateur sports; their players were being paid for their performances, and not secretly, either. Even Posey, who was luring players to the Loendis with something more than invitations to spend a few months visiting smoky, grimy, Pittsburgh, always publicly avoided discussing the subject of paying players. Jess and Ed lined up games against both black and white opponents, defeating most of them, and played on Sundays, as their Lincoln Giants had done, on "a day when businesses were closed and many Harlemites climbed the walls from boredom."[33] Midway through the season the McMahons agreed to play the Original Celtics, the top white pro team in the Northeast. Although the Celtics won, 41–29, on March 4, the game was much closer than that until the fourth quarter, the Commonwealths played well, and their popularity in Harlem continued to increase. This gave Bob Douglas cover to make his move and, backed by the Spartan Field Club management, he took the Braves out of the MBA. The amateurs were never again to control the black basketball agenda in New York. Romeo Dougherty, sports editor of the *New York Amsterdam News*, noted that hoop was going the way that baseball had gone long ago: "The crowd will go to see the professional games because the men are well up in the game and there's no thought of any crowd cheering for 'the game's sake.' They are with the proficient players and this thing of trying to tell us about a National Game and having us believe that it comes from a true love of the sport is all bosh."[34]

Loendi claimed another national black title in 1922–23. With Sessoms at center and Specs Moton added at a forward spot, the team had very little trouble with most of its competition, particularly the black teams it defeated to earn the title. It far outpaced the Baltimore Athenians twice and the Lincoln University team once. It also decisively defeated the Commonwealth Big Five, 51–27, at the Labor Temple on March 16, and 43–33 in New York two days later, after negotiations so involved and rancorous that the game itself was almost an anticlimax.

The game was not Posey's first contact with Commonwealth that season, and his initial experience had not been gentle. A member of the black wing of the Elks fraternal organization, he had played against them at the McMahons' casino on November 3 for an all-star team sponsored by Harlem's Monarch Elks Lodge. Commonwealth won the game, which featured a near free-for-all on the floor when Forbes, with the single referee looking elsewhere, slugged Posey. Cum's next visit to the casino was as a spectator on March 4 when the home team lost to the Celtics before a capacity crowd. Dougherty of the *Amsterdam News* wrote, "Those who saw, tell me that 'Cum' Posey's face took on an ashen hue when the announcer ... introduced the local players as colored champions of the world." By early March Dougherty was likely willing to seize on anything that smacked of a Posey weakness. He was a big booster of the Commonwealth Big Five and tired of Loendi's domination of Eastern basketball. He had been on Posey's case since the beginning of the season to agree to a championship match with Commonwealth.[35]

In December an uncredited article in the *Amsterdam News*, which was either written or influenced by Dougherty, said that "New York has been so fed up of Posey coming here and knocking teams over[,] the people are elated over the coming together of such a combination of the Commonwealth Big Five, the only basketball aggregation with any chance of humbling Loendi." In January Dougherty, with no pretense of journalistic impartiality, said Posey "has been hemming and hawing and refusing to answer telegrams, special deliveries, night letters and special couriers" regarding Commonwealth. This was at the point Specs Moton jumped Loendi to sign with the Commonwealths and, Dougherty, went on, if he [Posey] doesn't look out, we'll go and take most any man off his team and leave him on the rocks."[36]

Dougherty, who seemed to think of himself as practically part of Commonwealth's management ("We'll go and take most any man"), next accused Posey of bad mouthing Moton after Specs left him for the McMahons, and likewise denigrating other top players not on his team. Dougherty was not modest—he accused Posey of courting black newspapers "without backbone in sport," filling the columns of the papers, including the *Pittsburgh Courier*, with lies. His diatribe certainly did not cow the *Courier*, in which his "Eastern Sport Trails" column ran. Perhaps the *Courier*'s editors could feel all right about running this criticism, since an unsigned "Sportive Realm" column adjoining Dougherty's piece called for there to be a challenge series between Commonwealth and Loendi: "The public should get what it wishes.[37]

Posey wanted this series, too. He just wanted it on his own, lopsided terms. Surprisingly enough, given that in the McMahons he was dealing with veteran sports promoters who well knew the ropes, he got most things his way. Posey wrote Jess McMahon in early February offering a home-and-home series, with a number of provisions. Woodrow Wilson had formulated his 14 points in 1918 to try to bring about peace in Europe; now Posey had his 14, to encourage basketball warfare on the East Coast.

His letter opens with finger wagging at the McMahons, chiding them for discrediting Loendi in the newspapers and in letters to opponents, and for associating with Dougherty, "whom Loendi Club has learned through various experiences, financially and otherwise, to avoid." Posey excuses the brothers, though, since this is "their first year in basketball." (Of course, Jess and Ed were already running a top-flight black baseball team when Posey's Homestead Grays were unknown outside of Pittsburgh, and had been promoting sports in new York ever since.)[38]

Posey's letter attempted to dictate just about everything, big or small, that needed to be decided for a Loendi-Commonwealth matchup, including the game dates, the method for picking the referees, the rules to be used (intercollegiate), and how many free tickets were to be handed out (not very many). Other than the dates of the game, which Posey had proposed for late February and early March, but which wound up being played on March 16 and 18, the Loendi's boss got his way with the McMahons.

Many of Posey's demands, such as the free ticket limit, were fairly inconsequential and some of them, such as the stipulation that the team winning the 1922–23 series get the first game in the following season's challenge series, plus a more favorable share of gate receipts, were things the McMahons might certainly favor. But the brothers also gave in on the choice of rules. The collegiate (amateur) ones that minimized the dribble and emphasized passing were used, and some observers thought this might have favored Loendi, since Commonwealth, used to the pro rules, was a faster team. There was at least one mention later that the McMahons regretted giving in on this point.[39] Posey was the second highest Loendi scorer in the first game, with 14, but only scored five in the second. He had been pounding the courts for years, now, and as owner and chief talent scout, he had found others to carry the scoring burden. Legs Sessoms poured in 20 points.

The sweep of the Commonwealth Big Five was generally regarded as having handed Loendi another national black championship, but the keenly disappointed Dougherty was not giving up. In February, Loendi had been upset on an Ohio road trip. A team from the black American Legion post in Xenia, near Dayton, which included some of the best players in the Midwest, had edged them, 30–26. It was likely the first time Loendi had lost to a black squad. In a March 14 column Dougherty produced what he said were an exchange of letters between Posey and Dean Mohr, the Xenia coach, which the columnist claimed showed Posey's intention to thwart a rematch. Dougherty also alleged that a Loendi win over a strong black team from Perth Amboy, New Jersey, in April was tainted because only one of the Jersey team's usual starters made it to Pittsburgh for the game. Despite the columnist's protests, almost no one with an interest in black hoop, then or now, thinks anyone but Loendi was the 1922–23 champ.[40]

Posey's "14-point" offer to the McMahons had included provisions for continuing the series in 1923–24, but Loendi and the Commonwealth Big Five never met again. The McMahons, who were not making money off of home games, shut their team down after that season and went back to promoting boxing. Black basketball team owners kept the financial details of their business mostly to themselves, and generalized observations such as the one about the Commonwealths are the only evidence left of the businesses' viability at the time. But there was likely truth behind the generalizations, including one at the time about Posey's team that suggested "even Loendi suffered financially last year." This tidbit came in an un-bylined story in the *Amsterdam News* that was probably Dougherty's opening salvo for the forthcoming season, in which he stated that Sessoms and Ricks would both abandon Pittsburgh for New York City, leading to a headline: "Once Famous Pittsburgh Basketball Team All Shot to Pieces."[41]

Posey soon responded with a letter to Dougherty that the *Amsterdam News* ran intact, countering that "despite rumors, hopes and fears, Loendi will be on the court this basketball season." The team would abandon the "once-a-week realm of basketball" and play often, mostly in the Midwest, particularly in Cleveland, at the expense of games in the East. He asserted that Ricks would, in fact, be a Loendi.[42] Posey changed the shape of the Loendi basketball season to mirror to some extent his growing baseball operation. The Grays were developing from a local to a regional power, and had already discovered that money could be made in Cleveland, only 130 miles to the northwest. Potential turnout and profits increased when Posey took the baseball team and its reputation to places it wasn't usually seen, playing mostly in front of white crowds. Perhaps this could be true for basketball, as well.

Dougherty promptly publicized the McMahons' intentions to play Loendi's Pittsburgh archrivals, the white Coffey Club, noting that the brothers were "not ... at all enthusiastic to bring Posey to New York." (The game with the Coffeys seems not to have materialized.) While Dougherty might have accurately represented the brothers' thoughts, the story doesn't specify whether they objected to getting beaten twice by Loendi or to being one-upped in general by Posey, or both.[43] Consequently, the Loendis' only appearance at the Commonwealth Casino was on March 9, when they beat the Peekskill, New York, team from the white professional Hudson River League, 40–34. Posey was the second-highest scorer for his team, with 10 points.

But this game was the undercard contest that night. The main event was a 31–21 win by Commonwealth over the new challenger for black hoop dominance, Bob Douglas' Renaissance Big Five. Douglas had left the Spartan Athletic Club and persuaded the owner of the new Renaissance Casino in Harlem to allow him to put on games as an added attraction to the usual music and dancing. He also persuaded some Commonwealth players to jump to his squad, and in 1924, he was on the verge of establishing the longest-running dynasty ever in black basketball, eclipsing the efforts of Posey, the McMahons, Edwin Henderson, and Will Anthony Madden, among others. Douglas's "Rens" would play until 1949 and become one of the teams inducted en masse into the National Basketball Hall of Fame. But they weren't at that level yet. Not only did Commonwealth defeat them that March night, but Loendi had soundly whipped them, 26–16, in Pittsburgh in January.

Just after its appearance in New York the Loendis went to Atlantic City to play the Vandals and were upset, 45–40, in overtime. They beat the up-and-coming, youthful, Philadelphia Panthers, 35–27, in March, but then went to Chicago and lost unexpectedly, 29–22, to the veteran Eighth Regiment team, loaded with Midwestern basketball stars. Losing in Chicago and not playing Commonwealth at all, combined with the loss to the Vandals, eliminated Loendi from consideration for championship honors. W. Rollo Wilson, the *Courier*'s top sports columnist, eloquently said it was all over for Posey's five for the season: "And it is so ordered: Champions, city, state and national,

1923–24—THE COMMONWEALTH BIG FIVE, NEW YORK. 'The grandeur that was Greece, the glory that was Rome' will be a gratis preface on our part to any and all alibis emanating from Fullerton street, Pittsburgh."[44] Eighty-three Fullerton was, of course, the location of the Loendi Club.

So far as black national championships went, it was all over for Loendi, forever. The team would be together for only two more seasons, and it was considered for the black title in neither. The squad continued through the 1924–25 season to chew up local and regional opponents, rarely losing to any of them except for the teams at the very top of white independent ball in Pittsburgh. The city champions were picked much as the black national champs were: The teams that considered themselves first rate, and had their self-evaluations confirmed by beating most of their opponents played multi-game series. The local sports press anointed the winningest of the bunch as the champion.

Early in their existence the Loendis (including during their Monticello years) had been described as one of three teams that "dominated the situation in Pittsburgh for several years," and they were identified then as a potential city champion.[45] One of the other three, though, was Coffey Club, which season after season kept Loendi away from the title. It turned out that it was much easier to be the national black champion than to win the Pittsburgh title. The rivalry with the Coffeys went back to 1917–18, when the Monticellos had beaten them in their last year under that name. It continued through 1924–25, for a total of 15 games that were among the best-attended and hardest-fought in a Pittsburgh hoop season. The Coffeys won 11 times, but the outcome was almost always close, often decided late in the game. Coffey Club won by 10 points one night (as did Loendi another), and beat the black team by eight once, but seven of the games, including two wins by Loendi, were decided by one or two points.

The Coffeys, started at a Jewish settlement house, continued to be a Jewish team, built around longtime starters Moy Marks, Lefty Abrams, Buckets Sandomire, and Saul Adler. Although they seem never to have made it to New York City, despite the invitation from the Commonwealth Big Five, they played throughout the eastern part of the Midwest as well as the inland part of the Northeast, in Rochester, Cleveland, and Detroit.[46]

The first Loendi-Coffey game, on March 11, 1920, was emblematic of the rivalry. Coffey jumped out to a nine-point lead, but Loendi came back to go ahead, 20–19, at the half. Coffey worked its way back to a 36–34 lead and held on through an unsuccessful Loendi push in the last 40 seconds. The Labor Temple was sold out, 1,000 fans were turned away, and "so great was the jam at the hall that [a] riot call was sent to the Central Police Station, and the police quelled the disturbance with difficulty."[47] A Coffey 33–25 win in February 1921, despite a strong Loendi second-half comeback, was described as "a regular roughhouse game," which was a good characterization of many in the rivalry.[48] There were 36 free-throw attempts awarded by the referee in that game, but 61 in another in January 1922. The Coffeys were an excellent free-throw-shooting team, better than Loendi and other squads, and their edge at the foul line likely accounted for many of their wins.

The Loendi-Coffey Club rivalry even had its own disputed time-keeping incident, very similar to the one with Douglas's Spartans in 1921, although this time the game was resumed and completed. On December 20, 1923, at the Labor Temple, Loendi was in the midst of a comeback down 34–32, and had won a post-basket jump ball when, depending on the account, with as much as a minute or as little as a few seconds to play, a whistle blew from the scorers' table, signaling the end of play. It turned out that an over-enthusiastic member of the Coffey contingent, identified by the *Courier* as player Gimp Golumb, had grabbed the official whistle, and "gathered father time by the forelock." Posey and the Loendis protested, of course, but the orchestra retained for the post-game dancing, apparently thinking the contest was over, struck up a tune and fans began to pour onto the floor and do the fox trot. The officials properly decided that the game should restart, but it took 15 minutes to clear the mess. This time Coffey won the jump ball, and stalled out the restored seconds for the win.[49]

The other famous white pro team in Pittsburgh at the time was the Second Story Morrys. The team was founded by Maurice Goldman, who owned a popular clothing store of the same name on the second floor of a building in downtown Pittsburgh. Although the Morrys were a Jewish-owned team, the roster was multi-ethnic, and included Charles "Chick" Davies, later a renowned coach at Duquesne University. Loendi played the Morrys four times between 1921 and 1925, winning once. Besides the Coffeys and the Morrys, though, there was no other white team in the Western Pennsylvania area that could count on beating Loendi on any given night.

There was one white opponent from New York City, however, that could count on beating Loendi (and just about anyone else). The Original Celtics were the dominant team in the nation, formed after World War I to replace a team of the same name that had become inactive during the war (hence the "Original" tag). The team uniform featured a big green shamrock in the middle of each jersey, although many of the players who wore them were anything but Irish-Americans. This was a metropolitan team, representing the ethnic mixture of New York. One of the starters, Nat Holman, was Jewish and another, Joe Lapchick, was of Czech descent. Those two, with three other teammates, are in the Basketball Hall of Fame, as is the franchise in the team category.

The Celtics were in and out of early professional leagues, but played most of their games as independent barnstormers, winning upwards of 100 games a season, and rarely losing. They would play anyone, practically anywhere. A game with them was a lucrative box office proposition, and short-term notoriety would come to anyone who beat them. The Commonwealth Big Five could not top the Celtics in 1923, and the Rens couldn't either in March 1925, although they pulled off a 37–30 upset in December 1925 that helped start Douglas's team on the road to long-term fame. Posey booked three games with the Celtics in his team's prime years, but the New Yorkers won them all pretty easily, 48–27 in April 1923, 42–29 in February 1924, and 55–30 that April.

Posey said following the last loss to the Celtics that the team would retrench: "Instead of importing out-of-town talent, he intended to rebuild the Loendi machine, using local ability to do the trick." The decision to use only locals was likely a tacit admission that it was no longer financially possible to compete with New York for the top players.[50] In 1924–25 Sessoms and Ricks would be gone, although Moton was still on the team. The first order of business in October, though, was to find a new team name and some financial support. The members of the Loendi Club, which counted both Cum and his father as members, became concerned about the rampant professionalism of the squad they were sponsoring. It used to be that most Loendi players, such as Young and Betts, had day jobs and played, even if for money, as a sideline. But now the likes of Sessoms, Ricks, and Moton came and went depending on what the market for their services would bear. The Club had lost $500 in supporting the team in 1923–24, and it was felt that the business was "not so lucrative that any organization should foster a team which is composed of some men who refuse to do anything but play basket ball and good time."[51]

Sellers Hall, the former Monticello and all-around local promoter, stepped forward to be "responsible for the club in every way," thus addressing the money situation. Finding a new name was more difficult, however. A *Courier* sports columnist called "Expert," who was either Posey himself or privy to Cum's thinking, said that once the team could no longer call itself Loendi, revival of the old Monticello name would have been preferable. But the Loendi name was known to basketball teams and fans throughout the area, and it was important for that identity to be maintained. Posey's first stab at a new name was to call the team "Loenda," a close-shave skirting of the ban on using the club's name that almost immediately prompted scoffing.

"The Griddle," a *Courier* column full of inside jokes about the well-known in the Pittsburgh black community, announced the debut of "'Within the Law,' [t]he season's greatest novel by 'Cum' Posey. Read about 'Loendi' and the great name mystery. NO COPIES SOLD AT 83 FULLERTON STREET. For sale at local basketball games."[52]

It wasn't long before the team was using another variant, "Leondi." Leondi wasn't much of a change—sportswriters and headline composers at both the *Courier* and the white dailies had been frequently erring for years in transposing the "o" and the "e" in Loendi. Now they could use the mistaken spelling for real, although of course they still sometimes transposed the letters to call the team by the name that it could no longer use. The Loenda variation never caught on either as an official name or a typographical error. (In the text that follows, the team is referred to only as "Loendi," to avoid transporting the confusion of that day to this.)

Rollo Wilson, the black sports columnist, wrote in a literary, yet very readable style. A native Pennsylvanian, he nevertheless had a penchant for Scottish literature and history. He usually referred to the Hilldale Negro League baseball team, which was headquartered in Darby, a Philadelphia suburb, as "Clan Darbie." He liked to refer to Bob Douglas as "Rhoderick Dhu," a renegade Scottish clan chieftain celebrated in the writings of the poet Sir Walter Scott. The tone of Wilson's columns was genial and informative, but he didn't shy away from being a critic, either. He generally covered several subjects in a single column and liked to report on the doings of the many sporting figures who were his friends.

Cum Posey was one of those friends. He and Wilson probably met around 1914 or so, when Wilson was a student at the University of Pittsburgh's pharmacy school (he later worked for a time as for the City of Philadelphia as a chemist). Wilson was president of the Monticello-Delaney Athletic Association in 1916, when Posey was secretary and the star of its basketball team.[53] When Posey announced Loendi's name change, Wilson was one of those who would rather have seen the Monticellos revived, but his support for the team was never in doubt. "We are with you till Charon radios that there is skating on the River Styx," he wrote.[54] In February, though, Wilson was eloquently describing a basketball upset, in which "fading veterans" faced "exuberant youth." Posey's Loendis were involved, but they weren't the youngsters.

For the Loendis, the season featured several losses—of vitality through injuries and age, a particularly important game, their home court, and money. Worst of all, perhaps, was the loss of face for Posey. Not that the season was a total disaster. It featured a 25–15 wipeout of Coffey Club in March, at the Duquesne Garden, the city's best indoor sports arena. Coffey was ice cold from the floor, and actually scored no field goals in the first half. The crack varsity from the historically black Wilberforce College in Ohio went down to defeat, 37–32, on New Year's Night. Wilberforce's star Harry "Wu Fang" Ward wound up on Posey's team shortly afterwards and he would contribute a lot in those days when college athletes could drift over and play with the pros for a while and still retain their eligibility. The preceding season's loss to Chicago's Eighth Regiment team was avenged in February, and a black New York team (although not a top-flight one) sponsored by an American Legion post was also beaten that month.

But any hopes of competing for the national title were dashed by a disastrous road trip to Philadelphia in early February. The Philadelphia Panthers were a black team run by Harry Passon, a local white sports entrepreneur who also organized black baseball teams. The Panthers were a young outfit that hustled its way to a 15–1 lead after the opening jump ball and a clear 36–22 walloping of Loendi on February 6. On February 10, Posey's team lost again, 35–32, to the "Speed Marvels" of the Wissahickon Boys Club, a good local black team, as both Posey and Young went down to injury. Loendi barely beat the Panthers in a return match, 29–27, on March 27, when "the incomparable Cum Posey, still the master of the show, gave the kiddies some lessons in the art of playing basketball." But splitting with the Panthers, the only top-level black team that Loendi played more than once, and then losing what ought to have been a walkover with Wissahickon within the same week, put the team out of championship contention. Even to be in the hunt that season (and others afterwards) though, a team would have to play the Rens. Posey had sent Douglas one of his challenge manifestos, apparently something similar to the one-sided deal to which the McMahon brothers had agreed. But all that seems to have happened was that Douglas turned it over to Romeo Dougherty, who chastised Posey, wondered if he was entering his "dotage" and wrote of "the challengers who have descended to the level of the parasites of the game."[55]

There were three season-long problems with the Loendis. One was that they were, finally, getting older and more frequently injured. The Pittsburgh answer to questions about the team's viability each season was something like "We've got Posey, Young, and Betts, and we can always fill the other two spots with good players from somewhere." Of course, the "other two spots" over the years went to stars such as George Gilmore, Jim Sessoms, Pappy Ricks, and Specs Moton, but it was true that the dependable core of Pittsburghers was indispensable to the team's success. But Posey was 35 years old, and more frequently missing games because of illness and injuries. In fact, he started the season on the sidelines, playing his first game against Wilberforce on New Year's. Young was only 25 but was more often injured than Posey. Wilson, who was based in Philadelphia and also wrote for the city's black weekly, the *Tribune*, covered the Panthers' February upset for the *Courier*. He was familiar with the Philadelphia team, commenting in the game story that "the kids were just as good as I thought they were." Two weeks later he followed up with an elegiac entry in his column, comparing the upset of Howard University's crack team by the upstart Monticellos in 1912 with the game he had recently covered: "Another group of fighting youngsters. Another blasé team of champions…. Fading veterans facing exuberant youth. History DOES repeat itself, though the actors in the drama may assume other names and read other parts."[56]

The *Courier* had noted in December of that season that in the whole of the Pittsburgh area there were only three basketball floors that could reliably be counted on for black teams to call home and one of these, the Labor Temple, was available only because Loendi and other squads paid to use it. But the Temple was getting run down (Wilson referred to it as "in its senility"), and on March 1, 1925, the labor unions sold the building to the Society for the Improvement of the Poor, a major charitable group that converted it into a dormitory for transient men.[57] For the rest of the season the Loendis were also transients, playing as a visiting team in various places, probably with a reduction in its share of gate receipts since the home team, responsible for rent and other game night expenses, usually took more. As 1924–25 wore on the *Courier*'s game stories alluded to a drop-off in attendance, describing a "fair-sized crowd" for a local game on December 4 and noting that the team was "not drawing as well" as in the past. The reporter covering the Eighth Regiment game, while not naming an attendance figure, wrote that the crowd "clearly showed that professional basketball for the present season at least, is dead."[58]

This trend was not just a Leondi problem: the Coffey Club, for instance, merged with Ameritas, a white rival club, after this season due to lack of fund. And it wasn't even just a Pittsburgh problem. Sports historian Robert W. Peterson has noted that while amateur basketball was gaining in popularity about this time, the pro game was slumping badly: "One of the reasons was the constant jumping of players from team to team to find the top dollar. It was hard for fans to maintain interest in the hometown heroes when they could not be sure who would suit up for a game."[59]

Not everyone close to the Pittsburgh basketball scene thought the decline of the pro version of the sport was a bad thing. Ira F. Lewis of the *Courier*, who eventually would be Robert Vann's right-hand man in making the paper one of the most-read African American newspapers of the time, was the sports editor in 1925. He was very happy that professionalism was waning and felt that basketball was being saved by the emergence of new blood on young amateur teams.

He put a finger on another of the likely causes of pro ball's decline: There were simply not enough top-flight teams in the city to ensure true competition and keep fans filling the halls the way they used to. The top teams, including Loendi, packed their schedules with pushovers and played only one or two games a year against each of the other fives in their class. The result was that "the team that can beat you tonight, can beat you tomorrow night, the next night, and the next night, and so on." Lewis, like a lot of fans everywhere, was also fed up with the comings and goings of pros who would come to Loendi, then drift away for a better payday somewhere else. "A professional basketball player," he wrote, "is the most purchasable piece of humanity wearing a sport uniform."[60]

Posey told Rollo Wilson before the 1925–26 season began that "he would not be in the game in any way this season.... Posey's health has not been of the best during the past year." This led to a lengthy, although premature, farewell to Loendi basketball in Wilson's column. But when it became time to start the season, Posey was there with his team, although nothing was better, and some things were decidedly worse, than during the season before. Cum got hurt again, playing in a 49–13 shellacking by the Second Story Morrys on Christmas Day with a broken rib. The team forged a deal to play at Montefiore Hall in downtown Pittsburgh, but the arrangement fell through, forcing the cancellation of a potentially lucrative New Year's Day game against the Coffey Club/Amerita combine.[61]

There were no games against nationally ranked competition, white or black, and few against top-level local teams, either, which might have been a good thing considering how the Morrys had thrashed Loendi. Posey, who would in time be well known for his contributions to the black population in his home town of Homestead, took time from his team to coach a girls' team at the Clark Memorial Baptist Church, a major African American congregation that was right down the street from his home. The team was so successful that it began to play out of town squads, and the distracted Cum was "practically allowing the Loendi team to run itself."[62] Posey, ever the businessman, laid the blame for the awful season on the effects of the loss of Montefiore Hall as a home court, but he might have been well advised to heed his feelings from October and not struggle against all the impediments to putting a top-flight team on the court again.

While the basketball wasn't very rewarding, Posey as a "race man" (a black stalwartly pushing the prospects of African Americans) had a couple of small successes. On January 27 the team suffered a one-point overtime loss to a team in Uniontown, 50 miles southeast of Pittsburgh. It turned out that the Uniontown organizers had decreed segregated seating, and black fans complained in letters to the *Courier*. Posey responded in an open letter to the paper that he had known nothing of this when agreeing to the game, and "in all future contracts, there shall be a clause which will prevent such embarrassment." At the very end of the season Loendi entered the double-elimination Tri-State Independent Tournament in Pittsburgh, a big event for white teams. With several men suffering from the flu, the squad was dispatched quickly in the minimum of two games, but as Posey wrote in his *Courier* column, "The big thing accomplished was that the [racial] barrier … was broken down and the admittance of Loendi to the tournament, the clear playing of the club and the attitude of the fans, augers well for another season."[63]

When the next season began, Posey had changed the basketball team's name to match that of his nine, the Homestead Grays. What this meant was that the hoop team was now subordinate to the baseball team, and instead of vying for national honors, it shrank to a regional outfit while the baseball Grays were steadily moving from their regional status to become one of the very best black teams in the East, and then anywhere. Posey had ceased playing, although his sidekicks Young and Betts continued. They were joined by some Grays baseball players, in particular longtime Grays outfielder Vic Harris, keeping fit and earning a few dollars in the off season.

Posey also kept his hand in by being an occasional promoter in Pittsburgh, a youth teams coach, and a referee. (In the latter role, he had the chance in 1935 to blow the whistle on Pappy Ricks, now a veteran forward with the Rens, when the team was playing the Iron City Elks.)[64] But by 1925 all the accomplishments that later got Posey elected to the Basketball Hall of Fame as a player and team organizer had ended. Various writers started to summarize his career, beginning with Wilson's view of his importance to black sport in Pittsburgh in that slightly premature farewell in October 1925: "Cum was truly the father of basketball in Pittsburgh and to him must go the credit for putting the town on the map in that line." From New York, men with whom he had matched wits and hard knocks on the court praised him. Fats Jenkins wrote in 1943 that Cum had been "the greatest individual player that I ever saw." In 1942 Douglas named Posey as one of the five all-time great players in black hoop. Some writers recalled his temper, both on and off the court. Wendell Smith, the *Courier* sports columnist in the 1930s and '40s, remembered Posey as exceptional partly because he was "a fighting, fiery, dynamic personality on the courts. He was a good winner and a poor loser."[65]

Although he always reserved the right when writing or being quoted to point out his astuteness in the larger issues of black sport and to tout the success of his teams, Posey didn't toot his own horn about his personal accomplishments as an athlete. Most of the time when writing about the old days, particularly of Monticello and Loendi, he would even refer to himself as a player in the third person. There's no reason not to believe he wasn't pleased about the outright praise, though. There's also little reason to believe he objected to being described as a sore loser. His entire plan for success was to be a winner, and gracious losing had no place in the plan.

Chapter Three

"McGraw of the Sandlots"

The name "Homestead Grays" first surfaced in the Pittsburgh newspaper sports sections in 1903, and it belonged to a white amateur squad in the borough organized by Harry Haley, a 33-year-old grocery clerk. Haley had been running amateur baseball in Homestead for a few years but didn't seem to have much luck with the 1903 squad. Five of its games were reported in the local dailies, and the Grays won only one.[1] About eight years later, a team by the same name was seen on local ball fields, but this time with African Americans in its lineup and nearly 40 years of staying power.

A black team had existed in Homestead since around 1900, composed of youths who played amateur ball around the borough and called themselves the Blue Ribbon Club. The team at some point changed its name to the Murdock Grays. "Grays," or the alternative spelling, "Greys," was a common team name, and seems to have harkened back to a late nineteenth-century trend in the major leagues to name teams after the bright colors of the stockings they wore with their knickerbocker-style uniform pants.[2]

Then, in 1910, at a meeting at the home of John Freyl Alexander, a black laborer at Carnegie's Homestead steel works, the club was more solidly organized, primarily as a recreational outlet for black steelworkers at the works. Alexander became the club president and Jerome "Jerry" Veney, a Carnegie laborer who within a few years would cap a 40-year career at the mill by becoming the rare black locomotive engineer, was made playing captain. The team played mostly white opponents, since there were not enough black teams to create a single-race schedule. The Grays were popular and successful, and soon were sought after for games outside of the Pittsburgh area, and on days other than their usual Saturday playing date. This created problems. For one, the mill employees were loath to leave work and give up pay for weekday games, and they had no interest in spending additional time dealing with other clubs to schedule more games.[3]

A second impediment to the Grays' rising in the Pittsburgh baseball world was that Veney, a devout Christian who would become a trustee of his

African Methodist Episcopal church, refused to play on Sunday. Baseball on Sundays for paying fans was technically illegal all over Pennsylvania at the time, but local officials, who were tasked with upholding this so-called Blue Law, had varying appetites for enforcing it. The major league Pittsburgh Pirates either played Sunday games on the road in rival cities that condoned Sunday ball or just sat the day out. On the local level, authorities in Mifflin Township (adjacent to Homestead) banned Sunday ball in 1912. But there was Brunot's Island, located at the beginning of the Ohio River just west of Pittsburgh. It was accessible only by railroad bridge and ferry, so not in the backyards of anyone who might be affected by Lord's Day sacrileges. There a team named the Edward F. Dillons, sponsored by a police magistrate, played on Sundays in 1917.

These pressures for change created an opening for Posey, who had already demonstrated his sports entrepreneurial skills with the champion

The 1913 Homestead Grays baseball team. Posey, a regular outfielder, is third from the left in the second row. By the end of the decade, he was running the team, which he made into one of the most powerful black teams in America by the 1930s (Carnegie Library of Pittsburgh).

Monticello basketball team. His job with Railway Mail appears to have given him a work schedule flexible enough to play sports the year around, and he had made some road trips with his basketball teams. He had no qualms about playing on Sundays: throughout his career he was willing to play anytime, anywhere—so long as his conditions were met by the opponent, of course. Many accounts of the growth of the Grays under Posey's management have him in total control of the team by 1916. But the sports pages of the daily newspapers, in addition to reporting the outcomes of actual sporting events, also served in the early twentieth century as a sort of bulletin board that allowed managers of independent semi-pro and amateur teams to contact each other about scheduling games. Posey and Veney were listed as the men to see for the Grays through 1918, as was Posey's basketball teammate, Sellers Hall.

There may have been too many cooks stirring the Grays' broth that season. There was controversy in August when Hall called M.L. Kelly, who ran the crack P.J. Sullivan team from the Lawrenceville section of the city, to cancel a game that Posey had already booked. "I do not know whether or not there is any dissension on the Homestead club, but both Hall and Posey seem to be acting as managers," said Kelly. While Hall was essential to Posey's basketball operation in 1925, when he lent financial support to the struggling Loendis, the P.J. Sullivan situation was not the last time the two black entrepreneurs would lock horns over off-the-field decisions. In August 1925 Hall sued Posey and Charles Walker, who had replaced Alexander as team president, alleging that the Grays officials had reneged on an agreement to form a partnership. The Grays won the suit, however.[4]

While Hall had organized another good black team, the Pittsburgh Colored Collegians, he sometimes pitched for the Grays. Both black and white players with superior skills and a desire to earn some side money from their regular employment were known to suit up for multiple semi-pro teams. While regular salaries were as yet unknown for top level teams such as the Grays were becoming, players shared cooperatively in attendance money, when it was collected, and in "pass the hat" contributions by fans when the game was played at an unenclosed field where collecting admissions was next to impossible. Posey, in fact, played for four other baseball teams in Pittsburgh in addition to the Grays between 1911 and 1917 (and, as the not-so-mysterious Charles Cumbert, for Duquesne University in the spring of 1916). He first shows up in local newspaper game accounts in 1911, at age 20, as center fielder and leadoff batter with the Pittsburgh Colored Giants, a team organized by W.A. "Daddy" Clay, a veteran black steelworker at the Homestead mill who sponsored baseball teams for several seasons. The same summer saw Posey in the outfield for the Rippley Giants, run by Trummon H. Rippley, an African American construction worker. Continuing to play for Clay's Giants in 1912, Posey also made his debut with the Grays, showing up as the second baseman (with two errors among eight chances) in a late June loss to a local white team. He joined Hall's Colored Collegians for some games in 1913 and 1916, and he supplemented his work as a regular Grays outfielder in 1916 and 1917 with games for an integrated team of Railway Mail employees that played as the South Hills Athletic Club in the latter year.

In 1918 Posey stopped playing for other teams and became the Grays' regular left fielder, his role as player added to his booking and other administrative duties. While there would be others, including Walker, involved with running the team over the coming years, the Grays were now really Posey's team for sure. In retrospect, he seems to have had a long-range plan, or at least the ability to achieve his goals gradually, taking advantage of opportunities as they presented themselves. In the first couple of decades of the twentieth century black baseball went through the growing pains the white version of the sport had survived in the late nineteenth. There were many casualties of this growth on both sides of the racial divide, represented by teams, and whole leagues, that had started out with enthusiasm but had outrun their potential to make money and gone under. The Grays persevered, reportedly making money every season until the Great Depression hit, even though the coming effects of the Big Crash were already visible by the mid–1920s in the industrial sector of the economy, the basis of Pittsburgh's economic existence.[5]

To follow the Grays season to season through this period is to watch them grow from a very good local team, playing 40 or so games each year (and winning well over half), to a sought-after regional attraction that by the mid–1920s was dominating most opponents with a 75 to 80 percent winning rate in almost as many games as a major league team would play, in a season that was two to four weeks shorter. The Grays ranged over an area in Western Pennsylvania, Ohio, and West Virginia that could find them playing well over 100 miles from Pittsburgh. In 1924 they finally replaced a patchwork transportation system that included trains and streetcars for local games with two new seven-seater Buick autos that included extra baggage compartments. Riding in the Buick caravan, which sometimes included a third auto, was comfortable enough if the trip wasn't too long, but road trips just grew longer and longer as the team's reputation rose. Quincy Trouppe, who played for the Grays in 1932, recalled that "we organized a kind of Notre Dame shift, and when the ride became uncomfortable someone would give the signal and we'd all change positions on the rear and jumper seats."[6] The Grays seldom had a field they could call their own, although Posey struck up a friendship with Pittsburgh Pirates owner Barney Dreyfuss that allowed him to lease the Pirates' Forbes Field for major games beginning in 1924.[7] The lack of a home field may actually have been an advantage, allowing Posey to demand hefty shares of the gate, particularly at enclosed parks in larger cities, and avoid having his share reduced by the cost of home-team advertising and other expenses.

There was often significant money to be made by both teams. Pittsburgh sportswriters of the day referred to most local baseball that wasn't fully professional or amateur as "sandlot" ball, using the terminology usually reserved for youth baseball played on poorly manicured and often sandy fields. While news accounts of Grays games usually didn't include attendance figures, when the numbers made it into print it wasn't unusual for 4,000 or 5,000 fans to be reported. Local attendance records were often claimed to have been set when the Grays showed up at an opponent's park, as in nearby Bloomfield when the Grays played and defeated the J.J. Dean club before a "record crowd" on June 7, 1923.[8] Posey was able to drum up enough business to keep the Grays always on the move by playing any opponent who offered a game (even on Sundays, when possible) and by making sure the team's fortunes were well publicized in the local papers, which, unlike the dailies in some cities, were happy to cover the black teams as well as the white ones.

Posey, with his constant solicitation of games in the daily papers, pushed the Grays to upper bounds of the region's semi-pro activity, and he went right on booking from there. The team was playing an average of three games per week in 1920, in a season that began in April as soon as the weather would allow, and continued to around October 1, when most of the local teams had shut down the fields, many of their players being required for amateur and semi-pro football. By 1922 the Grays were averaging nearly five games a week and they hit six the following season. They played every Saturday around Pittsburgh and every Sunday somewhere in the region where Sunday ball was permitted, plus "twilight" games during the week after the mills and other businesses discharged their workers—the team's fans—for the day.

Once games were set for the coming week or more Posey made sure the papers had his schedule to publish. The stories on games coming up, probably inspired by press releases written either by Posey himself or under his direction, emphasized the difficulty it would take to beat the next round of opponents, even as the Grays were reliably winning around 75 percent of their games each season. In the days of newspaper publication when stories, headlines, and advertisements were set in metal type, the typographers who put together the pages would dump the day's type after the press run so that the metal could be melted down for reuse. For efficiency's sake they saved headlines that frequently ran verbatim, re-using them as "standing heads." "Homestead Grays Have Hard Schedule" appeared so many times over the summers that it could have been one of those standing heads.

As the number of games the Grays played each season approached and surpassed the previous season's total, the emphasis in stories about them was not so much the number of wins they had, but how they were climbing toward another team record in games played. Posey's team was said to have played 150 games in 1924, which *Pittsburgh Post-Gazette* columnist Jack Adams said was "the high water mark for the sandlotters to shoot at…. No semi-pro manager considers his schedule complete without booking the Grays. They are the first to start the season's activities and the last to put away their tools." It was unlikely that any other "sandlotters" would match the Grays in staying busy. The schedule that Posey put together far outstripped everyone else's, even the other crack teams. For example, a regular opponent, the Consumers of Harmarville, a community in Western Allegheny County about 20 miles from downtown Pittsburgh, had played only 71 games by mid–September when they suited up for the first game of the National Baseball Federation championship series.[9]

The Consumers were only one of the top-level semi-pro teams the Grays regularly played. Around the Pittsburgh area there were the Beaver Falls Elks, who like the Consumers could often be found advancing in national tournaments, the Fineview team from the North Side, and Bellevue from west of Pittsburgh proper, which became by the mid–1920s one of the regular opponents at Forbes Field. As was the case in other cities in those golden days for amateur and semi-professional sports, teams had sponsors from all segments of the community. Mining and heavy manufacturing were obvious supporters—some big companies, like the Homestead mill, had their own amateur company leagues in addition to semi-pro squads. The Consumers got their fairly unusual name from the Consumers Mining Company, which operated a coal mine in Harmarville. The National Tube Works in nearby McKeesport, manufacturer of more than 50 types of metal tubing, from sewer and gas pipes to flagpoles, backed a regular Grays opponent. The Grays played various teams from Ambridge, a borough 20 miles northwest of Pittsburgh, which were not only connected to local industry, but which actually came from a company town. The giant American Bridge Company, which had steel in the Golden Gate and Brooklyn bridges, among many others, bought the community from a failing communal religious sect and in 1905 incorporated it into a town named after itself.[10]

Beaver Falls was only one of several teams sponsored by Elks lodges, and Posey booked many games with Moose and American Legion opponents, too. As was the case in collegiate basketball, college baseball teams could play non-college teams. The nine from St. Vincent's College in Latrobe, 40 miles southeast of Pittsburgh, was regularly on the Grays schedule early in the semi-pro season before the school year ended. Teams were often run, or at least sponsored, by individuals with significant name recognition in the area's sports world or the community at large. Honus Wagner, the renowned Pirates shortstop who had retired in 1917, was a Pittsburgh-area native who owned a sporting goods store and was a leader in local amateur and semi-pro sports. He ran a team in Carnegie, where he lived. Speedo Laughran, an all-around athletic star at the University of Pittsburgh, had a team, as did Al Grayber, a former middleweight boxer turned local sports promoter. A consistent top-flight squad was named for, and probably funded by, Police Court Magistrate P. J. Sullivan, as was the team playing Sunday ball on Brunot's Island, named for fellow magistrate Dillon.

But with some exceptions such as the Dillons' perch on Brunot Island and Grayber somehow keeping Lord's Day enforcers at bay in Esplen, a neighborhood in the western part of the city where he held sway, Posey's desire for lucrative Sunday baseball had to be satisfied by getting the Grays on wheels and going to another part of Western Pennsylvania, Ohio, or West Virginia. The first regular Sunday opponent was a white team from Bellaire, Ohio, on the west bank of the Ohio about 60 miles southwest of Pittsburgh. The Grays played them twice in Bellaire and hosted them once (on a Saturday) at Forbes Field, winning two of three games. For the next few seasons the team found Sunday bookings closer to home, often in boroughs toward the outer edge of Allegheny County and in adjacent Westmoreland County such as McKeesport, Bridgeville, and Collinsburg, and on Brunots Island, of course. But small towns meant small games in terms of the level of competition and the dollars in the gate. There was little competition for sports fans on Sunday, and it was a day that could pay off handsomely for teams that could play. So further trips were added, with Cresson, 80 miles to the east, and Martins Ferry, Ohio, 60 miles in the other direction. As one of his players, Willis Moody, later observed, the Grays "couldn't help it but make money" off Sunday crowds.[11]

In 1921, as the Grays started to play more games than any of their local opponents, Sundays became days of travel to larger venues. Martins Ferry and Wheeling, West Virginia, opposite each other on the Ohio River, became favorite spots and the Bauers, a top team from Wheeling, became favorite opponents. The Bauers and Grays struck up a multi-year rivalry that saw them play on as many as seven different Sundays in the coming seasons, always in Wheeling. Sunday baseball was routine in Ohio, with both the major league teams in Cleveland and Cincinnati regularly playing on that day. The Grays found frequent competition in Cleveland, Alliance, Dillonvale, and Warren, all one-way trips of up to 80 miles, as well as longer jaunts topping 100 miles to Clarksburg and Parkersburg, West Virginia, and Cumberland, Maryland.

Another reason to make Sunday road trips besides the lucrative bookings was that things were getting too hot for comfort on Sunday baseball diamonds around Pittsburgh. Grayber Park in Esplen was a sure-fire site for the Grays until Sunday, July 30, 1922, when the *Pittsburgh Press* carried a notice that the scheduled game with the Beaver Falls Elks had been called off "by request of the county authorities." This followed by three months the wholesale charging of the entire Grays team, including Posey, and their opponents, the Heidelburg Firemen, for "desecration of the Sabbath" on April 23 in Carnegie when the Grays bested the Firemen, 10–4. The action, it was reported, came after a number of complaints to county authorities about Sunday ball, "most of which were registered by ministers."[12]

In 1924 the Grays avoided arrest, but lost their chance for a game at Collier, south of Pittsburgh near Uniontown, when Fayette County district attorney E. D. Brown "carried out his threat to drive a nail in the coffin of Sunday baseball in Fayette County." Although Collier was experiencing Western Pennsylvania's version of spring-like weather, which is to say there was "a high and piercing wind and cloudy sky," fans were in the stands and players were warming up when "County Detective A. B. Bell drove his automobile containing three state police and other officers out in the middle of the diamond and ordered the playing field cleared." D.A. Brown wasn't just picking on baseball, either. The next stop for Detective Bell and his officers after quashing the ballgame was the Uniontown Country Club, where Sunday golfers were shooed off the links.[13]

By the mid–1920s Posey's strategies to play all comers, drum up well-publicized multi-game challenges with strong opponents (usually an odd number of contests to ensure that one team could win more than half the games and wind up with bragging rights), expand the geographical area in which the Grays were well known, and schedule as many Sunday games as possible had made the team famous throughout the Tri-State coal and steel belt. The *Daily Post* opined in 1923 that "for the past three years the Grays have branched out until now they command a place alongside the best in the semi-pro division." A year later, Adams of the *Post-Gazette* called Posey the "[John] McGraw of the Sandlots."[14]

Because of the Grays' prominence, and quite possibly because of his family's reputation and his own sharpness, Posey had clout in the almost entirely white Pittsburgh semi-pro baseball world. In the off-season before 1922 more than 100 amateur and semi-pro teams organized the Greater Pittsburgh Baseball Association to better the state of competition in the area. Honus Wagner was elected president, and Posey was made a member of the board of directors, representing all the black teams.[15] That season, in an experiment that was not repeated, Posey tried to establish the Grays as more of a local, as opposed to a traveling, team. He secured Car Barn Field in Rankin, a borough across the Monongahela from Homestead, as a home grounds. Adjacent to the giant brick trolley car storage barn of the Pittsburgh Railway Company on Talbot Avenue, it had a covered grandstand, and the Grays played at least 17 games there. He also entered the Grays in the Association's season-ending playoffs, and nearly won the championship, losing October 7 in the final round, 6–5, to the Crafton Presbyterians.

But in 1923 the Grays were back on the road again, filling the role of everyone's favorite visiting team. The team became so well regarded that some began to wonder how it would do against white major league competition—a thoroughly theoretical question in light of the color line. The *Pittsburgh Daily Post* ran a sports section feature that answered questions from readers, one of whom stated in 1923 that "a gang of fans would like to see a game staged between the Pirates and the Homestead Grays." The *Post's* comment was "The Pirates might find a pretty stiff game if they should bump up against the Grays."[16]

The Grays, an all–African American team, and one that could swell the coffers of the local teams they came to play, appear to have been welcome wherever they booked games. But racial discrimination, even in the Tri-State Region, sometimes showed through. Often it merely took the form of ham-handed jests from sportswriters, such as the *Akron Beacon Journal's* observation before an early night game that "the real test for night baseball will come Sunday when the Homestead Grays come here. If fans can see those fellows, the lights are right." But comments were much more pointed in 1923 in Uniontown. *Pittsburgh Post-Gazette* sportswriter Gilbert Remley had a side job helping Posey book games in Western Pennsylvania, and the *Evening Standard* sports department took to referring to the Grays as "Remley's Monkeys." And, although it doesn't seem to have been noted at the time, when the Grays rented the Pirates' Forbes Field, the use of the ballpark did not include allowing Homestead or its visiting opponent to use the locker rooms. Three later histories of Pittsburgh black baseball all refer to black teams having to dress at the black YMCA in Pittsburgh before coming to the park.[17]

Playing the Grays meant occasionally putting up with on-the-field dissension, sometimes deliberately fomented by Posey himself. As field manager he was known to occasionally pull his team off the diamond in the middle of a game in protest after an umpiring call he disagreed with, occasionally sparking unruly fan reaction. The *Daily Post* reported in August 1920 that the Grays "almost precipitated a race riot" when they walked off in Johnstown after the local Independents scored the game's tying run on a disputed play at the plate. Posey likely initiated that incident, but he couldn't be blamed directly for one in 1919, when in McKeesport Tom Pangburn, called out at second on a close play, picked up the base and threw it at the umpire, hitting him in the side of the head. Fans rushed onto the field and a local amateur boxer, Johnny Ward, was kicked in the teeth by Pangburn when he closed with him. "From then on it was a free-for-all," the *Daily Post* reported, one that didn't end until Ward punched Pangburn in the face, drawing blood. The evening up of injuries seemed to work to calm things down, and the game was resumed and played out to an 8–4 Grays win.[18]

In August 1924 *Daily Post* columnist Fred Alger, after another Grays walk-off, this time against the Braddock Elks when an umpire refused to change a decision, wrote,

> Posey has been pulling this stunt regularly ever since he started piloting the Grays, and now that his team has become a big drawing card about the independent circuit he is becoming more independent than ever.... A lot of the big teams of the circuit would be justified in refusing to play the Grays after doing such an unsportsmanlike trick, but the drawing power of the Grays makes them a desirable attraction, even with these kind of faults, for it is often said that by booking the Grays for a number of games a lot of independent clubs are able to tide over their financial difficulties.[19]

The strategy of going anywhere within reason to find an opponent seems to have continued to pay off for the Grays, even when the area's industrial economy took a downturn, as it did in 1921, when several teams shut down as their sponsors and fan bases took financial hits.[20] No solid financial information exists for the Grays' early years, but in semi-pro baseball, and in professional black ball in general, the main indicator of a team's economic welfare was whether or not it existed from season to season. The Grays were always there. In addition to the claim that the Grays never lost money until the Depression, Posey later noted in one of his newspaper columns that player salaries increased every year from 1921 to 1931. Some small hints as to how this was possible come from newspapers' mention of money that the Grays didn't get. The walk-off in 1924 that drew Fred Alger's attention cost Posey at least $250, his guarantee of the gate. At about the same time the operators of the Cumberland, Maryland, team withheld half of a $209 payment when Posey split his squad on August 3, sending half to Cumberland and half to

Cleveland to play a Sunday doubleheader against the Browns of the Negro National League. The Cumberland folks apparently weren't advised in advance that they were not getting the full Grays team, and responded accordingly.[21]

It's not likely the Grays could command that sort of payment for just any game: the Maryland game was a Sunday contest, and the Braddock Elks were very popular. But the Grays played 20 times on Sundays in 1924, on the road in sizeable population areas, and if they regularly received an average of the Braddock and Cumberland guarantees each time, they would have grossed about $4,500 on Sundays alone. If they earned, say, half of the Sunday guarantee in each of their 100-plus other bookings, they would have grossed about $17,000 for the season, equivalent in contemporary standard of living terms to about $541,000 (before salaries, travel, and other expenses were deducted).[22]

Although the bulk of the Grays' games were with the white semi-pro squads of the Tri-State region, some were with a handful of black teams, including one that had black major league status. The Pittsburgh Keystones took its name from an 1880s black team in the short-lived League of Colored Baseball Clubs, the first attempt at forming an African American professional league. The twentieth century version of the club was founded in 1921 by Alexander McDonald Williams, an immigrant from Barbados who ran a billiard hall in the Hill District, Pittsburgh's main black neighborhood. Williams took a dive into black baseball in 1921 by founding the Keystones, who played at Central Park on Wylie Avenue, the Hill's main thoroughfare.

The newly organized Negro National League, the first black league with staying power, had been launched in 1920. Its powerful president, Andrew "Rube" Foster, was interested in consolidating power for the league at the expense of the major black independent teams of the Eastern Seaboard. He did this by establishing "associate memberships" for teams that were, sort of, league members. An associate club could not compete with the eight regular members for the league championship but could arrange to play potentially lucrative home-and-home series against full members. Perhaps more importantly, associate members were bound by the same rules against roster raiding that the NNL tried to enforce among its regular members. Associate teams' rosters were protected from all other NNL members, and, of course, other members' players were protected from the associates, too—which is what Foster really wanted to accomplish.

The Keystones, while not of the caliber of a regular NNL team, had a number of good players. Veteran pitcher William "Dizzy" Dismukes joined part-way through the 1921 season, and managed the following year. Among the other good players were pitcher-outfielder Oscar Owens, center fielder Willis Moody, third baseman Jasper "Jap" Washington and shortstop Gerard Williams. They anchored the Keystones, and shortly became part of the strong Grays foundation when Posey either lured them away to the Grays, or in some cases back to the Grays, where they had played before taking advantage of the opportunity to collect a regular paycheck for playing league ball. Like the other NNL owners, Alex Williams had his Keystones on salary from the beginning in 1921, a year ahead of the Grays. *Courier* sports editor Ira F. Lewis, in fact, thought that the Keystones would have been a serious threat to the Grays, speculating that if they had "remained another year the worry would have been up to Posey."[23]

The Keystones, as an associate league member in 1921 and a full member in 1922, were a rung above Posey's Grays in terms of national ranking. But Homestead dominated them on the diamond. It was natural for the two teams, the Grays with a powerful regional reputation and the Keystones with national status, to want to play multiple games against each other, and 1921 and '22 saw announcements of extended challenge series. As was the case with every kind of baseball in those days other than the organized white professional leagues, weather and scheduling problems, among other snags, reduced the total number of contests, at least those that can be found in the local newspapers, to a total of eight. The Grays won four of them and the Keystones one, there were two ties and a no decision. The no-decision game, which happened in 1921, and one of the ties the next season, said volumes about the level of competition between two black teams vying for the honorary title of black champions of Pittsburgh.

In the third game of the 1921 series Dismukes, by now the Keystones manager, pulled one of Posey's tricks out of his cap. When the umpire failed to heed Dizzy's plea to overturn a hit-batsman call, he pulled his team off the field. The fans, who had paid their money but had seen only three innings of baseball, were allowed in free to the rescheduled game the next night at Homestead Field, when the Grays beat the Keystones, 7–2. An advance for the 1921 series promised, "Intense rivalry, though of a friendly nature, exists and every battle will be hard-fought." But the first 1922 game was literally hard-fought, and none too friendly. A more or less dysfunctional contest on Friday, June 23, tied 12–12 after a combined 29 hits and 9 errors, broke up in the ninth inning when players got into a fist fight over a decision at first base and some spectators joined in. A scheduled game on Saturday was cancelled. When some members of the crowd, who had showed up anyway, threatened to set Central Park on fire because of the cancellation, the police ordered refunds to all the fans, who were then told to go home. The fight the day before seems to have been the cause of the game's being called off, although the press reported differing accounts of who was responsible. The *Post-Gazette* wrote that the Keystones had refused to play when the Grays put one of Friday's combatants in the starting lineup. The *Press* reported that the Grays had left the field just before the first pitch, again over something from the Friday fracas.[24]

The Keystones were just one of eight Negro League or big-city black independent teams the Grays played through 1924, usually at Tate Field, the Negro National League park in Cleveland, or as a special attraction at Forbes Field. Posey lured the Indianapolis ABCs of the NNL to Forbes on the first two days of August in 1918, and the Grays played them nearly even up, losing 4–2 (a Sell Hall five-hitter) and 2–1. The Tate Stars from Cleveland, owned by black businessman George Tate, also an NNL associate member, hosted Homestead in September 1921 and took three straight. The Tates invited the Grays over again in May 1923, with a substantially different outcome—Homestead won two out of three. The Grays had also hosted the then-independent Baltimore Black Sox, later a member of the first black league in the East, in July of 1921, and had defeated them, 7–3. as ace starter Charles "Lefty" Williams not only got the pitching win, but hit a grand slam homer.

It was in 1924 that Posey's plan to make Pittsburgh a stopover destination for Negro League clubs from both the Midwest and East headed to the other region began to really develop. Rube Foster's American Giants arrived for a three-game set at Forbes Field in late August and demonstrated why they were usually NNL champs by sweeping the series. As the *Courier* put it: "T'was a contest between Benny Leonard [a champion lightweight boxer] and [heavyweight] Jack Dempsey, with the inevitable result."[25] The Giants were followed in mid–September by the Detroit Stars, the league's third-place club, and this time the tables were turned. The Grays won all three games at Forbes, including a 7–0 one-hitter by Owens in the opening game. Homestead also paid another visit to Cleveland at the beginning of August, splitting a Sunday doubleheader with the Cleveland Browns, the Tate Stars' successors in the NNL.

The Keystones dropped out of the NNL in 1924, although they played on as a local black team. This was the beginning of an unsettled economic period when money could be made in professional or semi-professional baseball in Pittsburgh, but it could just as easily be lost, and Williams's baseball enterprise was not sufficiently successful to stay on the highest rungs of black ball. The mighty economic engines of steel production and coal mining, which had made the Pittsburgh area prosperous, were already tailing off: "Iron and steel production in 1929 was only slightly higher than in 1916. Coal and coke production declined each year after 1909, with the exception of the war years." To make matters worse for African American workers, the downturn coupled with new labor-saving devices in the mills, precipitated a significant loss of unskilled jobs, the ones most likely to be given to African American immigrants.[26]

Because of Posey's willingness to make his team the most heavily scheduled and widely traveled team around, the Grays had a reputation that made them fairly impervious to Pittsburgh's pre–Depression slump. In outlasting the Keystones, Cum survived the challenge of another black team in town, and not for the last time. In the 1920s, in fact, Pittsburgh was home to several other African American teams, although none enjoyed the league connections of the Keystones or seemed likely to challenge the Grays' dominance. Sellers Hall was in charge of several of them, or at least he had several names for what may have been a single operation. His American Giants of 1919 were followed by the Colored American Giants the next season, and then the team became the Pittsburgh Colored Giants. Whoever else was on each roster, Hall himself was usually the pitcher, and still a very good one.

Beginning in 1922 he fielded the Cuban X Giants, reviving the name of one of the top black independent teams of the late nineteenth and very early twentieth centuries. By 1923 he had taken over Central Park from the fading Keystones. Just as his Pittsburgh Colored Collegians of a few seasons ago likely had few collegians on it, his "Cuban" team had very few Cubans on it, although Pittsburgh sandlot star Ralph Mellix went as "Mellico" when pitching for the team to inject a little Latin flavor. Lewis, the *Courier*'s sports editor, was not impressed by this. He referred to the Cuban X Giants as "a collection of chattering jackasses, who could neither talk Spanish or play ball."[27]

In this particular column, though, Lewis bluntly summed up the state of black baseball in Pittsburgh in the spring of 1925. He strongly criticized Hall, the inveterate promoter, with taking inadequate teams on road trips to play NNL opponents such as the Detroit Stars, losing by "scores of 25 to 3, 18 to 2 and such scores." Hall had done a lot for black ball in Pittsburgh, Lewis agreed, but these fiascoes worked to "undermine the great reputation for colored baseball established by Posey and the Homestead Grays." But as for Posey, Lewis was responding to a charge from Hall's booking manager, Joe Ward, that Posey's arrangement with the good white clubs of the area forbade them from playing any other black team. Lewis didn't rebut this claim; in fact, he allowed as how it was Cum's "well known practice." So as the lagging Pittsburgh economy brought other black teams low, Posey in essence was putting a foot on their slumping backs to make sure they stayed down. In closing his column, Lewis had a good word for the black teams that were not the Grays. He noted that they provided a chance for numerous young players who could not crack the Grays lineup: "Posey does little developing [of young talent] now-a-days, depending on finished players with national reputations."[28]

Lewis had this correct, too. Just as Jerry Veney left the Grays lineup because of his objection to playing on Sundays, his immediate successors had also by and large been replaced, either because they didn't want to give up their day jobs for the incessant travel of the Grays' schedule, or because Posey had simply found someone better. The Grays of the late 1910s had several key players with substantial local reputations, such as Ben "Brother" Pace, Jerry Veney's brother John, Buddy Clay, and, of course, Sell Hall, who had played with Posey on other black teams such as Clay's Giants and the Colored Collegians. Grays box scores also featured some of Posey's winter teammates from the Monticellos and Loendis. Emmett Campbell and "Greasy" Betts, for instance, could be found in the infield, and beginning in 1918, W.S. Young caught. Young would play with the Grays until the mid–20s, remaining in the lineup even after his year-round sports boss had retired to the bench. While formally integrated teams were as unknown in Pittsburgh in those days as they were anywhere else in the country, occasionally black players suited up for white teams, and vice versa. Posey had played on the integrated Railway Mail team, and in the Grays' early years he sometimes recruited well-known local white players, including Johnny Pearson, regarded as the best white athlete from Homestead in those days, and catcher George "Ziggy" Walsh.[29]

Given the many opportunities for black players at the cooperative "pass the hat" semi-pro level, which the Grays had not yet abandoned, there was roster turnover season by season, month by month, and game by game. By 1918 and '19, though, the Grays lineup was beginning to stabilize. With a solid financial situation developing, Posey began to find a few players with actual credentials in national black baseball, such as Pangburn (of the flying base). Mostly, though, he began to attract the best local talent to play exclusively, or usually so, for the Grays. Since good pitching is the bedrock of any team, two of Posey's signings in this period can be said to have been the foundation of the early Grays.

Charles "Lefty" Williams came on board in 1918 and Oscar Owens, a right-hander, the following season. Posey recalled in 1926 that he had recruited Williams after playing against him at Homestead in 1917. Cum wrote in 1926 to celebrate his star's long-term presence on the Grays while some of his teammates had defected to the aspiring Keystones (and come back again when that team failed to prosper). But Williams had several more good years remaining in that left arm: He played until 1934, never for anyone but Cum Posey. He reportedly won 540 games for the Grays, including 17 no-hitters, against all types of competition. A native of Virginia who like so many blacks had migrated to Pittsburgh for a better life, Lefty was a street car company laborer playing ball part-time when he first caught Posey's eye. He may have been only five feet, six inches tall, and the clerk at the draft board where Williams registered in 1917 described him as "short" and "stout."[30]

Like Williams, Owens was an immigrant from the South, he and his family having left that region while he was still a youth. He joined the Grays in 1919 right after his discharge from the Army, when he already was 25 years old. A barber by profession, he was frequently accused of trimming opposing batters a little too close: "Owens is just about the champion pitcher in hitting batsmen with pitched balls ... Not a few of the seasoned vets have a healthy respect for Oscar's fastball." He had impressive durability, and in common baseball parlance he could be credited with a "rubber arm." He rarely missed a start, and sometimes started and completed both games of doubleheaders. He pitched for the Grays until 1931, with some time spent with the Keystones in 1921 and '22. Owens was a powerful hitter, too, and played outfield when not pitching. Owens was about the same size as Williams and, according to black baseball historian James Riley, this led to a rumor flying around in some towns in which the Grays played that the team had a pitcher who could throw with either hand.[31]

Whichever of the two was pitching, the results were usually highly favorable to the Grays. In 1920 Owens had a 19–6 record, and Williams was 14–5. As the Grays played more games each season as the middle of the decade approached, the two pitchers just worked harder, Owens was 29–9 in 1923, for instance, while Williams was 27–4. Each had a no-hitter, and Owens pulled off the "iron man feat" on August 25 when he pitched, and won, two games in a single day. He held the Beaver Falls Elks to two runs in nine innings at Forbes Field that afternoon, and then beat the crack Fineview neighborhood team, 11–4, in a seven-inning twilight game at the Fineview Park.

Another local star that Posey could depend on as the team began its climb from a local nine was second baseman Raymond "Moe" Harris. He had been a Gray since 1915 and was already a regular infielder when Williams and Owens put on Homestead uniforms. Harris played with the Grays until 1929 when, with Posey's support, he became a Negro League umpire for several years. Posey later recalled that "What 'Mo' needed [lacked] in natural ability, he made up in smartness." Harris "went out of the game as a player with the reputation of [a] perfect gentleman, who never rode umpires." Nevertheless, one of his favorite tactics when coming to bat was to unload a stream of nasty invective about an ump whose calls had been questionable, but direct it to the opposing catcher. The umpire would hear the insults but be powerless to give Harris the heave ho, since they apparently had nothing to do with him.[32] Jasper "Jap" Washington came from Fayette County, about 50 miles south of Pittsburgh, within Grays territory, to join the team in 1920, following discharge from his Army enlistment in 1919. He usually played first base but was versatile in the field and sometimes pitched against lesser opponents. He has been described as "a popular player" who "projected a mean image and was as tough as he looked." After a detour to the Keystones, he rejoined the Grays and played with them until the early '30s.[33]

But if the Grays were going to move beyond being a regional power, they would need to look beyond home for players, too, preferably ones who were ready for the starting lineup or rotation. The teams of the Negro National League and the new Eastern Colored League had plenty of those guys. Because Posey could circumvent the leagues' anti-raiding policies (since the Grays were independents) and because less financially stable Negro League teams sometimes went out of business, there began an incoming trickle of former league players that turned into a steady stream. His attempts to hire league players away from their teams were not always subtle. In June 1924 the *Courier* reported that "Manager Posey is planning on making an invasion of the Eastern [Colored] League. He stated Monday that up to the present time although the East has been after his men continuously, making all kinds of offers, he has refused to bother their men. But now it is a case of taking what he needs."[34]

Infielder Walter "Rev" Cannady had hit over .300 with the Cleveland Tate Stars in 1921 and was flirting with .400 early the next season when he became a Gray. Cannady continued to be a roving ballplayer, playing for a dozen more black teams, most of them major-league caliber, through the end of World War II, but he bolstered the Grays lineup for a few years (and made three return appearances), as well as taking a regular turn on the mound. He won 17 games in 1923 as one of the second-tier starters behind Owens and Williams.

The demise of the Keystones not only allowed Posey to recover the full-time services of Owens, Moody, and Washington, but for a short time it also brought him the services of Dismukes, the veteran pitcher, until he decamped for Indianapolis to rejoin the Negro major leagues. Willie Gray, the Keystones' fleet center fielder, got away, for a while. He signed with the Tate Stars, but when Tate's club also folded after the 1923 season he became a Gray until 1927.

Dennis Graham, likewise a fast and good-hitting outfielder, had been blocked from a regular starting role by veterans on the Atlantic City Bacharachs, but he was a Grays regular by 1924 and stayed for the rest of the decade. Graham was a college graduate, and, Posey later reminisced, the only player he ever fined for not arguing with an umpire. The first game of a doubleheader in Baltimore in 1929 against the Black Sox was exceedingly contentious, and between games Posey threatened fines for anyone who got himself ejected. Late in the game Graham was thrown out at second trying to stretch a single, in "one of those special Baltimore decisions." When Posey asked him if he thought he had been safe, Graham said he "was safe by a mile" but didn't protest for fear of being tossed and fined. Posey, his combativeness likely getting the better of him, and his own warnings notwithstanding, fined Graham $5 anyway for not arguing a very bad call. Cum liked Graham, though, and when he named the five best Grays hitters ever through the 1935 season, Dennis was one of them.[35]

Harry "Rags" Roberts, a catcher-outfielder, came from the Baltimore Black Sox in the middle of the '20s, and Joe Wheeler dropped in during 1923 to bolster the pitching corps and threw two no-hitters within the space of four days in September against lower-level opponents. Ed Rile, a right-handed pitcher who spent most of his career in the Midwest with the NNL, joined the Grays at the beginning of 1924 and was a highly dependable starter for the first half of the season, until he decided to rejoin the NNL with Indianapolis. As the influx of new non–Pittsburgh players meant the end of Grays careers for some original team members, the clock also ran out for Posey's playing career. He was not a regular after 1920, although he played the outfield fairly frequently in 1921, then less and less.

Posey's pickups from league teams were generally journeymen players, some a cut above that, but for 1924 he reached out to a bona fide star, John Beckwith. Only 24, Beckwith had already established two reputations. One was as a power-hitting, defensively versatile player that any manager might want. As to the other, as Riley diplomatically puts it, "His temperament and basic approach to the game contributed to his making the rounds of a variety of teams." Beckwith's signing in the offseason was sports-page headline news in the *Courier*, which quoted Ernest Gooden, a local ballplayer who had been in the NNL in 1923, describing how Beckwith, fooled by a pitch, had nonetheless hit a home run one-handed. The *Courier* did not report that Beckwith had been the centerpiece of an on-field brawl with a white team the previous October, when accused of deliberately missing a pitch as catcher so it would hit the umpire, and that the Chicago umpires' association had then refused to work anymore Giants games if Beckwith was in the lineup.[36] Beckwith had his problems with umpires. When he opened with the Grays in 1924 he was a little more than a year away from being suspended from the Eastern Colored League for waylaying an ump outside a ballpark and beating him up over a prior play-calling grievance.

Beckwith displayed both sides of his reputation in his short first stint with the Grays. He hit a home run in the season opener on April 19, but by early June Posey announced he had been released "for the good of the organization... We felt that we had to either let him go or ruin the morale of our club." Word got around, though, that Beckwith's particular transgression, aside from just being Beckwith, was to pull a gun on infielder Elmore "Scrappy" Brown during an argument. Eventually, though, Posey was able to forgive this star who could hit home runs, even with one hand off the bat. Beckwith was back with the Grays for a couple more stints in later years.[37]

Chapter Four

Posey: "Fans Love a Winner"

Posey's willingness to shop for the stars he needed to take the Grays to the next level paid off handsomely in the spring of 1925, when he signed a lanky Texan who was already a star, already regarded as one of the best black pitchers ever. Joe Williams was six feet, five inches tall, with a hawk-like profile befitting his partial American Indian heritage. Williams had pitched for the Brooklyn Royal Giants of New York City in the Eastern Colored League in 1924. Because the Grays were not a member of a Negro League, Posey could sign Williams at will, ignoring the complaints of the pitcher's former employer. But no one in New York seemed particularly interested in fighting to keep him. Williams was 39 years old that spring and had been pitching in high-level black baseball since 1910. When he departed for Pittsburgh he was deemed to have "about ended his active career." Williams had been a playing manager in previous years, and reportedly was going to be Posey's assistant on the Homestead bench.[1]

The talent evaluators in Gotham who were writing off Williams had it all wrong, though. He pitched for the Grays through the 1932 season, finally hanging it up at age 46 (many newspaper accounts had him in his 50s by then—it made for good copy even if inaccurate). Williams had a blazing fastball, which got him the nickname "Cyclone Joe," although by the time he got to the Grays he was known as "Smokey Joe." (As they say about fast pitchers, he "threw smoke.") He was enshrined in the National Baseball Hall of Fame in 1999.

He arrived in Pittsburgh in mid–April and immediately joined the Grays' starting rotation, showcased in a coveted Sunday game in Bellaire, Ohio, on April 26. He allowed only five hits and struck out nine in a 13–1 Homestead win. He similarly plowed through starts against the Grays' many semi-pro opponents, but his skills weren't just effective on weaker opponents: He two-hit the Kansas City Monarchs, the Negro National League champions, in a post-season exhibition game at Forbes Field on October 19.

Posey had intended to turn field management of the Grays over to Dizzy Dismukes, the longtime pitcher and manager who had been with the Pittsburgh Keystones a few years earlier. But Dismukes instead signed to manage the Memphis Red Sox in the Negro National League. This put Posey back in uniform, and the veteran Williams acted as team captain as well as a star pitcher. An un-bylined May 2 column in the *Pittsburgh Courier* extolled Williams' value:

> It has long been the custom of the Colored fans of Pittsburgh to see a great star in name, come to Pittsburgh much heralded, either in basket ball or base ball and in a few short hours turn into a prima donna or an autocrat, one is as bad as the other; this season we have seen a miracle come to pass. We have seen a pitcher recognized as the peer of all negro pitchers go out and pitch one solid hour of batting practice every day for two weeks, with the sun boiling down on him, then hit to the infield for forty-five minutes until the infielders could hardly stand it, and all the time he was encouraging the men to go get them and never a word of abuse.[2]

Smokey Joe Williams, one of the all-time great Negro League pitchers, was one of Posey's first star acquisitions in the mid-1920s as he remade the Grays into a nationally recognized attraction. Here Williams is in the uniform of the Lincoln Giants of New York, his last team before coming to Homestead (NoirTech Research, Inc.).

Plenty of starting pitching was a necessity if the Grays were going to continue to play on an almost daily basis, and they were, logging 158 games in 1925. In late May Posey added another first-rate pitcher, signing lefthander Sam Streeter. Streeter, unlike Joe Williams, was not unwanted by his previous employer, the Birmingham Black Barons of the NNL. In fact he had started the season in their starting rotation before being lured away to the Grays, which irritated NNL owners, tired of Posey's disdain for their roster reserve rules. Williams and Streeter joined a starting rotation that already had Lefty Williams and Oscar Owens, making Homestead's pitching among the best in black ball at the time. By the end of the season all four pitchers had more than 20 wins, and Owens was in the low 30s. Willis Moody, the longtime Pittsburgh player who spent several years with the Grays, thought Posey's focus on hurlers was excellent strategy, since there were plenty of good black position players available, but in the long run of a season, good pitching was indispensable.[3]

Posey also worked on improving the lineup, and one of his 1925 pickups had more long-term value to the Grays than even Joe Williams. Vic Harris was a 20-year-old left-handed hitting outfielder who had moved with his family from Florida to Pittsburgh when he was a child. Despite growing up in the Grays' backyard, he had gone west to the Negro National League to begin his career with the Tate Stars of Cleveland. He later recalled playing against Homestead as a Star in 1923: "We played against Posey's team, and I beat him with a home run."[4] He apparently got Cum's attention, because after moving to the Chicago American Giants after NNL operations in Cleveland folded, he left the Midwest in 1925 to come back home and play for the Grays.

Harris was beginning a long career in the Negro Leagues, most of it spent with Homestead. He was a steady influence in the lineup and Posey's replacement as field manager when the Grays dominated much of Negro League ball. As a player, his reputation was of one who played hard and slid with spikes high. As a manager, one of his players later simply said, "Vic didn't take no crap."[5] Not only didn't he take it from his players, he didn't take it from umpires, either, which led to a brush with the law. In October 1934 Harris's team at the time, the Pittsburgh Crawfords, was playing a barnstorming white team led by noted pitcher Dizzy Dean at Forbes Field. Harris beat out an infield chop and went to second on a wild throw, but Dean himself persuaded the home plate umpire, James Ahearn, to call Vic out for running out of the baseline on the way to first and interfering with the throw. When the decision went against him, Harris stalked in from second and, depending upon whose story is to be believed, either picked up Ahearn's mask and hit him over the head with it or just yanked it away from his face and let it snap back. In any case, he was hauled into criminal court on an assault charge, which was settled the following March with a conviction and six months' probation. Harris told an interviewer years later that Posey's constant friend Art Rooney helped get him out of the jam.

Posey had a longstanding rule against his players getting into fights on the field, particularly at the Forbes Field showplace, but Harris wasn't working for him at the time, so Cum couldn't take any action. He had an opinion, of course, which was that while "it would have been much better if it had not happened," Harris had been prosecuted because the Pittsburgh umpires association made it a point to pursue such incidents in court. And he had nice things to say about Harris, who soon would be back working for him.[6]

By the second half of the 1920s the Grays were becoming a team with a lineup and reputation that transcended Pittsburgh sandlot baseball. The team still played mostly in western Pennsylvania, eastern Ohio, and West Virginia, where it was so highly sought after by regional opponents, since it could fill their ballparks, that it could name its own financial terms for the privilege of showing up and beating the home team. Posey's ability to recruit very good players, and usually keep them, had the most to do with this continued success. But Ira Lewis of the *Courier* saw something more. In 1926, he wrote that Posey, previously content to be a highly competent but low-key executive, "got hep to the benefits of publicity and the wisdom of playing up his stars." The exploits of players such as Joe Williams, Oscar Owens, and John Beckwith began to be mentioned in the press, replacing the familiar stories of the Grays' lengthy schedule and efforts to push their win total ever higher.[7] The Grays were also becoming more of a well-developed business organization in other ways. At one time, a manager of another club could book a game with the Grays by calling Posey at home. As of the mid–1920s, though, the team had a clubhouse and office, at first on Wylie Avenue in the heart of the black section of Pittsburgh, later in Homestead. A small organization had grown around Cumberland Posey, one that included his older brother See, who drove one of the Buick touring cars that carried the team and otherwise provided support help, and Gilbert Remley, the white sportswriter and game arranger. Posey's partner, though, was a former mill worker named Charles Walker.

Walker, born in Charleston, West Virginia, had, like so many others, moved to the Pittsburgh area to work in the Carnegie steel mills. He identified himself as a molder helper at the Homestead works when he registered for the World War I draft, and his death certificate indicates he had lived in Homestead since 1898. A hero-worshiping 1931 feature story about Walker put him with the Grays around the beginning of the team's existence, in 1912, although the story gives him credit for the Grays progress up to then, and it gets around to mentioning Posey only in the third to last paragraph. At any rate, he clearly was important to the Grays. When John Freyl Alexander and Jerry Veney turned over control of the team, a milestone in the Grays' development into something more than a local semi-pro squad, Walker replaced Alexander as team president.[8]

Walker was a jovial, cigar-smoking presence with the team for years, as well as Posey's right-hand man in off-the-field matters. The *Courier* sports columnist William G. Nunn described him as "the power behind the throne of the Grays," Posey's "ever-present shadow and 'luckman' of the famous duo."

Posey and Walker were a team, and Posey gave him due credit for his work. But Cum also made it clear that the bulk of the responsibility was his. In 1928 he wrote in his *Courier* column, remarking on his release of some malcontented players, that the Grays were owned by Posey and Walker but "the former looks after the playing and has never been interfered with in any manner."[9]

Walker died in 1940 of heart disease, having been less active in team affairs since the early '30s. Posey devoted his October 12, 1940, column to his late partner, crediting him with being an integral part not only of the Grays but of the Loendi basketball team. "World's champions are not built overnight," Posey wrote; "They are built by the personality, cunning, ruthlessness of the governing powers." That sounds like a description of Posey himself by some baseball owner with whom he had locked horns, but he was ascribing these qualities to Charlie Walker. Cum described his late partner as his "Colonel House" for Loendi. (Edward M. House was an influential behind-the-scenes advisor to President Woodrow Wilson.) "He did not miss one practice of this team in seven years," Posey recounted, "and saw to it that no one else missed a practice." Some accounts of the team in those days identify Walker as the money man behind Posey. Cum said in his farewell column that Walker, like the Grays overall, had made some money when the team was a strong independent from 1923 to 1933, but Walker was always a renter in Homestead, not a homeowner, even when he was president of the club. It's unlikely that he had a profitable, illegal, side business such as numbers gambling or liquor. The men involved in those activities were constantly in the local papers, and there are no such mentions of Walker to be found there.[10]

Posey and Walker were able to capitalize on western Pennsylvania baseball's flagging economic situation in the late 1920s, but also on Pittsburgh's unique location between the geographic zones controlled by the Negro National League in the Midwest and its rival, the Eastern Colored League, on the East Coast. Regionally, the Grays dominated a shrinking market for top-flight semi-pro ball brought about by a recession in the manufacturing industries, including steelmaking. The income from the 170 or so games against semi-pro teams each season enabled the Grays to make successful offers to good black players on league teams. The leagues had rules against contract jumping, of course, but they didn't apply to a non-league team. And the Grays' contracts were sufficiently lucrative that when league teams came shopping for men on the Homestead roster, they usually left empty-handed. In the Tri-State region Posey was developing a reputation as a domineering team owner, although one with whom it was financially profitable to do business. Among other black team owners, he was regarded as a pirate.

After a post-war boom in the early 1920s, American manufacturing growth turned flat in the middle part of the decade, even before the Great Depression, as overproduction began to outstrip the buying capacity of consumers and inventories grew. Steel production was no exception, and Pittsburgh, being the Steel City, was particularly impacted. One way the economic slump played out was to reduce both sponsorship and attendance gates for the semi-pro baseball teams who actually had contractual commitments to their players. Fred P. Alger of the *Pittsburgh Daily Post* covered the top semi-pro, or "independent" teams, a group that included the Grays, although by 1925 they were anything but "semi" pros. (They just weren't, obviously, in white Organized Baseball, which kept them from being regarded as true professionals.) In June Alger said that business was bad because of the recession: "Few clubs are making enough to swim along on and at this time the situation is grave," the teams' financial "angels" having lost some of their enthusiasm. But "the one club that is getting the breaks this year is the Homestead Grays.... This club proves to be a saviour [*sic*] for most of the teams, for the games with the Grays always draw down a nice piece of change."[11]

A year later, though, while reporting that the independents' financial situation was even worse, Alger was also highly critical of Posey's increasingly draconian money demands: "The Grays are dictating their own terms this year ... with a certain feeling that [Posey] is 'grabbing' the gate receipts at some games.... Today one team gets all the crowds and the spectators hold off other games waiting for the appearance of the Grays." A month earlier Alger, who often admired the Grays in his *Daily Post* "Periscoping the Independent Circuit" column but was clearly bothered by the imbalance developing, reported that a manager of another team was saying that Posey took 75 percent of the gate receipts just for bringing the Grays to his field. Alger also reported that the Grays sometimes insisted that "a certain umpire" work their games; "it certainly has come to the point where Posey dictates to the white clubs of this section." Beyond the talk of the unidentified manager, a few definite examples of the Grays' favorable terms popped up. It was reported that the Grays had demanded a $250 guarantee (the minimum they would collect if the crowd was small) for a game in Warren, which was "one of the largest amounts ever paid to an invading club." Homestead was a regular visitor to Canonsburg to play the local Gunners, and in June 1928 the local *Daily Notes* encouraged fans to show up for that night's game, even though wet weather threatened: "The local management is signed up for a large rain guarantee [$125] which must be paid in case the game is called off, so do not take it for granted that if rain falls during the day the contest will be called off." The game was begun under "dark hanging clouds" and went four and a half innings before it poured with the Grays ahead, 2–1.[12]

The onset of the Great Depression a short time later had an even worse impact on the Pittsburgh semi-pros than the late '20s industrial slowdown. The number of top-level teams continued to drop off, and Posey began to look elsewhere for white competition to keep the Grays' almost-daily schedule in force. His financial demands and the Grays' often overwhelming talent edge might have contributed to this decline, but to Posey, it was just evolution. In a 1937 column, he maintained that Negro League and white semi-pros needed each other, and back in the day the Grays "never made the terms so great, although always demanding a fair percentage, that it would injure the opposing club." But the growing strength of Homestead, for which he did not apologize, led to a falloff in attendance at the parks of the teams that were always getting beaten, and "the clubs died natural deaths."[13] Posey often warned in his columns against killing the Goose that Lays the Golden Eggs, urging players not to demand too much from owners and owners themselves not to ask too much to play good opponents. In this column he seems at least to be acknowledging past criticisms of the Grays' dominance of western Pennsylvania baseball, but without admitting fault. When it came to keeping the Goose alive, Posey saw himself as a dedicated conservationist.

The "sandlot" game accounts didn't regularly include attendance figures, but while business was still booming game stories regularly had the Grays playing to crowds of up to 5,000. Homestead kept playing a few more games each year, and continued winning most of them, assuring their status as a superior drawing card. There were varying, but not too divergent, won-loss records published for the seasons from 1925 through 1928. Posey's version, usually published in his *Courier* column, tallies closely with game-by-game counts tracked in the sports pages. He reported that his team won 130 of 158 games in 1925, 140 of 163 in 1926 (a season that opened with 43 wins and four ties before the Grays were defeated), 141 of 166 in 1927, and 131 of 170 in 1928. A Posey-led team rarely let up on the opposition. There was talk that being badly beaten in a first encounter discouraged lesser teams from scheduling further games, although the Grays never wanted for someone to play, even on their own terms. Posey admitted in 1926 that some teams resented being beaten badly, but this didn't seem to bother him much. So far as he was concerned, the Grays "have become a great attraction because of their consistent winning and the popularity of the club in every town visited the past two seasons bears out the old saying 'Fans love a winner.'"[14]

Since it was so difficult to beat the Grays, any victory by a semi-pro team was the cause of much bragging on behalf of the victory. Even coming close had its honors. The West Newton club in 1927 was lauded for having "recently held the Homestead Grays to a 3–1 victory." The Grays' victory, that is. Pitchers who could beat the Grays, even sometimes, became regional heroes and were much sought after. Well-known semi-pros Steve Swetonic and Joe Semler, for instance, were brought in by the best white semi-pro teams to make multiple starts each season against Homestead. Swetonic, who went on to win 37 major league games with the Pirates from 1929 to 1933 before his arm went bad, and Semler, winner of 73 minor league games from 1931 to 1936, were the answers, according to the *Pittsburgh Press*, to Pittsburgh semi-pro managers' constant query, "Where can I land a twirler who can stop those fellows?"[15]

It was such a feather in a team's cap to have beaten the Grays during this period that some semi-pro promoters fabricated victories over Posey's team to spice up their advance publicity. This would only work outside of Pittsburgh, where the local dailies always kept accurate tabs on the team's doings. But news travelled more slowly in those days, and on June 2 the *New Castle News* reported that the Pittsburgh Broadways, in town for a game, had recently beaten the Grays, 3–1. The next day the *Connellsville Daily Courier* said that the Miller club of Pittsburgh had "put the skids" to the Grays. Both of these victories would have had to have happened during the Grays' season-opening 43-game win streak, which was meticulously documented in the Pittsburgh papers and made no mention of either supposed opponent.[16]

The real facts were good enough for most Western Pennsylvania sportswriters, who were pleased with what they saw. A writer for the *Altoona Mirror* in 1929 noted that "every player is a star. Each member of the team plays ball.... The team is in there to win and win is what the club usually does." This reporter commented on another facet of the Grays' performance: It clowned for the crowd in the fashion that was more or less expected of a traveling black team in those days, as there was a touch of the old minstrel show in a game involving a black team, even a world-beating one.[17] Going back to the earliest barnstorming black teams in the nineteenth century, a black team hitting a small town was expected not only to play baseball but to put on a comical side performance, usually by the men in the coaching boxes, or maybe by players on the field when the action stopped.

This is something that Posey, the consummate athletic professional, never talked or wrote about, but he kept reserve catcher and utility man "Rags" Roberts on the roster for years, despite the fact that Roberts was a marginal player at the Grays' demanding level. But Rags contributed to the Grays' appeal on a regular basis as its comedian. He pulled "vaudeville stunts" when coaching the bases, and put on "a boxing act, a one-handed dice game and baseball juggling that usually gets a big laugh from the spectators."[18]

Some white sportswriters occasionally used the Grays' abilities as a stepping-off point to speculate about how successful they would be in white baseball. A writer for the *Warren Tribune* stated in 1926 that "there is no gain-saying the fact that several of the Grays would be in the major league if they were white-skinned." A sportswriter for the *Uniontown Evening Standard*, having some fun in 1927 at the expense of the Pirates, halfway through suffering a World Series sweep at the hands of the New York Yankees, quoted an anonymous "disgusted fan" who asked "why [Pirate owner] Barney Drey-fuss didn't trade them for the Homestead Grays."[19]

As the top-flight semi-pro opposition in Pittsburgh began to thin out, Posey became more and more dependent on extended series with teams outside the city and its suburbs. In particular, the Grays thoroughly mined eastern Ohio for opportunities. The General Tires team of Akron was a regular opponent, the teams playing 10 times in 1926 and seven in 1927. (The Generals were willing to play, but not necessarily because they could win—they prevailed in only two games in each of those seasons.) The Grays played the Agathons of Massillon 11 times each in 1928 and '29, winning 17 of the games against a very good Aggies team that won 87 of 105 games in 1928.

As the '20s wore on, the best white teams moved toward congregating in leagues, both in the organized minors and on a high semi-pro level. A lot of Homestead's competition came from the semi-pro Ohio and Pennsylvania League, including the Agathons, the Beavers Falls Elks, and Akron's General Tires. The relationship was so close that at one point the Grays were made an associate member of the league, entitling them to schedule exhibition games with O&P members. (The protection given associated clubs from roster raiding by other league members wasn't an issue for the Grays, since all the other clubs were completely white and integrated teams were a long way off. But the guaranteed schedule rights with these better clubs was very important.) The Middle Atlantic League, a Class C minor league with teams in Charleroi, Jeannette, Johnstown, and Scottdale in Pennsylvania, as well as Wheeler, Clarksburg, Cumberland, and Fairmont in West Virginia, all places where the Grays often played, also scheduled a series of pre-season exhibitions against Homestead. Being in a bona fide minor league didn't change much when it came to playing Homestead—the Grays won most of those games, too.

The Elks of Beaver Falls, 40 miles northwest of Pittsburgh and an Ohio and Pennsylvania member, were one of the most frequent, and certainly the toughest, Homestead opponent. In 37 games from 1925 to 1928, the Grays won only 21 times and had a losing record, 7–8–1, that last year. Semler and Swetonic, who had the "Grays killers" reputation, both played for Beaver Falls, among other teams, as did Johnny Pearson, the star Homestead athlete who had been a white Grays fill-in years before. In Pittsburgh, the Grays' chief opponent was the top semi-pro team from the Homewood section of eastern Pittsburgh. The teams played 30 times in the last half of the '20s, with Semler pitching some of the games. The Grays won 18 of the tilts, a rather small share compared with their dominance of other local teams, and Homestead-Homewood series some seasons were billed as being for the "city championship."

Posey never again tried to develop his own home field for the Grays, as he had tried to do in Rankin in 1922. But for each season's choice games, he got his hands on the best ballpark in town, continuing to rent Forbes Field, the Pirates' home, when they were on the road. Forbes, in the Oakland section of the city east of the downtown business district, had been built in 1909 by Pirates owner Barney Dreyfuss, with financing by his friend Andrew Carnegie. It was a model of the early twentieth century steel and concrete park that was replacing the outmoded flammable wooden parks around the white majors as big league ball became ever more profitable. It featured ramps, rather than flights of steps, to make it easier for fans to get to and from their seats, and elevators to the third-tier luxury boxes. The Grays played premier Saturday games, Pittsburgh's equivalent of Sunday baseball since the sport was still banned on that day, featuring top local teams such as Homewood, regular semi-pro opponents such as the Akron Generals and Massillon Agathons, white major league all-star teams, and a growing number of black teams from the Negro Leagues or the touring teams a cut below black big league status. The Grays were booking Forbes for as many as 18 dates, some of which included doubleheaders, by 1926. No documentation now exists to detail the financial terms for the Grays' rental, but a rival black ball owner stated in 1930 that the Pirates were known to get 30 percent of the gross gate, which is in line with rental information at other parks at the time.[20]

While semi-pro baseball in the North was integrated—black teams playing white ones represented integration, although the teams themselves were almost exclusively of one race—there were seldom opportunities for the clubs in the white major leagues and the Negro Leagues to get together during the busy major league season. This was not the case after the season ended, however. Big leaguers' salaries ended when the major league season was over. This meant a less-glamorous off-season job for most major leaguers, some of whom postponed that reality by continuing to play into the fall on barnstorming "all-star" teams. Earle Mack, son of Philadelphia Athletics owner and manager Connie Mack and a coach on his father's team, was one of the predominant barnstorming organizers. His American League All-Stars played extended series with the Grays in both 1927 and '28, with interesting results.

The Macks won five of nine games in '27, and the teams split eight games the next season in close competition. The games were played in various cities that treated the Grays well, attendance-wise, such as Columbus, Ohio, and Jamestown, New York, but three of them were set at Forbes Field (and two others scheduled there were rained out).

The barnstorming squads regularly played Negro League teams, or their equivalents such as the Grays, and a close look at the results of these contests can provide some clues as to how high-level black players might have fared in integrated major league ball, if it had been allowed to exist. While it was true that the white teams had the title of "all stars" only because they bestowed it on themselves, there certainly were several major league regulars on each roster, and some of the men certainly could have played in the annual major league All-Star Game if it had existed in the 1920s. But frequently the talent level dropped off precipitously once past the name players. Earle Mack's connection with the A's ensured he would field a strong team, but his lineups against Homestead were not the equivalent of a regular big-league roster. Three of his players in 1927 had not played in the majors that year, and two others had played fewer than 10 games with the Athletics. Two 1928 starters also hadn't cracked a major league lineup that season, and the lineups featured a dead giveaway that the team was undermanned—starting pitchers played right field on their days off the mound.

On the other hand, future Hall of Fame outfielder Harry Heilmann of the Detroit Tigers, who had led the American League in batting in 1927, played both years, as did regular St. Louis Browns center fielder Bing Miller. The well-known Jimmy Dykes of the A's played third base in 1927, and future Hall of Famer Jimmie Foxx played that position in 1928. Heinie Manush of Detroit, also an eventual Hall of Famer, appeared in 1927. Mack's pitching, though, was about as good as anyone's. His rotation in the 1927 series consisted of four of the five most-used starters on his father's second-place team. Lefty Grove, Rube Walberg, Jack Quinn, and Eddie Rommel had combined for 62 of the A's 91 wins. Quinn and Walberg, joined by George Uhle of the Cleveland Indians, who had 12 wins in 1928, were Mack's starting rotation the next year.

Posey used his regular high-quality rotation against the American Leaguers—Joe and Lefty Williams, Oscar Owens, and Sam Streeter, along with right-hander Mervyn "Red" Ryan, picked up off Hilldale in the Eastern Colored League in 1927, and submarine-ball expert Webster McDonald, who had spent the season barnstorming in the West, in 1928. The Grays' field lineup was pretty much the same as it had been during the earlier stages of those seasons, although Posey added three ECL stars in 1927, catcher Raleigh

"Biz" Mackey from Hilldale, Martin Dihigo from the Cuban Stars, and John Beckwith from the Harrisburg Giants. In the case of Dihigo and Beckwith, the opportunity to play a few games against the American Leaguers at the end of 1928 presaged their appearance in Grays uniforms the next season, as Posey continued to operate outside the no-raiding rules of the two black major leagues to sign the stars he wanted more or less at will.

As Posey and the Grays occupied their geographical niche between the two Negro major leagues and the opportunistic business strategy he had created by ignoring the leagues' contract rules and outbidding their teams for their soon-to-be-former players, the leagues made attempts to curb what they saw as his excesses by trying to entice him into joining up, which was really the only way they could control the Grays. Posey wrote in his column in December 1925 that the Grays were being courted by both the Negro National League of the Midwest and the Eastern Colored League, but "the Eastern League is much better suited for association with the Grays." He was aware of the expensive travel costs that teams far from the Chicago-Kansas City-St. Louis axis of the NNL, including the short-lived Pittsburgh Keystones, had experienced as NNL associate members.

Despite his preference for the East, when push came to shove at the joint ECL-NNL winter meeting a month later, the Grays were still independent, and Posey appeared by no means sorry about it. The sticking point was the players he had signed away from both leagues, particularly the NNL. The ECL didn't have associate memberships, but seems to have offered Posey an informal version of one, which would allow him to schedule games with its teams if he would keep his hands off their players. They were mostly agreeable not to demand the return of the bulk of Posey's 1925 signees from their league, although they thought compensation was in order in one case, that of Gerald Williams, a veteran shortstop who had left the Lincoln Giants, and also opined that Cleo Smith, a third baseman from the Lincolns, ought to be returned. Before negotiations could progress, however, the powerful NNL president, Andrew "Rube" Foster, weighed in with demands for the return of Streeter and Vic Harris to his league. "It was then," the *Courier* reported, "that all negotiations ended."[21]

Posey, in his own view at least, wound up occupying the high ground above a swamp of less than scrupulous league owners who were meeting lower-than-expected revenues by imposing team salary caps, using the situation to take advantage of their players. In the same issue that reported the events of the joint league meeting a *Courier* article, though not quoting Posey directly, stated his position in detail. If he himself didn't write it, he probably dictated to someone in the paper's sports department:

Gerald Williams, Cleo Smith, Vic Harris, Streeter were signed to play at a stipulated salary.... These players are not going to be returned to any league clubs to be made an example of and be cut from fifty to seventy-five dollars a month merely because they wished to leave conditions which were not satisfactory. Any player on the Homestead Grays who desires to change to another club is free at all times to change and any good player who is in any club in either league will be offered a contact when the Grays' management feels they need this player and when he comes to the Grays, he will not be treated like a prince for one season and then made an example of to provide a Roman Holiday for men who do not hesitate to refuse a man his pay on account of an error and suspend a player indefinitely after two weeks on half pay, because he broke his leg while attempting to play good baseball. It is these things which are causing the real stars of the game to respect the word of the Grays' owners and it is best for the players that clubs of this kind exist.[22]

In 1926 Posey, losing no key players other than Gerald Williams, through illness, took it pretty easy on the other black owners. The only players of note he signed were Bobby Williams, who jumped the Indianapolis ABCs of the NNL to replace Gerald Williams, and pitcher George Britt, a pitcher and utility man spirited away from the Baltimore Black Sox to join the Grays' starting rotation. But beginning in 1927, with the leagues in ever-worsening financial and leadership trouble, the Grays' uniforms could have included a skull and crossbones symbol, so much was their boss a raider. Posey shook the very foundations of Negro League ball in January when he announced he had signed outfielder Oscar Charleston, regarded then and now as one of the best black position players, away from Harrisburg of the ECL, where he also was the field manager. The Charleston signing floundered because Posey wouldn't give the star, no matter how good he was, the multi-year contract he wanted, but the very attempt showed both Posey's audacity and the weakness of the leagues in combatting him. When Red Ryan deserted Hilldale, the Philadelphia entry in the ECL, that August, J. M. Howe of the *Philadelphia Tribune*, with irony, described the transaction as a colorful trade: "The Grays get Red and Hilldale gets Blue."[23]

In 1928, slugger Beckwith left Harrisburg after succeeding in prying a two-year contract out of Posey; center fielder Floyd "Jelly" Gardner, a serial team-changer, came from the Chicago American Giants, and Dihigo, a remarkably versatile pitcher and infielder from Cuba, jumped the Cuban Stars of the ECL. So likely was it that Posey would go shopping for the Grays' needs among existing rosters that on January 14, 1928, the *Chicago Defender* headlined a pre-season story "Posey Plans More Raids for Players."

While the influx of stars and other regulars accomplished the Grays' main objectives, winning as many games and drawing as many fans as possible, it was never the case that individual success allowed the players to get the notion that they were more important than management or the sport they were playing. Posey the field manager was still likely to raise hell with umpires and in an extreme situation pull his team off the field and forfeit a game in protest. On July 1, 1928, for example, he stood up a reported crowd of 10,000 to 15,000 in the second game of a Sunday doubleheader at the Lincoln Giants' Protectory Oval in New York over what he saw as lousy umpiring. But he made it clear that the right to act outrageously on the diamond was his alone and did not belong to the men wearing his uniforms. In 1925 he had told sports columnist W. Rollo Wilson that "the first player who starts a fight on Forbes Field, be he a Gray or opponent, will be arrested because I'll see that it is done, myself. No roughneck ball players are going to ruin the reputation we enjoy in the Tri-State district if I can help it."[24]

Despite his own ability to blow his top unapologetically and disrupt a game as a manager, Posey not only laid down the law to his men, he enforced it, too. After the 1927 season, which looked on paper to have been the usual Grays' success story (141 wins, 31 of them in a row), Posey was unhappy with the team's performance and partially cleaned house. In addition to those who underperformed on the field, he made it fairly clear that the existing group had not met his behavioral standards. "There were men on the Grays club in 1927," he wrote in one of his *Courier* columns, "who did not have the pep which is necessary to a championship baseball club. There is no room on the Grays for such men.... Players who spend their time on the field or on the street doing various things which tend to make enemies for the Grays will no longer have a place in the Grays' lineup."[25]

It was pretty clear that so far as Posey was concerned, being a Homestead Gray was an around-the-clock occupation. He would not tolerate dissipation off the field, stating before the 1928 season that "The tendency of players to make 'a night of it' before some games" would be stopped. A story Posey told Bill Nunn of the *Courier* in 1927 shows exactly when he, one of the few black owners who had been a player himself, would give his men some slack, and when he would draw the line. He had lured pitcher James "Nip" Winters away from Hilldale in the middle of the season, and

I suppose he felt that he could do as he wanted to with the Grays.... We have a strict rule which is enforced by Captain Joe Williams, that players must report on time—and be sober when they report. Winters went out Wednesday night and indulged in a regular "booze" party. When he reported Thursday, 15 minutes late, and with a "hangover," I immediately called his hand, told him to go back and that I would tell Joe Williams he was sick, to save him from being fined. When he insisted on going with the team, I became emphatic in my statements, with the result that he left. I told him, at the time, that while he might report to the Hilldale management intoxicated, and play, the Grays didn't tolerate drunkenness.... Winters apparently accepted the easiest way out, and hied himself back to his old haunts.[26]

Before the 1927 season, Posey, following up on the approach made to the Grays by owners of the Negro Leagues a year before, floated his own proposal, that teams from the ECL headed to the Midwest for exhibition games with NNL teams, and Midwestern teams making the trip in the opposite direction, stop in Pittsburgh for games at Forbes Field. He offered four games each month, which would give the Grays 20 good draws at Forbes. Posey said discipline would be observed during the games—in addition to the leagues' own rules, he proposed a hefty $50 fine for any player ejected from one of these showpiece contests. Importantly, in exchange for these lucrative dates, he would stop signing the leagues' players (except for Charleston, whom he thought he had in the bag for '27, although he promised to give Harrisburg suitable player compensation for the loss of its star).[27] Negotiations got complicated, though, apparently over the leagues' demands for the return of their players, and Pittsburgh did not serve as an official East-West stopover.

But the leagues were in bad shape, poor finances leading to failures of organization and discipline, and although the Grays had never been accepted as even a quasi-official member of either league, 1927 saw a marked rise in their games against league teams. The fragility of the leagues, though, particularly the ECL, meant that when the Grays played these "league teams," they were not necessarily members of a league at that precise time. In 1927, for example, the Grays struck up what would be an enduring rivalry with the Lincoln Giants. Their owner, Jim Keenan, had a good relationship with Posey, partially based on things they had in common—the struggles it took to make a go of it in semi-pro sports without a "safety net" of profits from some other business, and a refusal to take too much guff.

The Giants and the Grays played seven games against each other in 1927, six of which were won by Homestead. As a member of the ECL, Keenan's team should have had either formal or informal strictures against playing the Grays. But as it happened, when the teams met in August and October, Keenan had quit the league and could do as he pleased. He had been unhappy for some time with the way the ECL supposedly favored his New York fellow owner, Nathaniel Strong of the Brooklyn Royal Giants, when it came to booking dates. The last straw, at least for 1927 (the Lincolns rejoined the league in 1928) came when he was ordered to return a player, Estaban Montalvo, to the NNL, where the Cuban Stars had a claim on him that Keenan reasonably rejected. The Grays also played an NNL team, the Cleveland Hornets, three games at Forbes Field in late August, after the Hornets had dropped out of their league.

The dispute that had caused Keenan to take his team out of the ECL in 1927 was not an isolated incident—it was an early symptom of the league's death throes, and after starting the 1928 season in April, the whole organization collapsed by the Fourth of July. The death of the ECL promptly brought its member teams, dressed not in mourners' garb, but in baseball uniforms familiar to any fan who kept up with the black newspapers' sports pages, to play at Forbes Field, while the Grays would visit their home parks. Just because there was no longer an Eastern Colored League, and just because Posey had been a thorn in the league's side, didn't mean there wasn't money to be made playing baseball with the Grays. Homestead split eight games with the Lincolns, including the July 1 game in New York where Posey marched the Grays off the field in response to alleged poor umpiring.

In that game, the Grays were actually holding onto an 11–10 lead by the skin of their teeth in the bottom of the ninth when an umpire called a Lincoln runner safe on a force attempt at second base. It wasn't the first argument over one of his calls that day, and Posey led the Grays off the Oval. As might be imagined, the sportswriters who reported the event were influenced by where their newspapers were published. Thomas Lurry of the *Chicago Defender* saw that the throw definitely beat the runner to the bag, but that the arbiter, "who was on top of the play," ruled that Beckwith, covering second, didn't have his foot on the bag. Rollo Wilson in the *Courier* just said it was a bad call "by the same dumb umpire." The un-bylined report in the *New York Amsterdam News* acknowledged not only the points of view of both teams' supporters, but a third one as well: "Many of the fans were loud in their condemnation of the unsportsmanlike tactics of Posey and his team, while friends defended him. But most of the confusion came from those who had bet on the visitors to win and did not want to lose their money through a forfeited game."[28]

Eight games with Hilldale of Philadelphia, whose owner, Edward Bolden, ran one of the most consistently successful black teams on the East Coast, and had been the founding father of the ECL, also produced a 4–4 split. One of the Homestead wins was another proof that Smokey Joe Williams was far from over the hill—he three-hit Hilldale for a 6–1 win at Forbes Field on September 28. The Grays were more successful with the Baltimore Black Sox, winning four of five games in September, split between Forbes Field and the Sox's Maryland Park in Baltimore.

Although the Eastern Colored League had collapsed in 1928, there was an almost immediate interest in reviving black league ball in the East. The result was the founding of the American Negro League in the spring of 1929. Ed Bolden of Philadelphia was the consensus choice to head the league, as he originally had the ECL. Five of the six teams, his Hilldale squad, Keenan's Lincoln Giants, the Baltimore Black Sox, the Atlantic City Bacharach Giants,

and the Cuban Stars of New York, had been in the ECL. The sixth team was—
the Homestead Grays. Posey never explained publicly why he had decided
to stop being cagy about joining a league. The declining level of competition
in the Pittsburgh area brought about by the industrial recession, followed by
the beginnings of the Great Depression, balanced against the success his team
had when it began to play Eastern teams once the ECL broke up in 1928, may
have convinced him that the more prudent course was to join up.

Until then, he certainly had been outspokenly blunt about the shortcomings of organized Negro ball. In January 1927, he had used his "The
Sportive Realm" column in the *Courier* to mock the inability of league owners
to enforce their own rules. Picking on a five-year ban that had been adopted
for players who jumped their contracts to play for non-affiliated teams (the
Grays, for example), he maintained, "That is not worth the ink it took to
write it. Five years from now five-sixths of the magnates now involved in
Negro organized baseball will have followed the paths of C. I. Taylor or "Rube"
Foster [Taylor, the former owner of the Indianapolis ABCs, was dead, and
Foster, NNL president and owner of the Chicago American Giants, was in a
mental hospital, arguably in both cases from the stress of being a baseball
"magnate"], or will be broke if they keep building up defenses against players
and each other instead of getting fair umpires and getting rid of the rowdies
on the club and in the stands."[29]

In January 1928, he accurately diagnosed some of the ECLs' illnesses
and prescribed "drastic remedies." The first was to force Nat Strong, who controlled numerous ballparks in the New York City area as the leading game
booker there, to provide a permanent home park for his league entry, the
Brooklyn Royal Giants. The absence of home grounds for the Royal Giants,
as well as for the other New York entry, an Eastern version of the Cuban Stars
not affiliated with the NNL team, made those teams nomadic "visiting" clubs.
This confounded league scheduling and usually led to them playing fewer
games than other ECL teams. The Grays themselves may have been mostly
a road team, but they had Forbes Field for important games, for which they
were the home team.

Cum Posey also, as he had for his own team, called for more on-field
discipline (at which the ECL was notoriously lax) and encouraged an agreement with the NNL for inter-league games. If reforms, as difficult as they
were to achieve, were not brought about, Posey predicted, "there will be no
Eastern League within the next two years" and "there will be a mad scramble
for players East and West by the Eastern clubs" when the league structure
collapsed. It turned out that his prediction was uncannily accurate, although
he and Grays were far from just bystanders when it came true.[30]

As late at March 1928, he was insisting that the Grays wouldn't join a league unless they could keep their players (including those signed away from league clubs) and not be forced into a league schedule, conditions which pretty much eliminated joining either Negro League. But ideas for reconstituting a black league in the East frequently mentioned the Grays. In August 1927, the venerable John Henry Lloyd, a longtime star on the field and at the time manager of the Lincoln Giants (and an eventual Hall of Famer), talked with a group of black sportswriters and then refined the plan he had broached with one of them, Bill Nunn of the *Courier*. Lloyd's solution to the sagging ECL was to place a single club in each of six cities, including Pittsburgh. The Grays were the obvious choice for Pittsburgh, and Nat Strong's Royal Giants would not be the choice in New York. The loop would be governed by a "high commissioner" who did not have an interest in any of the teams. In April 1928, when the ECL owners were working desperately to keep their league going, a plan was floated to continue as a relatively unorganized "association," which would include the Grays (and presumably exclude pesky rules requiring Homestead to return ECL players to their former bosses).[31]

So the Grays becoming a charter member of the 1929 American Negro League after keeping league connections at arm's length for so long didn't exactly have the effect of a bolt from the blue. Posey seemed to be entirely in favor. He crowed in his March 9 column that "The outlook for colored baseball in the East has never been brighter." But the news in January that the Grays would be in the ANL drew sharply contrasting comment from two important contributors of the *Courier's* sports pages. Ira F. Lewis, who had little use for what in his opinion were semi-dysfunctional organizations passing for black baseball leagues, wrote that Posey had been "taken in" by the other owners: "Posey and his Homestead Grays had everything to gain by staying out of any kind of league combination." But Rollo Wilson, who was by no means blinded to the shortcomings of Negro baseball, saw great progress in the formation of the ANL, and of the Grays' role in it: "When Cum Posey ... became a charter member of the body, he made Pittsburgh fans a part and parcel of big-time Negro baseball."[32]

Historically, getting into league ball was a major step for Posey, Charlie Walker, and their Grays. The sweep of history in baseball, and in team sports in general, has been for teams with much in common eventually to concentrate themselves into leagues, to take advantage of the rivalries and dependable schedules that satisfy both the competitors and their fans. But as the season rolled along, there were a multitude of problems for the Grays. They may have run up spectacular winning streaks and percentages in the Tri-State region, but playing other top-flight black competition was different.

Homestead finished third among the six teams in the first half of the ANL's split season and fourth in the final half, with a league record of 34–29, a .540 winning percentage. The Grays' record was good, but not great, and since the two weakest teams in the league, the Atlantic City Bacharach Giants and the Cuban Stars, had a combined winning percentage of .288, simple mathematics dictated that, in a closed system where every win by some team is balanced by a loss by another, some squads were going to have sky-high winning percentages without necessarily being that good.

Like the rest of the league, the Grays feasted on the two weakest teams, winning nearly half of all their victories against the hapless Bacharachs and Cubans. But they were markedly less successful otherwise. The Baltimore Black Sox ran away with the season, finishing with a .700 winning percentage. Along with Hilldale, they won their season series with the Grays, while Homestead and the Lincoln Giants battled to a 6–6 deadlock. Even Rollo Wilson, Posey's friend, could only say by September that the legendary Grays were "perhaps the big disappointment of the season." It was bad enough to say that the Grays didn't play well, but Wilson also implied that in being inconsistent, they also had become boring: "Critics in the East considered Posey's aggregation only an ordinary team and lost interest in it."[33]

Posey had begun the 1929 season with pretty much a pat hand from the year before. But events, mostly beyond his control, sapped his lineup's strength. One was the Grays' inability to hold onto the excellent veteran submarine pitcher Webster McDonald, who played for them at the end of 1928 and at the beginning of the 1929 season. As the weather warmed in the Great Plains states, McDonald went back to Little Falls, Minnesota, where he played for a crack semi-pro team that, like several teams in that region, had a few black players. Playing ball on the Great Plains was a pretty comfortable existence, especially if one was paid well. McDonald told black baseball historian John Holway in 1970 that he made as much as $750 per month in Little Falls, plus bonuses for post-season tournaments.[34] The Grays could pay well, but not that well.

A more serious problem was caused by a banner headline trade in March, when the Grays shipped two versatile regulars, Dihigo and Britt, to Hilldale in exchange for former Gray Rev Cannady and shortstop Jake Stephens. Posey defended the trade in his *Courier* column, regretting the departure of Britt, "one of the most popular men on the team," but not particularly mourning the loss of Dihigo. The versatile Cuban, who could play almost any field position and pitch, too, "had a world of class and played some wonderful games but he was not the 'team player' as was Britt." Posey wrote that Dihigo "basked in the 'sunshine,'" leaving the implication that he may not have been just what a manager wanted when things weren't going his way. Given Posey's reticence in criticizing players by name (while being not at all reticent about getting rid of the ones he no longer had use for), this was fairly strong criticism of someone who eventually would join Posey in the Baseball Hall of Fame (and, in fact, got there first, in 1977). Anyway, Posey continued, the trade was good because the arrival of Cannady and Stephens "will be hailed with delight by the big majority of the Pittsburgh baseball fans."[35]

The return of the 25-year-old Cannady, who became the Grays' regular second baseman, displacing Mo Harris, one of the last of the early Homestead players to be forced out by better talent, was clearly a good pickup. But Stephens was another matter. The Hilldale shortstop, had a lot of attributes, not all of them contributing to success on the field. Negro Leagues historian James A. Riley described Stephens as "small, fast, aggressive, argumentative, temperamental, and controversial."[36] The small, fast, and aggressive traits made Stephens, although a light hitter, a star fielding shortstop, which was just what the Grays needed. What they got was Stephens' temperamental and controversial side. He played a few games for Homestead in April, but then skipped the club, reportedly taking some team equipment and $206 in advance pay with him.[37] Since Stephens had reported after the trade, Posey had no recourse with Hilldale, and he had essentially traded a star (albeit one with whom he apparently didn't see eye to eye) and a reliable starting pitcher who could also catch and play the field, for an upgrade at second base. Posey quickly signed journeyman E. C. Turner to play shortstop, but the Grays were clearly deficient at this key position.

The next setback for the team was not just a sportswriter's idea of a "disaster," but nearly a real one. On June 25, fresh from a 12–2 victory in Lewiston, Pennsylvania, over the Rayoneers, a team sponsored by the Viscose artificial silk mill (hence the team nickname), and en route to a league game in Atlantic City, one of three Grays touring cars, being driven by Posey's brother See, hit a rut at about 60 miles an hour and spun out of control. It overturned, and everyone in the car was injured to some extent. The passengers were all players: infielders Cannady, Jap Washington, and Stanford Jackson; pitchers Joe Williams and Oscar Owens, and outfielder Dennis Graham—half of the starting infield, a third of the outfield, and two of the Grays' best starting pitchers, in other words. Cannady was injured the worst. He was hospitalized in Lewiston and didn't return to the lineup until mid–July, which was also the period of time Owens was disabled. Although, like See Posey, the rest weren't badly hurt and soon returned to the lineup, they harbored various aches and pains that cut down on their effectiveness.[38]

The Grays forged ahead, arriving in Atlantic City in time for a single game with the host Bacharach Giants on June 26 and a doubleheader the next day. Playing with a patchwork lineup that had pitcher Sam Streeter in right field and outfielder Charlie Mason pitching, the Grays actually won two of the three games. But they lost five of eight league games while on the Eastern Seaboard as Cum Posey worked to reconstitute his crippled lineup. One move he made was, in retrospect, fairly brilliant. Jake Stephens was still under contract, even though he had defected to the lower-level Philadelphia Giants (who were based in New England, despite their name). An understanding was apparently reached in late June to encourage him to return to the ANL, at which time Posey traded him back to Hilldale for Britt, for whom he had been traded in the first place.

Ed Bolden, Hilldale's owner, may have thought he was getting a good deal, but it turned out that, for the loss of a valuable player, he was just inheriting Posey's headache. By the beginning of August, Bolden had suspended Stephens "for insubordination and slander" after a verbal confrontation with him. Bolden accused Stephens of demanding that Hilldale pay him for the two and a half months he was playing outside the league, and pointed out that in addition the shortstop had not repaid his debt to the Grays, nor to Hilldale, which had also advanced him money after the 1928 season. The irony regarding Stephens and Bolden was thick. When the first trade happened in March, Rollo Wilson of the *Courier* said that Bolden had agreed to it because "he was getting rid of men who were dissatisfied with the Hilldale management."[39]

In the process of making his way through 1929, Posey, perhaps predictably, managed to alienate other major figures in black baseball, particularly those in the Negro National League. The late Eastern Colored League had been created in 1923 in part due to a feud between Bolden and NNL President Rube Foster that included disputes over alleged roster raiding. The two leagues made a peace pact in 1924 that protected rosters and led to the first Negro World Series. The agreement, and the Series, continued through 1927, but both ended with the ECL's demise.

In 1929, there was substantial quarrelling over whether the protective rules had been re-instituted in writing or verbally, and whether they held any water. Cum Posey certainly didn't think so. In June, the NNL's Chicago American Giants suspended two players, Stanford Jackson (who was in the Grays' car crash) and pitcher Eddie "Buck" Miller, for disciplinary reasons. They promptly came east and signed with the Grays, although they were still under contract to Chicago. There were other disputes over who had legal rights to players who had switched leagues. But probably because Posey was involved, the supposed avarice of the Grays received the most scrutiny. The presence of Streeter in the American Giants' stands during a game against the Birmingham Black Barons in early July led to a sort of panic in the NNL that Streeter, who had played for the Barons, was a Posey agent sent to entice away Birmingham's great hurler, Satchel Paige. Streeter maintained he was in Chicago only to deliver a message to Stanford Jackson's wife, who had not followed him to Pittsburgh. At any rate, Streeter returned to the Grays, and Paige stayed with the Barons.[40] (Surprisingly, even though Posey had a sharp eye for talent and would sign anyone he wanted, if he could, and even though Paige was a serial team-switcher, Paige played only one game for the Grays, and that was an exhibition against a white all-star team).

The NNL power structure was also reportedly angry with Posey for cutting a deal with black Cleveland baseball promoter L. R. Williams to play Sunday games (which were still banned in Pennsylvania) in that city. However, it had been reported in March, when the deal was announced, that William C. Hueston, who had succeeded the seriously ill Foster as NNL president, had arranged the meeting, and while Cleveland had certainly been NNL territory, the league had no team there in 1929. For whatever reasons, Hueston stated in late August, when league championship races were getting hottest, that "several matters between the two leagues" must be settled before there could be a resumption of the World Series. Sportswriters assumed the "matters" involved Posey, and there was no post-season series, although there hadn't been one in 1928 due to the mid-season collapse of the ECL, and it isn't clear that one had been proposed in the first place for 1929. However, Bill Gibson, writing in the *Baltimore Afro-American* in October, said that "one of the reasons" that the Kansas City Monarchs, the NNL champs, didn't come east for a playoff was that Posey "insisted on 'stealing' players from the western circuit."[41]

While the declining economic situation for the majority of the Eastern Colored League's ticket-buying fan base was the primary reason for its demise, it was also true that the league had a number of operational problems that dissatisfied its most absorbed followers, particularly the baseball writers for the major African American weekly newspapers. The new American Negro League from the beginning had rules designed to cure the problems. Ed Bolden of Hilldale as president was given more executive power than he had had as the head of the board of commissioners of the ECL, particularly in policing on-field rowdiness, which was known to include attacks on umpires or other players.

Posey himself figured in one dramatic example of increased discipline. He was not exactly the antagonist, although the whole situation was exacerbated by his usual practice of baiting umpires over unfavorable decisions. At

Hilldale on May 17, he began riding the home plate umpire as early at the third inning, refused to leave the field when the ump tossed him out of the game, and was allowed to stay on the bench. With everyone thus set on edge, more fireworks broke out in the ninth inning. The potential tying run for the Grays was called out at the plate on a close play by the same ump. Somebody from the Grays pushed the umpire, and Homestead catcher Buck Ewing slugged the arbiter. Men from both teams poured onto the field, and Hilldale star and manager Oscar Charleston took a swing at someone, who turned out to be Posey. Charleston's poke apparently didn't connect with the Homestead manager, and it's not clear that he even knew whom he was swinging at. But both he and Ewing were suspended by the league, and Bolden fired Charleston as manager, although he retained the use of his superstar bat and glove.[42]

The league also stuck to other good rules. Rosters were limited to control payroll, the number of African Americans on its umpiring staff was increased, and compliance with the official schedule improved. But attendance was still down, finances were still a serious problem around the league as the Depression deepened, and 1929 would be the ANL's only season. Prospects for a 1930 season were already dimming by October of 1929, when Gibson of the *Afro-American* reported that "some of the baseball czars are not so optimistic about a baseball in the East next year.... While there has been no loud wail heard, it is sure that some of the baseball owners sustained painful if not serious injury in the region of the pocketbook." Gibson also forecast that even if there was a league, the Grays would not be in it. Posey, he said, "is reported to feel toward the league just as some of the members feel toward him—disgusted." Gibson predicted that Posey would go independent again, to regain his open recruitment advantage.[43]

Actually, by the time the edition with Gibson's column hit the streets, Posey had already started doing just that. After Negro League seasons ended, some teams would barnstorm, adding starters from other teams to their rosters. The Grays kept on playing after the ANL season ended, their lineup now including Charleston, third baseman Judy Johnson and, yes, Jake Stephens, as well as Clint Thomas, a hard-hitting outfielder from the Bacharach Giants, and Lincoln Giants second baseman George Scales, who had been obtained in a straight-up trade for John Beckwith at the end of August.

On October 5, the Grays arrived in Chicago for a five-game series with the American Giants that more or less wrapped up their season. Artistically, the series was no success for Homestead—the Giants swept them, five straight. Chicago had done what Posey had done, namely round up stars from other teams to augment its lineup. The American Giants had put together what amounted to an NNL all-star team, with a lineup that included three "borrowed" players, shortstop Willie Wells, center fielder James "Cool Papa" Bell, and first baseman George "Mule" Suttles from the St. Louis Stars. After the series, though, these men, all eventual Hall of Famers, reverted to being property of the Stars. Negro League ball was, in fact, dead for the time being in the East, and Posey hung onto Charleston, Johnson, Stephens, and Scales.

Chapter Five

Superb Teams,
but a Failed League

After spring training in 1930 in the resort city of Hot Springs, Arkansas, the Grays headed for a series of games against local competition in Arkansas, Louisiana, and Texas, wending their way toward St. Louis, where they won two games against that city's Negro National League team, the Stars. From there Posey sent word to the *Pittsburgh Post-Gazette* that "the Grays will have the strongest club in their history which is saying a great deal." Events changed Posey's mind, though. Rollo Wilson of the *Pittsburgh Courier* wrote in September of 1931 that "there is no doubt that Cum and Charlie [Walker] look on their 1931 outfit as the best one they ever bossed." And Wilson agreed with them.[1]

Negro League baseball was collapsing as the 1930 season opened. The failure of the American Negro League to survive more than a single season left the East without an organization. Rube Foster, the founding president of the Negro National League in the Midwest, died in 1930, and the demise of his increasingly rickety creation would not come far behind. The Depression undermined the leagues, as it did white professional baseball. The white major leagues began to feel a serious effect on attendance and revenue in 1931, which turned into a 40 percent attendance decline the following year. The minor leagues, more similar in the scope of their financial operations to the Negro Leagues and more sensitive to the worsening economic conditions, · had plunged from 27 leagues in 1928 to a mere 13 by the end of 1932.[2]

The black baseball state of affairs in the spring of 1930 was almost perfect for Posey's preferred methods of operation at the time. The Grays were again independents, with no black major league in the East and just a weakening one in the Midwest. This meant that Homestead could pick and choose its opponents, relying again on the drawing power of its reputation, avoiding potentially poor gates with substandard league teams that it would be forced to play along with the strong ones in a league schedule. More importantly, plenty of good players were available, and Cum Posey signed as many as he could. He told Wilson in August 1931 that the Grays were outspending other Negro League-quality clubs by $600 a month in salaries.[3]

For starters, the Grays retained the dynamic infield of Oscar Charleston at first base, George Scales at second, Jake Stephens at shortstop, and Judy Johnson at third that had been part of its barnstorming unit at the end of 1929. The group was successful in 1930, and history has validated Posey's choices: Charleston and Johnson were early inductees into the Baseball Hall of Fame when it began to enshrine Negro Leaguers, and Scales was one of 93 names in the initial round of potential honorees for a special black baseball election in 2006, although he did not survive that cut. Vic Harris remained a regular outfielder. To supplement him, Bill Evans, whose additional value as a substitute infielder would be appreciated when an injured Stephens missed part of the 1931 season, came from the Brooklyn Royal Giants. Chaney White, whom history has undervalued in his abilities as a hitter, but who was highly sought after in his day (as a fielder and baserunner, his

Posey advanced the Grays from being just a Pittsburgh regional attraction to one of the best black teams in the East by the early 1930s (author's collection).

nickname was "Reindeer," and he hit .346 for the Atlantic City Bacharach Giants in 1929), was the center fielder.[4] With Joe and Lefty Williams and George Britt still leading the pitching staff, there was little reason to go on a spending spree to keep the mound populated. Still, Posey added Darltie Cooper, a very competent journeyman hurler who had been with Hilldale in 1929.

Bill "Buck" Ewing, a journeyman catcher who had split a 10-year career between the Negro Leagues and lower-level regional black teams, began the season as the regular catcher. But in late July he suffered a hand injury, probably from absorbing a foul tip on his throwing hand. Posey turned to a strapping 18-year-old who was already developing a reputation in local sandlot ball. Josh Gibson appears to have caught his first game for the Grays on July 25 at the Pittsburgh Pirates' Forbes Field, subbing in mid-game for Ewing against the

Kansas City Monarchs, the premier Midwestern black team making a long Eastern swing. By September, Gibson was the Grays' regular receiver, beginning a momentous career noted for frequent and monumental home runs that got him nicknamed the "Black Babe Ruth" and elected to the Hall of Fame in 1972.

The influx of new talent meant, as it had in the past when Posey upgraded, the loss of some familiar faces. Dennis Graham was forced out of the outfield by the signing of Evans and White, and Jap Washington lost his first base spot to Charleston. The long-admired Oscar Owens left the club, too, which brought Posey some rare criticism in the black press, since Owens was a local guy and a longtime star. But he was back with the club before the season was over.

Negro League great Oscar Charleston joined the Grays for the team's outstanding 1930 and 1931 seasons, but was among several Homestead stars who jumped to the rival Pittsburgh Crawfords in 1932 (NoirTech Research, Inc.).

Ordinarily the Grays had held spring training not too far from Pittsburgh, usually 60 miles away in Wheeling, West Virginia. In 1929 Posey and Walker had taken their aggregation to Lexington, Kentucky, but in 1930 they assembled the team in Hot Springs. The "Spa City," as it was known, had long been the choice of white major league clubs for spring training, and the Pirates had trained there as recently as 1926. The Kansas City Monarchs of the Negro National League had trained there in 1928, and the Grays started the 1930 season, as well as 1931, at Hot Springs' Fogel Field.

Although Charleston had lost his managerial position with Hilldale in 1929 because of his role in the on-field brawl with the Grays, he was a natural leader and subsequently managed many Negro League teams. Reports back to the Pittsburgh newspapers had him taking charge of getting the rusty Grays into shape in 1930, at least those who were serious about their exercise. A five-mile jaunt "over the mountains" at 8 a.m. started the training day, with Charleston leading the run, although the *Courier* noted that there was also a smaller "walking group." Posey was with the runners, but Charlie Walker, "saying he didn't need any wind," was with the walkers.[5]   The Grays went through their usual early season schedule routine of playing exhibition games against teams from white minor leagues, particularly the Class C Middle Atlantic League, and semi-pro squads from the Pittsburgh area and Eastern Ohio. They didn't face a black team until a Memorial Day doubleheader against the Pennsylvania Red Caps on May 30, and didn't play an actual Negro League team until beginning a series with the Memphis Red Sox on June 7. This was the part of the schedule in which the Grays consistently got off to a roaring start against lesser competition. This year, Posey's moves to make the team as competitive as possible against the top black teams yet to come produced a lineup that mowed down the early opposition even more decisively than usual.

It had been true for years that regional semi-pro and minor league teams could expect to be defeated when the Grays came to their parks, their feelings assuaged by attendance and gate receipts well above normal. Now, in exchange for the money, they might also have to put up with being overwhelmed on the field. The Clarksburg, West Virginia, Generals of the Mid-Atlantic League took a 22–2 pounding on April 27, for example, and the semi-pro Akron Guards were beaten, 20–5, on June 1. Within a space of five days in late May, the Grays beat Pittsburgh-area teams, including archrival Homewood, by scores of 19–8, 10–4, 11–3, 11–0, and 14–4. An 11–5 win over top-level Book Shoe on June 5 put the Grays' record at 50–3.

After that, though, the Homestead schedule filled up with games against teams in the still-functioning Negro National League and those that had been in the now-defunct Eastern leagues. The Grays played those teams 56 times, and again were highly successful, winning 41 contests. They won every season series except the one against the St. Louis Stars, who took four out of seven. Beyond the wins, and the profits, the Grays' Negro League competition in 1930 helped accomplish two major milestones in black baseball, and in professional baseball in general: the proliferation of night games and the emergence of Yankee Stadium as a major black ball venue.

James Leslie Wilkinson, the founder and primary owner of the Kansas City Monarchs, was in many ways Posey's Midwestern counterpart. Also a child of a family that valued education, he had been a player as a youth and had been invested in black baseball since before World War I. Like Posey, Wilkinson personally had no other source of income, although he had a financial partner. Unlike Posey, Wilkinson was Caucasian, but no one in black ball seemed to mind. He was never known as a white businessman who manipulated other black teams for his personal advantage, a charge often laid against white booking agents such as Nat Strong of New York. Wilkinson's Monarchs were a charter member of the NNL in 1920 and rivaled Foster's Chicago American Giants as the cream of the league, just as the Grays were considered one of the class teams of the East, even as an independent.

In 1930, though, Wilkinson was scrambling for profits like everyone else. One of his solutions was to do as Posey was doing—market the Monarchs over a wide area of the Midwest, making them a widely sought-after attraction. But in 1930 he took Posey's "play anyone, any time" strategy and went it one better. His offer to play at any time of day included night time, even if the host's park wasn't equipped with lights. Wilkinson invested upwards of $50,000, all the money he had or could borrow, in a portable lighting system. A convoy of trucks manned by trained technicians went on the road with the Monarchs, setting up light towers at ball parks in cities and towns where the baseball day had always ended when it got too dark to play any longer. The lights, run by coughing gasoline generators, were hoisted and turned on for an initial game in Enid, Oklahoma, on April 28. Three thousand fans came out to see what was going on, and they were followed in droves by fellow baseball fanatics in other towns as the Monarchs played their way toward St. Louis. By the time they reached there for a series against the St. Louis Stars on May 17, Wilkinson had recouped his investment.[6]

Wilkinson wasn't settling for just a Midwestern tour, though. In July, his caravan loaded up again and proceeded eastward, spending most of its time in Pennsylvania and Ohio playing the Grays. The *Post-Gazette* reported on May 6 that Posey was "dickering" to bring the Monarchs and their lights to Forbes Field.[7] The negotiations with Wilkinson resulted in a dozen games, most of them at night, introducing night ball not only to the Pirates' ballpark but to Hooper Field, the Negro Leagues park in Cleveland, and other places familiar to the Grays such as Altoona and Sharon in Pennsylvania, and Youngstown and Denison in Ohio.

The games were preceded by a Kansas City advance party. Tom Baird, Wilkinson's partner, paved the way with sportswriters by explaining what they were about to witness. *Post-Gazette* sports editor Havey J. Boyle reported that Baird explained that the biggest question from folks who hadn't yet witnessed a night game, which was how in the world fielders could see fly balls, was immaterial: "it is, as a matter of fact easier to catch a fly ball at night than in the daytime. The blazing lights shoot high enough to keep the ball in sight," Baird assured the writer. This opinion was not universally shared by participants in some of the early night games. William A. Young, in a biography of Wilkinson, offers an opinion from one participant in Monarchs games: "As one player said, when a ball went so high you couldn't see it, 'you just looked up and prayed, dear Lord, bring it here.'"[8]

The Grays had a little practice before playing night ball against the Monarchs—they beat the semi-pro Akron Guards, 10–0, on July 14 at Akron, where the local park was already equipped with lights. (The already existing lights did not stop an *Akron Beacon Journal* sportswriter from wisecracking that "the real test for night baseball" would be "if fans can see those fellows," the black players.)[9] Although more games were scheduled, research in the newspapers of the region uncovers 12 Grays-Monarchs games, of which Homestead won 10. Seven of the games were at night, and six used Wilkinson's lighting system (a game in Akron on July 29 used that park's system). Three of the night games were at Forbes Field. The first one on July 18 was naturally much publicized in advance, and the action lived up to the ballyhoo.

Kansas City ran off to a 4–0 lead by the fifth inning, as the Monarchs roughed up George Britt, while the Grays could barely touch KC starter Chet Brewer's "sailers and sharp benders." But Darltie Cooper, the Grays' pitcher riding the bench, had a hunch about Brewer, who had a reputation for doctoring his pitches. Cooper "became suspicious of those mystic pitches," and the Grays began peppering the home plate ump with demands to look over the baseballs Brewer was tossing. For whatever reasons, Homestead batters started to hit Brewer, while Britt settled down. Charleston doubled in two runs in the bottom of the ninth to tie the game at 4–4, and the teams played on with no further runs until, at midnight in the bottom of the 12th, Ewing hit a shot that Monarchs reliever Dink Mothel couldn't hold onto with his bare hand, and Scales came home with the winning run.[10]

Pittsburgh Press sports editor Ralph Davis left the game account to one of his writers and used his space to evaluate the quality of the lighting and its future meaning for professional baseball: "The scene was a revelation to many doubting Thomases, who went to scoff and left the field, declaring that perhaps, after all, the national pastime, if it ever has to be saved, will find night performances its savior." Davis interviewed Pirates owner Barney Dreyfuss, who declared the exhibition "interesting, and [it] provides entertainment for many people who cannot get away from work for afternoon contests." Dreyfuss was not about to let shiny lights distract him from the generally conservative viewpoint held by most major league owners: "I don't think night baseball will ever replace the daylight brand popularity."[11] The first white

George Britt was a starting pitcher who could also catch and play the infield, making him a mainstay of Grays squads from 1926 through 1933. Britt, Oscar Charleston, Jud Wilson, and Vic Harris were known as the four toughest Negro Leaguers—Posey had them all on his team at the same time in the early 1930s (author's collection).

big league game under the lights wasn't played until 1935 in Cincinnati, and Forbes Field didn't get its permanent lights until 1940.

Havey Boyle in the *Post-Gazette* found the attendance for the first night games at Forbes disappointing, at least compared to pre-game predictions. As many as 15,000 fans had been foreseen for the July 18 game, but only about 6,000 showed, and about 4,000 the following evening. He took a humorous dig at Posey, implying that the low gate might have driven him a little off-center: "Financially, I am given to understand, the affairs here left much to be desired. Mister Posey ... was discovered under the grandstand cutting out paper dolls as he tabulated the receipts."[12] An average of 5,000 for a Grays game at Forbes wasn't bad, though, although the novelty of night ball would have been expected to raise that figure. But the Grays often did better in the other communities they played in regularly, and that was again true for the KC series. The initial game in Cleveland drew 10,000 fans, and a Sunday doubleheader in Sharon, the longstanding home for Sunday baseball banned in most other Pennsylvania municipalities, drew a reported 12,000 (although neither of those games was at night).

After the Grays and Monarchs finished touring Posey's environs, the two teams and the lighting trucks headed west to Kansas City for three more games in Muehlebach Stadium, the white minor league park the Monarchs used for their home games. Homestead continued to dominate, winning all three contests. The middle game, on August 2, was one of the most famous in Negro League history. Brewer started again for Kansas City under the lights, opposed by Smokey Joe Williams. Brewer, as the *Courier* put it, "gave a remarkable exhibition of emery ball pitching" (he used sandpaper to doctor the ball, in other words, as he probably had in Pittsburgh two weeks earlier). Williams had not made it to age 45 as a top-flight hurler by religiously following all the rules, either, and the *Courier* described his work as including "everything but a blacksmith's file." It was undisputable, the *Courier* reporter wrote, that "the opposing pitchers were cheating without the question of a doubt. An emery ball in daylight is very deceptive but at night it is about as easy to see as an insect in the sky."[13]

Posey admitted in an article he wrote six seasons later that skullduggery had been afoot: "Before the game, the writer and Mr. Wilkinson of Kansas City had an agreement that neither pitcher would use the 'emery' ball. The Grays got two men on base the first inning, when Brewer brought out his 'work' ... Joe Williams was then given a sheet of sand paper and the battle was on."[14] If modern sports marketing had been in vogue in 1930, the game could have been sponsored by a hardware chain. As Williams and Brewer toiled on through the night, they produced a double shutout that went 12 innings before it was decided in the Grays' favor, 1–0. Joe Williams wound up giving up a single hit, and he struck out 27 of the 36 men he retired. Chet Brewer fanned 19 and gave up a total of four hits. The last was to Chaney White, the Grays' center fielder, a fluke double that drove in Charleston, who had walked.

As soon as the marathon Grays-Monarchs series ended, Posey was busy setting up the next big challenge, a championship series against the Lincoln Giants of New York. Since there was no league in the East to produce a champion to challenge the Midwestern Negro National League for black honors, the rights to the mythical crown were asserted much as they had been when Posey's Loendis played for national black basketball championships. This was to say that individual team owners could declare their nines worthy of the title and challenge other worthies to beat them. Of course, many teams could claim this status, but only the best had their claims validated by the Negro sportswriters.

The August 9 *Courier* printed a letter from Posey to sports editor Chester Washington, proposing an 11-game series with the Lincolns "for the recognized champions of 1930." The Lincolns, Posey reasoned, "have beaten Baltimore [the Black Sox] so often that they must be considered the best in the Seaboard.... Personally, I think the Homestead Grays of 1930 the greatest club the Grays have ever had.... We are willing and anxious to play Lincoln Giants because we think we have a better club and because we think it would pay financially."[15] The Lincolns' owner, Jim Keenan, was another white owner of a black team who was, like Wilkinson, considered a colleague by Posey and other black owners. He had been in the black baseball business in New York since 1919 and was no pushover as a businessman. While sportswriters and hardcore fans waited impatiently, he and Posey engaged in a public exchange of offers and counteroffers, seeking leverage in scheduling and the split of gate revenue.

Only a week after the *Courier* printed Posey's letter, it ran a rejoinder from Keenan stating his desire to play, but doubting Posey's enthusiasm: "I understand his partner [presumably Walker] scouted the Lincolns for a week in Philadelphia and his report of their ability gives no comfort to Mister Posey." Keenan also complained that the proposed visiting team's percentage at Forbes Field was too low and held that out as another Posey stalling tactic. "We will play a series of nine, eleven or one hundred and eleven games if the Homestead Grays want to be reasonable and agreeable on terms," Keenan concluded.[16]

At the end of August, Keenan wrote simultaneously to the *Courier* and the *New York Amsterdam News* to accuse Posey of tossing up all sorts of road-blocks to a series he didn't really want to play, since he feared his Grays would lose. First, Keenan was mystified that Posey would propose to play "World's Colored Championship" games in Altoona and Beaver Falls, and at Edgar Thomson Field in the Pittsburgh suburb of Braddock. (If he had been better acquainted with the Grays' operations in Western Pennsylvania, he would have known that these were choice spots for good gates.) Then he offered to drop any demand for a gate percentage for games at Forbes Field, playing instead for a flat guarantee that Posey could set, thus giving up a chance for a potentially large profit from a very large attendance. Once Posey set a Pittsburgh guarantee, Keenan would do the same for New York games, but raise the Grays' visiting share by $200.[17] Posey didn't have much of anything to say publicly, but he stuck by his demands. The negotiations began to take on a marked similarity to those between him and the McMahon brothers (Keenan's former business partners) that set up the championship matches between Loendi and the brothers' Commonwealth Big Five basketball team in 1923. In that case, Posey stood pat and the McMahons wound up making several concessions, because even on terms that were mostly Posey's, there was no good reason to pass up a lucrative and prestige-laden series with Loendi.

Keenan had one very important card to play that wasn't in anyone else's hand, though. He could arrange for some of the games to be played at Yankee Stadium in New York. The Stadium was in only its eighth year of use as the home of the white major league champions, and in the first of many years of use as one of the major spots for important Negro League games. The Yankees rented out the park for many different kinds of athletic events to make money when the team was on the road, but before 1930 it had never been host to a game between black teams. This changed on July 5, when a doubleheader was played as a major fundraiser for the Brotherhood of Sleeping Car Porters, the union of Pullman porters being slowly brought to power by legendary labor and civil rights organizer A. Philip Randolph. The successful fundraiser led to a string of 225 games at the Stadium over the next 18 seasons with at least one black team involved. Sunday games at the Stadium became a major showcase for Negro League talent.

The Lincoln Giants had been the home team for the Pullman Porters' games, and with the aid of Roy Lancaster, a Brotherhood official and, like Yankees owner Jacob Ruppert, a member of New York's political powerful Tammany organization, Keenan was able to book six of the games against the Grays, including back-to-back doubleheaders on September 27 and 28 that wrapped up the 10-game series. The series opened at Forbes Field on Saturday, September 20, with the Grays sweeping a doubleheader. Lefty Williams was sharp in the opener, giving up eight hits as the Grays won, 9–1. The second game was something else entirely. Homestead had an 8–2 lead after two innings. The Lincolns tied the game at 8–8 in the top of the fifth, but the Grays scored five runs in the bottom of that inning. The Giants came back again, though, and actually led until the Grays tied the game at 16–16 in the bottom of the ninth, then pushed the winning run over in the tenth. Vic Harris, leading off and playing left field, had eight hits for the day. Charleston homered in the opening game, and Gibson had a homer and triple in the second.

Then it was onto the train to New York for a Sunday doubleheader at the Stadium, where the Giants stopped the Grays in the first game, 6–2, as righty Bill Holland outpitched Joe Williams. Former Posey favorite Rev Cannady, now the Lincolns' second baseman, had three hits, including a home run. Britt gave Homestead its third win of the series in the nightcap, though, with a five-hitter that produced a 3–2 win over Luther "Red" Farrell. The series next moved to Philadelphia, another hotbed of Negro League baseball, and the teams split on the 25th and 26th. Joe Williams rebounded in the first game in Philly to allow only seven hits. The Grays got 13 off of Holland and Connie Rector, including homers by Harris and Gibson, and won, 11–3. Righty Red Ryan mastered the Grays the next day, though, and the Lincolns won, 6–4.

The Grays took a four-games-to-two lead back to Yankee Stadium, but becoming the champs wasn't going to be easy. Homestead had a fifth win seemingly wrapped up in the first game on Saturday, the 27th, taking an 8–5 lead into the bottom of the ninth. But Lefty Williams walked the bases full, and when Joe Williams came in to shut down the threat, pinch-hitter Julio Rojo ripped his first pitch for a bases-clearing triple, then scored the winning run. The Grays won the second Saturday game, 7–3, for a five-games-to-three edge. This was the game when rookie catcher Gibson unloaded a legendary home run, reported to travel 460 feet into the left field stands. That was his second of the day—he had hit one in the first game, too.

But on Sunday the Grays lost the opener, 6–2, as Bill Holland outpitched Joe Williams again, by the same final score. Holland was another of those "iron men" who could start both ends of a doubleheader, and Giants manager John Henry Lloyd called upon him again to try to make the 10-game series a five-all tie. The strategy almost worked. Holland had given up a single run into the fifth inning, and Britt had yielded none, when an injury to a Lincoln star may well have tipped the series in the Grays' favor. In the top of the fifth, second baseman Cannady and Chino Smith, the Giants' outstanding right fielder, collided on a short fly ball, and Smith was hurt. He was replaced by Farrell, the left-handed starter who played the outfield when not on the mound. Farrell was a prodigious slugger, but not a particularly adept fielder. With two out in the top of the eighth and the score still 1–0, he misjudged a fly ball that Smith likely would have caught, which turned into a double. Then Homestead's Judy Johnson ripped a triple between the lumbering Farrell and center fielder Clint Thomas, and the Grays were on their way to a four-run inning. The Lincolns came back with two runs in the bottom of the eighth, but by then it had gotten too dark to play anymore. The Grays had a 5–2 win and the World's Colored Championship for 1930.

There is no financial information available for the games in Pittsburgh and Philadelphia, but the Yankees in 1955 and 1970 donated troves of old business records to the National Baseball Hall of Fame Library. The 1930 cash ledger shows total gross receipts for the three Stadium doubleheaders of about $13,340. The Yankees took the biggest share, $4,243, for rent and operating expenses, and Lancaster was paid $1,799 for arranging the games. The Lincolns took away $3,964, and the Grays $3,335.[18] To put Homestead's take into perspective, the club's share from those six games would nearly have covered the extra $600 a month in salaries for the full season that Posey and Walker were shelling out to maintain a top-ranked club.

The 1931 Grays featured a few lineup changes, which made the team even stronger than it had been the previous season. Judy Johnson, a native of Wilmington, Delaware, left to return to Hilldale in Philadelphia, which was only 30 miles from his hometown. But Posey promptly recruited an awe-inspiring replacement. Jud Wilson, who had been with the Baltimore Black Sox since 1921, was a driven man with a hot temper and a load of baseball skills. The skills, not his disposition, eventually put him into the Baseball Hall of Fame. While not Johnson's fielding equal at third base, he was a powerful hitter. His nickname, "Boojum," is said to have been derived from the explosive sound his line drives made when they hit outfield fences. Negro Leagues historian James Riley summarizes him thusly: "A fierce competitor, hard loser, and habitual brawler, the bull-necked Wilson was fearless, ill-tempered, and known for his fighting almost as well as he is known for his hitting." Riley ranks Wilson as one of the "Big Four of the big badmen" of black ball. In 1931, Posey had all four of them—Wilson, Charleston, Britt, and Vic Harris. It says something for Posey's own hard-nosed approach that he was able to channel their fierceness into highly competitive baseball without having it turn into the distracting misbehavior that he abhorred. It seemed he actually admired his tough leaders who had played for the Grays over the years. In one of his 1939 columns, he reported having asked a player, "What would the players do if Britt, Beckwith and Charleston were League umpires?" The answer: "The players would not argue on decisions."[19]

Jud Wilson, a slugging infielder, was another mainstay of the Grays' great 1931 team and returned during World War II. He is one of several Grays in the National Baseball Hall of Fame (author's collection).

Posey also bolstered the pitching staff with three major acquisitions, two of them with well-known reputations, giving him seven pitchers capable of starting against top-level opponents. Theodore Roosevelt Radcliffe had an impressive name—but his baseball nickname was even better. Ted Radcliffe, like George Britt, could catch as well as pitch, and sometimes he would play both positions in a double-header, starting one game on the mound and one behind the plate. This got him the nickname "Double Duty," which stuck with him the rest of his life.

Willie Foster was the younger half-brother of Rube Foster, himself an outstanding hurler in his day. Willie was a left-hander who eventually was voted into the Hall of Fame. Not surprisingly, he had spent the bulk of his early career with Rube's Chicago American Giants. But Rube had died in December 1930, and by May of 1931, Willie had signed with the Grays. Riley characterized Willie's ability as, "With a crucial game to win, Willie was the kind of pitcher a manager wanted on the mound."[20] Posey picked an annual Negro League all-star team in the *Courier* at the end of each season. He had named Foster to the team in 1930, and for this single season had the star at his disposal. The third pitcher was Roy Williams, a local talent. At age 22, he was a friend of the 18-year-old Gibson, but he had talent of his own and was beginning a 10-year career as a journeyman Negro League starter.

The 1931 Grays were acclaimed as the black champions and were one of Posey's best teams. Front row, left to right: George Britt, Lefty Williams, Jud Wilson, Vic Harris, Ted Radcliffe, Ambrose Reid, and Ted Page. Back row, left to right: Posey, Bill Evans, Jap Washington, Red Reed, Smokey Joe Williams, Josh Gibson, George Scales, Oscar Charleston, and Charlie Walker, Posey's right-hand man in running the team (author's collection).

The Grays won consistently at every level of competition. They were 143–22–2 overall and were 36–19–1 against the top black teams, including 12–8–1 against the Baltimore Black Sox, 7–2 against the St. Louis Stars, and 6–3 against Kansas City. At the end of the season, Posey, in his annual all-star article, also proclaimed the Grays the "undisputed National Championship team of the United States." And no one disagreed with him. While some Grays could be found on Posey's all-star teams, he didn't abuse his privilege as an owner with access to a printing press, and his picks were widely regarded as well-informed and fair. The 1931 team, though, was heavy with Homestead stars, getting six of the 16 slots. Joe Williams, Foster, and Radcliffe were among the pitchers, Gibson was the catcher, Charleston was at first, and Wilson was at third. No other team had more than three representatives.[21]

However, the champion Grays, due to circumstances beyond their control, were the leaders of a very sick movement. The Negro National League in 1931was down to six clubs from its usual eight, missing two of its flagship franchises of the 1920s. The St. Louis Stars had folded, and J. L. Wilkinson had withdrawn his Monarchs from the league, touring with his portable lights as an independent team. There were casualties in the non-league East also, primarily Keenan's Lincoln Giants, who had gone out of business after the thrilling marathon championship series with the Grays. Willie Foster later neatly summarized the situation for historian John Holway: "The team couldn't pay us, it was the Depression and nobody was working.... The people couldn't go to the ball game, and our bosses promised us so much money but didn't have it 'cause they weren't making it."[22]

In the spring, Posey wrote an article for the *Courier* about the prospects for black baseball in 1931. The season, he predicted, "has never had a more dreary outlook, should we take the financial outlook of the United States as a criterion." He, for one, did not. "All businesses which have been conducted in a safe and sane manner have weathered the worst part of the financial depression," he continued, and he saw no reason that black baseball shouldn't also survive. But not everyone who presented himself as a team owner could prosper: "Baseball at this time needs men with much knowledge of all things connected with the operation of big time baseball." This, of course, sounded like a typically self-assured Posey description of himself.

Posey, the man "with much knowledge of all things," presented a list of steps that should be taken to improve Negro League ball. For starters, scheduling could be centralized, instead of tolerating situations where "every club owner was maneuvering to get the best dates for his club and let the fellows who were timid about looking out for themselves, for some unknown reason, suffer the effect of a poor schedule." Despite his past pride in paying the

Grays as well as or better than other owners, he acknowledged at this point that "Players' salaries, especially in the east, must come down this year." He had no need for booking agents and thought that the other owners could do what he did to arrange games: "Get the addresses of all the baseball managers in the country and write them yourself."

Even if he thought players' salaries should be cut (and believed the best ones would understand, given the overall financial situation), he hadn't lost his insistence on discipline. "[White] big league players get very little respect from the fans and give those fans the utmost respect," he wrote, while "Colored players as a whole give the fans very little respect and demand the utmost respect for themselves, particularly before a home audience." And that was just his standard for behavior at the ballpark. After the game, "Club owners should fire players standing around the street in bedroom slippers, with no collar or tie; also for drinking in public after 12 o'clock at night or frequenting cabarets after 1 o'clock."[23]

Among Posey's main attributes as a sports team owner, in addition to his aggressive attitude and ability to find and procure top talent, was this fine-honed sense of organization. This plan for how a black league should be run was not mere hypothesizing on his part. There was a new league formed in 1932, and Posey was in charge of it. The new East-West League was born into a vacuum. The Negro National League had gone out of business the previous fall, leaving no black major league in the country. The Negro Southern League, usually considered a minor league, was elevated by default to major league status. It took in some teams from the NNL, but, as usual, suffered financially, particularly in these Depression times, from smaller fan bases in its major cities than in the industrialized north. As was often the case, some of its teams failed to finish the season, and the NSL sank back to minor league status after this sole season in the limelight.

There were rumors in the depths of the 1931 football season that something was afoot to produce a new black baseball league. Posey himself wrote in the October *Courier* article with his all-star team that "the time is now ripe for a colored league ... the baseball public can rest assured that a real league is in the process of formation." Sure enough, it was reported in January that a new league was being born, and Posey was the father.[24] Theoretically, he was one of three league commissioners, the other members of the triumvirate of owners being Lloyd Thompson of Philadelphia's Hilldales and George Rossiter, longtime boss of the Baltimore Black Sox. But it was clear that Posey was calling the shots. The owner who had deliberately avoided taking his Grays into leagues in the past in order to reap the unfettered rewards of independent ball was now, with tough financial times all around, the leading advocate of league organization as the way for black ball to survive. The East-West League stretched 500 miles along a northwest to southeast axis from Detroit to Washington, D.C. It also included, working from west to east, Cleveland, Pittsburgh (the Grays), Philadelphia (Hilldale), Newark, and Baltimore. There were also the Cuban Stars. There were always a number of black Latino players, primarily from thriving Cuban baseball, in the Negro Leagues. Probably for reasons of cultural comfort, they tended to congregate on a single team. The East-West entry was owned by white sports promoter Syd Pollock. He lived in New York City's northern suburbs, but his franchise didn't live anywhere—it had no home city and participated as a fulltime traveling team.

While Posey was enthusiastic in putting the East-West League together, he was aware of how owners had to take care not to repeat the business mistakes of the past few years. He gave a thoughtful description of the Negro Leagues during the past 10 years as having been "inflated," as had the stock market and other non-baseball businesses. By this he likely meant that the competition for players between existing teams and independent clubs throughout the 1920s had boosted salaries to the point where there was no longer sufficient revenue to support payrolls. It was likely no accident that a single new league, stretching across the northern part of the United States from the Midwest to the East Coast, and including most of the surviving major league-level teams, would severely constrict the free agent market in which players could shop for superior offers.

But Posey being Posey, and the Grays having the reputation they did, it wasn't difficult for him to go out and sign a raft of highly desirable newcomers. And he needed them. While there were eight teams in the East-West, he controlled two of them, or maybe three. He personally took over a new team, the Detroit Wolves, while his brother See oversaw the day-to-day operations of the Grays. Then there were the new Cleveland Stars, for the record owned by old Posey friend William S. Young, his teammate on the famed Loendi basketball squad of the early 1920s and a catcher for the Grays before the team got seriously professional. This led to speculation on the sports pages that Young was simply fronting for Posey, although Young stoutly maintained that it was his money, and no one else's, invested in the Stars.[25]

However many teams Posey controlled, he was also the head commissioner and chief spokesman for the East-West, holding sway over a black league in a way not seen since 10 years before, when Rube Foster had an iron grip on the Negro National. (Foster never owned more than one team, but he was president and secretary of the league so long as he was healthy enough to fill those positions, and was known to dictate player movements between teams in the NNL's early years to try to ensure competitive balance.) Posey's financial interests in multiple franchises also harkened back to the 1890s in the white National League, when owners controlled more than one team. This practice of "syndicate baseball" had its extreme downside, "when some of these groups decided to favor one of their franchises at the expense of the other. Most notorious were brothers Frank and Stanley Robison, who owned both the St. Louis Perfectos and the Cleveland Spiders, and moved all of the Spiders' best players to St. Louis before the 1899 season. The Spiders ended up as the worst team in Major League history." The Spiders' fiasco, when the team finished with a 20–134 record, led to the banning of syndicate ownership.[26]

Posey was not so obvious about it, but he did weaken the Grays a bit in favor of his new Detroit team. He moved two stars, Vic Harris and Lefty Williams, to the Wolves. The bulk of the Detroit roster, though, was gleaned from the late NNL, and the harvest was rich. The Poseys had contacted most of the roster of the late St. Louis Stars, and their efforts yielded center fielder James "Cool Papa" Bell, shortstop Willie Wells, and outfielder George "Mule" Suttles, all regarded as top talents in black ball. From the same team came pitcher Ted Trent, a top-flight right-handed starter, regular third baseman Dewey Creacy, and 19-year-old Quincy Trouppe, just beginning a long career as a catcher and outfielder.[27]

The Grays were also well stocked from the former St. Louis team—these guys wanted to play somewhere, of course, and why not for an organization with Posey's reputation? The Stars' 1931 regular first and second basemen, George Giles and Newt Allen, donned Homestead uniforms. The starting staff was bolstered after Lefty Williams' move by the signing of Harry Salmon, who had been pitching for the Birmingham Black Barons in the NSL, and Leroy Matlock and Joe Strong, formerly of St. Louis.

The Wolves, playing their home games at Hamtramck Stadium, which the Detroit Stars of the NNL had been using, zoomed to the top of the East-West standings with a 20–6 record, a .769 winning percentage, in early June. The Grays weren't far behind in third place at 13–6, a .684 pace. It might have been interesting to see the Grays step up the pace and catch the Wolves, but, in fact, the Wolves fell back to them in a sense—the Detroit franchise folded in mid–June, and the two rosters were combined as the Homestead Grays, one of several cutbacks that unsuccessfully tried to get the league through the rest of the season. This briefly gave Cum Posey, who again took over running the Grays, one of the dominating teams in all Negro League history: Bell, Wells, Harris, Trent, Lefty Williams, and Trouppe all joined from the Wolves to go with the strong team already assembled.

But it didn't last, not even a month. One of the extreme cost-saving moves adopted by the league in June was to stop paying regular salaries, even though the players had contracts. Henceforth, the clubs would dole out a percentage of each game's gate receipts to the players (with little paid out after a game with low attendance, and nothing if there was a rainout). This was a sure sign of a failing league. Bell, Wells, Giles, Allen, and Trouppe, among others, left to play for J. L. Wilkinson's independent Kansas City Monarchs, where according to Giles, "we knew we'd be paid every two weeks."[28]

The painstaking work by Posey and the other team owners that went into the formation of the East-West League could not counteract the terrible national economic conditions. "Lack of patronage has hit the entire circuit from Detroit to Washington, and not a single club has been able to cover up on the expenses necessary to promote the game," the *Courier* summarized the debacle. Posey himself admitted that "economically, we picked the wrong time." But, he added, "The East-West League has no regrets for the way it was organized and operated." It was truly an awful time to launch a new enterprise in America, particularly one with built-in vulnerabilities such as a professional baseball league, and in particular one catering primarily to a minority of the baseball-fan population.[29]

Posey may have had no regrets in the summer of 1932 (and probably wouldn't have admitted them if he had), but he also didn't have much money, and for the first time in his professional baseball life he had competition breathing down his neck for his dominance of Pittsburgh black ball. Posey had fended off challenges in the past, but this one would be hard to overcome.

There were still black semi-pro teams in Pittsburgh around 1930. A particularly strong nine was the Crawfords. The team began as a merger of the young black players on two integrated teams playing in the Hill District around Wylie Avenue. Although the neighborhood was the nearest thing to a central black community that the city had, "race didn't count that much on the Hill when it came time to choose up sides for a game," according to sports historian Rob Ruck. The leaders of the black players, Bill and Charles "Teenie" Harris, weren't related, although Vic Harris of the Grays was Bill's brother. In 1925, they persuaded their African American teammates to band together to form a very good amateur team that was sponsored by the Crawford Bath House, a recreation center and swimming pool at Crawford and Wylie avenues that served the Hill neighborhood and had a mostly black clientele. Jim Dorsey, an early Posey basketball teammate on the Monticello squad, was the nominal coach as head of the recreation center.[30]

The team underwent a few name changes in its early years, known sometimes as the Crawford A.C. team, sometimes as the Crawford Colored Giants. The roster also continually evolved, as the better players from teams the Crawfords had defeated left their clubs to join the victors. In 1928, the Crawfords played the tough black team from the Edgar Thomson steel works in nearby Braddock. Harold Tinker played for Edgar Thomson, and he recalled that "we were amazed that we could only beat them two to one or something like that. These kids were really hustlers." Tinker added that Bill Harris urged another of his brothers, Neal, to leave the Thomsons, "'Why don't you come down and we'll make this a real ball team?' So we quit Edgar Thomson and went down to play with these kids at Washington Park."

By this time, the Crawfords were the best black semi-pro team in Pittsburgh. They followed in the Grays' footsteps by playing and beating a wide range of opponents, mostly white, in Western Pennsylvania, reportedly winning 95 of 114 games in 1930. The Crawfords had the best black players in Pittsburgh not under contract to the Grays, and a manager, Harry Beale, who arranged games far and wide and saw to it that the team got publicity. The Craws had about everything they needed, except money. The team became so locally famous that they could draw upwards of 5,000 to a game, and they received a good share of the gate when playing outside of Pittsburgh. But city regulations prohibited charging to attend games at city-owned fields. It was permissible to pass the hat among the spectators, but many a fan contributed little or nothing for the privilege of watching the Crawfords play. A Memorial Day game in 1930 drew 6,000, for example, but a take of only $80. *Courier* sportswriter Bill Nunn took the cheapskates to task: "A nickel a person would see the youngsters on top. But no! Out of every ten people who pass through, nine of them have 'iron-clad' alibis. We say 'iron-clad' because very seldom does one hear the clink of silver. Copper pennies rattle in the box from the fingers of 'dressed-up' sheiks, who cleverly hide their contributions."[31]

The knowledgeable among Pittsburgh's sports fans knew how good the Crawfords were. Steve Cox, a white in the local sporting goods business who provided the team with equipment, helped Beale and Tinker, who had risen to be co-manager of the operation, book games with the better white squads. In 1930, he offered to buy the team for $1,000. Instead, Beale and Tinker sought out William Augustus "Gus" Greenlee, a well-known and well-heeled African American businessman, both an economic and political power on the Hill.

Greenlee was a native of North Carolina who had migrated to Pittsburgh to work in the steel mills. The mills drove the Pittsburgh economy, but Gus moved on to drive a taxi, the trunk of which, it being the Prohibition era, was filled with bottles of booze for sale. He was in the cabaret business by the early 1920s. He went on to open more cafes, including his most famous, the Crawford Grill, to found a musical booking agency, and to back a stable of black prizefighters that included light heavyweight champ John Henry Lewis. Greenlee was a big man physically, standing six feet, three inches tall and weighing over 200 pounds. More to the point, he was a big shot in Pittsburgh. He was a power in the political Third Ward Voters League, and he also had a big heart. He fed 700 homeless men at the Crawford Grill on Christmas night in 1931, and Chester Washington, who prowled Wylie Avenue for the *Courier* before he became sports editor, wrote, "It has been said of Gus by his friends that he has never hesitated to lend a hand when a worthy cause is presented to him."[32]

Greenlee supported his entertainment venues, sports interests, and philanthropy, through his domination of the then-illegal numbers gambling business on the Hill. Numbers gambling, at its core, is a simple operation. A bettor pays for the chance to pick a three-digit number, and if that is the winning number, he or she collects. There are more complex variations, but the triple-digit choice, with the winning number a random one, is the basis of the game. It is so easy to play, and so profitable for the "house," that state governments over the years have legalized it and taken it over as revenue-raising state lotteries.

But to make a lot of money off of the numbers when it was a private, underground venture required a lot of betting customers and a many-tentacled system of reaching them, collecting their money, and paying off the few lucky winners (since the three-digit number could be anywhere from 000 to 999, the theoretical odds on any bet were 1,000 to 1, far from a sure thing).

A history of the Pittsburgh African American community gave a detailed description of a large numbers operation spawned by Greenlee and his close business colleague, William "Woogie" Harris. The sprawling operation was said to have contained

Hundreds of stations, concealed in restaurants, fish shops, and news stands. The system by which they [numbers] are played is elaborate. Besides the hundreds of stations, many sub-stations exist, and for those who do not or cannot get to the station, 'writers' are sent out on regular routes to write up customers. All slips are written in triplicate—one for the customer, one for the sub-station and one for the central office. Pick-up men go to sub-stations to pick up the slips and the money collected from the writers. Writers get a percentage of the write-up and another percentage of any hit made on his book. Each sub-station gets a percentage on its turnover. A deadline is set at which all numbers must be in the main office—an elaborate organization of adding machines, counting machines, clerks, stenographers and accountants.... The central station pays off all hits; the hit money goes back to the sub-station and from there is delivered on the route by the writers or is called for.[33]

Rigorous law enforcement could smash such an operation, of course, but Pittsburgh was known as a wide-open city for gambling, illegal booze, and prohibition. The *Pittsburgh Daily Post* reported in 1926 that vice generated $5 million annually, cuts going to local politicians and police. All of those working in or otherwise profiting off of numbers operations had to be paid out of the betting proceeds. But since winning payouts, which in a world with no overhead or profit motive would have been 1,000 to 1, were generally made at only 500- to 600-to-1 odds, there was plenty of money to go around. Ruck interviewed several knowledgeable members of the city's African American community about Greenlee and Harris and reported that most of them believed the two numbers barons grossed $20,000 to $25,000 a day, if not more, an amount that gave them the current-day economic clout of a daily take of about $2 million.[34]

Even though law enforcement usually turned an indifferent eye to illegal gambling in the city, the occasional pinch was an occupational hazard. While Greenlee and Harris did not inaugurate playing the numbers in Pittsburgh, a veteran journalist "credited" them with being the first in the city to be convicted of running a numbers bank. Ray Sprigle of the *Post-Gazette*, in a five-part series on the numbers, wrote that Greenlee and Harris were hauled into court in 1926 by a perplexed police investigator. Inspector John P. Claney had taken them to Morals Court (the lower-level criminal court) to get things sorted out. He was pretty sure what the pair was doing was immoral. He just wasn't sure if it was illegal. "It's some new kind of racket they're pulling among the colored people up on the Hill," Claney explained to the magistrate.

> They sell these little slips with numbers on them for anything from a cent up. Then, somehow or other the clearing house totals for the Pittsburgh district enter into it [a clearing house sorted out cashed bank checks and forwarded them to the issuing banks—it published the dollar results of its work daily, which were used to derive winning numbers]. If the fellow that bought the slip wins he gets $7.50 for every cent he plays. The whole Hill district is going crazy over it. It ain't a gambling house, but it's gambling all right. I don't know what you would call it.

According to Sprigle, Claney and Magistrate Albert D. Brandon consulted with the city's lawyers, who suggested charging Greenlee and Harris with operating a lottery. So that's what Claney did, and the magistrate fined them each a hefty $50. The pair paid their fines with borrowed money and proceeded back to the Hill, where they soon became locally famous.[35]

If Sprigle's version of Claney's account to the magistrate was correct, the future numbers barons were paying off in 1926 at 750-to-1 odds, a generous return to winners. But in 1930, Greenlee and Harris made a major gesture to their customers that permanently cemented their reputations among Pittsburgh's black wagerers. There were many reasons for bettors to pick a certain daily number, ranging from the straightforward to the mysterious. On the exotic end were the purveyors of "dream books," a lucrative publishing trade which connected the content of people's dreams to suggested daily picks. Tips, though, could turn up anywhere. Starting in 1928, the *Courier* published a comic strip called "Sonny Boy Sam." Sam was a naïve young fellow who wandered the city, getting into scrapes that often made him the butt of a joke. But the subtext to his adventures was that the weekly panels were peppered with three-digit numbers, on signs, buildings, shirt collars—everywhere.

The simplest way to pick a number was to focus on personal data, such as birthdays, or even something as obvious as that day's date. The numbers was a great business to be in, unmarred in the long run by a bad economy (the betting population is so large and the average wager so small), police raids, or bad publicity. But the bank could be broken when fate, in the form of random chance, intervened. On August 5, 1930, an inordinate number of people, for reasons lost to history, played 805 (eighth month, fifth day). That was the day, according to Sprigle, when "just one little number nearly wrecked the numbers racket in Pittsburgh. Walk up to an old time numbers writer and say real quick, 'eight-oh-five.' Watch him turn pale, his knees go wobbly. See him gasp for breath."[36]

That number hit, and numbers operations all over Pittsburgh either refused to pay off or were wiped out. Greenlee and Harris paid their customers, though, by mortgaging their homes and pawning their possessions. They proved that honesty, even if you're doing something illegal, is the best policy. As Ruck wrote, "While most numbers bankers and writers were subsequently discussed with anger and contempt, Gus and Woogie were treated with a newfound respect ... 805 was an immediate financial disaster but a long-term godsend; it was the springboard by which they jumped to a position of dominance in the numbers business, not only on the Hill, but in many sections of Pittsburgh and throughout the tri-state region."[37] Their reputations were made. Thereafter, when Greenlee got into trouble over alleged lottery or election law violations (charges which he always beat), the newspapers would refer to him right away as the Hill's "numbers baron."

Among the many recipients of Greenlee's charitable giving were sports teams. Although not an athlete himself, at least not at the level of a Cum Posey, for example, he enjoyed sports, and "it didn't matter what kind of athlete you were.... Gus loved you and you'd get his money."[38] So agreeing to back the Crawfords was right up Greenlee's alley.

The growing success of the Crawfords naturally spawned interest in them playing the Grays. Ruck says that Posey put the confrontation off as the 1930 season rolled on to milk all the interest he could out of the potential rivalry, but when it did happen on August 23, the Grays were hosts in their "home park," the spacious Forbes Field, on a Saturday, the best day of the week. The game, which the *Post-Gazette* said the fans of the teams "have been looking forward to all season," was a close one.[39] Oscar Owens threw shutout ball until the seventh inning, and the Grays were up 3–0 when the Craws put two runs across. But Owens, with a big assist from a diving catch by Vic Harris in left with men on base, held them through the eighth. That was the last inning played due to darkness (the result of a 6:30 p.m. starting time—the game was the third of the day at Forbes, the Pirates having already swept a doubleheader against the Boston Braves). The two clubs played each other three times in 1931, the Grays winning twice.

But the Crawfords were in transition, as the Grays had been throughout the 1920s, from a strong local and regional team to one that could compete on a

William A. "Gus" Greenlee was the owner of the Pittsburgh Crawfords who challenged Posey's Homestead Grays for baseball supremacy in the mid–1930s. Greenlee was founder and first president of the second Negro National League in 1933, and he had a number of other occupations, including being one of the main numbers gambling bankers in Pittsburgh. Here he stands in his Crawford Grill club before a poster advertising light heavyweight boxing champ John Henry Lewis, whom he managed (Carnegie Library of Pittsburgh).

national level. Posey had done this very gradually, replacing original Homestead players with hires from the Negro Leagues on a gradual basis. Greenlee, being Greenlee, turned the Crawfords over almost completely during the 1931 season. He had hired veteran infielder Bobby Williams, who had been playing top-flight black ball since 1917, to manage the club in 1930. Williams also sent out feelers to players he knew, tipping them off to a new lucrative situation in

Pittsburgh, an oasis in the deteriorating black baseball employment situation.

The Crawford lineup at the beginning of 1931 looked a lot like the Grays of a few years before—it featured Jap Washington at first base, Moe Harris at second, Dennis Graham and Ambrose Reid in the outfield, and Rags Roberts as utility man, all good players pushed out at Homestead by out-of-town signings. Before the season was over, however, the Crawfords had their own high-class newcomers, including center fielder Jimmie Crutchfield from the Indianapolis ABCs and pitcher Sam Streeter (the former Grays hurler) and catcher Bill Perkins from the Cleveland Cubs.

Harold Tinker, a hometown Pittsburgher and the team's center fielder, recalled much later that in July, Greenlee gave his squad members an ultimatum—the Craws were becoming a full-time team, and every player either had to give up his day job and play ball, or quit the team. Tinker, who was beginning decades of involvement in sports and community service in the black community, decided to leave the Crawfords, but not before playing in the team's sole win over the Grays on August 1. It was a game which, in addition to the final score, showed just how far Greenlee was taking this team. Seeing the need to bolster his pitching staff, Greenlee had looked toward Cleveland again, where the Cubs were playing out the string in the fading Negro National League, and signed an up-and-coming 25-year-old right-hander. The new acquisition, Leroy "Satchel" Paige, "gassed up his reliable Packard and ... hit the road and drove the 135 miles to Pittsburgh nonstop, which did not take him that long given his penchant for driving at speeds that may have equaled his hundred-mile-an-hour fastball."[40]

On August 1, the Crawfords jumped off to an early lead, but the Grays came back against starter Harry Kincannon and tied the game at 7–7 after three innings. Enter Paige, who held the Grays scoreless for the rest of the game while his new teammates put over three more runs for the victory. Paige, who was the first Negro Leaguer elected to the Hall of Fame in 1971, is widely recognized as the greatest black pitcher from the era before integration, rivaled only by Posey's man, Smokey Joe Williams. Satchel, as inclined to follow the payday as any black player of those times, changed teams often, but he stayed with Greenlee in Pittsburgh through 1934, and then went absent without leave, playing elsewhere during salary disputes, before almost returning in 1937. Paige was in great measure responsible for some of Greenlee's best days as a major baseball owner, but then had a major hand in ensuring his worst.

Greenlee continued to add big name players in 1932. The difference was that several of them came from Posey's Grays, as the master raider now became the raided one. The change, as almost always, involved players acting in their own financial self-interest. Posey no longer had the money to pay them as they wished to be paid, and Greenlee could do so easily. The great Oscar Charleston defected in February, becoming the Crawfords' playing manager as Bobby Williams was demoted to player-coach. Charleston's move followed shortly after the defection of Josh Gibson. The young slugging catcher had signed a contract with the Grays in early February, but almost immediately signed a second one with the Crawfords. "Whether or not Gibson made the decision he did on the basis of the money involved is not definitely known," the *Courier* reported. But it's a pretty good bet that salary had a lot to do with it, although Gibson's friend, pitcher Roy Williams, also switched teams at the same time. Posey wrote in his column shortly after Gibson signed with Greenlee that he would be with the Grays or not play at all in Pittsburgh, but Gibson caught and slugged the ball all season, and did so for the Crawfords. There was a virtual stampede over to the Crawfords, as Rev Cannady, Cool Papa Bell, Ted Radcliffe, Jake Stephens, and Jud Wilson all left the Grays (although Wilson made an intermediate stop back with the Baltimore Black Sox before signing with Greenlee). In addition, third baseman Judy Johnson was enticed into leaving Philadelphia's Hilldale Club, and he brought with him hard-hitting outfielder Herbert "Rap" Dixon. Greenlee boasted that he lost $15,000 on the Crawfords in 1932. But he was aiming to have the best black team money could buy, so it was money well spent.[41]

In addition to the defections to the Crawfords, Posey also lost George Scales to the New York Black Yankees, who had replaced the Lincoln Giants as the dominant team in that city, when he was offered the chance to not only play second base, but be the manager. As the season went on, maintaining the Grays' roster became a constant effort of casting about for as good a level of players as possible who could fill in for those who had left. Jap Washington was a prime example. A key member of the Homestead infield throughout the 1920s, he had been forced off the team as Posey improved it in 1930, primarily by the signing of Charleston to play first base. The Crawfords were still building then, so Washington joined them. But then Charleston left for the Crawfords in 1932, again blocking Washington's starting hopes, and George Giles, Oscar's replacement on the Grays, went back to the Midwest upon the collapse of the East-West League. Although Washington, now 36 years old, hadn't been good enough to stay on the team before, he was more than welcome now as a dependable, but not superlative, addition to a picked-over lineup.

But as thin as the Grays' talent was in 1932, one of Cum Posey's signings that spring had a big impact on the team, and on Posey, too. Ray Brown, a native of Alger, Ohio, had played in 1930 for the Dayton Marcos, an independent black team, and for the Indianapolis ABCs in the Negro National League in 1931. Posey signed the 24-year-old for the Detroit Wolves when the East-West League began, and he shifted Brown to the Grays when the best of the Wolves were folded into Homestead in June. Brown never pitched for another Negro League team after that, playing for the Grays until 1945. Although he regularly played the outfield and was a good hitter, Brown, a right-hander, soon became the Grays' ace starting pitcher. He was known for a wicked curve and excellent control. According to James Riley, the baseball historian, Brown was so confident that "he would throw a curve with a 3–0 count on the batter." He was selected to two East-West All-Star teams and threw a perfect game in 1945.[42]

As did other Grays players, Brown lived at the Posey home during the season, but he became more than just a boarder. He and Ethel, the Poseys' oldest daughter, were married in 1937. The wedding was held on June 5, a Saturday, before a game between the Grays and archival Crawfords. Although newlyweds are supposed to receive the presents, Brown handed his new father-in-law a big gift that afternoon, when he six-hit the Craws to pace a 12–1 Grays win. As a player, however, being married to Cum's daughter was not an advantage—just the opposite, sometimes. For example, his teammate Buck Leonard said, Brown was a student in the off-season at Wilberforce University, a black college in Ohio. Posey insisted that Brown finish his studies in the spring before reporting to the Grays, an order in line with the family's respect for education. To the other players, though, it appeared that Posey was showing favoritism to him.[43]

There were times when Ray Brown seemed to be anything but the boss's favorite, though, and his temperamental attitude had a lot to do with that. While the star was a fierce competitor in any game he played in, he sometimes was less than willing to get into the lineup when he wasn't pitching. This was very un–Posey-like, and, as Leonard recounted, "Brown had an attitude about baseball that Cum just didn't like." Vic Harris, who managed Brown for years, once fined Brown $50 for refusing play on a pitching off-day and swearing at Harris in the bargain. But then, Harris wound up pleading with Posey not to increase the punishment. Posey wasn't with the team when Brown refused to play, but he called both manager and player to his office when the Grays returned to Pittsburgh. As they talked, Brown "started to raise his voice and use bad language. Cum Posey said, 'Now you're not only fined $50, you're suspended for ten days.'" After Brown left the office, Harris went to work on his boss, explaining that, if it hadn't been for the verbal abuse, he never would have imposed such a large fine in the first place. "I had it [the fine] cut to $10

... I talked him out of the suspension." So Harris managed both to get his decision upheld by his boss, and to make himself look good to Brown in the process. Brown seemed happy with the outcome—he offered to buy Harris a beer after the meeting: "That's just the way he was. He's bad one minute, the next minute he wants to buy you a beer."[44]

The changing status of the Grays and Crawfords in the spring of 1932 was hinted at in spring training, when Greenlee's team was the one to go to Hot Springs, while the Grays—and Posey's Detroit team—trained in West Virginia. Greenlee not only had many of the Grays' best ballplayers and a posh training site, back in Pittsburgh was his own ballpark, which seated 7,500 and was modestly named Greenlee Field. It was a monument to his success and, importantly, freed him from having to pay rent to the Pirates or anyone else to stage Crawfords home games. But unlike his team, the park was not entirely a Greenlee-funded project. A reputable source, in fact, had Greenlee owning only 25 percent of the Bedford Land Company, the firm that built and owned the field bearing his name. White businessmen owned more of the park than he did. The involvement of one of them, Joseph F. Thoms, was understandable—he owned the main piece of land on which the park was being built. The identity of the other investor, Joe Tito, a white numbers banker who dealt in bootlegging until Prohibition ended and he and his family bought the inactive Latrobe Brewing Company to go legitimate, clearly demonstrated that Gus Greenlee wasn't the only numbers businessman with money to spare. Tito's presence in the deal also suggested that sufficient capital for the project, which reportedly cost $100,000, was not available from the black business community.[45]

Once opened, Greenlee Field proved to have a major shortcoming—it lacked a roof over the grandstand, and fans complained about broiling in the afternoon sun during day games. This was partially solved by installing a $6,000 lighting system and playing as many night games as possible. Most importantly, the park was well situated for the team's fans. It was only a few blocks off Wylie Avenue, making it much more accessible than the Pirates' Forbes Field, about two miles to the east. Lewis Dial of the *New York Age* also pointed out the affordability of the park for the less-affluent fan. He wrote there were "nearly two thousand seats that go for a quarter and a like number for fifty cents, the boxes bring in six bits and at every game the S.R.O. [Standing Room Only] sign hangs out."[46] Greenlee Field was home to the Crawfords, but it was rented out for other sports, particularly boxing, in which both Greenlee and Tito were promoters, and for baseball games not involving the Crawfords. The fee for using the field was 20 percent of the gate, as opposed to 30 percent at Forbes Field. An occasional tenant was none other than the Homestead Grays.

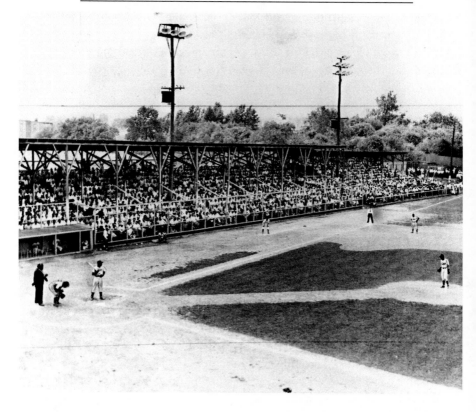

Gus Greenlee and some partners built their own ballpark, Greenlee Field, which seated 7,500 fans and was used for Negro League games in Pittsburgh in the mid-1930s, avoiding the payment of rent to the major league Pirates for Forbes Field. The park did not survive a reversal of Greenlee's financial fortunes, however, and was closed and torn down after the 1938 season (NoirTech Research, Inc.).

It would be difficult to say that Greenlee was more shrewd or energetic than Posey, or more committed to the success of black-owned sports franchises. Those qualities were all Posey hallmarks. But Greenlee had the money to pour into a money-losing, though famous, club and a ballpark built from the ground up, while Posey, his team existing from season to season, if not month to month, during the depths of the Depression, had none of his own to speak of.

Many who have written about Cum Posey have made a connection between his well-off parents, who lived an upper-middle-class life, and Posey's baseball operations that assumes he had access to family money to finance the Grays. Nothing could have been further from the truth. Clearly the Captain and his family lived well, but by the time he died in 1925, his funds were mostly depleted. Evan Baker, Jr., Captain Posey's great-grandson born in 1936, learned from his elders that by the time the Captain died "there was hardly anything." His father, in fact, had told him that when he was born in 1912, the family money "was almost all gone." Captain Posey's situation resembled that of one of those four blacks who helped establish Allegheny County in 1788. That man, Benjamin Richards, was a butcher, livestock dealer, and real estate speculator. At the height of his business success, he was regarded as among the outpost's wealthiest men, although "by mismanagement, he lost his estate."[47]

The primary beneficiary of the will dividing up the Captain's estate was his wife, but it was not Anna, the artistic community leader who was the mother of Beatrice, See, and Cum. She died on August 20, 1917, at age 56, of a brain tumor. Two years later, the senior Posey married again, to the widow of one of the men who had worked with him to save the *Courier* from bankruptcy. William N. Page was one of the four investors who bailed out the newspaper, who then quit what for an African American was a very good job, as secretary to an executive in the Carnegie Steel Company, to become the newspaper's business manager. Page had a longtime relationship with the Posey family—his first wife, Lucille Myrtle Lett Page, who died in 1912 of a chronic illness, was Anna Posey's first cousin. She had lived with the Poseys upon moving to Pittsburgh from Ohio to work as a stenographer and bookkeeper. Page remarried in 1913 to Bessie Taylor of Washington, D.C., but died of pneumonia in January 1916, while visiting her family in Washington.[48]

In 1919, Bessie Taylor Page and Cumberland Posey, Sr., were wed. While not the social leader that Anna had been, Bessie was an active, educated person in her own right. She was a graduate of Atlanta University, an historically black college in that city, and had taught school in Wilmington, Delaware, for several years before marrying Page. She survived the Captain by less than three years, dying unexpectedly in January 1928.[49]

The Captain's will, first made in 1920 but modified in 1924, left what turned out to be the bulk of his estate to his second wife in the form of a $19,000 payment (which would have the purchasing power of $260,000 today) specified in a pre-nuptial agreement. Most of the remainder of the estate was put into a five-year trust to be distributed equally to the elder Posey's three children. The 1924 modification, however, allowed for an advance of $650 to Cumberland, Jr., and $1,500 to See. The original 1920 will had See's share kept in the trust, with him eligible to receive only the income from his portion until he reached the age of 40. It seems the Captain may have originally meant to put his older son, who had dropped out of medical school, was running a billiard hall, and was on his second marriage (he was eventually to have four, as the first three ended by divorce), on something of an allowance.

Beatrice and her husband, Evan E. Baker, received a release from a mortgage that had been given them by the Captain to buy the house next door to the family home. Their bequest turned out to be the most valuable of the three made to the children, because by the time the trust expired and the county's courts doled out the proceeds, there was essentially nothing left. The final accounting showed a balance of $5,264, but $5,000 of it went to settle what appears to have been the Captain's last outstanding business debt. When Bessie died, her son, William Clyde Page inherited her entire $29,000 estate. She spent little time in Homestead after her husband passed on, and she was visiting friends in Brooklyn when she died. The Posey trust's assets were not impressive—for example, the large real estate holdings during Posey's years as a businessman had dwindled to the three family homes on 13th Avenue and a handful of rental properties in the area. Of the family's residences, the large Victorian in the middle of the three, where the Captain and Anna had raised their family, remained in the Poseys' hands, but was turned into apartments. Cum and Ethel remained next door at number 324, but they had to survive an attempt by the county in 1935 to sell the house for $3,306 in unpaid back taxes.[50]

Unburdened by financial problems such as these, Gus Greenlee's Crawfords, bolstered by the first-rate players he could hire away from other clubs, played the sort of schedule that had made the Grays famous. They used Posey's template of ranging around the Tri-State region in addition to playing in Pittsburgh, and then adding the better African American clubs to the schedule, both at home and in their opponents' far-flung cities. By the end of the 1932 season, it appeared that the baton of best black baseball club in Pittsburgh was about to be passed to the Crawfords. The *Times Mirror* of Warren, Pennsylvania, in an advance to a road-trip doubleheader, wrote of "The Pittsburgh Crawfords, successors to the Homestead Grays as the world's greatest colored baseball club." That verbiage likely came from a Crawfords press release—Warren was located almost 150 miles north, practically in New York State, and sportswriters there were unlikely to be keeping close tabs on black ball in Pittsburgh. But Rollo Wilson, a personal friend of Posey's since before 1920, although a sports columnist who could be relied upon to be a straight-shooter, wrote in September that "The Crawfords have taken the play away from the Grays and no longer do Smoky City fans consider Cum Posey's bunch the penultimate [*sic*] in baseball. A lot of them have a deep suspicion that the Crawfords are now the chosen people."[51]

This reversal of the pecking order did not inhibit the two teams from playing each other. They contested at least 18 times in 1932, in a number of locations that included Greenlee and Forbes Fields in Pittsburgh; Hamtramck Stadium in Detroit, which Posey controlled, and on Sundays at Elks Park in nearby Sharon, a community where the Sunday ban on baseball could reliably be flouted. Reputedly second-class or not, the Grays won 10 of the 18 games. The two teams also manage to outwit Pittsburgh's Sunday baseball law, or out-wait it, at least, in the first minutes of Monday, September 19. This was the final game of a four-game series that had included a Friday game and a traditional Pittsburgh Saturday doubleheader. The Sunday game was played by turning on the brand new Greenlee Field lights and waiting until 12:01 a.m. Monday to throw the first pitch. An estimated 3,000 fans showed and stayed into the night while the Grays broke open a tight game in the seventh and eighth innings to win, 5–1, as Joe Strong threw a three-hitter for Homestead.

Given the Crawfords' success and possession of its own home park, Greenlee's team would seem to have been an obvious choice for a slot in the East-West League. But the Craws weren't among the eight teams starting the season for a simple reason—Posey, the controlling force of the league, didn't want them. Greenlee, with his money and the advantages it was giving him, was dangerous competition. Posey had beaten out the Keystones in 1922 and had effectively neutralized Sellers Hall and other competing regional black team owners, partially by getting the Grays' best white opponents to refuse to play them in return for profitable bookings of Posey's team. But those were lesser threats to the Grays' hegemony, and Posey wasn't in a position to squeeze the Crawfords out of business. He could keep them out of the only available league, though, relegating them to lesser independent status.

Greenlee may have been a neophyte baseball owner, but he was well aware of the value that would be added to his team if it belonged to a black major league. In fact, he was present at a meeting in Washington, D.C., in October 1931, when a plan to form a league in the East, with the Crawfords alone representing Pittsburgh, failed to come to fruition. Soon after that, Posey announced the formation of the East-West League. Greenlee stated publicly the following February that Posey had made him an offer to join the East-West as an associate member, which would guarantee his team games with league member teams, but not a chance to compete for the championship. The terms, as Greenlee recounted them, were highly unfavorable, and in his opinion amounted to "a trap." He said Posey wanted him to sign a five-year contract stipulating that either Cum or See Posey would run the team, which would be composed mostly of "inexperienced youngsters." There was a guarantee of 40 games with league teams, but no promise that they would include lucrative Saturday dates, which Greenlee suspected would be reserved for the Grays. Greenlee rejected the offer: "I have a few scruples about means and ends."[52]

Gus Greenlee also had a publicity spokesman, well-known Pittsburgh journalist John L. Clark. Clark was later the first black political correspondent at the state capital in Harrisburg and covered two Presidential campaigns. He worked at one time for the black *Pittsburgh American*, but was best known in Pittsburgh for his "Wylie Avenue" column for the *Courier*, which covered business, social, and personal affairs in the Hill's African American community. Clark seemed to know everyone there. As a *Courier* editor wrote when he died in 1961, "No one but a man who loved Wylie Avenue—the street which started at the jail and ended at a church ... could have deified it, as did John Clark. He knew its moods. He knew the people who gave it life and color."[53]

Since 1929, Clark had been doing publicity for Greenlee's entertainment and other ventures, and he added the Crawfords and Greenlee's league aspirations to his duties. One of his main duties was to combat Posey in print. Given the Posey family's long relationship with the *Courier* and Cum's own presence on the sports pages, it might have seemed that Posey would have had the upper hand in the newspapers. But Clark's work nullified that, and Posey was again stymied. As early as January 1932, Clark was throwing stones at the new league, accusing Posey of having sabotaged the first organizational attempt that had included Greenlee's team, because it "would not eliminate the Crawfords or restore monarchical control of the baseball situation to 'Cum' Posey." Before the month was out, he was proclaiming that the East-West was primarily a cartel of black ball owners designed to suppress player salaries. Of course, this was true as far as it went—Posey was on record that the overall economic situation called for baseball spending cuts, including reigning in high player salaries. But that was the case to some extent in every professional sports league ever formed, and hardly a sinister East-West plot.[54]

It was usually Posey's strategy to side-step accusations of his controlling nature and assure readers of his column that he didn't have it out for a particular person or group, while simultaneously condescending to his critics. That was the case in his "'Cum' Posey's Pointed Paragraphs" column in the January 9 *Courier*, where he denied rumors of a baseball war between the Grays and Crawfords. But he took care to note that while the Crawfords were newcomers, the Grays were "a baseball institution." Greenlee, he allowed, "reserves the right to spend his money as he thinks best. Because the Grays have been in baseball for years does not give us the right to criticize others for entering baseball."

It was clear, though, that Greenlee and Clark were getting Posey's goat. In a bylined article for the *Chicago Defender* in February, he called the charge that he wanted to tie the Crawfords down to a five-year contract with the league as "ridiculous.... Where would I get the power to do this?" He claimed he had recommended Oscar Charleston to Greenlee as player-manager to enable Charleston to get the salary he desired, and in 1931 had "let" Greenlee use See Posey as his booking manager to inject experience into the Craws' "floundering" operation. He also derided Clark, a long-time crusader against vice on the Hill, for going to work for a numbers baron, and he alleged that Greenlee once told him he had hired Clark "to keep his mouth shut."[55]

In the long run, though, while the level of rivalry between Posey on the one hand and Greenlee and Clark on other was intense in 1932 and the years after that, there was little personal animosity. Posey wrote in his *Defender* piece of a "personal friendship of longstanding with Mr. Greenlee," and in a 1941 "Wylie Avenue" column, Clark noted that, after Greenlee was out of organized black baseball, his former colleagues rarely came to visit, but "Cum Posey, known as Greenlee's bitterest enemy, seldom comes to Pittsburgh without stopping at the [Crawford] Grill and chatting with Greenlee." That was the year that Clark was hospitalized for surgery, and Posey wrote a few "Wylie Avenues" for him. Even when their public feuding was at its zenith, the two were not opposed to making public appearances together, as in October 1933, when they were guests of the Rev. James E. Guy of the Nazarene Baptist Church in Pittsburgh for his annual baseball sermon, the subject that year being "Two Men Down, Three Strikes on the Batter and Three Balls in the Last Half of the Ninth Inning With a Pinch Hitter Coming to Bat No Runs, No Hits, Many Errors and Spectators Gone Wild."[56]

The black sportswriters who covered the new league frequently wondered in print why the successful Crawfords weren't a member, and were enthusiastic in June when the league (which is to say, Posey), allowed them and the New York Black Yankees to join as associate members. Of course, so far as the East-West League went, it was likely that nothing could have saved it at this point. Dial had written in the *Age* back in March that "One admirable trait about the commission chairman [Posey] is he knows when he has had enough and if all his plans miscarry it won't be long before the Greys [*sic*] and Crawfords will be playing each other."[57]

Chapter Six

Who Owns Pittsburgh?

Although Gus Greenlee and his Crawfords had been excluded from the revival of Negro League ball in 1932, he still believed that a league format was the best way to revive the black majors. With the failure of Posey's East-West League, the way was open for another opportunity to organize the black teams in the East's and Midwest's major cities and stage a revival of Rube Foster's Negro National League and the Eastern Colored League. Greenlee was anxious to take on this task, and in the end he was successful.

The league Greenlee put together was officially called the National Association of Baseball clubs, although, since it was the successor to Foster's league, it soon also became known as the Negro National League, and is recognized today as the second league to bear that name. The new NNL faced a number of early problems, which was not surprising since the poor economic conditions and chronic loose sense of organization among the owners that had brought down the East-West League were still in effect. The six-team league opened its season in late April, but only a month later growing pains included two teams shifting home cities due to a lack of attendance in one place and a lack of a permanent ballpark in another, the induction of a seventh club, and, inescapably, a revised schedule. *Pittsburgh Courier* columnist W. Rollo Wilson wrote on May 20, "If Gus Greenlee can carry his league through the present campaign this correspondent will be the first to congratulate him on performing a modern labor of Hercules."[1] Greenlee's forceful personality and ever-present numbers profits helped the league ride out these initial hardships.

But Gus Greenlee didn't just stop with being the power behind a new league. The white majors had inaugurated the annual All-Star game in 1933, played on July 6 at the Chicago White Sox's Comiskey Park. On September 10, the Negro National League played its first East-West All-Star Game at Comiskey. Greenlee was one of the three organizers. In the mid–1930s, Greenlee, who successfully brought diversions to black Pittsburgh ranging from illegal booze, through high-class musical entertainment, and then to widely popular numbers gambling, put his personal and financial resources to work for black baseball. While contributions toward the success of the new NNL and the East-West game were made by many team owners and others, he is due the lion's share of the credit for reviving black major league ball even while the Depression was still moving through its worst period.

While Greenlee provided the keystone for the new NNL, Posey played a much less prominent role, unless one counts his consistent and vociferous opposition to the new regime. Although the Grays and their principal owner had been a valuable member of the American Negro League in 1929, and while Posey had worked hard, although unsuccessfully, to launch the East-West League in 1932, his early association with the NNL can only be described as disruptive and obstructionist. Not surprisingly, the appearance of Posey the follower was significantly less attractive than that of Posey the leader, although some of his complaints against the league led by his rival were not without foundation.

While Posey had ignored the Crawfords in putting the East-West League together, the Grays were actually invited to be charter members of the NNL, even though it gave the league two teams in Pittsburgh and contributed an economically unprofitable tilt toward the Midwest. Besides the Crawfords and Grays, the pre-season lineup included the Chicago American Giants, Nashville Elite Giants, Indianapolis ABCs, Detroit Stars, and Columbus Blue Birds. Even before the league could capture fans' attention, though, there was a game of franchise musical chairs that hurt its image. The Chicago team had lost its ball park and moved its home games to Indianapolis, which was available because the Detroit franchise never got off the ground and the ABCs, fearing an unprofitable season in the city where they had been a charter member of the first NNL, moved to Detroit. Although the Baltimore Black Sox were admitted to the league in midseason, there was no representation from New York City or Philadelphia, historically major centers of interest in black baseball. The second half of the season fell apart, and only three teams, the Crawfords, Nashville, and Chicago, finished their schedules.

The absence of the Grays at season's end didn't mean that the team had collapsed. On the contrary, it continued to roam the East and Midwest and played until the end of October, well into football season. The Grays didn't complete their NNL schedule because the team left the league in June. Greenlee and John Clark, who had become league secretary in addition to holding the same position with the Crawfords, maintained that Homestead had been kicked out at a league owners meeting on June 23 when Posey got up to his old tricks, signing away two players from Detroit. Posey maintained that the Detroit management owed salary to outfielder Jim Williams and third baseman Jimmy Binder, making them fair game. No matter, the Detroit officials said, going after them without negotiating with us was a violation of the league constitution.

If the situation had involved an unhappy employer and a disgruntled employee, it would have been a case of "you can't fire me, I quit." It's most likely that Posey had every intention of pulling the Grays out of the struggling NNL and going back to independent ball. Posey wrote a letter to the *Courier* sports department, published on July 8, which clearly showed that the Grays management had been thinking about abandoning the league. "After due consideration," he wrote, "the Homestead Grays withdrew from membership in the Negro National Association. This step was taken mainly to assure the men associated with me, including players, and who have confidence in my judgment, that every effort was being made to uphold the caliber of the Grays Club, and to insure financial returns which would permit the Grays to keep their standing as the recognized leader of the colored clubs."

Posey was saying that his team could do better, both competitively and financially, if it was not bound to the struggling NNL. He pointed out the lack of profitable league locations other than Pittsburgh, and he took a shot at Greenlee's rule that the league would retain five percent of the gate receipts to finance league operations. This set the Grays back to 35 percent of gross revenues, since the closest thing they had to a home park was the Crawfords' Greenlee Field, and "The Grays had never played any games for less than 40 per cent any place." Posey's explanation also brought up what he saw as "obligations" to play the many independent white clubs of the Tri-State Region, "who furnished the games and money which made the Grays possible."[2] He did not say, but it was most likely true, that many of these games drew better than NNL contests outside Pittsburgh, and as a top regional attraction, the Grays were taking home much more than 35 percent of the gate (and probably often well over 40 percent, for that matter).

Lewis Dial, the perspicacious sports columnist for the *New York Age*, did say it, however. Recounting the details of the Grays' expulsion from the league, Dial opined that "The Grays have long been a stellar attraction in semi-pro circles…. It was probably the Grays' drawing power among the white clubs that played a big part in their leaving the League. They could play seven or eight games a week with nice guarantees and incur little or no expense, hence the cancelling of the League games, which would force the Poseymen to lay out some scrip on a prospect." So far as the "kidnapping" of Williams and Binder, "well it's part of Posey's creed to get what he wants regardless."[3]

Posey likely figured that, since he was leaving anyway, and since his roster had been raided by the team run by the league president, why not take a couple of desirable league players with him as he departed? He never showed the least bit of guilt for having signing Williams and Binder. He pointed out that, as soon as the Grays left the NNL, the Crawfords pounced once again and took his shortstop, Gerald Williams, whose salary was paid up to date by the Grays, while "Binder and Jim Williams had not received two weeks' salary for almost two months' play" while with Detroit. By this time, gaining and losing players was old hat to Posey, and you can almost see the nonchalant shrug when he wrote in his column that "one of the league clubs will surely suffer any time the Grays need a good man."[4]

After leaving the league (or being kicked out), Posey gave Greenlee credit in print a few times for the work he had put in toward establishing and running the NNL, but he primarily saw it as an example of an amateurish operation, with the various owners jockeying for their own teams' welfare and unable to deliver when it was necessary to pull together. Of course, except for the amateur part, that was a pretty good description of Posey himself at this point. Some of his criticism, though, went to the heart of conflicting business interests off the field that plagued Negro League baseball for its entire existence. In particular, he blamed the "sinister influence of the great booking agents of the East," white entrepreneurs such as Nat Strong in New York and Eddie Gottlieb in Philadelphia, whose control over ball parks outside of white organized baseball ensured them a percentage of the gate that would have ordinarily gone to the competing clubs, thus reducing the black teams' revenue in a year that was already fraught with economic peril.[5] The booking agents provided services such as pre-game publicity that eased the strain on the small Negro League front offices, and Gottlieb, in particular, was able to assist in getting the NNL a good deal to play in Yankee Stadium, a major venue that was profitable for everyone concerned. But the tension created by the requirement to pay white outsiders money that could have stayed in team owners' pockets was always an issue.

But Cum Posey made a lot of other observations, too, some of which amounted to just plain bitching about the NNL. The umpiring in 1933, for example, was "some of the worst umpiring ever witnessed by this writer." There also were very few young players who "rated" as high-quality talent, and he wasn't that impressed by the level of competition in the first East-West Game. His overall opinion of affairs in 1933 was expressed twice, once in his "Cum Posey's Pointed Paragraphs" column in the *Courier* on August 5: "Homestead Grays were an asset to the League [in drawing big crowds]. The League was no help to the Grays." Then in July, he said that "The Grays will be playing baseball when the present League owners and clubs have been

forgotten." Posey, deposed from his accustomed seat of power in black baseball, could be hypercritical and antagonistic (as he could be in better times,
too), but he had this one about right. When Posey's Grays won their last pennant with him in charge, in 1945, their ninth straight flag, only one of the
other owners and teams of 1933, Thomas Wilson and his Elites, by then based
in Baltimore, were still in the league.[6]

As the 1934 season dawned, steps were underway to correct the shortcomings of 1933. The league lineup for the second year showed a pronounced
tilt toward the East Coast, with teams in Philadelphia and Newark. There
were fertile opportunities in the East in a recovering economy (the U.S. Gross
Domestic Product ended a four-year slide in 1934) and, importantly, shorter
travel distances and lower travel costs. There were only two teams west of
Pittsburgh, the Chicago American Giants, who had a home park again, and
the Cleveland Red Sox, which, as Cleveland franchises often did, failed to
finish the season. Again, the NNL standings included only one Pittsburgh
team, the Crawfords. Posey had decided the Grays would accept an associate
membership only—they could play league teams and be protected from player
raiding (which they themselves could not do, either), but their games would
not count in the standings. Posey had announced in February that the Grays
would be involved in the league and would return to Forbes Field for home
games (which would undercut Greenlee's and his partners' revenue from
Greenlee Field). But the league banned the use of Forbes, and Posey accepted
that in exchange for an associate membership.[7]

Rollo Wilson, the *Courier* sports columnist, was made commissioner of
the league, bringing his generally optimistic outlook on Negro sports, coupled
with his view that they should be honorably conducted on the field, to the
NNL's inner sanctum. As the season opened, he wrote a piece as commissioner
for the black newspapers' sports sections, aimed at the players, stating that
"Negro baseball goes on trial Saturday with the opening of the League season.... Men who have lost thousands of dollars [the owners] are still enthusiastic.... The fans are going out to see you play baseball; when they want to
see fights, they know where to go.... If you disgust the fans by your conduct
afield, they will stay away from the ball parks and the owners will not need
any ball players."[8]

Posey and Wilson had been friends since their 20s, but one of the new
commissioner's first rulings aggravated the Grays' owner, and kept him aggravated for some time. Before the season began, two of his starters, including
the very valuable Vic Harris, had signed with the Crawfords. Harris not only
had been a starting outfielder for the Grays since 1925, but in 1933 Posey
made him the field manager. Harris's hard-charging attitude as a player likely

appealed to Posey as managerial material, also. Harris's pre-season warning to his players was to "play baseball every minute or don't play on the Grays." But a person's attitude doesn't pay his bills, and Harris and shortstop Leroy Morney, claiming the Grays were in arrears on their late-season 1933 salaries, went over to the Craws. The Grays protested, but Commissioner Wilson turned them down. His official opinion noted that Posey couldn't produce any receipts or cancelled checks proving he had fully paid the two players through 1933. Wilson also pointed out that, before being re-admitted to the NNL and its player-protection umbrella on March 10, the Grays were still suspended from the previous July. The team's players were presumably fair game during that period.[9]

The Harris-Morney situation, of course, contained echoes of the unpaid Williams and Binder being lured from the Detroit Stars to the Grays the season before. Wilson's decision, in fact, almost legitimized the Williams and Binder signings by allowing that, since the Grays were out of the NNL from July to early March, players they signed were their property. The two players, of course, had signed shortly before the league suspended the Grays. But no attempts were made to make them return of their old club, since it had gone out of business before the end of the season.

Posey saw no similarity between the Harris-Morney decision and his own previous actions. He maintained in his *Courier* column that the decision was "without precedent in any league."[10] As to a Negro League, he may have been technically correct. The history of high-level black baseball is replete with contract jumping but notably lacking in successful efforts to enforce that conduct. Posey was also steaming over the loss of two other players that spring, catcher Ameal Brooks, who signed with Cleveland, and pitcher Irv "Lefty" Vincent, who went to the Crawfords. The league ruled that both players belonged to the Grays. They were both replaceable, but as time went by and they never returned to the Grays, Posey continue to bring up their cases whenever those of Harris and Morney surfaced.

The Grays stayed with the league as the season went on, but Posey continued to take pot shots at it. In July, he announced that the Grays wouldn't participate in the second annual East-West Game. The game's organizers were Greenlee, Tom Wilson of the Elite Giants, and Chicago American Giants owner Robert Cole, who each got a share of the gate receipts. The rosters were selected by much-ballyhooed fan voting through the major black weekly newspapers. At about the time that voting started, Posey requested that fans not pick Homestead players. According to Lew Dial of the *Age*, Posey claimed that "the voting was not on the level, and he does not wish to participate in so nefarious a scheme."[11] Whether the results were fixed or not (as it turned out years later, Posey was not himself necessarily against creative East-West vote tabulating), it is true that, of the 12 players appearing for the East team, nine were Crawfords, while of the 12 who played for the West, seven were American Giants and three were Elites. Suspicion of the probity of the vote counting likely was a carry-over from 1933, when half of the East players appearing were Craws, and the nine players used by the West included seven American Giants.

Financially, Posey maintained, "No profit [from the game] is given to a worthy cause. It is an out and out private investment." Although the East-West Game was highly touted by black sportswriters as not only the Negro Leagues' all-star game, but a way to display black baseball's best to white fans, Posey was not alone in his suspicions. Frank "Fay" Young, one of the best-known black sportswriters, criticized the impending contest for its lineup imbalance favoring a few teams, and that so far as the initial 1933 game was concerned, "no one has named a charity or anything else which the net proceeds went to." In contrast, the net profits from the white majors' first All-Star Game in 1933 went to retired and disabled ballplayers. Dial pointed out that no financial information had been forthcoming after the 1933 game, and he also dwelt on the preponderance of Crawfords and American Giants on the teams.[12]

On August 5, the Grays, supposedly banned from using Forbes Field as a condition of rejoining the NNL, hosted there an interracial team from Fort Wayne, Indiana, sponsored by the Berghoff Brewing Corporation, a heavy contributor to semi-pro and amateur baseball in its home town. The game was a benefit for the National Association for the Advancement of Colored People, and had an additional special feature—the retired Smokey Joe Williams started for the Grays. He pitched two scoreless innings at age 49 before coming out of the game, and Homestead won, 5–1, before 1,200 fans. The day was a success, but within two weeks, Posey was claiming that use of Forbes Field had resulted in the cancellation by Greenlee of a choice Labor Day doubleheader with the Crawfords. The Grays "felt that they had a right to play where they pleased and that Mr. Greenlee or no one else should attempt to tell them where or who they should play," Posey wrote in a letter to the *Courier* on August 18.[13]

Greenlee fired back a week later with his own letter, saying that while Labor Day games had been contemplated with the Grays, nothing had been firmed up. This was partially due to Posey's refusal to pay a five percent booking fee to the booking office run out of Greenlee Field by his own brother, See, who had joined the exodus from the underpaid Grays to go to work for Greenlee. Greenlee claimed that, since the Crawfords were on the road on

Forbes Field, home of the Pittsburgh Pirates, the Grays' home field for their most important games for many years (Library of Congress).

August 5, where the Grays played was a moot point. That may not have been true, though, since by avoiding his ballpark, Posey was avoiding paying Greenlee a percentage of the gate, which instead went to the Pirates. The real reason Pittsburgh fans were denied a Grays-Crawfords matchup on a major holiday, Gus Greenlee wrote, was that "Posey's attitude resisted compromise at every point."[14]

Greenlee's letter may have actually been written by his henchman John Clark, and if so, it was one of the few times in this two-year span where Clark took after Posey under any name but his own. Pittsburgh fans of black baseball could be sure of a few things: the Grays and the Crawfords would play each other often, the Grays would win the lion's share of the games, and John L. Clark and Cumberland W. Posey, Jr., would put aside their personal friendship to fight tooth and nail for their business interests, in the process filling up the sports pages of the *Courier* and other black weeklies with copious explanations of the other's shortcomings.

After the Grays left the NNL in 1933, Clark published a detailed version of the affair, in which Posey allegedly told Clark before the June 23 expulsion meeting that he couldn't make Williams and Binder return to Detroit. The owners, having voted the Grays out that morning with Posey not having appeared to defend his organization, reopened the case when he did arrive, but "the courtesy developed into a waste of time, as Posey evaded direct questioning at every opportunity." Clark maintained that Posey showed no regrets of any kind over the situation until weeks later, and when he did, his regrets were mostly phony, larded through with claims of the injustices done to the Grays. "And so he continues in his own inimitable style of pity and sympathy for those who do not recognize the Posey rights, conclusions and acquisitions as superior to all others," Clark wrote.[15]

Posey certainly was good at staking out and defending his own positions. But while he sometimes had good words for Gus Greenlee's work on behalf of Negro Leagues ball, he consistently maintained that Clark had no business being league secretary, no matter what his opinions. Besides the fact that Clark was insufficiently versed in baseball management (he was one of the amateurs Posey looked down upon), Posey was aggravated by the fact that Clark was also the Crawfords' secretary. It was bad enough that the league president was a club owner (and of his chief rival for the Pittsburgh black baseball dollar), but it was doubly insulting that the president's day-to-day operations man also did the same job for the league. The situation was made worse by the fact that William "Dizzy" Dismukes, a highly experienced baseball man with ties to Posey as recently as the East-West League the season before, was to have been league secretary, but was deposed in favor of Clark as the 1933 season began.[16]

Although the Homestead Grays were out of the league in 1933, the team name had lived on in the NNL, existing on a sort of baseball life-support. This took the form of a slapped-together Akron Grays team, which played a few games in that Ohio city, where Cum Posey's team was a regular visitor, under See Posey's direction before soon expiring. This hijacking of the team name also annoyed Cum Posey. While he wrote that he wished his brother's team "makes a lot of money ... the sad part is: The club is financed and owned by Gus Greenlee."[17]

After a quiet winter, as the weather became baseball-friendly again, the feud between Posey and Clark resumed. In the June 16, 1934, *Courier*, Posey accused Clark of ignoring the truth: "Clark does not know facts; he is an ultra theorist and resorts to personalities to cover his shohtcomings [sic]." This was in response to a couple of salvos from Clark earlier that month. A June 2 piece was heavy with sarcasm regarding the Grays' declining financial situation and Posey's constant attempts to control the environment around him. Clark wise-cracked that Posey's constant criticism of the league may have been a result of his becoming partially unhinged by the pressure of trying to save all of society from adverse economic conditions while losing money himself: "We thought of the days when Cum Posey could spend more money in one night for a big time than the average man could earn in a month… [We] decided that the affected conditions had forced him to draw heavily on his financial reserve—and that he was somewhat upset mentally because he could not relieve the suffering of peoples as a man of his wisdom, wealth and philanthropy should." A week later, Clark dropped all attempts at a sophisticated approach and bluntly characterized Posey as someone "whose own stubbornness has brought about the 'breaks' which he claims have been against him" and who "throws mud at everything he can't control."[18]

The Grays had a mediocre 11–9 record when they left the league in 1933. The expulsion cancelled a highly anticipated July 4 doubleheader against the Crawfords at Greenlee Field, and the Grays played relatively few games in the Pittsburgh area after that. They were, of course, still welcome at their usual stops in the Tri-State area. In addition, they played two series in Buffalo and made a foray to New York City, losing a doubleheader to the crack Farmers semi-pro team on October 1. While the NNL ban was supposed to keep the Grays away from league teams, the disorganized end of the league's first season made games against the Crawfords, Chicago American Giants, and Baltimore Black Sox possible.

Back in the league's good graces in 1934, at least so far as being able to participate in the NNL schedule, Homestead played upwards of 35 games against NNL or Negro Southern League teams, winning or tying each series, according to game results that can be recovered today from the newspapers. While the events of 1933 had wiped out a July 4 doubleheader at Greenlee Field against the Crawfords, the two teams met there on that holiday in 1934 before 5,500 fans. For the record, the teams split on the day, but the Crawfords' win was spectacular. Satchel Paige threw a no-hitter, nearly a perfect game. He struck out 17 Grays, and the only baserunners came on a walk and an infield error.

The 1933 version of the Grays was lackluster by past Homestead standards as a result of the loss of standout players to the Crawfords and other clubs because Posey could not pay the top dollar salaries he had shelled out in the past. Vic Harris was still in the outfield that season; Williams from Detroit was proving to be an excellent acquisition; Ray Brown was pitching, playing outfield, and consistently hitting the ball; Morney, who played in the first East-West Game that year, was the shortstop after Chester Williams defected; and Harry Salmon and Joe Strong, acquired in 1932, were the other primary starting pitchers. James A. Riley, a thorough black baseball historian, published a biographical encyclopedia of black ball in 1994 based upon deep research into printed sources and interviews with the many Negro Leaguers living then. His capsule biographies of hundreds of players included unvarnished evaluations of their abilities by their peers. The Grays' 1933 roster also included catcher Rob Gaston, "average catcher defensively ... a little lacking at the plate"; outfielder Bill Evans, "defense kept him in the lineup"; Binder, "an average player" with "a workmanlike manner" at third. Other Grays players, such as pitcher Lou Dula, first baseman George McAllister, and second baseman John Terry, were good journeymen, but were either toward the end of their black big league careers or were going to have short ones.

In 1934, Harris and Morney had gone to the Crawfords, and regulars included catcher Tex Burnett, whom Riley described as a "mediocre hitter" and "fair receiver," and second baseman John Lyles, "an average ballplayer in most aspects of the game."[19] Outfielder Neil Robinson, a good hitter and perennial East-West all-star, boosted the offense for that one season he was with the club, and Pittsburgh native Harry Williams, brother of former Grays pitcher Roy Williams and an original Crawford from the team's amateur days, was also highly useful. But Posey was always on the lookout for new talent. Fortunately, he found a big dose of it.

Smokey Joe Williams may have retired to be a bartender in Harlem, but he had lost neither his interest in baseball nor his connection to the Grays. Walter Leonard of Rocky Mount, North Carolina, was an economic victim of the Depression—he had lost his job installing air brakes on freight cars for the Atlantic Coastline Railroad in 1932. Although he was, at age 25, a little old for a rookie, to stay employed Leonard turned his hobby, baseball, into his profession. A slugging first baseman, Leonard, whose nickname was "Buck," caught on with the Black Revels of Portsmouth, Virginia. As was often the case in the fluid world of black baseball, when a better team, the Baltimore Stars, came through Portsmouth to play the Revels, Buck and his brother Charlie left with them. This put Buck under the tutelage of one of the stars of the previous generation's black players, Ben Taylor. Taylor was the Stars' manager and regular first baseman, but was grooming Leonard to be his replacement.

The Stars soon went bankrupt. But Leonard, a hard-hitting, left-handed batter who was more mature than the average young player and didn't carry a burden such as excessive drinking or an attitude problem that weighed some prospects down, continued to catch the eye of veteran black players who could spot a comer. Star pitcher Dick Redding persuaded him to come to New York to play with his Brooklyn Royal Giants, an independent black team. In the chilly spring of 1934, Leonard stopped in at a Harlem tavern where Joe Williams was presiding behind the bar and talking baseball. Williams asked Leonard, "don't you want to get with a good team?" and suggested the Grays. Leonard was dubious about his chances of making the team, to which Williams, who had seen a lot of young players in his decades in uniform, answered, "Well, you could try.... I've seen you play two or three times and I think you can make the team."

Williams called Posey, who agreed to a spring training tryout for Leonard at the Grays' Wheeling, West Virginia, camp. The ever-canny Posey sent bus fare and spending money to Williams, whom he knew and trusted implicitly, rather than directly to Leonard, a stranger. Leonard and Tex Burnett, the catcher, took the same bus to Wheeling, where instead of it being rainy and chilly, as in New York, it was snowy and cold. It was made clear to Leonard that he was in Wheeling only on a "look-see" basis. Posey's plans had Joe

Vic Harris, left, and Buck Leonard had long careers as Grays starters and stars. Harris, an outfielder, also managed the team for several years. Leonard, the first baseman from 1934 through 1950, is one of the Grays enshrined in the National Baseball Hall of Fame (NoirTech Research, Inc.).

Scott of the integrated Fort Wayne Berghoffs as the regular first sacker. But Scott stayed with the Berghoffs, and Leonard won the regular job, paid a low, $125 a month salary. He stuck with the Grays for 17 years, becoming one of the building blocks of the coming Homestead dynasty and one of the best position players ever in the Negro Leagues. Josh Gibson eventually returned to the Grays with his home run stroke intact, and he became known as the "Black Babe Ruth." Leonard hit right behind him in the middle of the Homestead lineup, and naturally he became the "Black Lou Gehrig."[20]

And Posey brought in another important fellow in 1934 who, like Leonard, would be with the team for the entire time Cum Posey ran it, and longer. Rufus "Sonnyman" Jackson wasn't a baseball player (he did sponsor a black softball team in Homestead), but he contributed as much or more to the Grays' unparalleled Negro League success than any of the team's on-field stars. Jackson was an African American Homestead businessman, known for making legitimate money in the entertainment business, and illegitimate money from numbers. If Gus Greenlee had borrowed liberally from the baseball ownership primer that Posey might have written, it was now Posey's turn to avail himself of Greenlee-type financing. According to Evan P. Baker, Jr., Cum's grand-nephew, Jackson liked Posey, who took him into the Grays' management "because he needed his money." Jackson was not a silent partner—"he liked being associated with the team."[21]

The Homestead Grays became the "Homestead Grays Base Ball Club Incorporated" in April 1934, when articles of incorporation were filed with the state. There were 100 shares of capital stock in the new corporation, valued at $50 each. Charlie Walker, Posey's longtime partner, held 19 shares, Posey 20, and the corporation's lawyer, Theron B. Hamilton (who was also Jackson's personal attorney), had 10. Jackson held 51 shares, which made him the majority stockholder and eventually team president. As was the case when Walker became team president in 1918, there was no real question about who was in charge with the Grays. Posey was the boss, stock holdings notwithstanding. But Jackson became very active in team affairs, usually attending NNL meetings with Posey. He was the second-most important non-playing figure in Grays history, behind Cum Posey himself. In the spring of 1934, Sonnyman Jackson went right to work, pumping cash into the threadbare Grays. One of the first things he did was to buy the team a specially made Chevrolet bus, big enough for 17 passengers and the driver, a more economical way to travel than a convoy of touring cars.[22]

Jackson was born in Columbus, Georgia, in 1900 and, like so many other blacks from the South, migrated to Pittsburgh by 1927 to work in the steel mills. Entrepreneur that he was, though, he turned to more lucrative businesses. According to his widow, Helen, he ran a pool room and tailor shop on Dickson Street in Homestead, then went into the jukebox business at about the same time he invested in the Grays. He placed the record machines on a commission basis in restaurants and other places. Homestead historian Curtis Miner wrote that Jackson "cornered the market" on jukeboxes and slot machines.[23]

After Prohibition ended in 1933, he was a part-owner of the Sky Rocket Grill, at first in his building on Dickson, then at a separate nearby location, then up the hill on Amity Street when an expansion of the Homestead steelworks during World War II wiped out many blocks of lower Homestead. The Sky Rocket featured live blues and jazz, with name performers such as singers Lena Horne and Maxine Sullivan. To go along with the jukebox and café business, Sonnyman Jackson also owned a record shop, Manhattan Music, next door to the Sky Rocket on Dickson, that specialized in new and used "Popular and Race Numbers, Blues and Spirituals." He also owned other income-producing real estate besides the building at 508 Dickson (where the Grays also had their headquarters). As for the numbers business, Jackson was in it when Helen met him around 1930, and "was in the numbers until he died." Although Helen described the jukebox business as his main source of income, being a numbers banker couldn't have hurt. The Jacksons took a two-week cruise to Bermuda in January 1934, and the 1940 U.S. Census valued their home at 529 East Third Avenue in Homestead at $10,000. Only seven percent of homes in the entire Pittsburgh area were worth at least that much.[24]

While Posey's and Jackson's relationship worked well for both men, there were several things they didn't have in common. One was that Sonnyman Jackson seems to have been a true close friend of Gus Greenlee. Helen Jackson reported that her husband knew Greenlee well and that Gus was "a very nice guy." So far as being backers of hotly competing Pittsburgh baseball teams went, "they weren't really enemies, they just wanted to win ballgames." One documented occasion when Jackson and Greenlee were together was in March 1934, when both were hauled into court on gambling arrests. A police raid of the Belmont Hotel on Wylie Avenue, alleged to be the headquarters of the numbers business on the Hill, rounded up Jackson and 15 others, one of whom was Gus's brother George, along with evidence that the Belmont was the numbers headquarters. Greenlee was arrested nearby at his Crawford Grill, as police searched the premises and found six slot machines in the basement.[25]

Posey, the son of a Homestead family prominent even outside the African American community, belonged to the prestigious Loendi Club. Jackson's non-baseball business associates were considerably less reputable.

Emanuel McPherson (an African American, despite his nickname "Jew"), co-owner of the Sky Rocket, earned a Federal conviction in 1927, when investigators looking into the customarily tight relationship of local government and vice in the Pittsburgh area charged 17 people, including several Homestead borough councilmen, with conspiring to control the bootleg liquor business there. The council president and four other board members were found guilty, as were McPherson and three other traffickers in illegal liquor. Most of the defendants were sentenced to penitentiary terms, although McPherson received a sentence of probation. One of those sent to confinement was notorious bootlegger Joe Frank, widely reputed to be in control of illegal booze, drugs, and many other varieties of vice in Homestead. He, too, was Sonnyman Jackson's partner in the numbers business for a while, but only because his political clout enabled him to horn in and force Jackson to share the profits from the "night roll," a dice game that catered to inveterate gamblers after the daily number had been called.[26]

With Posey's help, Sonnyman Jackson got involved in Homestead politics, probably at least partially to insulate himself from pressure from politically connected rivals such as Frank. He wound up as Fifth Ward Democratic chairman as well as a major figure among all black Democrats in the borough. As Homestead's history shows time and again, one did not need a clean slate to attain power in the town's local politics, and Jackson had more than a few blemishes on his record. When he and McPherson got into disfavor with the state Liquor Control Board in 1940 over allegations that minors were being served in the Sky Rocket, it came out that he had been arrested five times between 1928 and 1934 for gambling and carrying concealed weapons.[27]

But Sonnyman Jackson did not draw a gun in 1935 when he quite likely became the only Negro League owner to be involved in a shootout. The *Courier* reported on April 1935 that Jackson had reported a $500 extortion attempt to the authorities, and he agreed to follow the extortionists' instructions to deliver the money in the dead of night at Brown's Bridge over the Monongahela, which connected Homestead to the Brown's Hill section of Pittsburgh. Except that the cash drop would be bogus, and Federal agents would be planted around the bridge. Jackson walked across the bridge from Homestead and left the package that was supposed to contain the $500. He was on his way back when the shooting began. Apparently the extortionists discovered they had been tricked and tried to escape when the authorities fired on them. If anyone was wounded in the shooting, no reports of it surfaced. The only piece of evidence left at the scene was the hat of one of the bad guys. Helen Jackson told the *Courier* that the attempted extortion was "the result of an old grudge by rival business and political enemies in Homestead." The newspaper didn't speculate about why Joe Frank drove up to the Homestead end of the bridge two minutes after the shooting.[28]

Helen, who helped run her husband's legitimate businesses and wound up a part-owner of the Grays after he died, was blasé when interviewed about Sonnyman's numbers business. "I never thought of it as gambling, no more than bingo," she told Rob Ruck. "I never seen nothing wrong with it." Jackson threw in with the Grays because "Posey was having a hard time ... he didn't have one penny to pay [his players]." Led by Greenlee, who dominated the NNL both personally and as owner of the league's best team, the revival of Negro League baseball by the mid–1930s depended upon the investments of numbers bankers. When the league expanded to eight teams in 1935, with a truly major league geographic span from New York to Chicago, six of the clubs, including the Crawfords and Grays, had owners who derived at least part of their income from the numbers. This, according to Helen, made perfect sense during the Depression: "Well, there wasn't nobody but them with the money."[29]

The National League that the Grays rejoined as full members in 1935 had undergone changes that set it on the way to being a stable Negro League. This was not to say that there weren't still growing pains. A major development, besides the presence of the Grays, was an eastward shift in franchises that by the end of the 1936 season had realigned the league as mostly an East Coast operation, with no teams west of Pittsburgh. This cleared the way for the founding of a second Negro League, the Negro American League in 1937, to cover the Midwest and South and establish the same structure for the black leagues as existed in the white majors—two equal leagues that could (and eventually did, beginning in 1942) send their champions to a Negro World Series, which hadn't been staged since 1927.

The major factor in the NNL's shift toward the East Coast was the establishment of two new franchises in New York City, the Brooklyn Eagles and the New York Cubans. Although the league had a presence in nearby Newark, New Jersey, with Charles Tyler's Dodgers, there had been no franchises in New York City since the demise of the American Negro League in 1929. A primary reason for this vacuum was the hegemony over semi-professional baseball in the New York area that belonged to Nathaniel C. Strong. Nat Strong had been in the sports booking business since before the turn of the twentieth century, and by the 1920s was the pre-eminent booking agent in the area.

The agents controlled the sport by controlling one of its prime factors, the real estate. Available ground upon which to build a ball park was relatively scarce in the New York area, and getting scarcer as the population of the city and its suburbs grew. Strong, as had agents in other metropolitan areas, made business arrangements with many park owners that allowed him to arrange games for their parks. On the one hand, the services agents provided ensured a steady flow of playing dates, which was good for the park owners and competing teams alike. Of course, these services did not come free, and Strong and the other agents took a percentage, up to 10 percent, of the gross attendance figure as payment. Negro Leagues teams had few choices about where to play in the New York area without doing business with Strong, and some black owners, Posey included, resented paying money to a white businessman that would have gone into their pockets had they been able to arrange games directly.

Strong was part-owner of the elite Bushwicks semi-pro team, which regularly drew five-figure crowds to Sunday doubleheaders in its Dexter Park on the Brooklyn-Queens boundary in the city, what amounted to a certified gold mine in terms of attendance revenue. Negro League teams always wanted to play at Dexter when they visited New York, but Strong, the controlling partner in the Bushwicks, would only pay them a flat fee as the visiting team's share. This protected the visitors from getting only meager pickings from a poor gate, but only torrents of rain could keep a crowd down at Dexter, so this protection was of little value. What was lost was the chance to reap extra hundreds of dollars from a sell-out crowd, which wasn't rare at all.

But Strong died of a heart attack in January 1935, and while his firm, Nat C. Strong Baseball Enterprises, carried on, his passing removed a barrier to Negro League growth in the New York metropolitan area. Max Rosner, Strong's surviving partner in the Bushwicks, dropped the flat guarantee at Dexter Park in favor of a percentage of the gate, encouraging more black participation in games there. Until then, Posey had refused to book his Grays at a Nat Strong ballpark. The *New York Amsterdam News* said he had "stood out longer than any other of the teams and absolutely refused to consider Dexter Park for more than six years," before bringing his team there and splitting a doubleheader on June 23.[30]

The two new New York owners in the NNL were numbers men, or rather, one was a formers numbers banker. Abraham Lincoln Manley, a native North Carolinian, had a numbers business in Camden, New Jersey, where he also ran a men's club, until prudence proved the better part of valor when white mobsters came around for a cut of his business. He moved to Harlem, where he met his second wife, Effa. Abe's strong interest in baseball, and his conviction in 1934 (which was not unfounded) that black baseball owners could be doing a better job of running a league, led the couple to campaign successfully for a franchise. After an unprofitable 1935 season as a tenant at the

Brooklyn Dodgers' Ebbets Field, which was too far from Harlem's 300,000 black residents to encourage African American fandom and too close to Dexter Park to withstand Sunday competition from the Bushwicks, the Manleys bought out Tyler's floundering Newark franchise in the off-season and merged the best of both rosters as the Newark Eagles.

Abe and Effa were different types of personalities—he was very easy-going and seemed to hate paperwork, but was a whiz at scouting and player evaluation. Despite only a high school education, Effa had a sharp business mind and handled the team's administration. She also had a sharp tongue and was never averse to expressing her opinions. But the two of them shared strong, progressive ideas about how to make black baseball better and stood together on issues at league meetings. In 1936, Posey lauded Abe as "the one man in the league who we are certain is for the best interest of the league and its members."[31] Posey likely wouldn't have been caught dead saying anything so complimentary about Effa Manley in print. They fought bitterly, two hard-headed, outspoken owners whose confrontation was undoubtedly driven in part by her determination to be a force in a thoroughly male-dominated business. Over the years, though, it turned out that they had many ideas in common as to how to make the Negro Leagues better.

Alejandro "Alex" Pompez was a native of Key West, Florida, where his father ran a cigar-making business and was an active supporter of independence from Spanish rule for his native Cuba.

Abe and Effa Manley owned the Newark Eagles in the National League. Although they were progressive owners and often agreed with Posey on how best to run the league, Cum and Effa both were hard-headed and sharp-tongued, and they sometimes clashed at league meetings, particularly the tumultuous 1940 one (NoirTech Research, Inc.).

Pompez had been involved in black baseball for about 20 years, running barn-storming teams of mostly Cuban players that, despite a lack of a home park, often were members of the Negro Leagues. In 1935, Pompez found a home for his New York Cubans, a key requirement to getting into the expanding NNL. He leased the Dyckman Oval, an enclosed park in Harlem, from the New York City parks department and poured $60,000 into renovations that expanded seating to 12,000 and included lights for night games. Pompez had this money because, like so many other NNL owners, he ran a very profitable numbers business in partnership with other Harlem bankers that was said to gross $5 million a year.[32]

The Philadelphia Stars, who were owned by longtime black baseball entrepreneur Ed Bolden and white Philadelphia booking agent Eddie Got-tlieb, were another mainstay of the league, as were Tom Wilson's Elite Giants. Wilson hailed from Nashville (where he, too, was reportedly a numbers banker) and had run the Elite Giants since the early 1920s. Wilson-owned teams had been members of the Negro Southern League and both the first and second Negro National Leagues, and Wilson was an officer, including turns as president, in both the Southern and second NNL.

The Elites were often successful on the field, but they abandoned their Nashville home to get closer to the NNL's geographic area and cut travel costs. This led, first, to an abortive move to Detroit, where there were problems leasing a park, and then to Columbus, Ohio, where there was a park, but not so many fans to sit in it. As the 1936 season opened, Wilson had relocated yet again, to play in the white major league Washington Senators' Griffith Stadium. In 1938, though, the Elites shifted one last time, to a very successful run in Baltimore. Wilson, one of the three owners who founded the East-West All-Star Game, was easy-going, although perhaps too much so to be a success as a league president. His nickname was "Smiling Tom," and one quote attributed to him as he tried to quell a dispute at a league meeting summed up his approach: "Let bye-gones be bye-gones, and let's get together and make some money."[33]

The other team outside the Eastern orbit, the Chicago American Giants, was owned by Robert Coles, who was league treasurer and, with Wilson and Greenlee, a founder of the East-West Game. Nevertheless, Chicago was in a very disadvantageous position due to the travel costs to reach the rest of the league (and vice versa). The Giants also had money problems and were expelled from the league at the beginning of the 1936 season for not paying their players.[34]

The American Giants' departure opened the door to an opportunity to shift the league's geographic center even farther eastward. The New York

Black Yankees were an independent club that could trace its lineage to the Lincoln Giants of James Keenan, which had played the momentous long series with the Grays in 1930. However, the current boss, the African American James Semler, had been dependent upon Nat Strong for bookings and financial support, which cast a pall over a potential relationship with other NNL owners.

As an independent, the Black Yankees were basically regarded as a drag on the league by getting better bookings in the New York area and being able to go after league players, although the team was never a financial powerhouse and had limited ability to draw stars away from the NNL. Cum Posey, who had worked to build the Grays from the ground up and had recently endured bleak times, but had always treated his players as well as possible, had little regard for Semler. He wrote in 1935 about how the New Yorker "in some mysterious manner has become the sole owner of the Baseball Club without spending a penny of his own or anyone else's money," except that of the Yankees players, who were grossly underpaid.[35]

After Strong's death, and with the Eagles added to the competition already posed by the Cubans, Semler made attempts to have his team admitted to the league, but was denied as late as the beginning of the 1936 season. In May, though, after the American Giants had been expelled, Greenlee and Eddie Gottlieb were authorized to speak with Semler, "with a view to adjusting any [and] all misunderstandings."[36] There were several "misunderstandings," including a lawsuit by Semler and William Leuschner, who had taken over Strong's booking organization, against the Eagles and Cubans for signing some Yankees players. All was resolved by June, though, when, with Semler agreeing to withdraw his lawsuit and the league granting anti-raiding protection to his current roster, the Black Yankees were admitted to the league in time to start the second half of the schedule. Alex Pompez of the Cubans, who knew unwanted competition when he saw it, cast the only dissenting vote.

The black sporting press gave credit for this reconciliation to the new NNL commissioner, Ferdinand Q. Morton. He had replaced Rollo Wilson after his strained year at the head of the league, when Wilson's decisions, no matter how well thought out, made enemies of his employers, including Posey. In a January 1935 column, columnist Romeo Dougherty of the *New York Amsterdam News* reprinted a letter Wilson wrote to the owners, in which he declared himself fed up: "If a Commissioner must be blackguarded by owners who object to decisions on points at issue between owners, then the League needs either no Commissioner or a group of new club owners." Wilson also zeroed in on a particular owner, unnamed but almost certainly Posey, who "went so far as to attack him [Wilson] time and time again in a certain newspaper, questioning his honesty and fitness."

Actually, although Posey had several bones to pick with Wilson on behalf of the Grays, and of course did so in his *Courier* column, Wilson's characterization of Posey's opinions was overstated. But Posey also joined in with the newly admitted New York contingent, the Manleys and Pompez, and fellow Wilson critic Robert Cole of Chicago, to get Wilson ejected from the commissionership that March. The drafting of Morton to be commissioner on the surface made the move look like an upgrade. Morton, a New York Democrat with much influence in the African American wing of the city's Tammany Hall organization, was the first black appointed to the city's civil service commission. But Morton had no particular baseball background, except as a fan, and at any rate the contentiousness of the Negro League owners proved as intractable for him as it had for Rollo Wilson. Morton was out after three years, replaced by a strengthened set of league officers, all of whom were owners (including Posey).[37]

Although the Homestead Grays were now full-fledged league members again, the 1935 and '36 squads produced mediocre results. The team finished in third and fifth place, respectively, in the first and second halves of the 1935 split season, and sixth and fourth in 1936. Dependable pitching was a problem both years. Ray Brown was the ace of the staff, although he was hampered early in the 1936 season by illness contracted while playing the previous winter on a combined Eagles-Grays team sent by the Manleys to Puerto Rico. Of the other veteran starters, Joe Strong, who had been with the Grays since 1932, was nearing the end of his career, as was lefty Willie Gisentaner. But it was the rare Grays season that didn't see the front office building for the future, and 1936 saw the debut of a pair of young left-handers who were to be mainstays of Homestead's pitching staff in the coming years.

Edsall Walker, 22, who hailed from Catskill, New York, in the Albany area, was pitching for a local black semi-pro team, the Albany Black Giants. Walker was six feet tall and 215 pounds, and he could throw hard, although he always had some control problems, which earned him the nickname "The Catskill Wild Man." Nonetheless, he was a Grays regular until 1945 and a starting pitcher in the 1938 East-West Game. Walker was signed in 1936 by See Posey, who had returned to the Grays' front office the year before, probably not coincidentally with the appearance of Rufus Jackson's financing. According to Walker, See was out looking for talent when he rolled into Albany and contacted former Grays infielder Elmore "Scrappy" Brown. He told Brown he was looking for ballplayers, and Scrappy said, "I've got one for you." Although See had recently worked for Cum's archrival, Gus Greenlee, when money was tight, he was clearly welcome back at the Grays front office. His duties soon included leading the team south for spring training each year, as well as booking non-league games. When his brother died in early 1946, See stepped into his shoes, running the team with Jackson for the few years remaining in its existence.[38]

The Grays trained in Atlanta in the spring of 1936, and when they headed north they took local pitching star Roy Welmaker with them. Welmaker, 22 and a student at Clark University, had been playing with the Atlanta Black Crackers in the Negro Southern League for the past few seasons after school ended, but easily made the jump to the black majors. He was a Grays hurler through 1945, except for 1940 and '41, when he opted to play in the Mexican League.

Some major moves were also made in 1935 and '36 to strengthen the rest of the roster. Vic Harris was reacquired in a trade with the Crawfords in the spring of '35 that gave up promising third baseman Andrew "Pat" Patterson. Posey promptly made Harris the field manager again. Harris generally played left field, alongside Jerry Benjamin, who like Welmaker came up from the Southern League. Benjamin was fleet of foot and a good hitter, and he held a spot in middle of the Homestead outfield throughout the Grays' glory years.

George Scales, the former Gray who would follow the money to whatever team he thought would pay him best, came from the independent Black Yankees in 1935 to play third base, but then went back to his old team the following season. He was replaced by Henry Spearman, a .300 hitter who spent most of time in the 1930s playing for the Grays. The question of who would play second base was solved for years with the acquisition of Matt Carlisle from the Southern League in 1935, and shortstop was likewise anchored for the future when Norman "Jelly" Jackson was picked up from the Cleveland Red Sox, whose one season in the NNL had ended in 1934. Neither Carlisle or Jackson were strong hitters, but surrounded as they were by sluggers such as Leonard, Harris, Benjamin, Scales, and Spearman, and with a set of strong-hitting pitchers such as Brown, Strong, Walker, Welmaker, and Tom Parker (possibly a better hitter than pitcher), offensive output from the middle of the infield wasn't a pressing need. With Josh Gibson launching homers for the Crawfords, catching duties fell primarily to Tommie Dukes, who could hit well but as a receiver was described by James Riley as having a good arm, but "was only moderately mobile behind the plate." There was talent on these Grays squads, but much of it had not yet matured, and at this point represented only an investment in a highly lucrative future. It was telling that when Posey named his annual all-star team at the end of the 1936 season, Leonard and Harris were the only picks from his own team.[39]

As the Grays weren't too distinguished in their return to full NNL status, so Posey was uncharacteristically restrained in his actions and comments concerning the league. Sometimes, he actually seemed to be enjoying being a part of the organization. As the 1935 season opened, he noted in his column that while the financial results of the 1934 season, while not in themselves so great, looked very good in light of the disastrous seasons just before, and "there never appeared a brighter future for Colored baseball than at the present time." A year later, he proclaimed that "league baseball is the salvation of Negro baseball."[40] He was especially pleased that expansion on the East Coast had undercut the power of the white booking agents. With the Black Yankees still not in the fold, he stated in February 1936 that getting all major league-quality black clubs into the NNL, either as full or associate members, would not only stabilize the league, but would end the paying of booking fees.[41]

The operational issues he did identify as mistakes were relatively minor, such as the decision by the league to send an all-star team in August to the prestigious *Denver Post* semi-pro tournament. The team, which included Ray Brown and Buck Leonard, plus See Posey as business manager, won the tournament, but followers of the Negro League teams complained that league play went on with diminished lineups. Posey admitted in November that the "Homestead Grays were a party to this and deserve the censure of the baseball fans in general. The best we can say is, this will not happen again, regardless of the money offered."[42]

Posey never let up on Gus Greenlee, though, still constantly making him an object of criticism for his possible conflict of interest in running both Homestead's arch-rival Crawfords and the league at the same time. Despite having agreed in 1932 to play Grays home games at Greenlee Field, in the spring of 1936, Posey announced that his team would be going back to the Pirates' Forbes Field. He said the reason the Grays had switched from Forbes was "because it appeared as though they were antagonizing to a Negro enterprise in not playing all home games at Greenlee Field." But the lack of a grandstand roof, exposing fans to "intervals of rains and burning sun," hurt attendance, and "We feel that the Homestead Grays have as much right to operate at any park as any other club owners." But Greenlee declared that the reasons Posey gave for switching back to Forbes Field were a "smokescreen." What was going on, he maintained, was that Posey was trying to harm his business. There was even talk that See Posey was at work trying to schedule Grays games for Forbes on dates that would directly conflict with the Crawfords at Greenlee Field, something that had been scrupulously avoided up to then (and which didn't happen in 1936, either, in the end). Greenlee vowed to continue playing at his ballpark, in which he said he had had invested

$50,000, even though Posey "hasn't a single penny invested there and he is not bound to respect it."[43]

But in addition to just fighting over the upper hand in Pittsburgh, Posey was now campaigning for Greenlee to be replaced as league president. Without mentioning Greenlee by name, he wrote in March 1936 that "Every player in the League and every local League fan knows the affairs of the League have been handled in a loose manner for two years. It is not possible to restore the confidence of the public under the present set-up of the league." In that same column, he urged rotating control of the league among veteran owners (as usual, exempting himself from the top spot). He mentioned Ed Bolden, Tom Wilson, and Alex Pompez as potential leaders, and not long after that Bolden took over as president for the 1936 season. Greenlee appeared to be distracted by managing his stable of prizefighters, particularly light heavyweight champion John Henry Lewis. He also apparently was getting tired of being the target of criticism from other owners (Posey had something to do with that) and having his authority constantly questioned.[44]

Even Greenlee, who could in the past boast of spending whatever it took to figuratively build the Crawfords and literally build Greenlee Field, was also apparently having money problems. Although it never eradicated the numbers in the Pittsburgh area, law enforcement officials did attempt to crack down on the business in 1936, with at least temporary effect. Like the other bankers, Greenlee's "numbers games were no longer immune to police vice squads." Greenlee himself was the subject of an arrest warrant that April after a particular numbers writer, arrested once again, fingered him as the guy he was working for. Greenlee voluntarily surrendered himself, but in court the writer had a change of heart—no, the fellow he worked for was named Gus all right, but he was a white man. The police court magistrate, trying to keep control of the case just in case some other evidence came up, sparred with Greenlee over when he could come back to court (a fight tour with Lewis was about to begin), and finally surrendered: "Well, when I want you I'll call you up or you call me in the next few days." Apparently, the judge never called.[45]

Posey and Jackson called Gus, however, to arrange a trade that would return Josh Gibson to the Grays. Posey later gave Jackson all the credit for pulling off the deal at the league meeting in March, and Jackson certainly supplied something that Posey didn't have, and Greenlee apparently needed—$2,500 in cash (this sum, as a share of the total output of the U.S. economy, would be equal to half a million dollars today).[46] Gibson was reportedly holding out for a 50 percent raise, which may have contributed to Greenlee's desire to trade him. The money aside, the deal on paper was very lopsided in favor of the Grays, since it also included third baseman Judy Johnson, like Gibson an eventual Hall of Famer. But Johnson, 36, chose to retire. Homestead gave up two starters, third baseman Spearman (to replace Johnson) and catcher Lloyd "Pepper" Bassett, a youngster beginning a long, productive career, who subbed for Gibson about as well as any available catcher could have in 1937.

Gibson complemented a Grays lineup that was long on hitters, with Leonard, Harris, Benjamin, and Brown all back from the 1936 team, complemented by the return of hard-hitting Jim Williams, a Gray in 1933 and '34, in right field and Cuban Javier Perez, who had a better-than-usual season at the plate, filling Spearman's slot at third base. Carlisle and Jackson continued to be dependable contributors in the middle of the infield. Brown was the ace of the pitching staff, and Edsall Walker and Welmaker continued to develop as reliable members of the rotation. Lou Dula, whose career with the Grays in the 1930s was plagued by arm trouble, had his only really good year, and Tom Parker, despite a high earned run average, started on a regular basis.

Josh Gibson, regarded as the premier home run hitter in the Negro Leagues, came to the Grays from a Pittsburgh sandlot team in 1929 and, with two breaks in service—to play with the Pittsburgh Crawfords and in Latin America— was the starting catcher for the Grays until his death after the 1946 season (author's collection).

The 1937 Grays were no longer the run-of-the-mill team that had emerged from the wreckage of the East-West League. They won both halves of the NNL's split-season schedule, negating any need for a playoff for the pennant. In the first half, the Grays ran away from their closest competition, the Newark Eagles, winning 21 of 30 games for a .700 percentage. The second-half standings seem not to have been published in any black newspaper (Joe Louis was defending his heavyweight boxing title again, and the bout sucked up many columns of the sports pages). But the *Courier* on September 11 acknowledged that, with a week to go in the season, the Grays had clinched the second half, too, "and they will play now just for the fun of playing for the fans that will turn out to see the champs."[47]

But elsewhere in Pittsburgh, disaster struck. Even with a league structure that supposedly barred players from jumping their contracts, there was often a way for a Negro League owner to successfully seduce dissatisfied player away from an opponent. Posey had done it in 1933 when he scooped up Jim Williams and Jimmy Binder from Detroit under cover of alleged unpaid wages. Greenlee had done it to Posey in 1934 when Vic Harris changed colors, also after being supposedly unpaid. But what happened to the NNL, mostly to the Crawfords, in 1937 was unprecedented. A reported 21 valuable Negro Leaguers, some of them key members of their squads, and 10 of them Greenlee's men, were lured away not by some unscrupulous American team owner, but by a Caribbean dictator's desire to dominate his country's baseball scene.[48]

Rafael Trujillo was commander of the Dominican Republic's national police when, in 1930, he turned a revolution against the country's elected president, Horacio Vasquez, into his own success story by keeping his armed forces out of the fray, then stepping in to seize power once Vasquez had been toppled. His rule, which lasted until 1961, when he was assassinated, was "one of the longest, cruelest, and most absolute in modern times.... He had Santo Domingo renamed Ciudad Trujillo, and he amassed a vast fortune for himself by taking ownership of virtually everything he touched—land, airlines, trading monopolies, manufacturers, and most sugarcane producers—in all as much as three-fifths of the nation's gross domestic product and workforce."[49]

As is often the case in countries controlled by dictators, their authoritarian rule is superimposed upon the democratic structure they overthrew, and there are still elections, although often meaningless. But the strongman still has to maintain popularity with the public. This was the case in the Dominican Republic, and part of Trujillo's campaign to stay popular was taking control of the Dominican summer baseball league. In 1937, he caused the two teams in the capital city to merge, and his henchmen took control of the new Los Dragones de Cuidad Trujillo (The Dragons of Trujillo City).

Black players from the U.S. had long spent winters playing ball in the Caribbean to supplement their summer salaries, but the Trujillo plan, to pack the summer league with the best American black players who could be hired, naturally ran smack up against the NNL season. To lure them away from the U.S., Trujillo's operatives and the other team owners paid Negro Leaguers far more than they could be earning in the States.

In addition to American blacks, several Cuban-born NNL players went south, among them Martin Dihigo, the former Homestead Gray all-around star. Their absences didn't disrupt any existing NNL team, since the New York Cubans, their U.S. team, had unexpectedly gone dormant. A calamity in his numbers banking business more serious than any that Greenlee ever faced had driven owner Alex Pompez out of the country. The white gangster

Dutch Schultz had strong-armed his way into control of the rackets in Harlem a few years earlier, and a special prosecutor, future New York governor and presidential candidate Thomas E. Dewey, was on the case. Pompez, a target of the investigators, slipped out of New York ahead of them and escaped abroad. Although he eventually surrendered to police in Mexico City, pleaded guilty to a reduced charge, testified in a major trial of a Schultz henchman, and returned to black baseball in 1939, his team was out of the league while he was out of the country.

The player the Trujillos wanted most of all was the Crawfords' star pitcher, Satchell Paige. Given Paige's career-long propensity to follow the dollar, they got him. In addition to agreeing to pitch for the Dragons, Paige accepted $30,000 to divide among himself and seven other Negro League regulars.[50] The players Satchell Paige had the closest contact with were his teammates, who formed the bulk of the group he persuaded to defect. Greenlee lost not only his star pitcher, but two other top-notch hurlers, Chet Brewer and Leroy Matlock; star outfielder James "Cool Papa" Bell; catcher Bill Perkins, and outfielder Sam Bankhead. The Crawfords were gutted, in other words, and fell from 1936 league champions to the second division, while the Dragons won the Dominican League pennant.

To add insult to injury, the Dominican League ended while the Negro Leagues were still playing, but Paige, Bell, Brewer, Matlock, Perkins, Bankhead, and many of the better players who had jumped other NNL clubs to go to the Caribbean threw in with a Ray Doan, a white promoter, when they returned to the states and played on as the Santo Domingo Stars rather than offering to return to their teams. The Stars went to the prestigious *Denver Post* Tournament for semi-pro teams, and won it. Then they played their way back east in a series of exhibition games that included two at Yankee Stadium, the Negro Leagues' premier showcase place in the East. Greenlee was in charge of booking the black teams into the Stadium at that time and apparently decided that, since fate had handed him a lemon in the form of his players' defections, he would go ahead and make some profitable lemonade out of the situation.

In addition to the extreme damage done to the Crawfords, the New York Black Yankees and Philadelphia Stars of the NNL were also hurt by the Dominican exodus. Only one player left the Grays, but he was vital to them. Josh Gibson was one of Paige's targets, and he took $2,200, a very hefty sum as black ballplayer salaries went, to leave the Grays for a couple of months. Gibson's biographer, William Brashler, portrayed the exchange between Gibson and Cum Posey as straightforward: "Posey, no doubt, did not like losing his star catcher for even a year, and he resented the jumping of Bell and the other Craws ... but he realized that he didn't have much choice with Gibson.

Rather than alienate him, he announced that Josh had received the okay of management before he went south." It is significant that when the Dominican Leaguers returned to the U.S., Gibson did not join the all-star team headed to Denver, but got back behind the plate for the Grays. A comment from his teammate Buck Leonard indicates that he had every intention of returning to Homestead after cashing in on his lavish Caribbean payday: "When he left to go down there, he told me, 'Buck, you hold them close until I get back.'"[51]

The NNL owners, whether they felt victimized personally or not, agreed that the departure of so many well-known players would hurt attendance. There were complaints to the U.S. State Department, which yielded no solid results, but in Pittsburgh two Dominican "scouts," consular office employee Luis Mendez and attorney Federico Niña, were arrested in early May after being spotted at Greenlee Field by Crawfords secretary John Clark. This was after Paige and some others had jumped their contracts, and Clark swiftly figured out what the two Latin Americans might be up to. They were charged with conspiring to defraud the Crawfords and Grays, and were held on bail until an attorney from the consulate in New York City arrived to spring them. Charges against Mendez and Niña were eventually dropped, but Niña's son told baseball historian Rob Ruck that "they were accused of robbing players from Pittsburgh. Of course, this was true."[52]

Greenlee, as league president, could not stop the exodus that primarily hurt Greenlee, the club owner. Clark, his right-hand man, had stepped down from the position as league secretary in January, which should have pleased Posey mightily. As 1937 moved along, it was apparent that Greenlee was being bypassed by the other owners, just as their teams, particularly the Grays, were moving past the Crawfords in the standings. The final insult of the season came when an interleague competition between the NNL and the new Negro American League, which included Midwestern franchises that had been shed by the NNL and former members of the Negro Southern League, decided to stage a series of post-season games billed as a World Series. There hadn't been a Series between two black leagues since 1927, and this one wasn't quite a matchup between each league's champions.

According to a Posey column in the *Courier*, NNL Commissioner Morton and NAL head Major R. R. Jackson decided that their leagues would be represented by the best men not only from the pennant winners, the Grays and the Chicago American Giants, but also from the second-place teams, respectively the Newark Eagles and Kansas City Monarchs, to work "for the best interests" of the league to present the strongest clubs possible and excite the public. The series was certainly in the best interests of the Grays (and Eagles), who won six of the seven games played.[53]

But John Clark, still at Greenlee's shoulder, conveyed his boss's opinion that Posey, Abe Manley of the Eagles, and Jim Semler of the Black Yankees "have been successful in getting over a low, ratty trick on Commissioner Morton" to palm off the games as a "degenerative 'World Series'" that not only gave the sport a black eye, but constituted a "deliberate scheme to sidetrack W. A. Greenlee" and avoid paying the league its usual 10 percent booking fee for games. Greenlee himself sent an open letter to the *Courier* laying out instances throughout the season in which Morton, Posey, Rufus Jackson, and the Manleys had undercut him, or tried to. He accused his fellow owners of selfishness and stated uncategorically, "I am not resigning as Chairman of the Negro National League."[54]

But the mogul who had, more than anyone else, been responsible for the revitalization of Negro baseball in the East was about done as a league president, team owner, and even an owner of his own ballpark. By the start of the 1939 season, Greenlee had shut down the Crawfords and had turned over his presidency to Tom Wilson, who had been league vice president. A possibly even bigger blow had fallen in December 1938, when the failing Greenlee Field was sold to the city, which tore it down for a housing project. Greenlee continued to express an interest in getting back into the Negro Leagues, but his relationship with his fellow owners was "marked by increasing tension and distrust."[55] He finally did get back into the game in 1945 with a franchise in the rival United States League, but the league, having been born just as black fans' attention was turning toward integrated baseball, barely lasted two seasons. Meanwhile, Posey had become a league officer in 1938, and his Grays had begun their long run of NNL pennants.

The end of Greenlee's Crawfords began a process that brought about a thaw in the relationship between Posey and Clark. "From 1932 to 1937 we belonged to different parties," Clark wrote in his "Wylie Avenue" column in late 1941, some months after Posey covered for him while he was hospitalized; "In 1938, Posey won. Since that year we have been getting closer to each other." Clark noted, however, "He's a damn bad enemy. Anybody connected with the Pittsburgh Crawfords will tell you that." When Posey died in 1946, Clark recounted that Posey had never doubted he would win the baseball war for Pittsburgh. According to Clark, Posey characteristically asserted that Greenlee never understood the economics of baseball entrepreneurship: "He liked the 'big fellow' [Gus] for many reasons, but maintained that his one shortcoming would always be his downfall."[56]

Chapter Seven

Posey in Homestead

Cumberland Posey, Jr., was best known in his hometown for the success of his baseball team, but he personally contributed to the general welfare of the borough, too. His efforts showed distinctive indications of his upbringing by the Captain and Anna. Among his first thoughts were the town's public schools and the welfare of its black residents, issues that were important to his mother. His work on the issues, though, had to be addressed through the borough's local political system, which included the sort of corruption that infected the City of Pittsburgh just across the Monongahela, plus a healthy dose of steelworker rambunctiousness and some racial prejudice. This required more than a touch of the hard-headed, racially impervious business attitude of his father.

By the time Posey the younger became fully involved in Homestead affairs in 1931, he had already shown his sagacious and combative traits in building his Grays into a strong regional, and then national contender, and he was about to begin his struggle with Gus Greenlee for Pittsburgh black baseball supremacy. But never, in his many years in baseball, had he faced the personal threats that came his way when he asserted himself in Homestead. In return for his efforts on behalf of better government, he was arrested twice, beaten up on a street corner once, and roughed up another time by a police officer.

Posey entered local politics in 1931 as the first African American ever elected as a member of the Homestead school board. He won one of two director seats up for election, finishing fairly closely behind the leading candidate and beating the other soundly. He won two subsequent six-year terms on the board with no problem and remained a Homestead school official for the rest of his life.[1] Although he broke the color line on the borough's school board, he did so as a candidate of the local political machine. Homestead's growth from a placid farming town to a minor industrial boomtown by 1930s was due almost entirely to the Homestead steel works and the business activities associated with it. Politicians in the borough recognized this and, particularly since the bloody steelworkers strike at the mill in 1892, aimed to keep antagonists of the company at bay. Homestead was a one-party town run by the Republicans, who in turn were under the thumb of the steel executives. "Local politics," according to historian Curtis Miner, "upheld the stability of the steel company simply by keeping things quiet and keeping the political process out of the hands of folks who would use it for purposes not friendly to Carnegie Steel."[2]

Up until the period during and after World War I, voter turnout in Homestead elections was usually light, held down by the political disinterest of European immigrants working in the mill and living in the tenement housing nearby. The borough's elected officials were likely to be friendly to the Carnegie firm, and sometimes were even its employees. But the two wards down by the river and near the steelworks, known as the "lower wards" because of their geographical location, began to show political life. Beginning with the 1917 election, "primaries once uncontested began to heat up." The ethnic area near the Monongahela became politically valuable and in 1921 was captured by a new breed of Homestead politician. John J. Cavanaugh was a coal miner who then became a Homestead policeman. As a beat cop, he had walked the streets of the lower First and Second Wards, and he had many connections there. He had held several minor positions in the local political machine, but foreswore it, temporarily, to form his own party and challenge a favored attorney and real estate agent for the burgess position. According to Miner, Cavanaugh "moved in a working class world" and made "obvious attempts to win the favor of his future constituency by presenting himself as a man of the people."[3]

Cavanaugh's election that November was fueled by votes from the two wards below Eighth Street, which was regarded as the dividing line between upper and lower classes. He lost the three upper class wards located farther up the hill, away from the river. He would soon return to being a Republican and win three more terms as burgess on that ticket. The borough's immigrant blue-collar population (which included blacks from the South) had swept Cavanaugh into the top office, and he had no problem repaying their loyalty. He recruited men of Eastern European descent with social and business ties below, not above, Eighth Street to be his political lieutenants, and became "regarded by many Homesteaders as a sort of paternal machine boss who looked after the interests of the community at large."[4]

Some of Cavanaugh's actions on behalf of his disadvantaged constituents were the sort that today would bring him praise almost anywhere. For example, he banned the Ku Klux Klan (at that time anti-immigrant and anti-Catholic in addition to being anti–Negro) from demonstrating in his town.

But relaxed official strictures on drinking, gambling, whoring, and other after-work activities that cheered up the end of a long, sweaty, day in the works also appealed to the hard-working mill workers. Lax enforcement of the laws against such activities (including the Volstead Act after Prohibition became the law of the land), were welcome, and in the Cavanaugh administration they were practically non-existent. William Serrin, in his history of the borough, reports that "Homestead, for years, had, along Sixth Avenue [the street where See Posey's billiard hall was located], one of the greatest, gaudiest sin strips in American, a wild, wicked place of whorehouses, taverns, and gambling houses."[5]

Of course, the authorities' steadfast ignoring of the obvious along Sixth Avenue and its adjoining thoroughfares came with a price. Payoffs from people in the vice businesses, collected by the police, were common, and as Miner puts it, "Political corruption seemed to be pathological." Vote fraud on Election Day, often involving people brought in from Pittsburgh to cast multiple illegal ballots for the machine's candidates, was endemic. More than one borough official faced charges for it. Violence at the polls was prevalent. In the 1925 election, in which Cavanaugh won his second term, "continuous battling all day" was reported at one polling place, and a poll watcher for Cavanaugh's opponent was shot dead at another after challenging nine voters suspected of being "repeaters." Cavanaugh's obituary in 1949 aptly characterized his years of power: "Politics as the Homestead burgess and his friends played it was no game." It also quoted an earlier interview in which Cavanaugh was remarkably forthright about his view of the voting process: "I never have fouled a ballot box, and I never will.... But of course, if somebody drops a few extra ballots into the box—or when a voter whom you know isn't [politically] right doesn't get to the polling place for one reason or another—that's just practical politics."[6]

There were almost 3,400 blacks, a sixth of the borough's population, living in Homestead at the time Posey ran for office. Many of them were voters, and many lived in the lower wards from which Cavanaugh drew most of his support. Although there's no indication that the burgess had any close connection with the Grays, the team paid proper attention to the political head of the community from which it got its name. In 1927, for example, when Posey and Charlie Walker were running the team, it sponsored a testimonial for Cavanaugh in a popular meeting hall in the lower wards, with Posey the organizer.[7]

The ensuing political relationship helped both men. Posey, of course, got a chance to work for the betterment of his town's black community (as well as all of the schoolchildren), and Cavanaugh was able to show his black constituents his regard for them. In Posey, he got the best of both worlds—an African American supporter who was popular in the lower wards because of his sports exploits, but who lived in the upper wards, where the burgess's support was thinnest. The relationship seems to have caught the attention of Homestead's blacks. On December 31, 1932, the *Pittsburgh Courier*'s "Talk O' Town" column featured a report from "Santa Claus" recounting his Christmas good deeds, including a meal for 700 persons at the Clark Memorial Baptist Church in Homestead: "Do you know who asked me to stop there? Cum Posey! He and Mr. Cavanaugh run Homestead like 'Sunny Man' [Rufus Jackson] runs the numbers."

By that Christmas, though, Cavanaugh's iron-fisted rule was on the verge of breaking down. He won re-election handily in November 1933, but across the river Pittsburgh elected William M. McNair as its first Democratic mayor since 1906. Right after the election, the *Pittsburgh Sun-Telegraph* stated, "As the 1933 election returns became final a morgue ambulance pulled up in front of Republican headquarters, allowing some Democrats to ask, 'What you got in there, the Republican Party?'" There were localized reasons for the Democratic upset—the incumbent Republican mayor, Charles H. Kline, had resigned after being convicted for misuse of his office in awarding city contracts, and his temporary appointed successor, the city council president, had filled Kline's shoes poorly. But the primary reason for the shift of voters away from the Republican Party lay 250 miles away in Washington, D.C., where Franklin Delano Roosevelt was settling in to his first year as president. One issue that propelled FDR to victory and brought about a realignment of political allegiances nationally was the perceived mishandling by Republican Herbert Hoover of the effects of the Great Depression. Unemployment had soared in steel towns as the demand for steel plunged. Homestead was no exception, with 50 percent of the workers from the Homestead works unemployed.[8]

Cavanaugh banned the Klan from his borough, but he was also strongly anti-union, a stance that won support from the steelworks management but began to grow out of favor with the suffering workers. The National Industrial Recovery Act, an early lynchpin of Roosevelt's economic recovery program, guaranteed workers the right to form unions. Homestead was no stranger to unionization, and there were plenty of residents who had sided with the steelworkers during the bloody Homestead Strike of 40 years before. Cavanaugh had personally been the brunt of ridicule in July of 1933 when Frances Perkins, Roosevelt's labor secretary, came to town to speak to steel workers about how the new administration could help them. She arranged a meeting in the borough hall, but discovered that local police were barring union officials and others from entering and had beaten up at least two men. Perkins immediately suggested that the meeting be moved outside to a nearby public park, but Cavanaugh and his police objected, citing an ordinance banning such gatherings.

As the *Pittsburgh Post-Gazette* paraphrased Perkins's account, "With Cavanaugh becoming 'more and more nervous' and the eager steel workers becoming 'more and more eager,'" she seized upon a handy solution. She adjourned the meeting to the nearby U.S. Post Office, a Federal building where the locals had no jurisdiction over the gathering, and a Catholic church where the police were likely not to want to interfere. The near rhyming of the adjective "nervous" and the distinctive title Pennsylvania gave to its borough mayors proved irresistible to the press. Cavanaugh became known as the "Nervous Burgess." He claimed in his defense that by trying to limit Secretary Perkins's exposure to disaffected workers, he had nipped in the bud a "Communist volcano threatening the entire business structure, as well as our Government" in the Pittsburgh area.[9]

Nothing more was heard about the red volcano, but events were erupting under the Homestead political machine. A major blast happened on March 11, 1934, when a group of reformers met before an overflow crowd in a downtown social hall to discuss the state of misgovernment in the state legislative district that included Homestead. Featured speakers dwelt on election fraud and high taxes, but the floor was stolen by someone who had been one of the machine's own. John J. McLean, by profession a dentist, was the borough controller, and until he fell out with Cavanaugh a few months before had been considered the burgess's chief lieutenant. This was McLean's first public appearance since the split, and according to the town's newspaper, the *Daily Messenger*, he "held the center of attention when he arose to speak." The *Messenger* reported that McLean "charged that Homestead politics was dominated by bootleggers and gamblers. He stated that he was dissatisfied with conditions as they existed as the clean living people had no say and he refused to take dictation from racketeers."[10] McLean not only went on to oppose his political mentor, but did so by switching to the Democratic Party. Success came to his forces at the next major election, when the Democrats took four of seven borough council seats plus all three school director positions up for election. In 1937, with the burgess position itself on the ballot, McLean overwhelmed Cavanaugh, leading a virtual Democratic takeover of the borough's politics. The night after the election, Homestead Democrats staged a mock funeral in front of the borough hall. This time there was no question who was supposed to be the corpse. There was merriment among the Democrats, and some drunkenness, too. A "slightly inebriated 'pall bearer' dropped the front end of the casket," and the man who was officiating the mock funeral implored the crowd to "Weep for your burgess, the old reactionary Republican is dead and delivered into the hands of the Democratic party."[11]

Among those who rode to victory on McLean's ticket was School Director Cumberland Posey, who had also switched parties when McLean broke with Cavanaugh in 1934, and was seeking his second term on the school board. One likely reason for Posey's switch was that the John McLean who was consolidating political power in Homestead was the same fellow Posey had coached in basketball at Homestead High in 1911, and who then had been a teammate of "Charles Cumbert" at Duquesne University a few years later. There was a longstanding personal relationship involved. It also became apparent, though, that like other McLean followers, Posey was getting fed up with the extreme corruption in the borough's government.

According to James E. Johnson, the *Baltimore Afro-American* newspaper's Pittsburgh correspondent, Posey's switch did not go over well with all politically inclined Homestead blacks because, after all, he would never have been the borough's first black school board member without Cavanaugh's help, and by defecting, Posey had "violated a principal of political trust." But, Johnson added, the younger element among the borough's blacks held the opinion that McLean, who was Cavanaugh's deputy in 1931, had done the most to ensure Posey's election, and so deserved Posey's allegiance. This version of Posey's initial try for office apparently was circulating around Homestead. The *Courier*, in a highly critical article about the Cavanaugh machine just before the 1935 election, claimed that Cavanaugh was prone to taking credit for Posey's election when talking to black audiences and blaming it on McLean when before white ones.[12]

One thing Cavanaugh clearly blamed Posey for was deserting him for McLean's organization. Johnson wrote on March 31, 1934, that the entrenched machine was "not asleep at the wheel," and particularly, "reports are floating about town that repeated raids were made on a beer garden last week in an effort to obtain a colored political leader, but the raids were to no avail." Two weeks later, Johnson identified the target as Posey, and was free to do so because Posey had, in fact, been arrested as an offshoot of a disturbance at a Homestead night club. The police were called to the downtown Manhattan Club about 3:30 a.m. on Tuesday, April 2, to quell a disturbance. They arrested several people, one of whom was Grays pitcher Joe Strong.[13]

The police returned to the club twice to keep the peace, and on their last visit, Posey approached the lieutenant in charge, Lawrence Albiez. From there the two men's stories diverged to the point that about all they later agreed upon was that the Manhattan Club and the police station were where the events occurred. Albiez's version was that Posey approached him, unsolicited, to try to get Strong released: "I told Posey to go away as I did not want to talk to him. Posey then hurled a vile name at me and I placed him under arrest, telling him he was charged with disorderly conduct." Posey was put in the police wagon and taken to the station. The acting police chief, John "Cup" Jenkins, known as Cavanaugh's enforcer in the vice-ridden areas of the lower wards, told the press that Posey had tried to "fix" Strong's case.

Posey's version was that he approached Albiez merely to find out how much Strong's bail was going to be, but Albiez "told me to get away, he did not want to talk to me." In Posey's version, it was the lieutenant who began spewing "vile names" and who arrested him right after that. Posey claimed that at the station, he was denied the arrested person's usual right to make a phone call, although Albiez said this was because post-arrest processing was still going on and that Posey eventually did make a call—to McLean. Posey also alleged that Albiez hit him on the shoulder with his blackjack, although all the police witnesses testified this did not happen. Everyone did agree that Posey then posted $50 bail and went home.

The burgess was also the police court judge in Homestead, so the case landed before Cavanaugh. It was decided before a courtroom so full of spectators that "it was impossible to move." Although he had one of his new political enemies square in his sights, Cavanaugh dismissed the disorderly case, on the grounds that the argument with Albiez had been "person to person." He also criticized the police for setting an excessive $50 bail on Posey—the ordinary bail in such a case was $15. Cavanaugh's remarks from the bench, as reported in the *Daily Messenger*, were so vague that it is difficult to tell whom he considered to have been at fault. He stated that he "had the greatest contempt for liars [one might think he meant his enemy Posey]" but he extended his contempt to "officers who do not perform their duties as they should."[14]

The *Messenger* played the story perfectly straight, not taking either side (the Pittsburgh papers barely covered the case at all). But the black *Courier* sided with Johnson of the *Afro-American*. Its front page headline read, "'Cum' Posey Framed," and it went on at length to relate his side of the story. Posey said that Lieutenant Albiez had ordered him into the sidecar of his police motorcycle after the arrest, but that he insisted on the police wagon for his own safety, telling Albiez, "you won't take me for a ride and beat me up." Posey also maintained that at the station, Albiez told him, "I am a white man and you are a nigger," apparently attempting to goad Posey into defending himself. "The arrest of Posey," the *Courier* reporter wrote, "is believed to have been the fore-runner of efforts to whip the recalcitrant politicians [who backed McLean] into line before the spring primaries." Johnson speculated in the *Afro-American* that the "humiliation" stemming from the arrest "was aimed to kill much of the Posey influence in Homestead," but any such effect seems to have been short-term at the worst.[15]

Cum Posey himself was far from intimidated in the fall of 1935, when he spotted some blacks he knew from Pittsburgh who had been driven over to register to vote in Homestead in time for the November election. He followed the carload of men, some of whom he described as ex-ballplayers, to watch them sign up to vote and then go back over to Pittsburgh. He wrote an open letter published September 5 in the *Daily Messenger*, accusing Cavanaugh's Republican machine of "all forms of intimidation and lying (which is natural to them) to offset the inroads of the Democratic Party in Homestead." He accused some Republicans of going beyond the usual bounds of political behavior in Homestead to drive a wedge between whites and blacks: "It is very hard to see how the white people and colored people with an ounce of brains cannot see how one is being played against the other."

Specifically, he said GOP operatives would go door to door to tell whites that equal rights legislation favored by Democrats "will permit Negroes to socialize with white people," and "then go to Negroes homes and tell them the Democratic Party voted against the Anti-Lynching bill." Like much political propaganda, these claims were not without some underlying general truth, but without specific relevance. Expansion of government-supported individual rights would probably lead to more social mixing of the races, but only if the private parties agreed to do so. Southern Democrats in Congress did work hard to kill anti-lynching legislation, but this had little or nothing to do with Pittsburgh. But so far as Posey was concerned, the Homestead machine's claims were "damnable lies."

A threat closer to home for Posey was an infiltration by the Republicans of the ever-stronger Democratic school board slate of candidates. Posey alleged that Cavanaugh's machine had persuaded King Taylor, an African American Republican Posey alleged was the brother of a man who ran a "moonshine joint," to switch his registration and run as a Democrat for an open school director seat (not Posey's, who did not run again until 1937) to dilute the chances of Posey's actual Democratic colleagues. Anyone had the right to run for office, Posey admitted, but "no man has a right to allow himself to become the tool of selfish unscrupulous small time ward heelers and grafters in an effort to discredit the entire colored population of Homestead."[16]

Six days after Posey's letter ran in the *Daily Messenger*, Taylor's brother George confronted Posey while he was standing outside the Grays office at 508 Dickson Street. "I've been looking for you for nearly a week," George

Taylor began, and an argument between the two over the letter about King Taylor ensued. Posey stood his ground on his opinion that King was being used as a tool of the Republicans, and he turned his back to head for his office. Then, as the *Courier* reported, "Taylor grabbed him, swung him around and struck Posey behind the right ear." Abraham Dorsey, who had been standing nearby, pushed Taylor away, but Taylor still managed to land another punch, this time under Posey's right eye. The fracas ended when two municipal firemen rushed in and, operating outside their authority, arrested both Taylor and Posey.[17] Nothing seems to have come of the arrest, and King Taylor's candidacy did nothing to retard the takeover of Homestead by the Democrats in 1935 and 1937.

The Manhattan Club and Dickson Street incidents, while ugly, took place among adults defending their respective political fiefdoms. But between the two there was another case, involving a young Homestead black man, which incensed both the borough's Democrats and its African American community in general. James Chapman, a 23-year-old member of an established local African American family, had been identified by the borough's police the previous August as being "the colored man who has terrorized women of the Homestead district for five weeks."[18] The actual case against him, though, seems to have consisted of only a single incident on August 11, 1934, when a black man crawled through a second-story bedroom window and attempted a sexual assault on 23-year-old Helen Sullivan before fleeing. The case went to trial in the Allegheny Common Pleas Court over in Pittsburgh in late January.

So far as the evidence from the scene of the crime, Chapman's attorney pointed out a number of inconsistencies. Miss Sullivan's description of her assailant and the clothes he was wearing did not resemble Chapman or any garb he owned. The Homestead police, with the notorious "Cup" Jenkins leading the investigation, presented only Chapman to the victim for identification, and a friend of hers testified that "she had admitted to him that she was uncertain as to Chapman's identity." The all-white jury quickly acquitted Chapman. The direction and speed of its deliberations may have been assisted in great part, though, by the trial judge, Michael A. Musmanno.

After the evidence is completed in a criminal trial, the judge is required to brief the jurors on the specifics of the law which they are about to decide has been broken or not. Musmanno went beyond that. "We feel it is our duty to state we have some doubt as to whether the identification of Chapman by Miss Sullivan as the guilty man is reliable," he reportedly told the jury. "He also hinted the 'psychological reaction' which might have caused Miss Sullivan, by constant repetition, to actually believe that Chapman was the man who had attacked her," the *Courier*'s account added. Armed with the facts and the judge's skepticism, the jury returned in 20 minutes with its not-guilty verdict.[19]

Musmanno apparently did not comment on the defense's other main line of attack, that Chapman's arrest and trial was the Homestead machine's way of getting back at his uncle, Abraham T. Dorsey, for switching his allegiance to the McLean Democrats. Chapman's lawyer, Joseph Passafiume, told the jury, "Jenkins has been on the police force in Homestead for 14 years. He runs that town. I say he knows every colored fellow who has been in Homestead six months. If he had had a proper description [of the assailant], he would have got that boy the first night. These officers are shooting at Abe Dorsey, Chapman's uncle, because he is the acknowledged leader of a political faction in the borough. That's who they're slapping at."[20]

Dorsey, a steelworker, was a neighbor of Posey's, the same man who tried to stop the assault on Posey by George Taylor seven months later on Dickson Street. He gave the *Courier* a lengthy statement after the trial that plumbed the depths of the disgust he had for Jenkins, and Jenkins for him. He said he left the Cavanaugh ranks

> Because of the change in complex [*sic*] that was shown by the organization when it allowed 'Cup' Jenkins to ruthlessly maltreat citizens of Homestead.... Jenkins was belittled by remarks made by me on the witness stand. So shaken was he that he told me to lay off him that he had too much money for me to beat him. It would be wise policy for Jenkins to curb his remarks regarding his money, for it is universally acknowledged that money is less honorable than virtue.[21]

Judge Musmanno's charge to the jury was typical of his view of jurisprudence—he was outspoken and known to back the underdog. He had volunteered for the defense of Sacco and Vanzetti in the 1920s, and forever considered them to have been innocent of the murder and robbery charges that led to their execution in Massachusetts. As a state legislator, he led the eventually successful fight to abolish private coal and iron police forces, known to resort to violence on the mining companies' behalf during labor disputes. Before his death in 1968, he had ascended to the Pennsylvania Supreme Court. Like Posey, Dorsey, McLean, and so many others, he had left the Republican Party to join the Democrats.

Several people testified at Chapman's trial as character witnesses, and Posey was one of them. His regular sports column in the *Courier* on February 2, 1935, opened with commentary on the trial just completed. Although he certainly shared Dorsey's opinion of Jenkins and the political machine, Posey instead devoted his column space to praise the judge: "The writer was a character witness for a boy in Homestead the past week. The charge against the boy was of a very serious nature and was preferred by a young lady of the opposite race. Despite any preponderance of evidence in favor of a defendant in cases of this kind, the usual verdict is guilty." But noting the not-guilty verdict, Posey singled out Musmanno's final words to the jury: "There are far too many cases in which a white woman accuses a colored man of rape wherein the jury, without due deliberation of the evidence, and with that prejudice that lies in their heart, will bring in a verdict of guilty with the thought in their minds, if he did not do it he would have done it if he had a chance. This, ladies and gentlemen, is the same as stringing a man to a tree and is legal lynching."

"This writer," Posey concluded, "is happy and proud to say that he was one of the many who parted from the strong Republican Organization's candidates for judges in 1933 and worked for the success of the candidacy of Judge Musmanno."[22]

In carrying out his school board duties, Posey was ever aware of his special position as a black man with some governmental influence, and more than once specifically stood up for his race. There were relatively small issues, such as when he joined with two black ministers to urge the school board to make an exception for a black youth basketball team to a blanket ban on outside groups using the high school gymnasium. The team should get to use the gym because, as one of the pastors explained, "every other place in the district is closed to us." At a 1945 gathering of Democratic candidates, Posey went on record as urging a county court judge to appoint a Negro bailiff, to provide a highly visible government job to a black man.[23]

In his multiple roles as school board member, owner of popular sports teams, and scion of a well-known local family, Posey had no trouble gathering local intelligence, and, at the *Courier*, he had the means to disclose it. He broke off his sports commentary in one of his 1938 columns to compliment Homestead Police Chief Thomas Conlon for his support of the borough's Depression-ridden black community: "Conlon took a one arm colored man into the relief office in Homestead and told the whole office force if they didn't quit investigating these colored people for three and four weeks while they are hungry he would go direct to the Governor and have the whole force removed."[24]

Posey was involved in the major reshaping of Homestead in the lead-up to World War II. In June 1941, the Homestead steel works were chosen for a $75 million U.S. government-financed expansion that would make the mill the largest provider of steel to the Navy's ship-building program. The program promised to boom the borough's economy, but the new industrial buildings had to be built somewhere. That place was the low-rent housing area near the mills, the lower wards below Eighth Avenue, which were virtually wiped out. In six months, 8,000 residents and many businesses (including Rufus Jackson's club) were relocated. The rush to clear space for the steelworks expansion (which events on December 7 proved was more urgently needed than the government planners had thought) emphasized the fast expansion of the works over consideration for the residents about to be displaced. The relocation affected the many racial and ethnic groups that lived in the lower wards, and African Americans were no exception. The *Courier* estimated that 5,000 of them would be forced to move.[25]

Nearly 1,400 buildings of all types were torn down in a matter of months, even while newcomers were migrating to the Pittsburgh area as all of the area's industries increased production. Housing was at a premium. A black mill worker's reaction, as quoted in the *Post-Gazette* in early July, was typical of the residents' early reactions: "Where am I gona go? That's what I'd like to know. Maybe I should go across the river and build a shanty." The black community had a mass meeting and appointed a committee of its religious, business, and government leaders to make sure its opinions would be heard. Posey was one of the members (as was Jackson). In the end, the dislocated found housing, but many had to leave Homestead to do so, heading for new and existing government housing in adjacent communities.[26]

As Posey took care of Homestead when the need arose, in the end Homestead also took care of him. He had health problems late in his life, beginning with a major operation in 1940, and an increasingly severe illness beginning in 1945 that was diagnosed as cancer in 1946. As early as 1940, Burgess McLean's administration appointed him as the borough's "ordinance officer," in charge of enforcing the many building, housing, and other municipal codes that regulated the day-to-day details of urban life. It's not clear how much Posey was paid, but his successor in 1946 started at a salary of $2,700 a year, an amount equal to $57,000 in contemporary purchasing power. Posey was, of course, also busy running the Grays and being a Negro National League official at the time. His grand-nephew Evan P. Baker, Jr., who as a youngster hung around the team a great deal, said much later he thought the municipal job was McLean's way of subsidizing the team run by his longtime good friend and supporter.[27]

Posey also had a social life among the elite of the Pittsburgh African Americans. He followed his father as a member of the prestigious Loendi Club in Pittsburgh, although, unlike the Captain, he seems not to have become an officer. He was a member of the Loendi billiards team, though, and won the championship for his club when his "steady, consistent fours and fives" were too much for his opponent from the black YMCA.[28] Posey also belonged, along with other Loendi members, including publisher Robert Vann and editor Ira Lewis of the *Courier*, to an even more exclusive black men's club, the

FROGS. The name was an acronym for "Friendly Rivalry Often Generates Success." The group in Posey's time was limited to only about two dozen select regular members, but it threw an annual "Frogs Week" of parties and other celebrations that was the social highlight of the black community.

He also belonged to the Improved Benevolent and Protective Order of the Elks of the World, the African American wing of the Elks fraternal organization which had been founded in 1898 for blacks who wanted to belong to this prestigious social group but, of course, were barred from the dominant white Elks lodges. In the early 1940s, Posey was the organization's national commissioner of athletics. He organized several Elks' Days at Negro League doubleheaders, including some at the choice Yankee Stadium location, with the multiple goals of providing entertainment for members and publicity for the organization, as well as raising funds for the IBPOEW. In 1942, he organized an Elks national basketball tournament at Harlem's Renaissance Casino, the home of the Rens, the team run by his old hoop rival, Bob Douglas, which now dominated black professional basketball. The quality of play was high. There were few restrictions on the players black Elks lodges could put on their teams—they had to be dues-paying members, and they could not have been members of the Rens or the Harlem Globetrotters, the two top black pro teams, within the past five years.[29]

What with the Grays, his Negro National League leadership role, Homestead politics and government, and the Elks, Posey was away from home quite a bit. "When he was home," his daughter Beatrice recalled, "he was the head of the household." When he was away, that role fell to his wife, Ethel. "I admired my mom for keeping things going. She was a strong woman," Beatrice added.[30] Ethel not only had a major role in raising four girls, all of whom went on to attend either college or nursing school, she also stepped into Anna Stevens Posey's shoes as a social leader in the Pittsburgh black community. Not only did Ethel carry out the woman's role in the Posey family, after her husband's death she took over Cum's duties in Homestead and, to some extent, with the Grays.

Cum Posey was halfway through his third six-year term as a Homestead school director when he died in the spring of 1946. Without missing a beat, the rest of the board members elected Ethel to finish out his term. Elected by the Homestead voters again and again, she served for 23 years. After her husband's death, supported by the Allegheny County Democratic organization, she went to work as a clerk in the county courts.

Longtime Pittsburgh black journalist Frank Bolden recalled Mrs. Posey as "very supportive of everything her husband did" with the Grays. In addition to allowing the Posey home to function in part as a boarding house for members of the team, "she mothered the young players and got them adjusted to urban living, introducing them to quality people in Homestead and Pittsburgh until they could be on their own."[31] But when Cum died, she inherited his half-ownership of the Grays, although Sonnyman Jackson and See Posey actually ran the team.

Beatrice Lee recalled that baseball was ingrained into the entire family's existence. The girls spent a lot time watching the Grays play; "Other children went to picnics on the Fourth of July—I was at the ball park."[32] But the value Cum and Ethel placed on education sent the girls as adults away from Homestead after high school, into a considerably wider world than could be seen from up the hill on 13th Avenue. Their early adulthood was a time when blacks were emboldened to stand up for their rights, and then to reap the benefits. The Posey daughters took part in both the striving and the reaping.

The oldest daughter, mother Ethel's namesake, the one daughter who did not attend college, was in nursing school at Mercy Hospital in Philadelphia at age 21 in 1935 when she, the hospital's nursing supervisor, and a young physician went to court to complain that a movie theater in the city had forced them into segregated seating, a crime according to a recently passed state civil rights law. The case went to trial in April 1936, with only the nursing supervisor and doctor as the complainants. It was the first prosecution under the new law, and the defendants, the theater manager and his assistant were found not guilty. Ethel had apparently withdrawn from the case, quite possibly because by then she had moved back to Homestead. She and the Grays' ace pitcher, Raymond Brown, were married in June of 1937.

Daughter Ethel's second husband, J. Louis Maddox, was well known in The Hill District as an aide to visiting black musicians, chauffeuring them from their hotels to the spots where they would be playing, and then taking care of them after their shows. "I knew all the good restaurants in the Hill and I took them there after the last performance. It was also Prohibition and I knew all the drugstores where I cold hustle some gin," Maddox told a *Pittsburgh Press* writer in 1982 covering Lou's reunion with Count Basie, who was in the city for a performance. Maddox himself wrote a book about that period, *Jazz and the Era of Swing*.[33]

The Poseys' second daughter, Mary Elizabeth, born in 1915, married a local man, Oliver C. Palmer, in September 1940. But she filed for divorce by the following March. The divorce wasn't granted until 1946, though, possibly because Palmer, a radio repairman in civilian life, was serving as a shipboard radioman on the Liberty Ship S.S. Fitzhugh Lee in the Merchant Marine during World War II.[34]

Mary's second marriage in 1947 took her to New York City and into a different world. Her husband was Lewis Sparkman Flagg III, the son of a prominent Brooklyn lawyer. Louis S. Flagg, Jr., was active in Democratic politics and in 1954 became the first black judge in the Municipal Court in Brooklyn. He did so by entering the previous fall's election campaign against the white choice of the Brooklyn Democratic machine, defeating him in the primary election with the backing of a strong grass roots organization that included future congresswoman Shirley H. Chisholm.[35]

Louis Flagg III also became a lawyer and carried on the family's barrier-breaking tradition. After active duty in Europe during World War II, he joined the National Guard and eventually retired as a major. He practiced law in Brooklyn, including stints with the district attorney's and U.S. attorney's offices there. In 1962, he was appointed as a lawyer in the Interior Department in Washington, D.C. He and Mary lived there for the rest of their lives (due to his military career, both are buried in Arlington National Cemetery), where she graduated from Howard University with honors in 1973, at age 58.

Three of the five women of the Posey family take in a game at Griffith Stadium in Washington, D.C., during the Grays' pennant-winning years. Left to right, front row: Cum's wife Ethel, daughters Ann and Mary (NoirTech Research, Inc.).

The youngest daughter, Beatrice Kathleen (usually known by her nickname, "Bumps"), born in 1921, went to college at Duquesne, but left during her sophomore year to work in Washington for the Department of the Navy as a stenographer. While in Washington, she enrolled in Howard University, and she graduated in 1945. She moved to New York City to do post-graduate work at the City College of New York and became a social worker for the school department's attendance program, specializing in home visits to families. In 1946, she married attorney John Howard Boxill, nephew of the legendary Rev. John Howard Johnson, longtime pastor of St. Martin's Episcopal Church in Harlem. In 1963, she married Lemuel Lee, Jr. She was active in women's social and community groups and vacationed (with the Flaggs) in the historic upper class black community in Oak Bluffs on Martha's Vineyard. In the 1970s, she joined, and was a New York chapter officer, of the Coalition of 100 Black Women, a now-national volunteer organization promoting equality for the black race and its female members. After retiring in New York, Beatrice moved to Atlanta to live with her daughter, Nancy Boxill, and continued her volunteer work for Cascade House, a shelter for homeless women and children.[36]

The third daughter, Anna (Ann), born in 1917, also went away to school, at Kentucky State College in Frankfort. Although integrated as a university today, it was a black college when she attended for three years through 1941. She returned to Homestead in 1941 to work in the county treasurer's office (hired by John McLean, who held that post in addition to Homestead burgess) and finish her education locally. But she didn't stay long. According to a *Courier* social column that December, she had "eloped!" back to Kentucky to marry Alex C. Harper of Lexington. She returned to live with Harper at the Posey home on 13th Avenue, and like her mother and sisters, she was active in black Pittsburgh society. But she died on January 21, 1945, at age 27, after being hospitalized for a severe internal infection.[37]

In a long "Wylie Avenue" column devoted to Posey after his death in 1946, the perspicacious John Clark summed up Cum Posey's relationships with his family: "Of his parents, he liked his mother best. She was cultured in the arts, devoted to her family, had high aspirations. He loved his wife, because she was a fine woman, understood him, and did such an excellent job in rearing his four daughters. And he was proud of his daughters."[38]

Chapter Eight

The Championship Years

Early in the 1938 season, Wendell Smith of the *Pittsburgh Courier* described the defending Negro National League champion Homestead Grays as "The New Gas House Gang," the Negro Leagues' equivalent of the aggressive, rowdy, and highly talented group of St. Louis Cardinals who had excelled in the white majors only a few years before, winning the 1934 World Series. Smith wrote that the Grays "play the game for all they can get out of it. Every ball game is palyed [*sic*] as though it meant the difference between life and death. They ask for nothing and give nothing in return." Cum Posey took a little unwarranted offense at the analogy. He responded in his own *Courier* column a week later that "Perhaps Homestead Grays are an arrogant, ungrateful, 'Gas House Gang.'" But he added, in a much more Posey-like frame of mind, "We never heard of any club winning pennants by patting the opposition on the back."[1]

However the Grays of the mid–1930s until the end of World War II might have been labeled, they were the best team in the NNL and the most consistent winner in all of black major league ball. Beginning with the 1937 season, when they finished climbing out of the hole dug by the combination of their own poor finances and Pittsburgh rival Gus Greenlee's riches, the Grays won nine straight NNL pennants, depending upon how one views 1939, when they won both halves of the league's split season, but lost to the Baltimore Elite Giants in a playoff championship held in lieu of an interleague World Series. With See Posey scouting for new talent, Rufus Jackson bankrolling salaries, and Cum Posey pulling it all together, the Grays in short order became a juggernaut, with a stable lineup and starting rotation disrupted to any great extent only by the loss of players to the military and defense industry work during World War II and the continued blandishments of Latin American leagues luring away talent. But these were problems that all Negro Leagues teams had to face.

One advantage that the Negro Leagues had during the war was prosperity. The black leagues profited from a set of circumstances created by the worldwide hostilities that had a negative effect on the rest of professional baseball. The white majors suffered a decline in attendance of more than 20 percent between the 1941 season through 1943, although attendance began rising again in 1944. The minor leagues, though, were severely impacted, mostly by the loss of talent to the war effort. Organized baseball had 41 leagues in 1941, but only a dozen or fewer during any of the war years.[2]

But despite losing dozens of players to the war effort, the home front economic boost from the massive productivity surge needed to keep soldiers, sailors, and flyers supplied and supported made the war years the most profitable ever for the Negro Leagues. For example, in the vicinity of Newark, New Jersey, an NNL city, shipbuilding boomed along the Hudson River, and the little Federal Telephone & Radio company had 11,500 people at work in 44 locations by war's end. The Newark airport was turned over the military as the landing place for flights of new airplanes to be loaded onto ships at Port Newark for shipment overseas. The Prudential Insurance Company had just built a new 20-story headquarters downtown, but its first occupants were 10,000 government workers processing the allotments taken out of service members' pay to be sent home to their families.[3] After subtracting all the working-age men who went into the Army, Navy, and Marines, there weren't enough workers in the North to fill all the new jobs. This triggered a second twentieth-century migration of African Americans from the South, following the one that had sent defense workers north during World War I.

Black ball historian Neal Lanctot summed up the cause and effect of the period on the Negro Leagues:

> Between 1940 and 1944, the number of black unemployed had dropped from 937,562 to about 151,000 while the percentage in war industries more than doubled from less than 3 percent to 8.3 percent. By September 1944, about 1.5 million blacks were employed in war industries, concentrated heavily in league cities.... The heavy war employment also stimulated a continued heavy migration to major urban centers, providing both leagues with thousands of new customers eager for entertainment.[4]

While the black population grew in cities such as Newark, Chicago, Philadelphia, and Pittsburgh, at the same time government rationing of gasoline and automobile tires curtailed everyone's entertainment-seeking travels. So the base of fans for big league black baseball grew, while at the same time they became something of a "captive audience" for the Negro Leagues. While never abandoning their Pittsburgh fan base, Posey and Jackson seized upon these events to lead the Grays to play before one of the fastest-growing and most baseball-conscious black populations in the country, in Washington, D.C., and combined championship play with booming attendance and profits.

The squad that had won the 1937 pennant mostly stayed together for the Grays' long pennant run, at least until the war started to deplete the ranks.

Josh Gibson was the regular catcher and star home run threat, except for the 1940 and '41 seasons, when he defected to the Mexican League. (Rufus Jackson could not always outspend Latin owners bent on acquiring top talent). Buck Leonard never went anywhere, except out to first base, where his fielding was highly regarded, and up to home plate, where he was a feared left-handed slugger, always making these appearances in a Grays uniform. After his initial professional year with the independent Brooklyn Royal Giants, Leonard never played for any other Negro League team than the Grays, from 1934 through 1950, when the franchise disbanded as the black leagues were gradually going out of business. The seasons he was teamed with Gibson provided the Grays a monumental one-two punch in the middle of the batting order. As James A. Riley put it, "While Gibson was slugging tape-measure home runs, Leonard was hitting screaming line drives both off the walls and over the walls."[5]

Leonard's abilities were appreciated by Negro Leagues opponents and by black ball's fans. The annual East-West All-Star Game held in Chicago's Comiskey Park was the biggest single event of any Negro Leagues season, much bigger than the Negro World Series. The players were picked by the fans, voting by way of printed ballots clipped from the major black weekly papers. Leonard made his first appearance in the East-West classic as a reserve in 1935, and he was back as a starter nine times from 1937 through 1946, missing the game only in 1942, when his season was interrupted by a broken hand. With a final appearance in 1948, he had appeared in the game 11 times, more than any other Negro Leaguer. In 1944, Posey picked an all-time all-star team for the Negro Baseball Yearbook, and he put Leonard at first base, "because he is one of the steadiest and most dependable ball players of any age and because he is the master fielder and for the greater portion of his career, has been the most terrific hitting star ever to work on any infield."[6]

Ray Brown, Posey's ace starter, was also a constant presence in the Grays' rotation from 1933 through '45 (although he did spend the greater part of the 1939 season in the Mexican League following the contract dispute with Posey during which Brown unilaterally shopped his services to the Newark Eagles).[7] Brown was not only a reliable, key player in the Grays' success, in 2006 he (along with his boss and father-in-law, Cumberland Posey, Jr.) joined Gibson and Leonard as a member of the National Baseball Hall of Fame.

Gibson had gone to play in Latin America during the winter of 1939–40, first with a Negro League all-star team for six games in Cuba, then to the Santurce club of the Puerto Rican winter league. Posey and the Grays expected him back, but instead he went to Venezuela for the summer, in the early days of an eventually successful campaign to establish professional ball there. Gibson went for a salary of $700 a month and travel and living expenses, plus a

Ray Brown, trotting home after hitting a homer, was the ace of the Homestead pitching staff for years and doubled as a good-hitting outfielder when he wasn't on the mound. One of the Grays who roomed with the Posey family during the season, he wound up marrying Posey's daughter, Ethel (NoirTech Research, Inc.).

$1,000 signing bonus, considerably better than he could get in the Negro Leagues, even from the Grays. His Venezuelan summer proved to be shorter than expected—the country's league failed to finish the season, and he wound up playing and starring for Vera Cruz in the Mexican League. He was far from alone. Wendell Smith of the *Courier* wrote in the spring of 1941 that "the last time I checked there were at least 25 ball players who once romped in the Negro National League now cavorting in the Mexican League."[8]

The Grays' star catcher was expected to return to them in the spring of 1941. Posey and Jackson had gone so far among NNL owners as to favor little or no punishment for contract jumpers from 1940, trying to clear the way for his return. Gibson actually signed a contract with Homestead, but then didn't report—the $500 a month the Grays would pay him for six months in the U.S. paled in comparison to the $800 a month (for eight months) he could get to return to Vera Cruz. This time Posey and Jackson were not so supportive. They went to the Allegheny County Court of Common Pleas and sued Gibson for $10,000. Gibson, playing dynamite ball in sunny Mexico, failed to show up and defend himself in court, and the Grays were declared the winners by default. As compensation, the team was awarded title to Gibson's house in Pittsburgh (not likely worth $10,000, but enough of an asset to make the suit appear successful).

But the court's decision notwithstanding, the dispute between Gibson and the Grays was really a standoff. As William Brashler, a Gibson biographer, puts it, the suit "failed in its primary goal, to get Josh back with the Grays, and Posey, being a far from a malicious, vindictive, man, had little interest in taking Gibson's home in Pittsburgh away from him." Gibson's two children from his first marriage were living with his late wife's relatives, and he himself was spending most of his time out of the country, so the seizure of the property had little effect on him. As Brashler puts it, "Posey knew it and let the prosecution ride until he could think of a better way to get his star attraction back." The outpouring of attendance and profits for Negro League teams during the war solved Posey's problem. He could soon afford to pay Gibson more than $1,000 a month (and give him back his house) as salaries all over the black leagues skyrocketed, and Gibson, along with other Negro Leaguers who had gone south, returned home.[9]

Anyway, the last thing the Grays management needed was an empty house. What they really required was a catcher. The headline on the April 5 *Courier* story reporting the team's departure for spring training in Orlando, Florida, was about manager Vic Harris's chief challenge once the team got settled down South: "Harris Seeking Veteran Catcher." Other candidates were tried, but the primary receiver for 1941 was the same guy who had held the position the year before, Gibson's understudy, Robert "Rab Roy" Gaston, who hit .218 in 1940 and .250 in 1941 as the starter.

(Since the Negro Leagues and independent black teams often did not keep reliable player statistics, and since newspaper coverage of games was spotty in some locales, assembling a complete set of individual season numbers has been a task carried out by black baseball historians for years. The most complete data today can be found at the www.Seamheads.com website, a wide-ranging Internet repository for current baseball news and historical material that includes a Negro Leagues Database. The data includes box score information from many games between Negro League teams and with major independent squads. While in some seasons, available box scores and game stories are spotty, Seamheads has a high percentage of games for the 1938–45 period covered in this chapter, providing a sample size that can be used for evaluation of the individual Grays during the pennant-winning years.)

Gaston's low output notwithstanding, the Grays were so loaded with talent that they could well afford to start a journeyman catcher for a couple of years. Seamheads' career stats for Leonard in league play from 1937 through 1945, the span of the Grays' nine-year pennant run, show him hitting .350, with a .607 slugging percentage. Gibson did even better, hitting .386 and slugging .743 in the seven pennant-winning years he was around.

Vic Harris was the regular left fielder until the war, when he got a job in a defense plant, relinquished his managerial position to veteran Jim Taylor, and played only part-time on weekends. By 1945, when he resumed the managerial reins, he was 40 years old and well past his prime as a player. But he was ever a dependable member of the Grays, and he hit .296 during the pennant run. Most of the time he played alongside perhaps the most underrated regular on the team. Jerry Benjamin had come to the Grays in 1935. He was a fixture in the outfield for most of the rest of its existence, a good hitter and fielder, and a superior base stealer. He owned center field, except during the 1939 season, when he jumped the club in July, but not for an exotic location such as Mexico or Venezuela.

Instead, he showed up in Toledo, Ohio, playing for the Crawfords, the organization that had been Gus Greenlee's Pittsburgh powerhouse, now barely hanging on under different ownership in the rival Negro American League. Although Benjamin's cover was thin and soon blown, he did appear to have tried to disguise his presence on the Toledo roster by using the last name of Christopher. It's not fully clear why Benjamin left the Grays, although Posey had tried to trade him to Newark for star third baseman Ray Dandridge, and Riley states that Benjamin had not wanted to report there. Posey leaped upon the information, published in a St. Louis newspaper, that Benjamin was hiding in plain sight in center field in Toledo. He filed a complaint with American League president Major R. R. Jackson, maintaining that Toledo had broken the anti-raiding pact between the two black major leagues. (Since the Negro Leagues needed, but never did get, an independent commissioner overseeing all of its professional baseball, these cooperative pacts were necessary to maintain peace.) Former Grays star and manager Oscar Charleston, now managing Toledo, shrugged and said he had a guy named Christopher, not Benjamin, and the NAL officials took his word for it. "We cannot see how the American League club owners can hope for continued peace between the two leagues when they shut their eyes to an open and shut case such as this one," Posey fumed in his *Courier* column at the end of the season.[10]

It was never wise for club owners to cross Posey by signing one of his players. No one knew the ins and outs of acquiring someone else's talent better than Posey, and Benjamin was back with the Grays uniform in 1940. It's hard to imagine Posey being anxious to trade Benjamin, although Dandridge, an eventual Hall of Famer, would have been an outstanding acquisition. At any rate, Benjamin usually hit over or near .300, and he had a batting average of .307 during the pennant years.

Posey's ire over the temporary loss of Benjamin was balanced by the distress he caused other owners when important players from their rosters suddenly became Grays. The pennant skein began with a return appearance in right field by Jim Williams, one of the Detroit players whose signing by Posey in 1933 had gotten the unrepentant Grays kicked out of the NNL in its first year. The controversy that had surrounded Williams' initial tour with Homestead was old news when he was traded to the Toledo Crawfords in 1939. But the circumstances surrounding his replacement, David Whatley, stirred up acrimony all over again.

Whatley, a speedy runner and a high-average, although not powerful hitter, had played for the Birmingham Black Barons of the Negro American League in 1938, but was signed by See Posey to a Homestead contract during training in Florida the following spring. It's not entirely clear if Whatley was still bound to the Black Barons, but so far as Cum Posey was concerned, his signing was a "reprisal" against the NAL for its Chicago American Giants signing one of his players in 1937, then making matters worse by not refunding to the Grays advance salary Posey had fronted the man.[11] Whatley gave way in 1943 to a somewhat motley combination of right fielders (Harris when he wasn't working, Ray Brown when he wasn't pitching, and even Gibson once in a while). But in 1944, the Grays acquired 18-year-old Dave Hoskins, who hit .328 that year and .272 the following season as the regular right fielder. Hoskins was also a good pitcher, a frequent starter for the Grays. He was young enough to still be in his prime when white professional baseball integrated in 1946, and he crossed the old color barrier in 1949. He made it up to the Cleveland Indians in 1953 after going 22–10 in the Texas League, and he went 9–3 with a 3.99 earned run average that year, the first of two he spent in the majors before settling into a role as a top-level minor leaguer.

The loss of Harris as a full-time outfielder created an opening in left, and Posey filled it with one of the best men ever to play Negro Leagues ball, even though he was already 40 years old when he signed in 1943. James "Cool Papa" Bell, an eventual Hall of Famer, had played for both of Posey's teams, the Detroit Wolves and the Grays, in the failed East-West League in 1932, then jumped to Greenlee's Crawfords through 1938, when he began playing primarily in Latin America. Bell, a superlative center fielder in his prime, was pushed over to left by the presence of Jerry Benjamin, but filled the position well from 1943 to '45, batting .355, .322, and .299.

His arrival didn't come without controversy, as he was one of seven players the Grays, Philadelphia Stars, and New York Black Yankees were accused of pirating from the NAL. The two league presidents, J. B. Martin of the NAL and Tom Wilson of the NNL, reached an agreement that ordered the return of all the players to their original clubs, but Posey fought back bitterly. First, he claimed that Bell, who had returned from the Mexican League to play for the Chicago American Giants in the NAL in 1942, had been there only because Wilson had claimed the rights to him for his Baltimore Elite Giants, then had released him to Chicago on approval of Bell's last Negro Leagues employer, Gus Greenlee of the Crawfords. Posey claimed that he had contacted Greenlee, who denied any such arrangement. Posey then delved into several disputes between the two leagues, cloaking his actions in the argument that the NAL had broken the "peace treaty" between the leagues so many times that it ought to be dissolved. His argument was successful. The Grays were allowed to keep Bell, although other disputed transactions were reversed. This earned him criticism from Wendell Smith about his "holier than thou" attitude, but it undoubtedly mattered much more to Cum Posey that he got to keep Cool Papa.[12]

In the infield, while Leonard was always at first base, there was significant turnover, especially as the war loomed over the horizon. The keystone combination from the late 1930s, Jelly Jackson at shortstop and Matt Carlisle at second, remained intact until 1941, when Jackson decided to remain at home in Washington, D.C., to work in a defense industry. "It may be one of those work or fight propositions," Posey opined in his column.[13] Jackson was back in 1944 and '45, though, when the team was playing many games in his home town, this time as the regular second baseman. Carlisle was the regular second sacker through 1942, but as his batting average dropped into the low .200s, he was pushed out of the starting lineup. Carlisle lost his starting spot to Howard Easterling, a rising star whom Riley describes as "a complete ballplayer."[14] Easterling joined the Grays as their regular third baseman in 1940 and hit over .300 in three of the four seasons he played with the club. He was drafted in 1944, however, and didn't get back to the Grays until the war was over.

The major infield addition during the nine-year pennant run was Sam Bankhead, who came to the Grays in his prime in 1939 at age 28 after starring for the late Crawfords team. He was anticipated by management to be a long-term anchor for the infield. In five seasons for Homestead, Bankhead hit .275 with some power and good speed on the bases, but his great talent was in the field. He could play almost anywhere and reputedly had a cannon for a throwing arm. As Riley sums him up, "He was a player's player," and clearly a fan favorite too, being voted to seven East-West All-Star lineups. There was only one drawback so far as the Grays were concerned—Bankhead was Josh Gibson's closest friend, and he went with Gibson to the Mexican League for the 1940 and '41 seasons, returning to the Grays when Gibson did. Bankhead did not get sued—he may not have signed a contract with Posey and Jackson for either of those seasons, and he didn't own a house they could go after, since he and his family were renters.[15]

With new young players to fill out rosters at a premium at all levels of professional baseball during the war, the Grays, like other teams, reached back into the past to recruit role players. As in the case of Bell, Posey went back in Grays history to 1932, the year of the troubled East-West League, for his wartime replacements. Cool Papa, in fact, was a relative spring chicken compared to a couple of returned infielders. Jud Wilson was 44 years old when he returned in 1940. Wilson, another eventual Hall of Famer who played for the Grays, primarily filled in at third base, although his presence was very important in 1942, when he took over first base while Leonard was recuperating from a broken hand. Jud Wilson suffered from epilepsy, which was sometimes apparent when he was on the field. At bat, though, he continued to hit hard, with a .302 Seamheads average and some extra-base power during his last stint with Homestead. To further back up the infield in 1944, Posey reached back for 42-year-old Walter "Rev" Cannady, who like Bell and Wilson had last played for him in 1932. Cannady was only a year away from the end of his Negro League career, but he went out in style, hitting .328 as a Grays reserve.

Ray Brown was the winning pitcher in 35 percent of the Grays games from 1937 through 1945 in which Seamheads is able to credit the pitching win. His season total included 10 or more wins in six of the nine seasons, and a 16-2 record in 1940, when he was 32. Seamheads credits him with a 2.87 ERA during that period. Edsall Walker is credited with 47 wins, almost 20 percent of the nine-year total. More to the point, he got almost 30 percent of the wins that Brown didn't earn. Although they had help, year in and year out, the two of them were the mainstay of the Grays' rotation against Negro League and other top competition. They started regularly and relieved when necessary. Walker once recalled pitching five times in eight days, as a starter and from the bullpen.[16]

Roy Welmaker, the left-hander from Clark University in Atlanta who had joined the Grays in 1936 with Walker, was a reliable starter, missing only two years of the pennant run when he went to play in Mexico with Gibson, Bankhead, and so many other Negro Leaguers. Roy Partlow, another lefty, joined the Grays in 1938 and spent the best years of his career in the rotation. Like Brown and many other Homestead pitchers, he could hit, too.

Valuable hurlers who spent only a part of the 1937–1945 run on the mound for the Grays included Hoskins, the regular right fielder in 1944 and '45, who Seamheads records as having had a 5–2 won-lost record and a 3.60 ERA in 1944, and J. C. Hamilton, a lefty who was a good pitcher, but was best known in his day for his golf game. Hamilton was good enough to play in amateur tournaments, and he reportedly could hit tee shots that approached 400 yards.[17]

Eighteen-year Negro Leagues veteran right-hander Ernest "Spoon" Carter spent four seasons with the Grays and is credited with a 14–2 record in 1943. Another veteran, Terrence McDuffie, was only with the team for a single season, 1941, but went 9–3, the second-best record after the ace, Brown. McDuffie, a self-promoter who acquired the nickname "The Great," was described by Max Manning, a Newark Eagles teammate later on, as a man "who believed he could do anything in the world and would tell you that, too."[18] McDuffie came to the Grays in a trade that could perhaps only have happened in the Negro Leagues, particularly during the Latin American player raids just before World War II. Posey acquired his contract from the New York Black Yankees before the 1940 season in a five-player trade, but didn't get the great one's services until a year later, when McDuffie returned from a sojourn in the Mexican League.

The potentially best Grays hurler of the pennant years had a brief career with the team due to the war and then to professional baseball integration. John Wright, a native of New Orleans, joined the team in 1941 and pitched well, but blossomed in 1943, when he went 18–3 with a 2.54 ERA. But then he entered the Navy, where he was stationed stateside pitching for crack service baseball teams. He was discharged in time to rejoin the Grays for the end of the 1945 pennant push and would undoubtedly have remained in the Homestead rotation. But he had caught the eyes of Brooklyn Dodgers scouts, and Dodgers President Branch Rickey signed him to spend the 1946 season with the Brooklyn farm team in Montreal, where he roomed with Jackie Robinson and became one of four Negro Leaguers to play for Dodgers minor league squads as the long-standing barrier against blacks in Organized Baseball fell.

Although they kept on winning, the Grays were getting a little gray around the temples, particularly in the field, where the 12 most-used players in 1945 averaged 36 years of age. Wendell Smith wrote in his *Courier* column that the team had won the pennant on heart alone—"It's no secret that the champions are creaking at the knees." In the spring of 1944, the paper's sports pages featured a form that young players aspiring to be members of the Grays could clip out, fill out, and mail to Smith at the sports department, where he presumably forwarded them on to the Posey brothers and Jackson. An accompanying story stated that the team would "throw the doors open to all young players." Not much resulted from the effort, though—Uncle Sam had dibs on the group from which future baseball stars might emerge.[19]

While the Grays always finished first in their long nine-year run, this was not to say they didn't have competition for the pennant, sometimes quite keen. Their frequent pursuers were league president Wilson's Baltimore Elite Giants. Looking for a city that would support his team, Wilson had moved the Giants from his home town of Nashville to Columbus, Ohio, and Washington, D.C., before settling in Baltimore in 1938. The Giants finished third in 1939, but the league had decided on a post-season tournament matching the first-place Grays and the fourth-place Philadelphia Stars in one bracket and the Giants and second-place Newark Eagles in the other. Homestead topped Philadelphia, three games to two, to reach the finals to face the Giants.

For the most part, Baltimore's stars didn't have the long-lasting luster that shone from eventual Grays Hall of Famers such as Leonard, Posey, Brown, Bell, and Wilson, but the best Elites were well known as top-ranked players of their day. Jim West at first, Sammy Hughes at second, Felton Snow at third, Henry Kimbro in center, and Bill Byrd on the mound were very familiar to East-West All-Star Game voters and spectators. The team did have two future Hall of Famers at catcher, though. The venerable Raleigh "Biz" Mackey was easing back at age 41, mentoring and giving way to 17-year-old Roy Campanella.

Homestead started the championship series off on September 16 in Philadelphia with a 2–1 win, as Partlow beat Byrd with a four-hitter. The next day, a Sunday, brought a 7–5 Elites win at home in front of 10,000 fans at Bugle Field in Baltimore. A second game of a scheduled doubleheader resulted in a 1–1 tie when the Baltimore curfew law kicked in after five innings. Baltimore won back in Philadelphia, 10–5, on Saturday, September 24. The next game was at Yankee Stadium on Sunday. It could decide the NNL title, and it would decide the winner of the Ruppert Cup, a trophy the Yankees awarded each year to the Negro League team with the best record at its ballpark. Fifteen thousand fans showed up to see what would happen. The Elites took home all the hardware as Baltimore left-hander Jonas Gaines shut out the Grays, 2–0. The kid, Campanella, had four hits on Saturday and singled through the box on Sunday to drive in one of the Elites' runs.

Toward the end of the Grays' run, they regularly had to fight off the Newark Eagles to win each season's pennant, and sometimes it was close. The Eagles had been established in the NNL in Brooklyn in 1935 by the husband-wife team of Abe and Effa Manley. But after a season of mediocre attendance at the Brooklyn Dodgers' Ebbets Field, they moved the team to Newark. The Manleys, beginning with what amounted to an expansion team in Brooklyn, invested in younger players and gradually improved the squad. They nearly won the second half of the 1943 season, which would have forced a pennant playoff, finally trailing the Grays by a half-game.

The winner of the first half of the 1944 season, the last games of which were scheduled for July 4, wasn't determined until later in the season, when a contested game from July 2 was replayed. The Eagles had won the first game that day, 11–7, and the Grays took the second, 14–5, which gave them the lead in the standings. But the Eagles protested, successfully, that the Grays had used an ineligible player in the second game, an important one so far as the outcome went. Roy Partlow wasn't on the Homestead roster at that point in the season, but showed up in Newark on July 2 and pitched and won the nightcap. The game was ordered replayed on August 18 and was tied, 4–4, after six innings when the Grays opened up on former teammate McDuffie, coasting to an 8–4 win that effectively gave them the pennant.

It was again necessary to beat the Eagles at the end of 1945 to clinch first place. Newark was right behind the Grays for the second-half title but lost a doubleheader to Homestead on September 2. The Manleys' enthusiasm for younger players, a sensible course in the long run, hampered the club during the war when several of their best were called into the services. But in 1946 they were all back, including future Hall of Famers Monte Irvin, Larry Doby, Leon Day, and Biz Mackey, and this time Newark broke the Grays' pennant skein.

Claiming the 1944 flag also required Posey and Jackson to overcome a boardroom challenge, in addition to winning on the diamond. As that season's Negro World Series, pitting Homestead against the Birmingham Black Barons of the Negro American League, was about to begin, Philadelphia Stars owner Edward Bolden went public with a claim that his team, not the Grays, should be in the Series. In effect, he accused Posey of hi-jacking the league standings. On September 4, Labor Day, the Grays and Cubans played a doubleheader in Detroit, drawing about 12,000 to the Tigers' Briggs Stadium. Surprisingly, the Cubans won both games, which would have put the Grays in a bind in the tight pennant race with Newark and Philadelphia.

Posey, however, claimed that the doubleheader was a replacement in the schedule for a night game at Griffith Stadium in Washington, so only the result of the first game should count in the standings, the second being an "exhibition game." Bolden accused Posey of abusing his position as league secretary to wait until a week before the game date to inform league officials that only the first game would count. It seemed, Bolden said, that "they waited to see how the race stood before deciding whether they needed to play one or two league games in Detroit."[20]

Bolden's appeal was unsuccessful, possibly because Posey had outmaneuvered him with Tom Wilson and the other officers, but also possibly because trying to sort out a Negro League schedule toward the end of the season was a confusing task that league officials just weren't up for. The leagues dutifully constructed and announced their proposed schedules each season. But even with the best of intentions, it was difficult to stick to the plan. Every league had to contend with rainouts, but in the case of the black leagues, where almost all teams were renters of parks owned by other teams that had first call on available dates, it was hard to make up lost games. Added to that confusion was the fact that many league teams *did* count some of their games as exhibitions, electing to play each other in excess of the number of head-to-head confrontations dictated by an originally balanced schedule in order to maximize the profits that usually flowed from the meeting of two Negro League squads.

Nevertheless, *New Jersey Herald-News* sports columnist Oliver "Butts" Brown correctly pointed out that the entire pennant-race mess, from the Grays' replayed game with the Eagles to the Detroit situation, "allows the pressing need for a Commissioner who will rule with an iron hand."[21] That was something the Negro Leagues never had, at least not since the iron-fisted Andrew "Rube" Foster was in his prime as the president of the first Negro National League in the 1920s. Generally, the league president and the other officers were club owners as dedicated to the welfare of their own teams as they were to that of the league. None of the attempts over the years to establish independent presidents or commissioners were successful. William C. Hueston, Foster's successor in the first NNL, and Isaac Nutter, last head of the Eastern Colored League, lost their positions when their leagues collapsed due to the effects of the Depression. W. Rollo Wilson and Ferdinand Q. Morton of the second NNL and Major R. R. Jackson of the NAL in the 1930s were eventually forced out for, of all things, trying to exercise authority over the owners.

Posey was a frequent campaigner for independent oversight of the Negro Leagues, particularly for a commissioner of both leagues once the NAL was founded in 1937. But such a person didn't exist in 1944, and there is no reason to believe that Cum Posey, with his overpowering desire to be a winner, wasn't above playing with the league schedule to get the Grays over the finish line in first place that year. If so, he would have hardly been the first Negro Leagues owner to do so.

As relations between the NNL and the newer NAL improved, the Negro World Series was resumed in 1942. One had not been held since 1927, when the champions of the first NNL and the ECL had squared off. As perpetual league champions, the Grays appeared in four straight. They were not as dominant in the Series as they were in the regular season, splitting the four with the NAL champs. They defeated the Birmingham Black Barons twice, in 1943 and '44, but were swept by the Kansas City Monarchs in 1942 and the Cleveland Buckeyes in '45.

The first loss to the Monarchs was on September 8 at Griffith Stadium, the Grays' most successful venue, where 24,000 fans showed up. Homestead was shut out, 8–0, by Satchel Paige, who went five innings, and Jack Matchett, who relieved him for four. The Series moved on September 10 to Forbes Field in Pittsburgh, the Gray's second-best place to play, and they were blanked for seven more innings until scoring four runs in the bottom of the eighth to lose, 8–4. Three days later, the teams played again at Yankee Stadium, the favorite ballpark for everyone in the Negro Leagues. Estimates of the crowd ranged from 20,000 to 30,000, but the score was very precise—Paige and Matchett again dominated, and the Monarchs won, 9–3.

The Grays' backs were against the wall in Kansas City on September 20, but they had added some extra backs. Three Newark players, star pitcher Leon Day, second baseman Lenny Pearson, and left fielder Ed Stone, started, as did shortstop Bus Clarkson, a member of the Philadelphia Stars. Day, despite a steady stream of Monarchs complaints that he was defacing the ball to increase its movement over the plate, pitched a five-hitter with 12 strikeouts, and the three new position players combined for five hits, as Homestead won, 4–1. A meeting of the owners and other officials from both teams, along with a representative of the NAL, was convened the next day, and the presence of the "ringers" led to the result of the game being thrown out. The Grays contended, accurately, that there was precedent for World Series teams borrowing from other squads in the case of injuries, and that the Grays had some injuries, including shortstop Sam Bankhead's broken arm.

Kansas City's response was summed up by team secretary William "Dizzy" Dismukes, a longtime Posey protégé now working for the Monarchs. "We didn't play the Homestead Grays," he said, "we lost to the National League All-Stars."[22] Posey and Jackson maintained that the Monarchs had agreed before the series began to allow the Grays to use substitutes, but rather meekly submitted to Kansas City's demand. The Series was resumed in Philadelphia's Shibe Park on the 29th, and the Monarchs put an end to all controversies by winning, 9–5.

The 1943 Series was nip and tuck—the Black Barons won the opener in Washington on September 21, and there was a 5–5 tie in Baltimore two days later. Then the Grays took two in a row before Birmingham won a wild one, 11–10, to tie up the series. From there, the teams alternated winning, but the first and third games were won by Homestead, which took the series, 4–3–1. As was usually the case for a black World Series, the games moved around among several potentially lucrative venues rather than just shuttling back and forth between the two teams' home parks. The Negro Leagues, after all, were playing to a fan base that was a distinct minority of the population, and for the most part had incomes below the national average, and moving the attraction to a new group of ticket buyers was deemed good business. The 1943 series was played in Washington; Baltimore; Chicago; Columbus, Ohio; Indianapolis; Birmingham, and Montgomery, Alabama. The most distant of the cities were 750 miles apart. But according to several of those involved, the Series should have gone 300 miles farther.

According to major sports columnists Wendell Smith of the *Courier*, Fay Young of the *Chicago Defender*, and Dan Burley of the *New York Amsterdam News*, Winfield Welsh, the Black Barons' manager, and Posey, acting without approval of either league (which had left organization matters to the two competing teams), decided on their own to extend the Series and play the final game in New Orleans. But the Montgomery promoter complained, and J. B. Martin, the NAL president, put a stop to the extension without informing New Orleans black baseball promoter Allen Page, who was busy setting up the contest. The final game, which the Grays won, 8–4, was played in Montgomery on October 5. However, the two teams continued to play, in games that were advertised in Birmingham as Series contests. The columnists were highly critical of the disorganization in what should have been a Negro Leagues showcase event. The way Smith saw it, the black baseball fans had been given a "kick in the pants," yet again. Young concluded that the mess was just another argument in favor of a strong Negro Leagues commissioner. Burley wrote that the "chance to make a lot of gold had both Posey and Welsh in a stranglehold from which they didn't want to become unentangled."[23]

When September of 1944 rolled around, Smith and Young, along with Sam Lacy of the *Baltimore Afro-American*, were named to a three-member "Arbitration Commission" that would oversee the conduct of that year's World Series, pursuant to an inter-league agreement designed to impose order on the proceedings. Among the rules they were empowered to enforce was a requirement that both clubs submit a list of eligible players, the only ones who could be in uniform, and that those players had to have belonged to their respective teams not later than August 10.[24] In addition, the Series was mostly confined to the home parks of the two pennant winners (two at Rickwood Field in Birmingham for the Black Barons and one each at Forbes Field and Griffith Stadium for the Grays). New Orleans got the second game, likely to make amends for Page's being stranded in 1943.

Circumstances conspired to give the Grays an advantage over the Black Barons even before the Series opened on September 17. Just before that date, four Birmingham players were injured in auto crash as the team was returning home from an exhibition game, and three of them were badly enough hurt to miss the Series. If Negro League teams had possessed minor league player development programs, the Barons might have secured decent replacements,

The 1944 Grays were the eighth of nine straight Homestead pennant winners. A starting lineup photographed before a game included, from left: Jelly Jackson, Ray Battle, unidentified, Sam Bankhead, Josh Gibson, Buck Leonard, Dave Hoskins, Jerry Benjamin, and Cool Papa Bell (NoirTech Research, Inc.).

but by and large the black teams had no such organizations. Leroy Morney, a 35-year-old reserve infielder nearing the end of his career, was added to the roster, but otherwise the Black Barons played shorthanded.

The Grays nearly swept the Series, winning the first two games in Birmingham and New Orleans, getting shut out, 6–0, in Pittsburgh, but bouncing back in all respects. Ray Brown threw a one-hitter on September 23 back in Birmingham, and the offense supplied nine runs. With Welmaker pitching, the Grays wrapped it up, 4–2, in Griffith Stadium before 10,000 fans only eight days after the Series began. In 1945, though, the squad that Wendell Smith thought was "creaking at the knees" was quickly brought to its knees by the Cleveland Buckeyes, who not only swept four straight games, but shut the Grays out twice, limiting them to a mere three runs in the four games. As a *Courier* headline on September 22 put it, "Cleveland Has Grays Reeling and Rocking."

As the national economy recovered from the Depression, and as the two Negro Leagues, despite their management shortcomings, became more financially stable and began to resemble their white counterparts, rivalries between the black teams became the centerpiece of barnstorming trips. It had been the case for years that top black teams would play a league game at home or at an opponent's ballpark (or, sometimes, somewhere else where black ball had proven to be popular), and fill in the schedule gaps by bouncing from city to city, or to smaller communities, to play local teams. Posey's energetic travel schedule for the Grays in their earlier days had the team crisscrossing Western Pennsylvania and Eastern and Central Ohio, constantly in search of a game and a share of the gate.

By the end of the 1930s, though, it was becoming commonplace for two Negro League teams to hook up and go barnstorming together over a considerable geographic distance, playing each other nearly every day. In July of 1938, for example, the Grays and the Memphis Red Sox of the NAL (when it came to inter-league play, the Negro Leagues were way ahead of the white majors) played a doubleheader in Pittsburgh, then faced off five more times in Indianapolis; Zanesville, Ohio, and two Pennsylvania towns before winding up with a coveted Sunday game in Yankee Stadium. In 1941, the Grays and the Elite Giants put together a pre-season jaunt out of spring training in the South that included 13 scheduled games in a 25-day period from New Orleans; to Nashville; up to Ohio and Pittsburgh; on to Washington; back north to Harrisburg, Pennsylvania, and then to the Elite's territory in Baltimore and Richmond. As was the case in the roaming schedule for the Negro World Series, the rationale for black baseball barnstorming had always been that, with a minority fan base that usually earned less than its white contemporaries, it was best not to oversaturate a location, but keep the excitement spread from place to place, including among white audiences that didn't usually see black athletes. Now, though, this strategy was being pursued by pairs of top black teams, rather than one black squad and a local opponent, likely white.

In the case of the Grays, at least, this switch to joint barnstorming coincided with the waning of the strong semi-pro tradition in Western Pennsylvania. In 1938, Posey wrote a letter to *Pittsburgh Post-Gazette* sports editor Havey Boyle explaining why the Grays no longer played many games locally. Boyle reproduced it in his June 16 column.

> The main reason is because there are no white semi-pro teams of the strength and following of the Beaver Falls Elks, Jeanette, Bellevue, Sharon, Youngstown, Charleroi, Homewood, West Newton, Uniontown, National Tube of McKeesport, Akron General Tires, of former years. All of these clubs were stronger than Class C clubs of organized baseball.... Homestead Grays from 1921 to 1929, were able to maintain a salaried club and not play one game over 150 miles from Pittsburgh in a season. It would be suicide to attempt a schedule of this kind.... The local district white clubs can not furnish much opposition for the Grays to attract a paying crowd.[25]

The damage done to local industry and business by the Depression had undercut the financial sponsors for many locally-famous semi-pro clubs. When the industrial recovery brought about by World War II pumped money back into the Western Pennsylvania economy, the armed forces draft took away the teams' raw material, the young players.

Less than two months after Boyle reprinted Posey's letter about the collapse of local baseball, the Grays put on an exhibition to honor it. The Grays had proclaimed this the 25th anniversary of their founding, and announced an oldtimers' game that would pit past Grays stars against their old white foes at Forbes Field on August 7, sharing a doubleheader bill with a current Grays-Newark Eagles contest. "Muscles which are now prone to creak and legs and arms which have been slowed by the onslaughts of Father Time, are being limbered and loosened," Chester Washington of the *Courier* reported.[26] The game went five innings, and the graying Grays beat their erstwhile competitors, 5–2.

Few former Grays notables had been overlooked. Smokey Joe Williams travelled from New York, started for the old Grays, and faced the first three batters, to whom he "failed to show the famous 'fire-ball,'" but "he did use an effective change of pace and a tantalizing curve ball."[27] At age 52, that may have been all that was left of his repertoire. Oscar Owens, who harkened back to the first great squads of the 1920s, and Sell Hall, who went all the way back to the team's first years, also took the mound. They were caught by John

Veney, an original Gray, the brother of one of the team's founders, and W. S. Young, another regular from the '20s. Two of the umpires for the league game, Pop Turner and Moe Harris, switched to players' flannels and relived their time with the team. Shortstop Bobby Williams, first baseman Jap Washington, and outfielder Willis Moody, who all broke in with the Grays in the '20s, were there also.

When on the road, the present-day Grays showed up in many of their usual haunts, such as Columbus, Cleveland, Toledo, Akron, Altoona, and Harrisburg. But they also could be found playing at least once a year in cities such as Louisville, Cincinnati, Detroit, Indianapolis, Newport News, and Buffalo, almost always in tandem with another major black team. In 1941, Dan Park, a sports columnist for the *Times Herald* in Olean, New York, a regular Western New York stopping place for the Grays, reported that Posey's team had made $9,729.60 (a precise number that he must have gotten from Posey or some other Grays official) playing a doubleheader in Detroit against the Elite Giants on August 3. That was a lot of money for a Negro Leagues date, but 23,312 fans showed up. "Colored teams have taken to playing league games in cities where their players are unknown and draw capacity crowds," he wrote. "One of the reasons is the dash the negro players inject into the game." Another reason, Park added, a little, but not much, ahead of his time, was "the outstanding playing ability of the colored players, many of whom could make the major league grade."[28]

The change in the opponent mix, if anything, made a team's travel schedule even more arduous. In the case of the Grays, for example, the out and back trips from Pittsburgh to play 40 or 50 miles from home were being replaced by interstate travels to the Midwest, the New York City area, or the near South. Living on the team bus had become second nature to a successful player. Grays pitcher Edsall Walker noted that the travel became so routine that a comfortable break provided by a rainout while barnstorming was actually disrupting to the sleep schedule. Given a night in a hotel or rooming house, "we couldn't sleep, we'd walk the street all night, and sleep in the bus the next day, on those reclining seats."[29]

One area that Walker recalled as fun to visit was the New York metropolitan area, for the high level of baseball competition. By 1939, when the NNL settled into the structure it was to maintain through the end of its existence in 1947, there were four league teams in or within 100 miles of New York. As the Grays worked their way east, they could play the Philadelphia Stars at their Parkside field and the Newark Eagles in the minor league Ruppert Stadium, then the New York Black Yankees and Cubans, who used various city and Northern New Jersey parks for their games. But no visiting

Negro Leagues team would limit its foray to the area without scheduling as many games as possible with its many high-quality semi-pro teams.

Regular Grays opponents included the Lloyd Athletic Club of Chester, Pennsylvania, right outside Philadelphia, the Belmar Braves and Red Bank Pirates from those Jersey Shore towns, and the East Orange Baseball Club near Newark, one of the best teams west of the Hudson River. Crossing the Hudson, though, reaped even bigger rewards, because the region's epicenter of semi-pro ball lay in Brooklyn. A game with the Bushwicks, the team on the Brooklyn-Queens borough border owned by baseball entrepreneur Max Rosner, provided a consistently lucrative return. Rosner's Dexter Park seated 15,000, and those seats could be counted on to be mostly occupied for a Sunday doubleheader. Rosner, who no doubt appreciated the "exotic" nature of all-black clubs in the region's otherwise white semi-pro world, paid visiting clubs a percentage of the gate, backed up by a good rainout guarantee.

Posey had boycotted the Bushwicks early on as a protest against co-owner Nat Strong, the dominant New York booking agent who was widely seen among black ball executives and sportswriters as unfairly squeezing Negro teams' profits. But after Strong's death before the 1935 season, Posey was happy to do business with Rosner, as well as with Rosner's younger brother Joe, who ran another strong Brooklyn semi-pro outfit, the Bay Parkways. By the time the NNL included the New Jersey-New York trio of the Eagles, Black Yankees, and Cubans, the Bushwicks were always part of a Grays eastern swing, either for a Sunday doubleheader or a midweek night game. The rosters of the Bushwicks, Bay Parkways, and the other top semi-pro teams were made up of the cream of the crop of former high school and college stars, plus fellows who had been minor leaguers and, occasionally, major leaguers. Since the teams usually played about twice a week, players who wished to increase their baseball second incomes often appeared in more than one uniform. The lineup of the East Orange club on Saturdays, for example, often contained several Bushwicks, and a fan from Brooklyn who might travel to the Jersey Shore to see the Red Bank Pirates in a weekday game likely would notice some familiar faces from the Bay Parkways.

Although their players might get around a bit, the Bushwicks team itself, with its large park and enthusiastic fan base that could fill it, rarely travelled for games, even within the metropolitan area. But the business relationship between Posey and Rosner was so strong that when the Grays established their second home in Washington, the Brooklyn team took to the road for games there, as well as at Forbes Field. On July 5, 1943, the day the Fourth of July was generally celebrated that year, since the Fourth had fallen on a Sunday, the Bushwicks appeared at Forbes Field for a doubleheader. Nine thousand fans turned out, a good number for the Grays in Pittsburgh, as Homestead won both games. The next day, the two teams met for a single game in Washington, and 10,000 fans showed up at Griffith Stadium, as the Grays won again, 11–3. The Brooklyn team made single-game appearances again at Griffith on August 24, 1944, and June 28, 1945, and again, the Grays won. Over the years, the Grays were usually triumphant over the New York semi-pros, but victory was considerably less certain against those opponents than in the other non-league matches.

While the Grays were winning pennants with regularity, they were not profiting at the gate so easily, at least in the late 1930s. The national economic recovery from the Depression, which had seen the Gross Domestic Product climb by double-digit percentages each year since 1933, stalled out in 1938, and while it began to climb again the next year, it was not until 1940 that the 1937 level had been noticeably exceeded. The effect was felt at Grays headquarters—as Grays historian Brad Snyder puts it, "Posey cared about winning, first and foremost, but he also cared about making money, and in the late 1930s the Grays weren't making money in Pittsburgh."[30]

In July of 1939, Rufus Jackson, undoubtedly not speaking just for himself, told the *Courier* about his disappointment with attendance in Pittsburgh, and said, "in all probability the Grays will make their home grounds in Washington, D.C., at Griffith Stadium next season."[31] The team did not abandon Pittsburgh, but forged a rental agreement with the Washington Senators of the white American League to play an increasing share of its home games at Griffith, about 250 miles from Forbes Field. Appearances increased from nine dates and 17 games in 1940 to a high of 26 dates and 38 games in 1943, concentrating on the prime Sunday doubleheaders, plus weekday night games after the Senators equipped their ballpark with lights in 1941.

Posey, one of whose reputations was as someone as cunning as a fox, was now doing business with someone whose actual nickname was "The Old Fox," to the benefit of both. Clark Griffith had been a star major league pitcher in the nineteenth century and, as a player organizer, was a key behind-the-scenes figure in the founding of the American League. He began a field managerial career in 1901, running the Chicago White Sox, the Cincinnati Reds, the New York Highlanders (later the Yankees), and finally the Senators. He invested in the Senators in 1911 while managing them, and with another investor bought a controlling interest before the 1920 season. He owned the team until his death in 1955.

The Senators had won the AL pennant three times between 1924 and 1933 and had taken the World Series in 1924, but by the time Posey and Jackson showed an interest in sharing Griffith Stadium, the Senators could usually be found in the second division, hovering not far above last place. Attendance accordingly declined, and profits with it. The team owed $124,000 to a bank in 1934, which led to the sale that off-season of Griffith's son-in-law and best player, Joe Cronin, to the Boston Red Sox. After the Old Fox's death, his wife Addie told a reporter that "He never had any money to spend.... It was always throwing money into the club—every cent we had."[32]

Griffith did have a valuable intangible asset, though it wasn't of his own making. His team, and its ballpark, sat in a hotbed of fervent African American baseball fans—a lot of them. The national government in the District of Columbia had been a major employer of blacks since after the Civil War, and the black population grew there during the 1930s as it did in other American cities, primarily due to migration of Southern blacks seeking better working and social conditions. Washington's black population increased 41 percent between the 1930 and 1940 censuses, to 187,255, in contrast to the size of the black population in Pittsburgh, which had barely budged from the decline of the steel industry through the Depression. In all of Allegheny County, which can reasonably be thought of as containing the Grays' home fan base, there had been only an eight percent growth rate, to 90,060. Not only were there perhaps double the number of black baseball fans in Washington, they were known to be enthusiastic supporters of the sport, as Senators fans: "Blacks considered Griffith Stadium their ballpark and the Senators their team."[33]

Washington Senators owner Clark Griffith was one of the owners of teams in the white major leagues with whom Posey had close business connections. The relationship was mutually beneficial—use of the Senators' ballpark gave the Grays access to a large and enthusiastic black fan base in Washington, while Griffith collected rent whenever the Grays played there (Library of Congress).

Despite the reservoir of passionate baseball fans, Washington had not been a welcoming place for black teams until the Grays moved in. There had been four previous attempts to put down roots by franchises in the Eastern Colored League, the East-West League, and the second Negro National League. They all failed, the most recent an attempt by NNL president Tom Wilson to locate his Elite Giants there in 1936–37 before moving to greener pastures in nearby Baltimore. Black fans followed the Senators, although from segregated seating in the right field bleachers, and seemed incapable of warming to Negro Leagues teams.

Although the Grays drew fairly well in their first two years as part-time Washingtonians, it can't be said that they were anywhere near to seizing the interest of the Capitol's baseball fans. The team drew in the mid-four figures for games, which was good, but not great, although the comparative closeness of Pittsburgh and Washington (for barnstorming baseball players, anyway) meant the Grays could play an opponent at Forbes Field on Saturday, then hop on the team bus and ride through the 260 miles to Washington during the night to play a doubleheader, sometimes against the same team, on Sunday, thus providing two profitable playing dates in a major league stadium in a weekend.

Things changed drastically before the 1942 season. Faced with the possibility of a protest march in the summer of 1941 organized by leading African American labor leader A. Philip Randolph that could have numbered up to 100,000 marchers, President Roosevelt signed an Executive Order banning discrimination in defense industry hiring. This brought many more blacks to DC to take government jobs related to the war effort. The black population of the district, which was already increasing rapidly, boomed even more, shooting up 50 percent between the 1940 and 1950 censuses. Not only did the executive order created more jobs for African Americans, it increased the quality of those jobs. By November 1942, half of the federal jobs belonging to blacks were clerical or professional positions.[34] There were more black baseball fans in town, with more disposable income in their pockets—potential Grays fans, in other words.

Snyder, whose book *Beyond the Shadow of the Senators* provides an in-depth account of the Grays coming to Washington and the simultaneous creep toward integration of professional baseball, points to an underappreciated factor in the Grays' success in the national capital. When the team first began to play regularly at Griffith Stadium, Posey and Jackson hired a local white sportswriter, Joe Holman, to be their publicist. But Holman, who didn't seem to have any deep regard for black baseball, could not get the team substantial coverage in the local daily papers. Prospects were dim enough that the *Chicago Defender* reported after the 1941 season that the Grays were mulling over abandoning their new home due to the low attendance.

But in 1942, Holman was replaced with a black sportswriter. Art Carter was the sports editor of the *Afro-American* chain of black weeklies, which included a Washington edition. He took on promoting the Grays as a part-time job and greatly improved how the team was viewed by black Washingtonians. As Snyder tells it, "The secret of his success was his courtship of the black elite. He augmented the Grays' upper-class black fan base by chartering an informal yet exclusive club of fans to whom he gave season passes." He gave out freebies to prominent federal employees, businessmen, faculty at Howard University, and, importantly, black preachers. As they attended Sunday afternoon doubleheaders, the men of the cloth were likely to bring many of their Sunday morning flocks with them. As a Washington sportswriter, Carter also had a good relationship with Griffith.[35]

Snyder identifies two other immediate reasons besides Carter's hiring for the Grays' popularity and attendance taking off in 1942. One was Clark Griffith's rescission of a long-standing ban on interracial games at his stadium. The other was Satchel Paige. In 1934, Paige had humiliated the Grays while with the arch-rival Pittsburgh Crawfords with a no-hitter that was nearly a perfect game and featured 17 strikeouts. Now 36 years old, Paige was no longer the totally dominant hurler he had been in the 1930s. He seldom even pitched a complete game any longer, and he couldn't be guaranteed to be as nearly unhittable as he once had been. But he was wildly popular with fans, who turned out enthusiastically to see him pitch.

On Sunday, May 17, 1942, a modest crowd of 4,463 at Griffith Stadium saw the Grays split a doubleheader with the Elite Giants. Two weeks later, Paige made his only appearance in a Grays uniform, on loan from his Kansas City Monarchs for a game against the white Dizzy Dean All-Stars. The Grays' opponent was supposed to have been the Bob Feller All-Stars, but Feller, in his pitching prime but currently in the Navy at Norfolk, Virginia, turned out not to be available. Dean, who hadn't pitched even semi-regularly in the majors since 1939, stepped in to lead the white team. The Grays scored three runs in the first, Dean's only inning, while Paige hurled five, giving up an unearned run and striking out seven. The Grays wound up winning, 8–1.

The big thing about the game, though, was that 22,000 fans showed up, swamping the ticket windows and constituting the largest attendance ever at Griffith for a non–American League contest.[36] Some of the fans may have come out to see Cecil Travis, the Senators' star third baseman, who had journeyed from the Army's Camp Wheeler in Georgia to play for the All-Stars. And this was the year the already legendary Josh Gibson had returned to the Grays lineup. But future attendance booms coincided with the appearance of the Monarchs as Grays opponents, and it is more likely that folks rushed to the park to see Paige pitch. Kansas City returned on June 18, and Paige hurled the first five innings of a pitchers' duel that Roy Partlow and the Grays won, 2–1, in 10 innings. The stadium nearly sold out at an estimated 28,000 attendance. The earlier exhibition against the Dean All-Stars notwithstanding, Snyder identifies this thrilling game as the night that "black Washingtonians accepted a Negro League team originating in Pittsburgh as their own; it was the night the Homestead Grays truly became the *Washington* Homestead Grays."[37]

Back again on August 13, the Monarchs and Grays went 12 innings in a night game before Dave Whatley drove in Vic Harris with the winning run. This time Paige pitched the whole game, and 20,000 were said to have seen it. Finally, in the Negro World Series opening game played in Washington that season, 24,000 more folks came out to see him start and go five innings for the win. The pattern continued for the next few seasons. The Grays would draw well playing other clubs at Griffith Stadium, sometimes nearing or just topping 10,000 fans. Then the Monarchs would hit town with the prospect of Paige pitching, and attendance would go up as high as the low 20,000s. (It should be noted that the Paige box office magic worked for the Grays in other locales as well, as it did for so many Monarchs opponents. More than 10,000 turned out at Forbes Field in June 1943 for a Monarchs game, and the two teams drew more than 12,000 to Shibe Park in Philadelphia that September.)

Carter noted in his September 5, 1942, column that the Grays had already drawn an official count of 102,690 to Griffith that season, with the World Series game that drew about 24,000 still to be played. While special events like the East-West All-Star Game at Comiskey Park in Chicago could draw upwards of 40,000 fans each year, and the four-team doubleheaders at Yankee Stadium and the Polo Grounds in New York could sometimes hit 30,000, the attendance the Grays were generating on a regular basis was outstanding for a Negro League team. As a result, *New York Amsterdam-News* columnist Dan Burley wrote after the 1942 season, the Grays had earned "a cool $100,000 last year."[38] That same season, while the Grays were drawing comfortably over 10,000 fans to each playing date at Griffith Stadium while winning the NNL pennant, their hosts finished next to last in the American League and drew 403,493 fans, only a little over 6,700 per playing date. While comparisons between individual white and Negro major league teams are difficult to make due to a number of factors, one could surmise that the Washington-Homestead Grays were the best major league team in Washington, D.C., that season.

It is likely that Clark Griffith wouldn't have found the comparison, should it have been made in his presence, completely embarrassing. Griffith's team and Posey's Grays had developed a symbiotic relationship that helped both franchises. The Grays used the Senators' spring training site in Orlando, Florida (Negro League seasons began later than those of the white majors, so there was no conflict for the facilities), and ordered uniforms and equipment through the Senators' accounts with sporting goods suppliers. The white team's ticket manager, John Morrissey, managed stadium affairs, including the printing of tickets and the lining up of security and other game-day personnel, for the black games.

This relationship paid off in both directions—the Grays made the money in Washington that made them the most profitable Negro League team, with the Senators receiving a substantial share. The arrangement with the Grays was that Griffith's team would receive 20 percent of the gross gate, and the Grays would pay for the personnel, tickets, and other game-day expenses from their share. The Senators would keep profits from concession sales. This was a pretty standard arrangement for Negro League use of a white profes-

Beginning in 1940, the Grays played some of their home games at Griffith Stadium, home of the Washington Senators. By the middle of World War II, the stadium was the team's primary home park, and they frequently drew upwards of 20,000 fans to a game (Library of Congress).

sional team's park, but rarely was paid attendance so large at a black game on a regular basis. Snyder estimates that Griffith took in $60,000 from Grays games in 1942, and perhaps $100,000 in 1943, when the black team played more games in Washington and may have drawn 225,000 or so fans.[39]

The Senators were far from the only white major league team to profit from providing an upscale venue for black games. The managements of all three teams in New York, the Yankees, Giants, and Dodgers, rented their parks on off-days to Negro League teams (and for other sporting events, too). The Yankees, whose Yankee Stadium became a major black baseball location, had a winning trifecta—they also rented the minor league parks they owned in Kansas City and Newark to the Monarchs and Eagles. Generally lacking the capital to build their own ballparks, these arrangements were very positive for the black teams, and the use of major and high minor league parks gave Negro Leagues games an additional air of success, not to mention additional seats to sell to the growing wartime fan base.

But while doing business with owners like Clark Griffith may have been good for Negro League baseball as a business, it was not necessarily good for the Negro League players. The explosion of interest in the black leagues just before and during the war, and the participation of black soldiers, sailors, and airmen in the conflict, was bringing about talk about how the white majors might be ripe for integration. Griffith's cooperation helped make the Negro Leagues a stronger organization, but he realized two things. One was that if the best black players joined the heretofore white majors, the Negro Leagues, and his important profit stream, would collapse. The other was that it would take a very brave big league owner to sign the first black player, who would have to be even braver. He told black Sam Lacy of the *Washington Tribune* that while integration was coming, "A lone Negro in the game will ... be made the target of cruel, filthy epithets.... I certainly would not want to be the one to have to take it."[40] He did not add that the owner who stepped forward to upset decades of segregation would face opposition, too, and he didn't want to be that person, either.

It was not that Griffith desired an all-Caucasian, American-born team. He was a leading importer of Cuban baseball talent, which he determined was "easier to find, cheaper to sign, and more reliable on the field." It happened that, although his Cubans came advertised as Castilians (Caucasians), this might not have been exactly so, although there was no one in the American baseball sports industry with the ability to trace their heritage in their home country. The most attention toward the racial identity of the Senators' Cuban players during the war centered on one of the best, Bobby Estalella. Estalella was likely a light-skinned mulatto (born of mixed-race parents), and, according to a biographer, "Many of his teammates and a few prominent sports-writers of the era considered him to be black."[41]

The tension between running the Negro Leagues as successfully as possible, and doing justice to the black league's discriminated-against players, grew as the war years went along. It was one of many issues that Cumberland Posey, not the successful owner, but the league official, would deal with.

Chapter Nine

Executive Decisions

In 1938, as his rival Gus Greenlee's hold over the Negro National League was coming to an end, Cum Posey, who had been kicked out along with the Grays in the league's initial 1933 season, became a league officer. He was elected secretary and held that position, with occasional additional duties as treasurer, through the end of his time as a Grays owner. Although he was always a league officer from 1938 on and, as might be expected, an outspoken one, he never was president. He never ran for the position and never seems to have wanted it. His approach to power and responsibility in the NNL was similar to the way he ran the Grays. Charlie Walker or Rufus Jackson could be the club president, and could have an important role, but there never was any real doubt as to who was actually in charge. Posey could never be said to have been fully in charge of the league, but he exerted a strong influence on everything that went on.

So far as Posey's official duties went, he applied himself to the league's routine business—setting up season schedules, getting league standings and individual player statistics out to the teams and the black press, and making sure the loop's umpires were doing their jobs and getting paid. By the early 1940s, with his league responsibilities combined with his active government and political involvement in Homestead, he seems to have delegated considerable responsibility for the day-to-day running of the Grays to the rest of the team's management—Rufus Jackson to share responsibility for major decisions, his brother See to handle scheduling and act as team secretary, and John L. Clark, his former foe when with the Crawfords, to handle public relations. In 1941, he informed Effa Manley that he was recommending that league president Tom Wilson fine the Grays, his own club, since See had not sent him from a road trip the team box scores necessary for compiling player statistics.[1]

Being secretary also gave him chances to meddle in league business when he had the very Posey-like inclination to improve things unilaterally. For example, he informed Effa Manley that his striving on behalf of the NNL

The Grays' brain trust poses at Griffith Stadium before a game. From left: See Posey, travelling secretary and scout; co-owner Rufus "Sonnyman" Jackson; Posey, and Washington, D.C., Elks official Russell J. Bowser. Posey is wearing an elaborate Elks fez as the national athletic commissioner for the black wing of the Elks, and this was one of several special games honoring the association staged throughout the Negro Leagues (NoirTech Research, Inc.).

the previous season had included "juggling votes [for the league's East-West team] so we could get three men from each team and have the public think they were picking them."[2] This was possible because the *Pittsburgh Courier*, where Posey had an in as a columnist, was the place for fans to mail their ballots. If parity among the NNL teams was his intention, he didn't do a bad job—15 players got into the lineup for the East, and 12 of them were split equally among the Grays, the Newark Eagles, the Philadelphia Stars, and the New York Cubans.

Being an NNL officer also gave him an opportunity to take part in solving bigger problems, such as lobbying federal officials to exempt the Negro Leagues from strict wartime gasoline rationing, which grounded their team buses for a time and threatened their very existence. And while he already had a soapbox in the form of his newspaper column, his increased status within the league enhanced his orations about black baseball's shortcomings and his firm views on how to fix them.

From the beginning of his time within the power structure, the seasoned baseball veteran strongly and consistently expressed the opinion that the problems assailing the Negro version of the National Pastime could best be corrected by experienced baseball men (such as himself). That baseball management should belong to the sport's veterans wasn't a new attitude for Posey—it was the one which had bolstered him through the lean years while Pittsburgh black ball was being controlled by Greenlee, and which led him to later confide in John Clark that he knew he would win in the long run because Greenlee never really understood the business of baseball. He had yet to be voted in as secretary for the 1938 season when he, in general terms, used his *Courier* column to criticize the NNL's "hit or miss style." The problems, he maintained were ingrained and went back to the league's founding, when its defective constitution "was written by men who had never played, umpired, or looked in a rule book." By June, highlighting the decisions of some owners to ignore the official schedule in favor of more lucrative exhibition games, he said the league would be better off without "some members wishing to enjoy the league prestige with no idea of attempting to do right."[3]

Although the economic effects of World War II, which hurt white semipro and professional baseball, paradoxically gave a boost to the Negro Leagues, they were still plagued by long-running areas of disagreement and dysfunction. These included the undependability of schedules and published standings, the raiding of rosters by baseball entrepreneurs, often from Latin America, and sometimes from the leagues themselves (of course, Posey himself was fingered a few times for this), and how much power and money the highly organized white booking agents should get for assisting in scheduling the black teams away from their home parks. Another subject that constantly came up in the councils of the NNL, and in the other black league, the Negro American League, was whether or not the two loops should have an independent commissioner in charge of both organizations, just as the two white major leagues had.

Seen from the distance provided by history's perspective, these issues have clearly correct choices: regular scheduling, respecting player contracts, and an independent commissioner were good, progressive moves, and taking the opposite tack reeked of disorganization, selfishness, and the triumph of insider politics. Posey, it has to be said, was usually on the right side of these issues, at least in theory. In the case of disputed player signings, for example, he always maintained that the anti-raiding rules had already been broken so badly (by someone else) that he felt entitled to his share. He often beat the drum at league and joint NNL-NAL meetings for an independent commissioner, and once was named to a committee to find one. But while he had candidates in mind, they weren't necessarily those that other owners favored. In the end, the two leagues never had a strong chief executive who wasn't a team officer until the NNL hired one in 1946, at a point where black ball had been so weakened by the integration of the previously white majors and minors that it was too late to save it. Posey operated as a league officer in much the same fashion as he did as a successful team owner—he gave his opinions freely and forcefully, and he tried to make his desires become reality. It was considerably harder to sway his fellow Negro League moguls, though, than it had been to persuade players, managers, and umpires.

By the time Posey became a league officer and his Grays the perpetual champions of the NNL, the league was usually composed each season of six teams—the Grays, Philadelphia Stars, and Baltimore Elite Giants outside of the New York metropolitan area, and the Newark Eagles and New York Cubans and Black Yankees within it. Although, as in the case with the Grays' Posey and Jackson, an individual team might have more than one owner with a voice at league meetings, each team had only one vote. Alliances among the teams were fluid and often depended on the issue under consideration. Sometimes there were fine distinctions within the important issues themselves that affected how the teams' votes lined up. The economic interest of each franchise was always a primary consideration for its ownership team, although some owners, Posey included, also took the longer view that a well-organized and respected black league was good for business as well as speaking well for the black race. Once one had invested time and effort in founding a Negro League team, it could be a source of great pride to be a "race man" (or woman, in the case of Newark co-owner Effa Manley). But it would be considerably less satisfying, as Posey could have told you from experience, to be one who was broke.

The product the NNL and NAL sold to its fans was dependent on as high a quality of players as could be obtained, and once hired, then held onto in the face of competing demands for their allegiances. The establishment of both Negro Leagues on a fairly sound basis by the late 1930s, with a set of enforceable rules, mostly put an end to intra-league roster raiding. Poaching on the other black major league, though, was far from unheard-of. And the Negro Southern League, the leading Negro minor league, which had no firm protection from its major league counterparts, always presented possible good pickings for the big league teams.

As early as February 1938, after its first year of operation, the NAL owners at their winter meeting "agreed to respect player rights and contracts, also not to dicker with, sign, or play against any suspended player or players" from the NNL. This was reported in the *Courier* by none other than Cum Posey himself. He attended the meeting, representing the NNL, and sent back a dispatch.[4] Throughout 1938 and the opening of the following season, comity seemed to prevail, with joint meetings of the two leagues and agreement to play inter-league games on a regular basis in the second half of the season.

But things turned disagreeable over the fate of the team that had used to be Gus Greenlee's Pittsburgh Crawfords, and the players on the roster. The franchise had been acquired by a group of Toledo, Ohio, businessmen and moved there as an NNL team to begin 1939, only to draw poorly and be allowed to move to the NAL. The Toledo group had been assured by NNL President Tom Wilson that they would have the rights to the players on the 1938 team, but three of them, catcher Pepper Bassett, pitcher Theophilus Smith, and outfielder Dan Wilson, appeared on NAL rosters at the beginning of the season. "It Looks Like War," read the headline over the column by the *Courier's* Chester Washington on May 6, and if so, it would be because of "that time-worn and antiquated practice of stealing ball players."[5] Washington, writing from Pittsburgh, could be seen as a supporter of the National League in this matter, but Frank A. "Fay" Young of the *Chicago Defender*, published in the heart of American League territory, had a decidedly different viewpoint: Bassett, Smith, and Wilson had not signed Crawfords contracts for 1939 and thus were free agents. This, Young pointed out, could not be said for David Whatley, under contract to the Jacksonville Red Caps but playing right field for the Grays.[6] Posey, of course, felt he was justified. Anyway, his signing didn't bother any consciences in Pittsburgh, because it was "a reprisal" for the Chicago American Giants having previously signed a Grays player away.

The Negro Leagues player disputes of 1939 ended as did most of these cases—the owners and league officials involved pointed fingers, the black sporting press seized the opportunity to again chastise them for poor management, and the players stayed put. An exception was the grand dispute of 1943, in which five teams—the Grays, three other NNL clubs, and Cleveland of the NAL—were ordered to return 10 players to their previous teams. The dispute had raged for weeks, the playing of the annual East-West All-Star Game was in jeopardy at one point, and grievances unrelated to this round of player snatching were aired. Posey, for example, defended his signings, including the veteran star outfielder James "Cool Papa" Bell, with the mostly irrelevant argument that the American League had broken the multi-topic inter-league agreement by allowing its teams to play the travelling Ethiopian

Clowns. The Clowns featured players in African war paint and grass skirts, and they were supposed to be boycotted by all black major league clubs for an implied mockery of the African nation of Ethiopia, which had been conquered by Benito Mussolini's Italian Army in the run-up to World War II.[7]

The player returns were worked out at a joint meeting of both leagues in Philadelphia in June, described as "an uproarious one with many heated words being exchanged and old differences and dislikes aired freely as the various club owners smoked black cigars, walked the floor and got grievances off their respective chests. Everyone present, it was reported, was charged with violating the player agreement."[8] While Posey's airing of the Clowns complaint likely did little to bolster his case, his more relevant argument was that Bell, having been a National Leaguer for years before going to Santo Domingo with other stars in 1937, and then staying to play in Latin American for several years, had always been NNL property, his partial year with the Chicago American Giants of the NAL in 1942 notwithstanding. At any rate, when the dust settled, Bell was the only one of the 10 players involved to be allowed to stay with his new team, and he was very valuable to the Grays for the duration of the war years.

Player raiding had always been second nature to black baseball owners, given the generally weak enforcement of contract rights in the Negro Leagues. But the war years made these signings more tempting given the general loss of talent to the military and to defense industry jobs that exempted those holding them from the draft. Bell, for example, was signed by the Grays to fill a major void created when player-manager Vic Harris became a part-time player because of his defense job. Negro League owners, as was the case with their white baseball counterparts, were helpless before the needs of the war effort. But they also faced a threat to their rosters from the burgeoning Latin American summer leagues which was in a way more serious, since the best black players were the specific targets.

The leagues made attempts to hold their players, who were being offered significantly higher salaries from teams in Latin American leagues bent on improving the quality of their play. Sizable suspensions were threatened for contract jumpers, including a proposed three-year ban to be imposed on players who headed south in 1940. In addition to hoping to bring the players pause, there was also a theory that this would somehow undercut the big salaries offered in Latin America: "It was felt here that when the foreign owners learn that players they bring to their clubs are under a three-year ban and out of a job in the States, their value in service, rated in dollars and cents, will be greatly diminished."[9]

But the owners decided in the spring of 1941 to allow the defectors to return for payment of a relatively puny $100 fine. Posey was in favor of this. He had written Abe Manley of Newark the previous December that "I think we should get all players back from Mexico, if we can. Otherwise our league is too weak to charge the prices we charge, especially when white semi pro clubs beat us consistently [sic]."[10] Posey wrote this during the period when he thought he had his star, Josh Gibson, convinced to return from Mexico, only to have Gibson turn around and head right back south in the spring of 1941. That's when the Grays sued him.

The reversal of attitude by the Negro Leagues was no different from that following the departures of the core of Greenlee's Crawfords and other top-rank players to Santo Domingo in 1937. Punishment for the contract breakers must have seemed very tempting. But as Grays manager Vic Harris told Wendell Smith just before the 1941 season opened, with Gibson gone again and star pitcher Ray Brown rumored to be joining him (although he didn't), "These leagues in Puerto Rico and Mexico are hurting all the Negro National League clubs.... We can't ignore the fact that all the good ball players are playing on foreign soil." Smith agreed—"Last time I checked there were at least 25 ball players who once romped in the Negro National League now cavorting in the Mexican League.... Ball players are always going to go where they can make the most money."[11]

The owners tried various schemes to keep their players in the country. Effa Manley cooked up a plot to have the New Jersey draft boards of future Hall of Famers Ray Dandridge and Willie Wells, among those who had gone to Mexico, revoke their family based draft deferments and force them to return to the U.S., presumably to play for her. She got nowhere. She and other owners had tried to enlist the U.S. Department of State to put pressure on Mexico to stop the player defections. But the need to keep up good relations with Mexico during the war, to have access to its precious metals and migrant labor supply, resulted in the fadeout of government help to the Negro Leagues. "It looks like the war has played right into the Senors' hands," Wendell Smith observed.[12]

But there were more successful, although not necessarily socially acceptable, ways to deal with the crisis. Rufus Jackson demonstrated one during the 1943 season when he spotted A. J. Guina, the Mexican consul in Pittsburgh, eyeing Grays players during a game at Forbes Field. Although Guina was on a sort of baseball espionage mission, he lacked the qualities that make a good spy. He walked into the park during a July 10 doubleheader against the Cleveland Buckeyes and asked someone who looked as if he might know where he could find Sam Bankhead and Howard Easterling, half of the Grays' starting infield. The guy he asked was Jackson, who, according to Smith's account in the *Courier*, "detected Guina's Latin accent and became suspicious. He asked the diplomat if he were Mexican, and when he found his suspicions were correct, proceeded to escort Guina out of the park." Guina claimed that negotiations were already well underway with the two players, who had "double-crossed the Mexican government" by changing their minds about leaving the states. Guina told Smith that he had gone to the ballpark to confront the two (and to scout Gibson and Buck Leonard, the Grays' two biggest stars). He also maintained that Jackson did much more than "escort" him out of Forbes, and charged him with assault. All charges were dropped shortly thereafter, the Grays' roster stayed intact, and Jackson declared himself satisfied and ready to keep defending his players: "I don't care if they send Pancho Villa."[13]

The player raiding between the two leagues and among the member clubs was something which might well have been quelled by a unified independent authority over the Negro Leagues. This was just what the white majors had done when they created their commissionership in 1920 and hired a Federal district judge, Kenesaw Mountain Landis, who gladly wielded the far-reaching powers given him. In February of 1938, after the Negro American League completed its first season, the topic of a commissioner came up at the first joint NAL-NNL meeting, and there actually was an attempt to name one. But the vote ended in a standoff between the two leagues, with Robert R. Jackson of Chicago favored by the NAL and Joseph H. Rainey of Philadelphia the candidate of the NNL. The American League had brought up the idea of a commissioner (Jackson was their league head), and despite the failure to elect one, the National League owners put themselves on the record in favor of reconsidering the matter at a later joint meeting. But when the two leagues met again in June, the National Leaguers had lost interest.[14]

An effort to elect Jackson the following year seemed close to success, but also failed. According to sources, it was partly because of Posey's opposition. The *New York Amsterdam News* reported that, at a joint meeting of the two leagues' owners held in Pittsburgh in June, Jackson seemed to have the required nine of the 12 owners behind him, before Posey and Effa Manley of the Eagles began lobbying against him, and NNL President Tom Wilson, who had been in favor of Jackson's election, "succumbed toe [*sic*] squawks of the Newark and Homestead contingent" against electing a man from the other league. But it may have been that Wilson wasn't really in favor of Jackson. Posey wrote the Manleys in 1941 after a sit-down meeting with Wilson over several league issues that Wilson was in favor of a commissioner, but "he wants the commissioner to be a man who leans toward the East [his NNL, in other words]."[15]

The attempt to elect Jackson in 1939 was about as close as the two leagues ever came to replicating Judge Landis's rule of the white majors. In 1945, Robert R. Church, Jr., of Memphis was nominated by NAL president John B. Martin of the Chicago American Giants and William C. Hueston by Posey. What might have been expected to be a split six-six vote along league lines was altered only by the Manleys voting for Church, but that still left him two votes short of election.

Over the years, the list of men proposed as possible commissioners (or a similar independent "czar" for the NNL) was an impressive roster of prominent blacks from the East, Midwest, and near South. Jackson, who had been a National Guard major with a black regiment during the Spanish-American War and was thereafter referred to publicly as "Major R. R. Jackson," was a member of the Chicago Board of Alderman and a former Illinois state representative, had run successful businesses, and had been an official for Chicago black baseball teams. Rainey, the grandson and namesake of the first African American member of the U.S. House of Representatives, was a court magistrate in Philadelphia at the time his name came up for the commissionership. He had been a reporter for both black and white newspapers in Philadelphia, and at one time he was editor of the city's black weekly, the *Tribune*. He also was a member of his state's Athletic Commission, the board that licensed boxers and approved prizefights in Pennsylvania.

Others whose names were put forward were William H. Hastie, a Federal district judge and dean of the Howard University Law School during this period and later territorial governor of the U.S. Virgin Islands and a federal appellate court judge; Church, a prominent businessman and politician who had founded the Memphis branch of the NAACP; Dr. Clilan B. Powell, publisher of the leading black New York weekly newspaper, the *Amsterdam News*; Samuel L. Battle, a New York parole commissioner who had been the city's first black police officer; and Hueston, a high-ranking attorney with the postal service who had been president of the first Negro National League after its founder, Andrew "Rube" Foster, was incapacitated in 1927.

Both leagues had from time to time already elected their own commissioners to act as independent arbiters of contract disputes and other matters. But the owners turned out to be loath to give these men the power needed to fully run their leagues. Ferdinand Q. Morton had been turned into a figurehead NNL commissioner and was in the process of being forced out, as had happened to his predecessor, W. Rollo Wilson. Major Jackson had a longer tenure as NAL commissioner, but the *Defender*'s Fay Young described his status by 1941 as "sort of an honorary position if one could even call it that."[16] Since the leagues could operate, more or less to their members' satisfaction, without independent control, it isn't so surprising that widespread agreement on a strong commissioner proved so elusive.

The situation in finding an independent NNL president was no different. Hueston, whom Posey had nominated for overall commissioner in 1939, was his favorite for the league job, too. In 1942, when the Negro Leagues were coping with the stateside effects of war mobilization, he wrote Effa Manley, a strong supporter of Rainey for league president, that the man elected should be someone "who knows the problems of Negro Baseball" and "who has connections with some of the heads of the various agencies" in Washington. "I think Judge Hueston knows baseball," he added.[17]

In the end, it was too difficult for any candidate to become head of the Negro Leagues, or National League head, for that matter. Posey mused in 1943 that "there are bigger obstacles in trying to elect a commissioner of Negro Base Ball than the Germans encountered at Stalingrad." He blamed "the voting cliques who thrive in each league, and the money each league president gets from the East-West Game [Martin and Wilson each received a portion of the game's profits in lieu of an annual salary]." Oliver Brown, sports editor of the *New Jersey Herald-Tribune*, who covered the Eagles, seconded Posey's specific criticisms in a 1944 column about the failure of the leagues to hire a commissioner. But Brown also included in his list of barriers to success Posey himself, who Brown said wouldn't want anyone to be in charge who would make him play by the rules.[18]

Sportswriters for the black weeklies, who favored better-organized leagues, used the inability to elect an independent commissioner as a starting point to criticize black baseball's shortcomings, such as contract-jumping players and unpredictable scheduling, that made the Negro Leagues look plainly inferior to the better-organized white ones. William E. Clark of the *New York Age*, who didn't write regularly on black baseball but was perceptive when he did, pointed out that when the club owners try to run the NNL themselves, "There is bound to be the selfish motive," and ensuing disorganization. Black baseball was ripe for being burlesqued in the media, and when "these same club owners allow the league affairs to be conducted in such a ludicrous fashion, they make themselves the natural target for comedy."[19]

While the black leagues consistently took a beating from the sportswriters for their lack of central organization, it should be remembered that the white majors, with two leagues co-existing since 1901, hadn't hired Judge Landis to wield his non-appealable power until the 1919 Black Sox World Series fixing scandal came along and the press and public clamored for action. The Negro Leagues, well-organized or not, got along without facing that sort of crisis until major league re-integration began to undermine them in 1946.

Then the sea change of racial integration was so profound that it was too late to solve mere operational problems.

Publicly, Posey was in favor of independent control of the Negro Leagues, even if he might have been protective of his own domain when it came to selecting someone to be in charge. But his favorite idea, which he could never put over, was to merge the two leagues into one, dropping weaker teams and creating a single strong loop that "would soon be universally recognized as the third major league of baseball." He went so far in the fall of 1938 as to write several owners to outline what his strong league would look like, inviting them to attend an organizational meeting. His plan was to build on existing franchises in Pittsburgh, Philadelphia, Newark, Chicago and Kansas City, with additional teams from some combination of Midwestern cities such as Columbus, Indianapolis, Detroit, and St. Louis, and franchises in the Baltimore-Washington area and in New York City. Another requirement would be that "We must have clubs in the league who have home parks. We must keep clubs who own their park at home as often as possible."[20]

Many of the points in Posey's plan soon came to fruition in the East, when the Elite Giants moved to Washington, then Baltimore, and the Cubans and Black Yankees joined the NNL, representing New York. But the American League, as early as January 1939, turned him down flat, because his league structure completely eliminated the Southern teams that were often among the NAL's ranks. In a few years, Posey began to see both league presidents as impediments to the survival of black baseball, dear to both his heart and his pocketbook, particularly as integration loomed. He never had a good working relationship with J. B. Martin, whom he found to be "a fine fellow to associate with in a social way" but who was in thrall to the white entrepreneurs, particularly Chicago booking agent Abe Saperstein: "Doc [Martin was a pharmacist] goes along, gets his fifteen hundred dollars from the East-West game as president of the N.A. League and follows orders."[21]

Wilson had replaced Greenlee as NNL president in 1939, and Posey later described his own election as secretary as a way to placate the owners who opposed Wilson. As the years went on, though, the two found themselves allied more often than not on league issues. But Posey became progressively disenchanted with Wilson's laissez faire attitude toward league operations. After the 1942 season, Posey wrote that "Despite the fact the Homestead Grays have been one of President Tom Wilson's most ardent supporters, we feel that he and President J. B. Martin, of the N.A.L., should resign in favor someone who is in a position and willing to help Negro baseball over the present emergency."[22]

What Posey considered an emergency was really more of a trend, the increased encroachment of white booking agents into the power centers of the Negro Leagues. White investment, and even hands-on involvement, in black baseball was nothing new—two of the most powerful black teams of the late 1800s, the Cuban Giants and the Cuban X-Giants, were owned and operated by John Bright and Edward B. Lamar, Jr., respectively. One of the founding owners of the first Negro National League in 1920 was a white man, J. Leslie Wilkinson, of the Kansas City Monarchs (who, with his team, was still going strong in the 1940s). But the nature of a black team's incessant barnstorming travel and small front office staff created a need for assistance in arranging games across the wide geographic stretch that Negro League teams travelled in search of a solid financial bottom line. This help often came from "booking agents," who had gained control of the use of parks in metropolitan areas and could decide who played there.

There were two ways of looking at this arrangement. The assistance that the agents provided in terms of scheduling games and providing pre-game publicity took a burden off the small Negro Leagues front offices. But the services came with a price, usually calculated as a percentage of attendance revenue, the size of which black owners and sportswriters often found oner-ous. It was hard to break this grip the booking agents had on a geographic area, because they were not just serving the black clubs—they often controlled all baseball played at non-major league parks in their regions. The sharing of black baseball's revenue with white men had been prevalent for some time, and white assistance was probably important to the Negro Leagues' survival during the Depression. But the explosion of profits beginning with the nation's industrial upswing to prepare for World War II, as historian Neil Lanctot puts it, "resulted in an increasingly critical reexamination of their roles as booking agents, team owners, promoters, and park proprietors."[23]

In the early days of the Grays' rise to prominence as a nationally known team, Cum Posey had frequently been critical of the agents' power. Whenever possible, he and his staff made their own arrangements in Western Pennsyl-vania and the Midwest. But by the 1940s, he had plenty of critical things to say about the bookers, some of them, some of the time, anyway. Posey was certainly a "race man" when it came to advancing black baseball (or basket-ball, or local government in Homestead), but he could strike up a good rela-tionship with powerful whites when it suited his purposes, such as his relationships with owners Barney Dreyfuss and his son-in-law and successor William Benswanger of the Pittsburgh Pirates and Clark Griffith of the Wash-ington Senators, and his hometown political mentor, John McLean. His reac-tion to the increasing power of the white agents in the 1940s was classic Posey—money equaled power, and if whites were making money off black ball that could have gone to the African American owners, that was bad. However, if the process produced additional money for him and his partner Rufus Jackson, then it was good.

The tension over white agents led to an explosive Negro National League winter meeting in February 1940 that threatened to overturn the leadership structure of the league and got intensely personal among some of the owners, including Posey. The issue on the table at the meeting was who should have booking rights (and the resulting fees) from Negro League games at Yankee Stadium. The underlying issue was how far white executives should be allowed to go in controlling and profiting from the black games.

NATIONAL LEAGUE OFFICERS AND MEMBERS

Officers and members of the Negro National league which met in a two-day session in Chicago and held a joint meeting with the Negro American league on Saturday. Left to right, back row, are: Bill Semler, New York Black Yankees; Vernon Green, secretary of the Baltimore Elite Giants; Bill Leuschner of Nat Strong's booking agency, New York; Alex Pompez, New York Cuban Stars; Ed Gott-lieb, Philadelphia Stars, and S. H. Posey, Homestead Grays. Seated: Allen Page, New Orleans promoter; Ed Bolden, Philadelphia Stars; Cum Posey, Homestead Grays and league secretary; Tom Wilson, president of the league and owner of the Baltimore Elites; Abe Manley, Newark Eagles and treasurer of the league, and Mrs. Effa Manley, Newark Eagles.—Photo by Gushiniere.

The Negro National League owners and others involved with the league sat for a group portrait several days after a rancorous winter meeting in February 1940 that included a shouting match over the scheduling of games in Yankee Stadium and an attempt to vote out the league officers. Some still look unhappy. Cum Posey is third from the left in the front row, uncharacteristically partially hidden, and See Posey is standing on the far right (*Chicago Defender*).

The first time New York Yankees owner Jacob Ruppert had allowed his team's ballpark to be used for Negro games was in 1930, when he lent it to a railway union, the Brotherhood of Sleeping Car Porters, for a fundraising doubleheader between two top Eastern black teams, the New York Lincoln Giants and the Baltimore Black Sox. The success of that doubleheader led to several other games that season, including a portion of the "championship" series between the Grays and the Lincolns. Thereafter the Negro Leagues rented the Stadium for one to three doubleheaders a year, but it did not become a popular, not to mention profitable, venue for black baseball until 1939, when 11 games were played on six dates, with an average attendance of about 13,000. Yankee Stadium was excellently located for Negro Leagues games, not far from the burgeoning black community in Harlem and on a subway line. Plus, it was Yankee Stadium, home to the winningest team in the white majors, whose diamond was graced over the years by stars such as Babe Ruth, Lou Gehrig, and Joe DiMaggio. To play there was, in a way, to proclaim that the Negro Leagues were something special.

By the war years, the NNL was scheduling a dozen or more dates at Yankee Stadium, mostly Sunday doubleheaders. The games continued to draw well, and as at Griffith Stadium in Washington, D.C., the biggest crowds, upwards of 25,000, showed up when Satchel Paige was on the mound. Yankee Stadium may have been the House That Ruth Built, but it was frequently sumptuously furnished with fans when Paige pitched.

In addition to increased demand from fans with more money in their pockets, the success of black baseball at the Stadium beginning in 1939 had a lot to do with the selection of an agent to work with the Yankees management on behalf of the NNL. Edward "Eddie" Gottlieb is more famous in the sports world for his basketball accomplishments. He was a founder of an amateur team from the South Philadelphia Hebrew Association (known handily as the SPHAS) which turned semi-pro, then fully professional during organized basketball's earlier days. Then Gottlieb bought the Philadelphia Warriors of the National Basketball Association and became a powerful figure in the NBA. All this eventually earned him a place in 1972 in the Basketball Hall of Fame, where he was waiting, so to speak, when Posey was inducted in 2016.

Gottlieb's involvement in the Negro Leagues did not earn him a Baseball Hall of Fame plaque, although he was sufficiently noteworthy to have been on the first committee to elect Negro Leaguers to the Hall in 1971. In 1940, he was a powerful booking agent on the East Coast and a co-owner with Edward Bolden of the NNL's Philadelphia Stars. Initially, a drawback to use of the Stadium was the Yankees' preference to charge a flat sum, as much as $3,000, for one day's use of the park. This cut heavily into the portion of the gate available to the black teams playing there. Gottlieb, well known in the Eastern sporting world, had the sort of relationship with the Yankees front office that Posey had with Clark Griffith in Washington. Gottlieb made a deal with the Yankees—in exchange for promising many more playing dates, which generated income for the team on days when it was on the road and the Stadium would otherwise lie idle and unproductive, the Yanks changed their rental fee to 25 percent of the gross gate, with a minimum of $1,000.[24] This arrangement transformed black baseball at the Stadium. The Yankees' share of the gate, which had been as much as 40 or 50 percent, dropped precipitously, freeing up more profit for the black teams. One might think the rest of the NNL owners would have been very appreciative of Gottlieb's efforts, and Posey, for one, was. But the 1940 winter meeting, held at Gottlieb's offices at 507 Market Street in Philadelphia on February 2, was, instead, vitriolic.

In this case, the problem wasn't that the Yankee Stadium games weren't making money (the NNL was in its best financial shape ever). The first issue was that Gottlieb was taking a large, but not usurious, 10 percent cut of the net gate (after the Yankees' share and expenses) for his efforts. The second issue was that, whatever the percentage, it was going to a white man. Three ownership teams were up in arms about these matters: Abe and Effa Manley of the Newark Eagles, Alex Pompez of the New York Cubans, and Jim Semler of the New York Black Yankees. This was not a coalition built for all time— Newark had opposed the readmission of the Cubans to the league in 1939 after a two-year hiatus, and the Manleys generally did not think much of Semler, who was the least competent owner in the league when it came to managing money.[25]

Semler and Pompez objected to Gottlieb getting the Stadium booking business in "their" town. Semler, in particular, wanted to promote the games, claiming he had "been ignored as if he were nothing," although the long and heated discussion brought out evidence that some of his past booking efforts had been far from spectacular. Wilson pointed out, for example, that three dates in 1938 at Downing Stadium on Randall's Island in New York had netted $12 for the participating clubs, and he noted that the league, and Federal tax authorities, were still looking for ticket sales and entertainment taxes that should have been collected at Yankee Stadium and the Polo Grounds at games promoted by Semler in 1938. But it was the Manleys, Effa to be precise, who steered the debate into deep water. "The race issue," the *Chicago Defender* reported, "something which has been kept out of the league meetings before, was brought up by Mrs. Manley who declared, 'the league ought to be run for colored by colored.'" She was also quoted as shouting over a cacophony of voices that "We are fighting for something bigger than a little money!"[26]

The three New York area teams—half of the league's voting power—had more up their collective sleeve, too. When it came time to elect league officers, they tried to depose Wilson by nominating Powell, the physician and newspaper publisher, for league president. It was another attempt to put someone at the head of the league with business or government experience who wouldn't have an interest in one of the teams. The Manleys, Pompez, and Semler all voted for Powell. Posey and Ed Bolden, casting the Stars' ballot, went for Wilson, and Wilson created a tie by voting for himself. The New York contingent actually had an entire insurgent slate in mind, intending to also depose all the incumbents, including Vice President Bolden and Secretaries Posey and Gottlieb. But Wilson, who was caught by surprise when Semler voted against him, so much so that he "almost broke into tears," ruled that since the presidency was unresolved, no votes would be taken on the remaining posts.[27]

As the argumentative meeting continued, the "hot words," in the account of one reporter, "grew hotter" until Posey reportedly jumped up and stormed out of the meeting. This likely was about at the time that Effa Manley went on a tirade about the "handkerchief heads" in charge of the league. A "handkerchief head," in African American slang, is a black person considered to be subservient to white control. The phrase is said to refer to the bandannas worn by Negro house servants at Southern Plantations before the Civil War. Effa Manley, to use a more familiar pejorative, had just called the black heads of her organization, all of whom undoubtedly considered themselves race men to some extent, "Uncle Toms." And if racism was going to be injected into the debate in Gottlieb's office, why not some sexism, too? On the way out of the meeting, Posey confronted Abe Manley and, according to the *Defender*'s man on the scene, "shouted that he would not be back until Abe Manley could keep his wife at home where, Posey said, she belonged."[28]

There wasn't much chance of that ever happening. The Manleys were united in their views of what was best for the Eagles. And what was best for the Negro Leagues. Effa, in fact, recounted that they got involved in 1935 when her husband mused that he could run a team as well as any of the existing NNL owners, leading in short order to their founding the Eagles.[29] Abe Manley, like Gus Greenlee, Pompez, Semler, and Rufus Jackson, had made a lot of money as a numbers banker, although the threat of violence from white gangsters in his Camden, New Jersey, base of operations led him to retire prematurely and move to Harlem, where he met his wife.

The couple divided up the responsibilities of running the Eagles according to their differing temperaments and abilities. Abe had no patience for the administrative side of the business—he liked to drink and play cards with the players, scout for new talent, and frequently get in his field manager's hair by looking too closely over his shoulder. Effa had given up riding the team bus to road games—she tried it once and could clearly sense she was crimping the guys' style. Although only a high school graduate, she had administrative skills and business sense. With the Eagles, tasks such as scheduling games and negotiating player contracts were her responsibility. Away from the ballpark, she was active in civil rights, including an effort in Harlem to get more blacks employed in the community's retail businesses, and in Newark, the New Jersey NAACP. Randy Dixon of the *Courier* once referred to them as "Affable Abe and Effusive Effa."[30]

As the only woman owner in what was still an overwhelmingly male-dominated business, Effa Manley was never an NNL officer. But Abe was sometimes the league treasurer, a job he would not seem to have been fitted for. Except that his wife did all the financial work. As owners, they favored the league adhering to regular scheduling, strong player contract controls, and reliable publicity. Although Posey would be likely to cut a corner or two in adhering to these standards whenever he thought it vital, those were standards that he favored. Where he and the Manleys differed most was one of the issues at stake in Eddie Gottlieb's office—whether an outsider to the Negro Leagues, no matter how well qualified, could run a black league.

The election of officers was put off until February 24, just ahead of the scheduled annual joint meeting with the Negro American League in Chicago. In the meantime, the fallout continued, both in public and private. Posey used his *Courier* column in the February 17 issue to give his side of the story. He defended the Yankee Stadium deal in great detail, pointing out that having the experienced Gottlieb booking the games had not only reduced the Yankees' share of the gate, but had made it possible to greatly increase the number of games played, since Gottlieb footed the advance rental payment the Yankees required, and used his own liability insurance. "The promoter took all the headaches, the league clubs walked into the Stadium, and twenty minutes after the game was over, walked out with their shares," which totaled $16,000 for all of 1939. Gottlieb made $1,100.[31]

Also, in typical Posey sidewinding fashion, he criticized Effa Manley: "we have never heard so much senseless chatter and baying at the moon as was done by one party," but never identified her by name. She responded in a letter in which she reminded him that she had a file of previous correspondence between the two, and "apparently your memory has played you some cruel tricks." She also threatened to publicize Posey's apparent changes of position, whatever they were, and "if you persist in your unjustifiable attacks in the *Courier* you leave me no other alternative."[32]

Posey had calmed down considerably a few days later when he wrote back. Not that he was happy: "All this mess at the league meeting was not necessary (you, for some unknown reason, are always attempting to force some one, who don't know a thing about base ball, on the league [as president]). You admit you don't know anything about the game, but still get mad and insulting with every body who disagrees with you." But he was getting philosophical and was showing a bit of humor about the clash: "Personally I got a kick out of the whole thing as it gave a lot of people whom we thought were friendly, a chance to get some thing off their mind. I am still ready to keep my mouth shut at league meetings if you do." Posey and the other NNL officers had been criticized by the New York-area black press, and he seemed sure that the city's half of the league had put the journalists up to it. But his attitude about this, too, was calm: "When you have the writers of New York and Newark write about me, I think, well that gives President Roosevelt a rest from them. When I write about you, then think of the space you are taking up, which would be allotted to Eleanor."[33]

He was certainly right that the New York area black press took the side of the Manleys, Pompez, and Semler. Dan Burley of the *Amsterdam News*, in particular, blasted the entrenched faction for its closeness to whites: "Wilson and his cohorts want Yankee Stadium run like it has been with white boys chasing balls; white ticket takers; white everywhere, even on the sound trucks that advertise coming attractions on Seventh and Lenox avenues and on 135th Street [the heart of Harlem, in other words], while thousands of capable Negroes stand idle as Gottlieb gives off the benefits of the New York promotions to members of his own race." The February 24 edition of the *Amsterdam News* also carried a biting editorial cartoon showing a hungry-looking Gottlieb, with knife and fork in hand at the dinner table, being served a sumptuous meal of "NNL Promotions" by three subservient black waiters labeled "Cum Posey," "Tom Wilson," and "Ed Bolden." It was likely the only time that the well-known and well-regarded Posey had been so caricatured in print, in a cartoon or otherwise.[34]

But even in his February 17 letter, written two weeks after the blowup, Posey was already trying to bring the National League back together. He was proposing an owners meeting in Pittsburgh just before the meeting with the NAL, so "we could at least arrive in Chicago with some semblance of cordiality towards each other." He planned on including dinner at the Loendi Club, to which the press would also be invited. It's not clear that the preliminary meeting took place, but the owners all went to Chicago, where another presidential ballot produced another three-three tie. Alex Pompez then proposed that the incumbent officers be continued for another year, and everyone decided that would solve matters for the time being. The matter of Gottlieb's 10 percent fee was also somewhat resolved at the 1941 winter meeting, when he agreed to return two percent of his booking earnings to the league treasury.[35]

The letters between Posey and Effa Manley after the league meeting were only a small portion of the correspondence that passed back and forth between them over their years as team owners. Most of the things they covered were purely routine, such as scheduling and finances, especially in the years when Abe was treasurer and Effa was handling all of that business. But there were several exchanges about league politics that showed how they aligned on the big issues. One of the most interesting was in the fall of 1941. In October, Manley wrote Posey a long letter detailing a number of things, major and minor, to which the league needed to attend. It included another plea to take the Yankee Stadium bookings away from Gottlieb, based in no uncertain terms on a racial argument: "If we had the money in the league treasury that Has [*sic*] been put into the o-fays pockets, we would be able to do a lot of things."[36] (The irony in Effa's racial equity stance, particularly the use of a slang disparagement toward whites, is that in her later years, when she was a spokesperson for the rediscovered history of the Negro Leagues, she claimed to be genetically white. She based this on what her mother Bertha had told her about herself being white, and Effa's birth having been the result of an affair Bertha had with a white businessman. The truth about the father's genetics, or his true identity for that matter, is unlikely to be found. But genealogical work by descendants of Effa's half-sister strongly indicate that Effa's mother was, at least in part, Caucasian).

Mrs. Manley's position on Gottlieb was unchanged, but Posey, responding a month later, agreed with her. He came out strongly for league control of bookings in the white majors' parks "and not as a promotion to further individuals' prestige and pocketbooks." He was shortly planning a trip to Nashville to see Tom Wilson, to tell him that "I want him as President of the Negro National League to get Yankee Stadium away from Gottlieb." There is no indication of any major falling out between Posey and Gottlieb since Posey had so forcefully defended him in February 1940. It just appears that in Posey's eyes, Gottlieb had run his course as a financially useful intermediary for the Negro Leagues. By the end of the 1941 season, Posey had the Grays established in two major league parks, Forbes Field in Pittsburgh and Griffith Stadium in Washington (although attendance at Griffith didn't take off until the following year), and had just participated in a return of black ball to Briggs Stadium in Detroit that had drawn more than 20,000 fans. He had every reason from his own experience to think that the league could pull off its own bookings.[37]

At this point Posey, the man who seemed to make connections easily with major league club owners and other prominent whites in organized baseball, had it in for the whites involved in the Negro Leagues, and the blacks he thought were assisting them. In that same reply to Effa Manley, he included a list of baseball men whose actions upset him. On it were several whites: Gottlieb; William Leuschner, a booking agent in New York City who had a financial interest in the Black Yankees; J. L. Wilkinson and Thomas Baird, co-owners of the Kansas City Monarchs; Abe Saperstein, a powerful agent from Chicago, and Syd Pollock, white owner of the independent Ethiopian Clowns and a Saperstein associate. He also threw in Negro American League President Martin; Horace Hall, an officer along with Martin of the Chicago American Giants of the NAL, and Fay Young, sports columnist for the *Chicago Defender*.[38]

Posey also used his *Courier* column to trumpet the threat from the whites to continued black control of the Negro Leagues. His main target was Saperstein, who had been booking basketball and baseball teams in the Chicago area for about 20 years, and who had already created the Harlem Globetrotters, the most well-known barnstorming black basketball team. Among Saperstein's jobs was to publicize the annual East-West All-Star Game, and he also had financial connections, as booking agent or actual investor, in more than one American League team. Posey saw him as dominating the Midwestern-based NAL, and he feared that East Coast white agents, presumably Gottlieb and Leuschner (who between them had a majority of the best ballparks in the region under their control, plus partnerships in two NNL teams) would make similar inroads into the NNL. "It is up to all who have any interest in organized Negro athletic enterprises to stop Saperstein, Pollock or any others who are attempting to monopolize them," he wrote in October. He was so fed up with league officials who would not stop them (J. B. Martin, for sure, and likely the other league president, Wilson), that the next month he pined for the return of his old foe, Gus Greenlee, who was making noises about getting back into baseball, as opposed to "the pious, and hypocritical crowd who are bowing and scraping [to the whites]."[39]

Posey had no success in ousting the booking agents. But in 1943, he was deeply involved in an ultimately successful effort to fight off an unintended consequence of the war effort that some in black baseball thought might kill off their livelihood. As the United States' involvement in World War II increased, rationing was imposed on many kinds of goods and services, including transportation. Since a substantial portion of the world's rubber production was in Pacific Ocean countries that had been captured by the Japanese, there was a serious vehicle tire shortage. New tires were rationed and then, in late 1942, gasoline use was also restricted to reduce the mileage on the increasingly worn tires on American vehicles.

Those vehicles included privately owned buses. They were the preferred mode of transportation for travelling entertainment outfits such as bands and theater groups, as well as baseball teams below the level of the white major leagues, where travel was almost exclusively by train. The restriction on buses exacerbated the outright loss of young players to the armed services as the number of white minor leagues shrank.[40] But the Negro Leagues weren't planning on closing. The migration to the wartime industrial work where their teams were located was increasing, not lowering, profits. As had the white majors, the black teams had made plans to hold spring training in the north, near their home cities, to avoid the long trips to warmer climes. At the 1943 pre-season NNL meeting in January, the big worry wasn't a supply of gasoline, which reportedly would be made available in unlimited quantities to the leagues by the Office of Defense Transportation, but a shortage of players due to the military draft. "The owners now find themselves with plenty of gas," the *Courier* reported, "but it may develop that they'll be without a diamond cargo to haul around this summer."[41]

John L. Clark, the former National League secretary now working as the Grays' publicist, predicted on March 6 that "Although some Negro teams are going to feel the restrictions that war has caused, especially in the way of gas and rationing of tires, most of them in the two organized league [*sic*] should have an unprecedented year financially ... The majority will play in nearby boom towns where people spend freely and like sports after a hard day of work in a defense plant."[42]

But Clark likely changed his outlook, as the black ball owners changed theirs only a few days later, when ODT head Joseph B. Eastman announced a directive that would, in fact, ban baseball bus travel. Posey, representing the NNL as its secretary, and J. B. Martin, the NAL president, both had asked for clarification of the order as it pertained to the Negro Leagues, and they got it, in a most unsatisfactory way.[43] If the black teams wanted to travel from city to city, Eastman ruled, they could use the railroads, just as their white counterparts did. Except that the number of non-league games the white majors played was minuscule compared to those on the leagues' championships schedules, and financially were only a minor part of their income. For Negro Leagues teams, though, the non-league barnstorming games in smaller cities and towns not easily accessible by train or commercial bus usually amounted to more than half of those played each season. They were financially crucial. As sportswriter Jim Schlemmer in Akron, Ohio, explained it, "in years past the Homestead Grays, for example, would play a morning game in Findlay or Lorain, an afternoon game in Cleveland or Akron and a night game in Youngstown or Canton ... on the same day." But now, "There is no hope for these teams to carry on if they are forced to travel by train or on public buses. The trains and buses do not go where the Negro teams want to go, nor when they want to go."[44]

The Grays' schedule in 1943, as measured by games that got reported in the major newspapers, both white and black, found them in major cities, where they mostly played Negro League opponents, with some games against military all-star teams and top-ranked semi-pro clubs such as the Bushwicks of Brooklyn mixed in. The primary route of travel for the team was back and forth between its two hometowns, Washington and Pittsburgh, where it played a total of 50 games on 34 different dates.

In June, Posey said that forcing the black teams to travel from city to city by railroad day coach was expensive: "Homestead Grays during the past week made a trip to Buffalo, Niagara Falls, and Erie, Pa. During this trip the Grays paid more money for taxi fares after getting off the trains than it would have cost to make the whole trip in their bus." Deciding to travel by train was one thing, but sometimes finding room on the train along with servicemen and other travelers kept off the highways by gas rationing was another. Buck Leonard, the Grays' first baseman, recalled the team having to ride in the baggage car on one trip, because all the seats were full and the conductor refused to allow them to stand in the aisles. Posey realized that road travel, with fewer games and higher travel costs, was a money-losing proposition for the black clubs: "The clubs of 1943 who are not drawing at home are in a precarious position." He certainly wasn't throwing in the towel, though: "Despite this, the clubs or organized [black] baseball are determined to carry on at least for the 1943 season."[45]

Posey certainly was carrying on. Despite his cool feelings toward Martin as NAL president, this was no time for personal politics. The two, with help from others, began immediately to lobby Washington. Washington Senators owner Clark Griffith, with whom Posey had developed a mutually valuable relationship over the use of the Griffith Stadium, stepped up almost immediately to arrange a meeting for Posey and Martin with the ODT on March 6.[46] At Eastman's request, Posey quickly surveyed the NNL teams, and by March 13 he had put together a report on bus usage and the relocation northward of spring training in 1943 (the Grays would train in Akron).

As for the upcoming regular season, Posey had worked with Gottlieb to devise a possible schedule that "can cut our League schedule mileage to less than one half by keeping the opposing clubs in the same league city for two and three days instead of one and by using day coaches." His report also emphasized the importance of Negro Leagues ball: "We have built our league through 25 years of steady work. We have never had a breath of scandal attached to any of our games…. We are now recognized as the Major league of Negro baseball by the public, both colored and white." The report to the ODT lacked some regular Posey touches—no indication that he, above all people, knew what was correct, and no criticism of anyone else. He was in an entirely different situation here from his usual approach to league affairs. His fortunes, and those of his fellow owners, were on the line, and he was going to be entirely reasonable in defending them.[47]

Griffith wasn't the only prominent white to go to bat for the Negro Leagues' bus use—U.S. Sen. Harry S. Truman was among those supporting a petition drive in Kansas City. But Eastman, while sympathetic, was unmoved. The only concession made was to entitle the black teams to a monthly gasoline allowance of 360 to 470 miles, which was a drop in the bucket compared to the usual barnstorming use of a Negro League bus. So the black teams got on the trains, for the most part, while Posey and others continued to lobby the ODT. Success came in June, largely through government recognition of the problems facing the Negro American League. The NAL had four franchises in the Midwest, but also teams in Birmingham and Memphis. The combination of rail travel and the small monthly gasoline allotment was insufficient to allow the two Southern teams to meet the other four on a regular schedule. Accordingly, the ODT in June allowed the league a monthly quota of 2,000 miles of bus travel, limited to the Southern states. The NNL convinced the government in 1944 to allow it the same ration for Southern use, even though none of its teams were located south of Washington which, as the national capital, was easily reached by rail. As the war went on and the Negro Leagues buses continued to roll, suspicions were raised more than once about why leagues with few locations in the South needed these Southern exemptions, but no official action against the National or American resulted.[48]

Chapter Ten

"Baseball Has Lost Its Greatest Name—Cum Posey!"

The issues, routine or contentious, that Posey and the other owners dealt with were usually ones that had to be faced every season in some form or another. No matter how they were dealt with, Opening Day came around each year, and the black leagues played on until fall. But as the war moved toward its end, an existential issue faced the Negro Leagues when the white majors and minors were (finally) re-integrated, with the first acknowledged black players since the nineteenth century on previously white rosters. The long-closed door cracked open for Jackie Robinson in 1946 and Larry Doby in 1947, then kept widening as a trickle of the best African American ballplayers, becoming a stream of black talent, flowed into Organized Baseball. From the historical perspective, this long-awaited arrival of black players was a momentous event in the story of the progress of racial equality in America, something to which no black citizen should have been opposed.

But the door only opened for the players. The owners and executives of white ball had no use for their black ball colleagues, at least not as equals. The black teams' owners nonetheless held out hope for some time that a merger of the two races' leagues was possible. This put the black owners, particularly the progressive ones like Posey who favored more rights and opportunities for their race, in a difficult spot. Successful integration could deprive them of their best players, and many of their black fans might follow those players to Organized Baseball's ticket windows. The demolishing of baseball's color barrier, in other words, could put them out of business. There was no way a Negro League team owner, not even the canny Cumberland Posey, could successfully deal with this situation without appearing to be lukewarm, at best, to the historic goal of integration.

Financially, the war years were the best the Negro Leagues ever experienced, even with the travel difficulties and loss of players to the armed services. But percolating below the surface was the major societal change of integration, being heated up by the war itself. Well over a million American blacks enlisted or were drafted during the war, and their service, often in combat, raised the question of why, if they could serve their country, they faced segregation of various kinds, official and otherwise, at home. This argument came to apply to baseball players, too. For several years before the war, a handful of well-known white journalists such as Heywood Broun, Westbrook Pegler, and Jimmie Powers had publicly endorsed the entry of black players in the white majors. In 1939, Wendell Smith of the *Pittsburgh Courier* visited all eight teams in the white National League, interviewing managers and players on the question of whether or not blacks should be allowed to play. He found a high degree of acceptance from the major leaguers. In the newspaper's home town, Paul Waner, the Pirates' star outfielder, who had played against Negro Leaguers in winter ball in California, told Smith, "I have seen any number of Negro ball players who could have made good in the big leagues." His manager, Pie Traynor, said that "Personally, I don't see why the ban against Negro players exists at all."[1]

But managers and players, however they felt, weren't going to be the driving force in integrating professional baseball. The team owners, and their employees, the baseball commissioner and league presidents, were the ones who would make it happen, if it ever did. In December 1943, the editors and publishers of the country's major African American newspapers were granted a hearing on the subject by the white major league brain trust. The major league commissioner, Kenesaw Mountain Landis, opened the meeting by stating, "I want to make it clear that there is not, never has been, and, as long as I am connected with baseball, there never will be any agreement among the teams or between any two teams preventing Negroes from participating in organized baseball." Some of the black press was thrilled by Landis's statement—Smith called it an "unqualified, official bombshell." Dan Burley of the *Amsterdam News* was considerably less impressed. He called Landis's statement an "opening wedge," but maintained that "the majors don't intend to do anything unless forced to do so."[2]

Less than two years later, Brooklyn Dodgers President Branch Rickey signed Kansas City Monarchs infielder Jackie Robinson to a minor league contract, and Robinson opened the 1946 season as a regular with the Dodgers' top farm team, the Montreal Royals of the International League. He was followed across the color line by other Negro Leaguers, usually the younger stars (and the eternally young Satchel Paige, who went to the majors in 1948). The effect on the Negro Leagues was immediate. The fans of black baseball, who had also always liked white major league baseball, started turning even more of their attention and ticket dollars to the clubs that boasted integrated rosters.

Effa and Abe Manley's Newark Eagles were surrounded by the Jackie Robinson phenomenon. As a Montreal Royal, he played in both their back yard (against the Jersey City Giants) and in their very home, Ruppert Stadium in Newark, which they rented from the Newark Bears, another International League club. In 1947 he was promoted to the parent Dodgers, who played 88 games in New York City, 77 at home in Ebbets Field and 11 more in the Giants' Polo Grounds. As a result, Eagles attendance dived from 120,092 in 1946, when they won the Negro World Series, to 57,119 the next season. The attendance falloff for Negro League games actually preceded Robinson's appearance in Montreal and Brooklyn. The Grays, who had consistently pulled five-figure crowds to Griffith Stadium during the war, saw the head count for dates there drop to an average of about 5,000. Brad Snyder surmises that "Maybe it was the impending end to the war, maybe it was all the talk about integration, but large numbers of black Washingtonians rarely flocked to Griffith Stadium in 1945 to see the Grays play."[3]

There certainly was talk of integrating baseball in 1945, and some action, although an important portion of it was clandestine, and the part the public could see contributed nothing directly toward putting black players on white teams. On April 6, Joe Bostic, an African American New York sportswriter, showed up at the Dodgers' spring training site at Bear Mountain, north of New York City, with two Negro League veterans, former Grays pitcher Terris McDuffie and first baseman Dave Thomas, and demanded that Brooklyn give them a tryout. They were given a look, but nothing came of it. Ten days later, Smith of the *Courier*, working with Boston city councilman Isidore Muchnick, who had been pressing the Red Sox to integrate, brought Robinson, outfielder Sam Jethroe, and infielder Marvin Williams to Fenway Park for a tryout. Unlike McDuffie, age 37, and Thomas, all of 40, the three players the Red Sox looked were all in their athletic prime, and prime candidates as well, as their subsequent careers proved. In addition to Robinson, Jethroe later made the integrated majors and was named the National League Rookie of the Year in 1950 with the Boston Braves, while Williams went on to play high-level minor league ball. Nonetheless, the Red Sox couldn't see their way to signing any of them in 1945.

There was action outside the ballparks, too, particularly in New York, where the state had passed a law that spring creating an anti-discrimination commission (one reason the Dodgers had acquiesced to the Bear Mountain tryouts, even though McDuffie and Thomas were clearly too venerable to become major leaguers, was to not fun afoul of the new law).[4] A labor-backed group, the Citizens Committee to End Jim Crow in Baseball, was active, too, its work being championed by the American Communist Party newspaper, the *Daily Worker*. Among the dozens of dignitaries on the committee was a sole Negro Leagues executive, Effa Manley. The Jim Crow Committee was planning on picketing outside New York's major league stadiums that summer, but was dissuaded by Mayor Fiorello LaGuardia and Dan Dodson, the chairman of the Mayor's Committee on Unity.

As part of his duties, Dodson had called on the presidents of the city's major league teams. Rickey of the Dodgers had let him on a secret—he had a plan to integrate his team, but he was working quietly and deliberately toward it. Outside interference would only disrupt his covert operation, which had been in the works since 1943 when, again in secret, he had let the Dodgers' owners in on his eventual plans to sign black players. Rickey actually had Dodgers scouts out evaluating talent, including Robinson, supposedly to staff the Brooklyn Brown Dodgers in the upstart United States League. This was an otherwise under-funded and under-talented upstart opponent to the established Negro Leagues that existed less than two full seasons, beginning in the spring of 1945. In the end, the USL didn't accomplish much other than to provide a smokescreen for Rickey's plan, although it did bring together the tee-totaling, highly religious Rickey and Posey's old nemesis-opponent-friend Gus Greenlee, whose non-baseball career involved the numbers business and night clubs, and who was owner of a USL franchise.

After Robinson proved to be almost immediately of major league caliber, the dominoes began to fall. Cleveland Indians owner Bill Veeck signed Larry Doby of the Newark Eagles in the middle of the 1947 season, integrating the American League. The St. Louis Browns signed two Negro Leaguers, outfielder Willard Brown and infielder Hank Thompson, later that season. Doby, Brown, and Thompson were immediately put on the big league clubs' rosters, where, under immense pressure, they bombed. The Indians stuck with Doby, who became a hard-hitting outfield star. Brown and Thompson went back to black ball, although Thompson would return to the majors as a regular on the integrated New York Giants teams of the 1950s. Doby and Brown, for his Negro League accomplishments, would eventually get into the Hall of Fame. Robinson may have been an historic signing for the Dodgers for the 1946 season, but Rickey also recruited four other Negro Leaguers that year for his minor league system. He signed catcher Roy Campanella and pitchers John Wright, Don Newcombe, and Roy Partlow.

Veeck paid the Eagles $15,000 for the rights to Doby, and Rickey gave the Philadelphia Stars $1,000 for Partlow, but the other players, Robinson included, were signed to Organized Baseball contracts for no compensation to their previous teams. Rickey saw the future, which was well populated with Negro ballplayers, but his vision had no place for Negro League executives. Standing side by side with Greenlee at the introductory press conference for the USL in May 1945, Rickey "betrayed no sense of irony when he denounced the existing Negro American and Negro National Leagues as 'organizations in the zone of a racket,'" pointing out the inadequacy of their player contracts, which contained no reserve clause (the language that bound a player to his team for the forthcoming season unless he was traded or released).[5]

It's not at all clear that, even had the Negro Leagues precisely emulated the procedures of the white majors, they would have been accepted into Organized Baseball's fellowship. Opening the doors to black employees (the players) was one thing, but sharing the profits from success was something else entirely. At any rate, the consistent failures of the two black leagues to correct their various administrative and operational shortcomings over the years now came back to haunt them at the hour when their entire existence was on the line. Some of the deficiencies, such as player raiding, Posey had abetted. Some, such as allowing control of the black version of the game to escape the hands of African Americans, he had opposed. But at the end of 1945, he was unquestionably fighting for the Negro Leagues and getting frustrated when their status didn't improve.

Robinson signed with the Dodgers organization in October 1945. On November 1, Posey drafted an open letter to Major League Baseball Commissioner Albert B. "Happy" Chandler that, edited by someone else and eventually signed by him and league presidents Wilson and Martin, noted Robinson's signing, as well as overtures being made to other players to join either Brooklyn's minor league organization or the Brown Dodgers of the USL. "We are not protesting the signing of Negro Players by white organized baseball," the letter stated. "We are glad to see our players get the opportunity to play in white Organized Baseball."

What Posey, Martin, and Wilson objected to was "the way it is done," which was signing the players without compensation. "The Negro National & American Leagues have constitutions, keep minutes of their meetings and have player contracts just the same as any baseball league of white organized baseball," they maintained, citing the successful civil breach of contract case against Josh Gibson filed by the Grays in 1941. So, they continued, the proper way for the white system to acquire black players was through "deals made between clubs involved [meaning money changing hands]."[6]

The letter, undoubtedly with some behind-the-scenes work by Posey, also brought forth support from Clark Griffith of the Washington Senators.

He wrote Posey that "I have written the Commissioner calling his attention to the fact that <u>custom</u> makes <u>Law</u> and that the Negro National and American Leagues are under this custom entitled to every consideration and fair dealing from Organized Baseball."[7] But the letter to Chandler, like Griffith's letter, was an acknowledgment that the Negro Leagues were already at a disadvantage. There was no claim here to equality, only that the black leagues would be willing to act as a conduit to train and promote good black players to the majors.

In a January 10, 1946, letter to Effa Manley, Posey, who had only two months more to live, expressed extreme frustration with what he thought was lack of progress toward building a protective carapace around the leagues. He referred to the failure to elect independent league presidents and asked, "do you realize we have not made one single change for the better since Negro baseball was called a 'racket?'" He mentioned an effort, which proved to be unsuccessful, but which he supported at this late date in his and his league's life, to elect Samuel L. Battles, a New York parole commissioner who had been the first black policeman in Manhattan, as NNL president. "It is just pure selfishness by Dr. Martin, Gottlieb that keeps us in this present position," he wrote. "I am tired of catching hell to perpetuate unworthy office holders."[8]

As to the possibility of a breakthrough of black players into white organized ball, Negro League owners had often been quoted as favoring it. Martin, who said he was speaking for all the owners in the NAL, said in 1943, "I want it clearly understood that we are not opposed to any move which would advance Negro players to the major leagues." Effa Manley told sports editor Nat Low of the *Daily Worker* in 1942 that she was "pulling for [her Eagles' best players] to make the grade." Posey had been even more positive about Negro Leaguers' abilities, as far back as the late 1930s. In a 1938 column, he held that "Practically every player of the Negro National League can play well enough to belong to some League of Organized Ball. They would rate from Class D Leagues [the lowest minor leagues] to the Major Leagues." He named a dozen black stars, including his top three players, Josh Gibson, Buck Leonard, and Ray Brown, as "worthy of tryouts" by big league clubs. A year later he wrote that "it is a d--- shame that every other race on the face of the globe can join and enjoy the fruits of Organized Baseball except the Negro, than whom there is no more loyal American citizen."[9]

But during the wartime years, as integration seemed to become more possible, owner support for it included expectations that the black leagues would benefit when their players crossed the color line. Manley's 1942 statement included the rosy prediction that, as was the case when the white majors drafted from minor league teams, the Negro teams would fare well, because "it improves them, because many hundreds of new stars take up the game, and interest generally is heightened by the addition of new talent." In addition to vowing that the NAL owners wouldn't stand in the way of their players, Martin added the caveat, "We only ask that if and when the majors decide to admit Negro players, they will give us the same consideration in regards to the acquisition of these players that they give to the minor leagues."[10]

At the same time that Manley and Martin were saying that they were expecting (or hoping for, as the case might be) fair treatment from white baseball, Posey was of a different mind. He saw the best approach for the Negro Leagues as not to eventually acquiesce to the loss of players, but rather to strengthen black baseball to the point at which it could meet white major league teams head-on. As he described it in a June 1942 column, this would include his "one league" idea. "We think the logical step is to work for one Negro major league playing every day baseball. Then at the end of the season meet the clubs which win the pennant in the [white] National league and American league." His briefly outlined scheme did not include any mention of integrated teams, and he admitted that "This may appear like the selfish desire of one who is a part of organized Negro baseball, but it is logical and can be worked out." His self-interest was evident in other ways, too. The try-out at Fenway Park in 1945 that featured Robinson and Jethroe was originally to have included Grays outfielder Dave Hoskins. But Posey wouldn't release him without an option on his services from the Red Sox, who seemed to have minimal enthusiasm for showcasing the players, much less signing them, so Marvin Williams took Hoskins's place.[11]

That August, he devoted an entire column to the question of integration and clearly discussed its promise and peril:

> As a Negro we have felt deeply the inability of owners of Negro baseball clubs to place star Negro players in that realm of financial security which surrounds star white players. As part owner of a baseball club in the Negro National League, we have sought in many ways a solution which would repay us for the many years of financial losses, to obtain recognition for the clubs of organized Negro baseball, and thus for the players on the 12 clubs of organized Negro baseball.

He knew that integration of baseball was an issue to now be reckoned with. "It is a problem long discussed, and recently, an answer demanded as to the direct yes or no.... We do not know what the answer will be. It has become a national crisis." He was well aware of the silent barrier thrown up to black players: "We would be a hypocrite to state that we do not think there is a tacit understanding which prohibits Negro players from entering white organized baseball."[12]

But the demand for a reckoning was quickly making nuanced positions on the issue untenable. The sporting press, particularly at the black weeklies, wanted action, and so increasingly did politicians who were gaining anti-discrimination weapons such as the New York law. African American men and women were in the military, some being killed or wounded, and the question of why they should have to come home to a segregated America was being asked over and over. The public view of Negro League team owners boiled down to believing that either they were foursquare for the breaking down of the color line at any secondary cost or they were guilty of impeding progress. For example, Effa Manley had a long track record, both in and out of baseball, of working for civil rights and against discrimination. But she was bitterly criticized after the 1946 season when she (as probably the only owner who could get away with this) forced Rickey to abandon the uncompensated signing of star outfielder Monte Irvin. The fact that she subsequently sold Irvin's contract to the New York Giants for $5,000 did little to un-tar her reputation at the time.

Posey came in for criticism, too. One of the points he often made during the long integration discussion was that black ball was now thriving in great part because of its ability to play at white major league parks, which both accommodated big crowds and burnished the black leagues' reputations just by being allowed to take the field there. Too much politicking for integration, he warned, could disrupt that profitable arrangement. This brought him pointed criticism from columnist Burley in the *Amsterdam News*, who mocked him: "Posey ... pointed out with a trembling finger the danger such 'agitation' might bring to pass if the colored club owners even so much as raised a whisper against the grave injustice and downright indecency of barring colored players from organized baseball."[13]

So far as Posey's reputation as being less than enthusiastic about integration went, it didn't help him in the eyes of the black writers that he had close ties to Clark Griffith, one of the white major league owners most antagonistic to Rickey's integrationist steps. Griffith began to criticize Rickey in the spring of 1945, when Rickey announced his participation in the USL, maintaining that the Dodgers' president was contributing to the undermining of the existing Negro Leagues. It did not go unnoticed that the Negro National and American leagues, for which Griffith was going to bat, provided much-needed revenue for the Senators through games that the Grays booked at Griffith Stadium. Wendell Smith charged that "Clark Griffith's defense of the present Negro leagues is not motivated by anything but his own selfish interests. He makes money by renting his park to the Homestead Grays. He doesn't want any one fooling around with that profitable mellon [*sic*]."

Smith compared Griffith to segregationist Congressman John E. Rankin and U.S. Sen. Theodore G. Bilbo, and further blasted him as someone to be ignored: "No individual who denies the citizens of the country in which he lives and thrives an opportunity is worth listening to. There is nothing any guy can say to me who waves the flag in the shadow of the Capitol and at the same time sneers at the citizens doing the saluting."[14]

In February 1946, Smith turned his entire *Courier* column over to Posey, who wrote on the state of the Negro Leagues. "His observations are worth studying carefully," Smith wrote in an introduction, "because he is one of the most successful operators in Negro baseball." According to Posey, a lot was wrong with black baseball at this challenging time of its existence. He didn't mention any shortcomings that had not already been discussed, but he made it clear that the Grays "violently oppose these old schemes and new methods, which are for the good of Organized Negro Baseball but will be profitable to those who are attempting to put them over in the league." He laid black ball's shortcomings at the feet of three men. Two of them, Eddie Gottlieb and Tom Wilson, he assured his readers, he held in personal respect.

The problem with Gottlieb was still that he controlled too many Negro National League bookings in the east, and took too big a percentage cut of the gate for his services. Posey had vociferously defended Gottlieb at the 1940 NNL winter meeting, but he had stopped taking his side long since, and now even reached back in time to criticize his fellow owner. He noted that Gottlieb had been a part-owner of the Philadelphia Stars since 1934, during the Depression, and "We doubt if Eddie Gottlieb lost any money in booking from 1934 to 1940 while the clubs, who were losing money, paid him ten per cent." Regarding Gottlieb, he concluded that "Eddie Gottlieb is honest in his dealing, and a good baseball man, but he must come to realize that the Negro National League was not organized for his benefit."

As for Wilson, he was "one of the best liked men in baseball" but "has allowed himself to be dominated by Dr. J. B. Martin in all controversies between the two leagues." He blamed the influence of Martin (aided by Gottlieb) on Wilson for there not being enough potentially profitable games between NNL teams, since playing dates in the NNL's eastern territory were used to host barnstorming NAL teams, although the American League did not return the favor in its Midwestern area.

Posey's text didn't have anything personally bad to say about Martin, although whoever wrote the sub-headlines throughout the column added "Martin Rules Like Dictator." Otherwise, Posey's evaluation of the NAL president was one criticism after another. Martin, he maintained, had too much control over the annual East-West All-Star Game, which was played in Chicago, his home city, each year, was afraid of Midwestern booking czar

Abe Saperstein, who Posey long believed was a much worse problem for the leagues than his Eastern counterpart Gottlieb, and was a major roadblock to the election of an independent commissioner. Posey also pointed out the conflict of interest created by the ownership of the NAL's Memphis franchise by two of Martin's brothers.

He criticized a move to appoint Wilson and Martin as the delegation to deal with Commissioner Chandler and other white baseball leaders to resolve the uncompensated signings of black players, without simultaneously "getting our house in order." Posey had been for and against many things in his long career as a black baseball man, his opinions often colored by what was good for the Homestead Grays, but not necessarily for everyone else. But now he laid down a multi-point agenda of what must be fixed if the black leagues were to survive: "Haphazard schedules must be a thing of the past. The cities that support Negro Organized Baseball are due [the East-West Game], and Chicago should have no monopoly on it. These and other reforms will automatically come to life if club owners cease to be officers."

At the end of the column, he once more raised the idea of a well-organized black league holding its own against the white majors: "The baseball public is more interested in seeing Negro baseball properly operated than they are in having white organized baseball clubs pay for players secured from Negro Organized Baseball clubs."[15]

Unfortunately, other than through his writing, Posey was unable to do much to influence the future of the Negro Leagues at this point. In January he began a business letter to Effa Manley with the comment, "I have been very sick." His health had been failing since the previous summer. According to his daughter Beatrice, there was some question about just what was ailing him: "There wasn't the ability to diagnose things as well in those days. First they told him he had an abscess on his lung, then a tumor, and after awhile they said he had inoperable cancer." Neither he nor Rufus Jackson had attended the joint NNL-NAL off-season meeting in Chicago in December, an absence that Mrs. Manley thought had killed yet another chance to elect Battles as an independent league president, since it reopened the door for Tom Wilson to run yet again for reelection.[16]

Posey and Jackson were at the Hotel Theresa in Harlem for the follow-up meeting February 20 and 21 when the president would be elected, but Posey never left his hotel room. (Jackson cast the Grays' vote for Battles, but the Manleys' Eagles vote was the only other one for him, and Wilson was reelected, 4–2). Posey had gone to New York for the meeting against his doctor's advice, and he was bedridden at home upon returning to Homestead. His longtime political partner, Homestead Burgess John J. McLean, came to visit him, became alarmed at his condition, and persuaded him to be admitted immediately to Pittsburgh's Mercy Hospital. He died there on March 28. Although he was never officially discharged, *Pittsburgh Sun-Telegraph* sports editor Harry Keck reported that Posey left Mercy on March 27 to be taken out in an automobile: "'Drive me down through Homestead,' he had requested on that ride. 'I want to see the old home town again.'" Shortly after returning to the hospital, Posey was put into an oxygen tent, but he lapsed into a coma and died. Somewhere around the time he left for his farewell trip through Homestead, he signed his half-interest in the Grays over to his wife Ethel.[17]

The funeral services, at the Clark Memorial Baptist Church just down the street from the Posey home, drew people, about half white and half black, "from all walks of life." The list of pallbearers, actual and honorary, 31 in all, described Posey's wide-ranging influence. McLean was among them, of course, but so was a judge and the Homestead state legislator. Former Grays Jap Washington, Dennis Graham, and Oscar Owens were there, as was the team's current star, Josh Gibson. From the basketball days were W. S. Young of the Loendis, and Charles "Chick" Davies, legendary Duquesne coach (after Posey/Cumbert's time), and a friend of Posey's since their Homestead days. Art Rooney, owner of the football Pittsburgh Steelers and a longtime Posey supporter, was an honorary bearer, as was J. B. Martin, the Negro American League president with whom Cum Posey so often disagreed, and Gus Green-lee, his old Pittsburgh baseball opponent. The *Courier*, whose pages his father had financed and for which he had written, was represented by Managing Editor William G. Nunn, Chester Washington, and John Clark.[18]

The eulogies began to flow in immediately after Posey passed. McLean said that "Mr. Posey was one of the finest friends I ever met, regardless of race or color." Gus Greenlee said, "Although at times we opposed each other bitterly, I always held the greatest respect for Cum as a friend, associate and rival. There will never be a figure to replace the militant Cum Posey in the world of sports." The *Courier* sportswriters, with whom Posey had sometimes sparred even as his column ran alongside their work, lauded him. Chester Washington wrote that "Sometimes a brilliant athlete soars like a fiery sky-rocket and spreads his name in glittering letters across Sportdom's lofty skies … and then some stars quickly fade like an exploding star-shell when their athletic careers are over, and fade from the sports world into oblivion. But not so with Cum."[19]

Wendell Smith honored the late sports pioneer with an eight-stanza poem titled "Game Called" that recalled the 1910 classic of the same name by Grantland Rice. Smith compared Posey's death to a determined batter facing the hurler of death:

The Master Pitcher wound and threw
That one last ball—straight and true!
As the gallant batter swung and missed,
His star descended in the evening mist.

There'll be no cheering in the stands today
The Captain of the team has passed away.
Put down the ball, that's the end of the game
Baseball has lost its greatest name—Cum Posey![20]

When Posey was in the hospital, he told his daughter Beatrice, "I want to live until opening day," and he had plans to attend the Grays' Washington opener in early April. But he passed just as the team was headed for spring training in Jacksonville, Florida.[21] The season that opened without him, the first in more than three decades where he was not a presence on a baseball field, saw the Grays playing fairly well, but not nearly as well as in recent years, and their nine-year pennant streak was broken. The Manleys' Newark Eagles, lurking on the Grays' tails in recent seasons, far outpaced all competition to win the National League pennant and then the franchise's only Negro World Series. Homestead's performance fell off in the second half of the season, and the Grays only managed to finish third. In 1947, Alex Pompez's New York Cubans, who had edged past the Grays for second place the previous year, finished first (the Grays fell to fourth). Homestead bounced back in 1948 to win both the pennant and the World Series over the Birmingham Black Barons, but that was the last flag anyone would win in the Negro National League. Integration of Major League Baseball had worked as the black teams' owners had feared—fewer and fewer fans were coming to their games, and the NNL disbanded after that season. Some of the teams in the league joined the Negro American League, which lasted until 1963 as a shell of its former self, when it "finally collapsed, a development that concerned few African American fans, many of whom were unaware of the league's continued existence."[22] See Posey and Rufus Jackson elected to play as an independent team after 1948, but the Grays folded after the 1950 season.

Many of the team's main men had already departed by then, one way or another. Ray Brown, who had fished around for better salaries in the past, but had always wound up playing for his former father-in-law Cum Posey's team, finally left for the Mexican League in 1946, where he played until 1949. Then, like other black players when Latin American baseball began to decline, he went to Canada, where he played in the minor leagues until 1952.[23]

The great Josh Gibson departed tragically during the 1946–47 off-season. Gibson had turned 35 that December, but although he wasn't that old, he had become a shadow of the Negro Leagues' most dominating long-ball threat.

His drinking increased, he lost weight, and possibly most importantly, he was dealing with the realization that his brilliant career was about over. During a mid–January weekend, he complained of a severe headache, and he died in his sleep on January 20 of a cerebral hemorrhage.[24]

Rufus Jackson died March 6, 1949, at a Pittsburgh hospital of respiratory failure, having been in declining health that forced him to give up his Grays' management role after the 1948 season. See Posey took control of the team until it went out of business. Then he passed on August 25, 1951. He was a patient in the Homestead Hospital after suffering a spinal fracture in a fall at his home in July, but seemed to be recovering when he had a heart attack. See, who physically resembled his burly father, the Captain, as his brother had more of their mother Anna's lithe physique, had put on quite a bit of weight over the years since his football and basketball playing days. He had also suffered from high blood pressure and diabetes for some time, likely contributing to the stress his injury caused. As was often the case in the Pittsburgh black community, *Courier* columnist John L. Clark had the last word: "'See' Posey was known all over the United States. He was a determined money-getter, an expert card player and uncanny booking agent. But the majority of people who came in contact with him, young and old, remember him as a 'year-round Santa Claus.' Nothing was too good and no amount money too high for people he knew, liked, or were in need."[25]

As Robinson, Doby, Campanella, and the other Negro Leagues stars flourished in the now-integrated major leagues, they were quickly followed by younger outstanding black players such as Willie Mays, Hank Aaron, and Ernie Banks, then others, including black Latin Americans who, if they had been around in the 1930s and '40s, could only have played big league ball for teams such as Alex Pompez's New York Cubans in the Negro National League. In 1963, the last season for the last, threadbare black league, African Americans and black Latinos dominated the major league leader boards, especially in the National League, where the likes of Aaron, Tommy Davis, Vada Pinson, Willie McCovey, and Maury Wills won the major batting and base stealing titles and Juan Marichal tied for the most pitching wins.

The Negro Leagues at that point were not just history in the sense of having existed in the past—they were mostly forgotten history. But they were about to be revived. Robert W. Peterson, a former New York City newspaperman turned magazine writer, remembered watching Negro League games as a boy in his home town of Warren, Pennsylvania (the Grays often played there— he probably saw them). He embarked on a quest to track down and record the oral histories of surviving black players. The interviews, along with hours of pre-internet research in the old newspaper files of actual libraries, yielded in

1970 a book, *Only the Ball Was White*. Its effect on baseball history was, as Negro League historian Larry Lester later wrote, "a catalyst for change. We learned that to celebrate the Major Leagues without recognizing the Negro Leagues was like one hand clapping."[26]

Peterson was followed in short order by other writers, particularly John B. Holway, whose *Voices from the Great Black Baseball Leagues*, which came out in 1975 and was followed by more of his works, was particularly valuable for its oral history interviews. Other authors and interviewers, along with filmmakers, followed, and the body of information about the Negro Leagues continued to grow. Peterson's book, in particular, helped bring the Negro Leagues back to the attention of baseball insiders, a few of whom were already pushing for the black stars from the segregated era to receive what is arguably the sport's highest and finest honor, election to the National Baseball Hall of Fame.

Boston Red Sox star Ted Williams surprised the 1966 induction audience when he used his acceptance speech to state that the best Negro Leaguers should also be in the Hall. Bowie Kuhn, the commissioner of the majors at the time, agreed and pushed for their recognition. The Hall's trustees at first proposed a separate (and hardly equal) display for Negro League greats that would keep them from having the iconic bronze plaques in what is known as the "Plaque Room," where Williams and the other white inductees are enshrined. But public resistance to this idea quickly brought about full honors for the black players.

A special committee was formed to select the honorees. The pitcher Satchel Paige was the first to be inducted, in 1971. Then Gibson and Leonard were admitted in 1972, followed by Newark Eagles outfielder Monte Irvin, James "Cool Papa" Bell, Judy Johnson, and Oscar Charleston successively in the next four years. The selection process ended in 1977, when John Henry Lloyd, the star Negro Leagues shortstop of the 1920s, and Martin Dihigo were inducted. So not counting Paige's one-game stint as a Homestead Gray in an exhibition game, six of the first nine Negro League electees—Gibson, Leonard, Bell, Johnson, Charleston, and Dihigo—had spent significant time in a Grays uniform, all recruited by Cumberland Posey.

After the special committee shut down in 1977, the responsibility for selecting further Negro Leaguers was handed off to the Hall's standing Veterans' Committee, which by then existed primarily to give a second chance to stars not inducted by the Baseball Writers' Association of America, the main voting group, as well as to comb the earlier years of major league history for players whose careers had ended well before the BBWAA began voting in 1936. The Veterans' Committee, over a stretch of 20 years, put nine more Negro Leaguers into the Hall, including three more Grays, pitching mainstay Smokey Joe Williams in 1999 and pitcher Bill Foster and shortstop Willie

Wells, who each spent only a season with the team, in 1996 and '97, respectively. So of the first 18 Negro Leaguers to make the Hall, nine of them had been Grays (although Wells was with Homestead for only a few weeks in 1932, he had opened the season with the Posey-run Detroit Wolves).

So far as Negro Leaguers entering the Hall, nothing happened for a while. But in the mid–2000s the Hall of Fame administered a grant from Major League Baseball to compile an extensive written and statistical history of black baseball in America. Not long after the process was finished, the Hall announced that a special committee of 12 (which included Robert Peterson and other historians who had worked on the project) would be convened in 2006 to consider further figures from the Negro Leagues, plus the period before the founding of the first Negro National League in 1920, when the best black teams played as independents.

The work of the first special committee and the Veterans' Committee had produced an excellent start to the process of recognizing blacks from before integration. But except for the election of Andrew "Rube" Foster, president of the first Negro National League, in 1981, no Negro League owners had been admitted. The 2006 special committee's work fixed that—Posey and three of his contemporary owners, J. L. Wilkinson of the Kansas City Monarchs, Effa Manley of the Newark Eagles, and Alex Pompez of the New York Cubans, were voted in. In addition to the four owners, 13 players whose careers ranged from the 1880s to the 1960s were enshrined. They included two more Grays, pitcher Ray Brown and infielder Jud Wilson, bringing the Homestead total to 12 (including Posey).

While there are other qualified black baseball candidates for the Hall who have yet to be admitted, they are unlikely to get in. Since the 2006 election, the Hall abolished its Veterans' Committee, replacing it with standing committees tasked with examining the qualifications of players, managers, umpires, and executives from different baseball eras. The Negro Leaguers, and their independent predecessors, fall under the Early Baseball Committee's purview. But current rules limit that committee to meeting only once every 10 years, its next vote scheduled for 2020. On such a stringent schedule, with the cream of black talent already enshrined, it's difficult to imagine the cases for remaining Negro Leaguers succeeding in competition against the much larger pool of pre-integration major league eligibles.

The Naismith Memorial Basketball Hall of Fame is named after James Naismith, the actual inventor of the rules of basketball at a YMCA in Springfield, Massachusetts, in 1891. (The baseball hall is in Cooperstown, New York, to honor the "invention" of the game in 1839 by future U.S. Army Gen. Abner Doubleday, a claim long since debunked.) While the 35 black baseball figures in the Cooperstown hall and Alexander Cartwright, unlike Doubleday a true early developer of the sport, are the only honorees not connected with major league baseball, the basketball Hall's scope extends beyond men's and women's professional hoop to the college and international game. The Basketball Hall of Fame had paid some attention to early black basketball several years ago. In 1972 it inducted Bob Douglas, whose New York Renaissance succeeded Posey's Loendi club as the champion black squad in the last half of the 1920s decade, and had already honored the entire Rens squad in its team category in 1963.

In addition to its regular three-step election process, the basketball Hall established "Direct-Elect" committees for certain categories in 2011. One of them was the Early African American Pioneers committee, entitled to elect one person from a pre-determined list each year. Edwin B. Henderson, the coach of the Howard University team that Posey's Monticellos upset in 1912, was the third elected by this committee, in 2013. Posey himself was the fifth, in 2016.[27]

This gives Posey the distinction of being only the second person to be elected to two professional sports Halls of Fame. Robert "Cal" Hubbard had been a lineman for nine years in the early days of the National Football League, primarily with the Green Bay Packers. Upon retiring from pro football, he turned to his second occupation, baseball umpiring. He had worked as a minor league ump in the football off-season, but in 1936 joined the American League staff. In 1951, following an off-season eye injury, he became an umpire supervisor for the league, working until 1969. By then he had already become a charter member of the Pro Football Hall of Fame, elected in 1963. He was inducted into the Baseball Hall of Fame in 1976.

Upon Posey's death, *Courier* writer John L. Clark filled his entire "Wylie Avenue" column with an account of his long relationship with Posey, which summed up his old friend's most distinguishing qualities. They had known each other since their high school years, had what Clark called a five-year "battle of words" in the 1930s when he was working for rival baseball owner Gus Greenlee, and had ridden side by side in the '40s in Posey's car when Cum had hired him to help promote black sports through the Elks. In the early years, Clark wrote, "Cum was the first Negro I had ever known who set out to make money out of baseball. All others took the game as a sideline, a diversion—an excuse to get away from work or home for a full day." Even when "battling with his back to the wall, he was determined, confident, frank about his position on all matters…. He was genuine, he mimicked nobody. Whether in baseball, politics, club life, sports writer, secretary of the Negro National League or member of the Homestead School Board, he was just 'Cum' Posey, nothing less."[28]

Chapter Notes

Chapter One

1. Helen A. Tucker, "The Pittsburgh Survey: The Negroes of Pittsburgh, 1909," at *Information Renaissance*, www.info-ren.org/projects/btul/exhibit/afamsur.html.

2. Abraham Epstein, *The Negro Migrant in Pittsburgh* (Pittsburgh: University of Pittsburgh School of Economics), 23.

3. John Bodnar, Roger Simon, and Michael P. Weber, *Lives of Their Own: Blacks, Italians, and Poles in Pittsburgh, 1900–1960* (Urbana: University of Illinois Press, 1983), 64.

4. Laurence Glasco, "The Black Experience," in *City at the Point*, ed. Samuel P. Hays (Pittsburgh: University of Pittsburgh Press, 1991), 70.

5. *Ibid.*, 73.

6. Laurence A. Glasco, ed., *The WPA History of the Negro in Pittsburgh* (Pittsburgh: University of Pittsburgh Press, 2004), 260–262.

7. Tucker, "The Pittsburgh Survey."

8. "C. W. Posey Is Victim of Illness," *Pittsburgh Courier*, June 13, 1925.

9. Thomas C. Ewell, "The Smoky City," *Colored American* IV, no. 2 (December 1901), 136; 1870 United States Census, for Winchester, VA. s.v. Alexander Posey, accessed at https://www.Ancestry.com.

10. "C. W. Posey Is Victim of Illness," *Pittsburgh Courier*, June 13, 1925.

11. Ewell, "The Smoky City," 136–137.

12. "C. W. Posey Is Victim of Illness," *Pittsburgh Courier*, June 13, 1925.

13. *Ibid.*

14. Carole Wylie Hancock, "Honorable Soldiers Too: An Historical Case Study of Post-Reconstruction African American Female Teachers of the Upper Ohio River Valley" (PhD dissertation, Ohio University, 2008), 331.

15. *Ibid.*, 314–319.

16. William Serrin, *Homestead: The Glory and Tragedy of an American Steel Town* (New York: Random House, 1992), 36.

17. *Report on the Population of the United States at the Eleventh Census: 1890, Part I* (Washington, DC: Department of the Interior, 1895), 551.

18. *First Annual Edition—1890, Directory of Homestead, Munhall, Six Mile Ferry, and Adjacent Parts of Mifflin Township, Allegheny County, Pa.* (Pittsburgh: M. P. and J. R. Schooley, 1890), 185; "A Mysterious Attack," *Pittsburgh Press*, July 17, 1894.

19. Serrin, *Homestead,* 23.

20. Ewell, "The Smoky City," 138; Evan Posey Baker, Jr., interviewed by author, June 15, 1995.

21. 1900 United States Census for Homestead, PA, accessed at https://www.Ancestry.com.

22. Glasco, *The WPA History of the Negro in Pittsburgh*, 265.

23. "C. W. Posey Is Victim of Illness"; Laurence Glasco, "Taking Care of Business: The Black Entrepreneurial Elite in Turn-of-the-Century Pittsburgh," *Pittsburgh History* 78, no. 4 (Winter 1995–96): 179; "Afro-American Notes," *Pittsburgh Press*, December 3, 1899.

24. "Pittsburg, Pa." *Black Diamond* 24, no. 22 (June 2, 1900): 612; Ewell, "Smoky City," 138.

25. "Big Suit for Alleged Slander," *Pittsburgh Daily Post*, March 14, 1903.

26. "Business Men Under Arrest," *Pittsburgh Daily Post*, June 6, 1897; "Seeks to Auction Off the Merrill Contract … Coal Men Are Sentenced," *Pittsburgh Daily Post*, April 10, 1898; "Sheriff's Custody Questioned," *Pittsburgh Press*, April 22, 1898; "River Intelligence," *Pittsburgh Post-Gazette*, August 23, 1898; "Mercy for C. W. Posey," *Pittsburgh Daily Post*, October 20, 1898.

27. *Pennsylvania Negro Business Directory* (Harrisburg, PA: James H. W. Howard & Son, 1910), 40; Hancock, "Honorable Soldiers Too," 330.

28. "Capt. Posey, of Homestead, Assaulted by Four Men," *Pittsburgh Press*, July 17, 1894.

29. "Thief Attacks Girl," *Pittsburgh Post-Gazette*, April 9, 1907.

30. "Gang of Young Robbers Is Broken Up by a Woman," *Pittsburgh Weekly Gazette*, October 4, 1904.

31. Ewell, "The Smoky City," 138; "Explaining the Measures of Worth," *Measuring Worth*, measuringworth.com/explaining_measures_of_worth.php.

32. Mary O'Hara, "Club Steeped in History Celebrates 80th Birthday," *Pittsburgh Press*, October 31, 1974; "Afro-American Notes," *Pittsburgh Press*, March 9, 1913.

33. "Colored Women's Clubs," *Pittsburgh Daily Post*, October 13, 1901.

34. Glasco, *The WPA History of the Negro in Pittsburgh*, 284; Twentieth anniversary booklet of the Loendi Club, 1917, Detre Library and Archives, Senator John Heinz History Center, Pittsburgh, PA.

35. "Old-Time Athletes of Homestead High School Throw Off the Years at Reunion," *Pittsburgh Press*, April 6, 1933. The photo caption identifies Cum Posey, but the image is of See.

36. "Seward Posey in Virginia," *Homestead Daily Messenger*, May 23, 1905.

37. "'Cum' Posey's Pointed Paragraphs," *Pittsburgh Courier*, December 12, 1931; "'Cum' Posey's Pointed Paragraphs," *Pittsburgh Courier*, December 8, 1934.

38. "Afro American Notes," *Pittsburgh Press*, April 2, 1905; E-mail exchange with Daniel Zyglowicz, California University of Pennsylvania Archives & Special Collections, March 16, 2018; "Let's Go Shopping," *Pittsburgh Courier*, September 9, 1933.

39. Evan Posey Baker, Jr., interview.

40. *LaVie* (Penn State yearbook), 1911, 288; *LaVie*, 1912, 287; "Local Players on Teams at Old State," *Pittsburgh Press*, April 17, 1910.

41. "Seniors Win Opening Contest at State," *Pittsburgh Post-Gazette*, December 4, 1910; "State Five Opens," *Pittsburgh Post-Gazette*, December 11, 1910; "Defense of State's Eligibility Code," *Pittsburgh Press*, February 26, 1911.

42. Arthur R. Ashe, Jr., *A Hard Road to Glory: A History of the African American Athlete 1919–1945, Vol. 2* (New York: Amistad, 1993), 108–109.

43. E-mail to author from Carol Miller, supervisor, Transcripts & Certification, Office of the University Registrar, University of Pittsburgh, May 23, 2016; Cum Posey, "Posey's Points," *Pittsburgh Courier*, November 14, 1942.

44. E-mail to author from Dr. Kimberley J. Hoeritz, University Registrar, Duquesne University, May 11, 2016; Rob Ruck, Maggie Jones Patterson, and Michael P. Weber, *Rooney: A Sporting Life* (Lincoln: University of Nebraska Press, 2010), 41.

45. Rob Ruck, *Raceball: How the Major Leagues Colonized the Black and Latin Game* (Boston: Beacon Press, 2011), 36–37.

46. "Duquesne University Floor Squad Closes Very Successful Season," *Pittsburgh Daily Post*, March 12, 1916; *Duquesne Monthly* 30, no. 4 (January 1923): 45; "'Cum' Posey's Pointed Paragraphs," *Pittsburgh Courier*, November 23, 1935.

47. John T. Taylor, "Notes of the Local Amateur Athletes," *Pittsburgh Press*, December 17, 1914.

48. *Duquesne Monthly* 23, no. 6 (March 1916): 223.

49. Robert W. Peterson, *Cages to Jumpshots: Pro Basketball's Early Years* (New York: Oxford University Press, 1990), 4, 49.

50. *Duquesne Monthly* 24, no. 4 (January 1917): 134.

51. *Duquesne Monthly* 25, no. 5 (February 1918): 181.

52. "Afro-American Notes," *Pittsburgh Press*, March 3, 1918; "Afro-American Notes," *Pittsburgh Press*, February 10, 1918.

53. "Dukes Make Fine Record, Zitzman Chosen as Captain," *Pittsburgh Press*, June 18, 1916.

54. "Duquesne Plays at Westminster," *Pittsburgh Press*, June 3, 1916; "Cinch for Cecil," *Pittsburgh Press*, June 4, 1916.

55. "Duke Quintet Has Two More Games to Play," *Pittsburgh Post-Gazette*, March 9, 1919; "Duquesne Endows $1 Million Cumberland Posey Fund to Assist Minority Students," *Duquesne University Magazine* 12, no. 2 (Winter 2014): 24.

56. Ruck, Patterson, and Weber, *Rooney: A Sporting Life*, 29, 52.

57. *Ibid.*, 51.

58. *Ibid.*, 235.

59. E-mail to author from Dr. Kimberley J. Hoeritz, University Registrar, Duquesne University, July 21, 2016.

60. "Homestead," *Pittsburgh Courier*, October 14, 1911; "Afro-American Notes," *Pittsburgh Press*, May 1, 1912, 42; "Afro-American Notes," *Pittsburgh Press*, May 1, 1912; "Chevaliers Will Play 'Cabin to Congress,'" *Pittsburgh Courier*, May 18, 1912; "Afro-American Notes," *Pittsburgh Press*, March 3, 1912.

61. Interview with Beatrice Lee by the author, November 27, 1995; Evan Posey Baker, Jr., interview.

62. "Delaney Rifles Defeat Wilberforce Uni-

versity," *Pittsburgh Post-Gazette*, November 29, 1912; "Afro-American Notes," *Pittsburgh Press*, November 23, 1913; "Homestead Does Well," *Pittsburgh Press*, October 24, 1915; "Pollard May Play in Colored Clash Here," *Pittsburgh Press*, October 12, 1917; "Grays to Play Football," *Pittsburgh Press*, September 18, 1921.

63. World War I draft registration card for Cumberland W. Posey, Jr., accessed at https://www.Ancestry.com; *Polk's Homestead City Directory, 1925* (Pittsburgh: R.L. Polk, 1925), 409.

64. Beatrice Lee interview; Evan Posey Baker, Jr., interview.

Chapter Two

1. Will Anthony Madden, "All-American and All-Star Teams for Basketball Season 1915–1916," *New York Age*, April 13, 1916.

2. "Basketball and Football," *Pittsburgh Courier*, December 16, 1911; "Sporting News," *Pittsburgh Courier*, January 13, 1912; "Local News," *Pittsburgh Courier*, May 27, 1911; "Local News," *Pittsburgh Courier*, February 3, 1912.

3. Rob Ruck, *Sandlot Seasons: Sport in Black Pittsburgh* (Urbana: University of Illinois Press, 1987), 126.

4. "Hall, Colorful Sports Figure, Promoter, Succumbs in New York," *Pittsburgh Courier*, February 24, 1951; "Sellers McKee Hall," *Pittsburgh Music History*, https://sites.google.com/site/pittsburghmusichistory/pittsburgh-music-story/managers-and-promoters/sellers-mckee-hall.

5. Cum Posey, "Posey's Points," *Pittsburgh Courier*, January 9, 1937; "Posey's Points," *Pittsburgh Courier*, March 15, 1941.

6. "Afro-American Notes," *Pittsburgh Press*, February 25, 1912.

7. "Basketball Game and Dance, *Pittsburgh Courier*, March 2, 1912.

8. "Monticello 24, and Howard 19," *Pittsburgh Courier*, March 16, 1912.

9. *Ibid.*; "Local News," *Pittsburgh Courier*, March 16, 1912; "In the World of Sport," *New York Age*, March 14, 1912; Cum Posey, "Posey's Points," *Pittsburgh Courier*, December 19, 1942.

10. "Says Monticello Quint Has 'Cold Feet,'" *New York Age*, January 23, 1913; "Monticello Answers Howard," *New York Age*, February 6, 1913; "Howard's Position," *New York Age*, February 13, 1913.

11. "In the World of Sport," *New York Age*, March 20, 1913.

12. "Pittsburghers Victorious," *New York Age*, January 2, 1913.

13. "Afro-American Notes," *Pittsburgh Press*, March 2, 1913.

14. "Monticello Quint Opens Season," *New York Age*, November 13, 1913; "Loendi Defeats Howard," *New York Age*, February 12, 1914.

15. "Howard, 27, Loendi, 14," *New York Age*, January 15, 1914; "Afro-American Notes," *Pittsburgh Press*, January 25, 1914.

16. "Colored Society Sees Basketball," *Pittsburgh Press*, February 7, 1914; "Loendi Defeats Howard," *New York Age*, February 12, 1914; "Afro-American Notes," *Pittsburgh Press*, February 15, 1914; *NIKH* (Yearbook, College of Arts and Sciences, Howard University) 1 (1914): 79, at http://dh.howard.edu/cgi/viewcontent.cgi?article=1092&context=bison_yearbooks.

17. "Afro-American Notes," *Pittsburgh Press*, September 27, 1914; "Afro-American Notes," *Pittsburgh Press*, December 13, 1914; John T. Taylor, "Notes of the Local Amateur Athletes," *Pittsburgh Press*, December 27, 1914.

18. "Basket Ball Summary," *New York Age*, April 26, 1917.

19. "Monticello-Delaneys Defeat Pittsburg Independents," *Chicago Defender*, March 31, 1917.

20. Anne Madarasz, "Sports History: The Early Days of Pittsburgh Basketball," Pittsburgh Sports Report (February 2006), http://www.pittsburghsportsreport.com/2006-Issues/psr0602/06020110.html.

21. "Afro-American Notes," *Pittsburgh Press*, December 1, 1918.

22. "Colored Basketball World's Champions, 1907–1925," Black Fives Foundation, at ttp://www.blackfives.org/champions.

23. Claude Johnson, "'Pimp' and 'Lyss': The Immortal Young Brothers," Black Fives Foundation, at http://www.blackfives.org/pimp-and-lyss-the-immortal-young-brothers.

24. Ruck, *Sandlot Seasons*, 32–33; "Charles A. Betts," *Pittsburgh Post-Gazette*, July 6, 1978.

25. "Big Football Contest in 'Phil,'" *Chicago Defender*, January 3, 1920; "Machine All Primed for Loendi," *Chicago Defender*, January 10, 1920.

26. William White, "Loendi Crushes the Red and Black Machine," *Chicago Defender*, February 7, 1920, 11; Ted Hooks, "The Sporting World from All Angles," *New York Age*, February 7, 1920.

27. Bob Kuksa, *Hot Potato: How Washington and New York Gave Birth to Black Basketball and Changed America's Game Forever* (Charlottesville: University of Virginia Press, 2004), 81; "About Leondi's Captain," *New York Age*, February 14, 1920.

28. "Vandal A. C. to Play St. Christopher February 12," *Chicago Defender*, January 29, 1921.

29. "Loendi-Spartan Braves Game in Gotham Ends in a Row," *Chicago Defender*, January 15, 1921; Sport Editorial, "Basketball Gets Black Eye," *Chicago Defender*, January 15, 1921; Kuksa, *Hot Potato*, 101; "Cum Posey Reminisces: The True Story About a Watch," *Pittsburgh Courier*, May 2, 1936.

30. Kuksa, *Hot Potato*, 102–105.

31. "Amateur Teams Warned Against Professionals," *Pittsburgh Press*, December 26, 1920.

32. "Loendi Team Barred by M.B.A. Charged with Professionalism," *New York Age*, March 18, 1922.

33. Kuksa, *Hot Potato*, 111.

34. "The Sportive Spotlight," *New York Amsterdam News*, February 28, 1923.

35. "Professional Basketball Season Opened in Harlem," *New York Age*, November 11, 1922, 6; "The Sportive Spotlight," *New York Amsterdam News*, March 7, 1925.

36. "Commonwealths Win," *New York Amsterdam News*, December 16, 1922, 5; "Poor Old 'Cum' Posey," *New York Amsterdam News*, January 10, 1923.

37. Romeo L. Dougherty, "On the Eastern Sport Trail" (column), *Pittsburgh Courier*, January 20, 1923; "Sportive Realm," *Pittsburgh Courier*, January 20, 1923.

38. "The Sportive Spotlight," *New York Amsterdam News*, February 14, 1923.

39. Kuksa, *Hot Potato*, 117; "Commonwealth Players Did Not Have a Chance," *New York Amsterdam News*, March 21, 1923.

40. "The Sportive Spotlight," *New York Amsterdam News*, March 14, 1923; "Public Hollers on Fake," *New York Amsterdam News*, April 11, 1923.

41. Kuksa, *Hot Potato*, 129; "Once Famous Pittsburgh Basketball Team All Shot to Pieces, Says Report," *New York Amsterdam News*, September 19, 1923.

42. "'Cum' Posey Tells of Plans for this Season," *New York Amsterdam News*, October 17, 1923.

43. "McMahons Planning to Bring Famous Coffey Club Here to Play Their Team," *New York Amsterdam News*, October 24, 1923.

44. W. Rollo Wilson, "Eastern Snapshots," *Pittsburgh Courier*, April 12, 1924.

45. "Strenuous Week for Coffey Club," *Pittsburgh Press*, March 23, 1919.

46. "Coffey Club Had Long Reign as District's Floor Leaders," *Pittsburgh Post-Gazette*, February 4, 1933.

47. "Coffeys Beat Loendi Five in Fast Tilt, 36–34," *Pittsburgh Post-Gazette*, March 12, 1920.

48. "Coffeys Win from Loendi in Rough Game," *Pittsburgh Daily Post*, February 4, 1921.

49. "Premature Whistling Assists Coffeys to Nose Out Loendis," *Pittsburgh Post-Gazette*, December 21, 1923; "Coffeys Use Shrewd Scheme, Beat Loendi Five, 34–32," *Pittsburgh Courier*, December 29, 1923.

50. "To Reorganize Loendi Machine Next Season, Declares Posey," *Pittsburgh Courier*, April 12, 1924.

51. "Loendi Club Will Not Foster Basketball This Season," *Pittsburgh Courier*, October 4, 1924.

52. "Sell Hall Backing Present Leondi Five," *Pittsburgh Courier*, January 3, 1925; "Sport—Pickups," *Pittsburgh Courier*, November 22, 1924; "The Griddle," *Pittsburgh Courier*, November 15, 1924.

53. "Afro-American Notes," *Pittsburgh Press*, August 20, 1916.

54. W. Rollo Wilson, "Eastern Snapshots," *Pittsburgh Courier*, November 15, 1925.

55. "Leondi '5' Wins from Panthers," *Pittsburgh Courier*, April 4, 1945; "Sport-Theatrical … and Other Comment," *New York Amsterdam News*, March 18, 1935.

56. "Leondi Is Beaten by Panthers," *Pittsburgh Courier*, February 14, 1925; W. Rollo Wilson, "Eastern Snapshots," *Pittsburgh Courier*, February 28, 1925.

57. W. Rollo Wilson, "Eastern Snapshots," *Pittsburgh Courier*, January 10, 1925; "Afro-American Notes," *Pittsburgh Press*, March 1, 1925.

58. "Leondi Wins from Attawa Club, 72–23," *Pittsburgh Courier*, December 13, 1924; "Chicago Next Opponent of Rebuilt Leondi Quintet," *Pittsburgh Courier*, February 7, 1925; "Chicago Loses to Leondi '5,'" *Pittsburgh Courier*, February 21, 1925.

59. Robert W. Peterson, *Cages to Jumpshots*, 80.

60. Ira F. Lewis, "The Passing Review," *Pittsburgh Courier*, March 7, 1925.

61. W. Rollo Wilson, "Eastern Snapshots," *Pittsburgh Courier*, October 31, 1925; "Played Xmas Night with a Broken Rib," *Pittsburgh Courier*, January 9, 1926.

62. "Clark Memorial Girls in Tip-Top Condition for Invasion of N. Y. Quint," *Pittsburgh Courier*, February 20, 1926.

63. "Uniontown Fans Protest 'Jim Crow' Ruling at Game," *Pittsburgh Courier*, January 30, 1926; Cum Posey, "The Sportive Realm," *Pittsburgh Courier*, March 27, 1926.

64. "Holy Cross 5 is Beaten by Detroit A. A.," *Chicago Defender*, March 7, 1931; "Schneider Quintet to Meet Renaissance," *Pittsburgh Post-Gazette*, January 2, 1932; "Renaissance Beats Elks," *Pittsburgh Post-Gazette*, January 7, 1935.

65. W. Rollo Wilson, "Eastern Snapshots," *Pittsburgh Courier*, October 31, 1925; Clarence "Fat" Jenkins, "My Greatest Thrill: It Was a Great Day When Rens Won Title," *Pittsburgh Courier*, March 20, 1941; Wendell Smith, "Smitty's Sports-Spurts," *Pittsburgh Courier*, February 7, 1942.

Chapter Three

1. 1900 United States Census, for Homestead, PA, s.v. Henry Haley, accessed at https://www.Ancestry.com; "Among the Amateurs," *Pittsburgh Post-Gazette*, August 15, 1901.

2. John Thorn, "The Color of Baseball," *Our Game*, May 4, 2011, https://ourgame.mlblogs.com/the-color-of-baseball-2ebd78ffed0b.

3. Ruck, *Sandlot Seasons*, 128; "Homestead Grays, an Institution," *Pittsburgh Courier*, August 27, 1955; John L. Clark, "Homestead Grays Founded 32 Years Ago," *Chicago Defender*, June 13, 1942.

4. Harry Keck, "Sullivans Post Forfeit for Games with Grays," *Pittsburgh Daily Post*, August 19, 1918; "Asks Receiver for Colored Ball Club," *Pittsburgh Press*, August 12, 1923; "Case Against Grays Dismissed by Judge Kline," *Pittsburgh Courier*, September 1, 1923.

5. John L. Clark, "Homestead Grays Founded 32 Years Ago," *Chicago Defender*, June 13, 1942.

6. "Grays to Go on Trips in Buick Cars, *Pittsburgh Courier*, May 3, 1924, 7; Quincy Trouppe, *20 Years Too Soon* (Los Angeles: S&S Enterprises, 1977), 66.

7. "Cum Posey's Pointed Paragraphs," *Pittsburgh Courier*, February 13, 1932, 13; "Afro-American Notes, *Pittsburgh Press*, March 9, 1924.

8. Tom Birks, "Record Crowd Watches Deans Blanked by Grays," *Pittsburgh Post-Gazette*, June 8, 1923.

9. Jack Adams, "Championship Contests Mark Closing of Semi-Pro Season," *Pittsburgh Post-Gazette*, September 21, 1924; Fred P. Alger, "Harmarville Tackles Baltimore's Best," *Pittsburgh Daily Post*, September 13, 1923.

10. "History of Ambridge," Ambridge, PA, borough website, http://ambridgepa.govoffice2.com/index.asp?Type=B_BASIC&SEC={BCB0E638-3DBD-4220-B2AC-F93A7A934590}

11. Interview with Willis Moody by Rob Ruck, Archives and Manuscript Collections, University of Pittsburgh Library, Pittsburgh, PA.

12. "Game at Graybers Called Off, *Pittsburgh Press*, July 30, 1922; "Sunday Ball Leads to Prosecutions," *Pittsburgh Post-Gazette*, April 27, 1922.

13. "Police Prevent Collier Game; Suit Planned," *Pittsburgh Daily Post*, April 21, 1924;

"Sunday Golf Forbidden by Fayette Ban," *Pittsburgh Daily Post*, April 22, 1924.

14. "Homestead Grays Have Strong Club," *Pittsburgh Daily Post*, March 4, 1923; Jack Adams, "Championship Contests Mark Closing of Semi-Pro Season," *Pittsburgh Post-Gazette*, September 21, 1924.

15. "Enthusiasm Marks Mammoth Meeting of Local Independents," *Pittsburgh Post-Gazette*, February 27, 1922.

16. "Answer to Query," *Pittsburgh Daily Post*, September 25, 1923.

17. "Real Test," *Akron (OH) Beacon Journal*, July 12, 1930; "Matchmaker Albright," *Uniontown (PA) Evening Standard*, August 4, 1923; "Monkeys Make Monkeys Out of Elks Ball Nine, *Uniontown (PA) Evening Standard*, September 18, 1923; James Bankes, *The Pittsburgh Crawfords*, (Dubuque, IA: William C. Brown, 1991), 25; William Brashler, *Josh Gibson: A Life in the Negro Leagues* (Chicago: Ivan R. Dees, 2000), 59–60; David C. Ogden, "Black Baseball at Forbes Field," in *Forbes Field: Essays and Memories of the Pirates' Historic Ballpark, 1909–1971*, David Cicotello and Angelo J. Louisa, eds. (Jefferson, NC: McFarland, 2007), 62.

18. "Grays Forfeit to Johnstown," *Pittsburgh Daily Post*, August 8, 1920; "'Almost' Riot Adds Thrills to Ball Game," *Pittsburgh Daily Post*, September 15, 1919.

19. Fred Alger, "Periscoping the Independent Circuit," *Pittsburgh Daily Post*, August 2, 1924.

20. "Unions to Meet Homestead Grays Here on Labor Day," *New Castle (PA) Herald*, August 5, 1921.

21. "Cum Posey's Pointed Paragraphs," *Pittsburgh Courier*, March 4, 1933; Fred Alger, "Periscoping the Independent Circuit," *Pittsburgh Daily Post*, August 3, 1924; "Grays Lose Purse," *Pittsburgh Daily Post*, August 6, 1924.

22. Measuring Worth website, www.measuringworth.com/uscompare/relativevalue.php.

23. Chester Washington, "Sez 'Ches,'" *Pittsburgh Courier*, March 21, 1931; Ira F. Lewis, "The Passing Review," *Pittsburgh Courier*, April 25, 1925.

24. "Keystone and Grays Series Opens Thursday," *Pittsburgh Daily Post*, August 21, 1921; "Keystone Game Stopped," *Pittsburgh Post-Gazette*, June 24, 1922; "Game Off, Ticket Money Returned After Threats, *Pittsburgh Post-Gazette*, June 25, 1922; "Umps' Statement on Central Park Game," *Pittsburgh Press*, June 28, 1922.

25. Cum Posey, "The Sportive Realm," *Pittsburgh Courier*, September 6, 1924.

26. John Bodnar, Roger Simon, and Michael P. Weber, *Lives of Their Own*, 117, 187.

27. Ira F. Lewis, "The Passing Review," *Pittsburgh Courier*, April 25, 1925.

28. *Ibid.*

29. "What Is This," *Pittsburgh Daily Post*, July 27, 1924.

30. Cum Posey, "The Sportive Realm," *Pittsburgh Courier*, January 9, 1926; James A. Riley, *Biographical Encyclopedia of the Negro Baseball Leagues* (New York: Carroll & Graf, 1994), 846; World War I draft registration card for Charles Henry Williams, accessed at https://www.Ancestry.com.

31. Commonwealth of Pennsylvania Veteran's Compensation Application for William Oscar Owens, accessed at https://www.Ancestry.com; Fred Alger, "Periscoping the Independent Circuit," *Pittsburgh Daily Post*, June 22, 1924; Riley, *Biographical Encyclopedia*, 593.

32. Cum Posey, "Posey's Points," *Pittsburgh Courier*, January 9, 1937.

33. Commonwealth of Pennsylvania Veteran's Compensation Application for Jasper Washington, accessed at https://www.Ancestry.com; Riley, *Biographical Encyclopedia*, 818.

34. "Beckwith is Released by Homestead Grays," *Pittsburgh Courier*, June 21, 1924.

35. Cum Posey, "Posey's Points," *Pittsburgh Courier*, January 9, 1937; "Cum Posey's Pointed Paragraphs," *Pittsburgh Courier*, December 28, 1935.

36. James A. Riley, *Biographical Encyclopedia*, 69; "Beckwith Signs to Play with Homestead Grays in 1924," *Pittsburgh Courier*, December 22, 1923; "Near Riot Breaks Up Giants-Pyotts Game, *Chicago Defender*, October 13, 1923; "Umpires Hired to Work, Not to Run Ball Club," *Pittsburgh Courier*, October 20, 1923.

37. "Beckwith is Released by Homestead Grays," *Pittsburgh Courier*, June 21, 1924; "Periscoping the Independent Circuit," *Pittsburgh Daily Post*, June 22, 1924.

Chapter Four

1. "Joe Williams and Other Prominent New York Baseball Players Go to Pittsburgh," *New York Age*, April 18, 1925.

2. "Sport—Pickups," *Pittsburgh Courier*, May 2, 1925.

3. Willis Moody interview.

4. John Holway, *Black Giants* (Springfield, VA: Lord Fairfax Press, 2010), 104.

5. *Ibid.*, 103.

6. *Ibid.*, 102–103; "Cum Posey's Pointed Paragraphs," *Pittsburgh Courier*, February 23, 1935; "Umpire's Attacker Paroled 6 Months," *Pittsburgh Press*, March 1, 1935.

7. Ira F. Lewis, "The Passing Review," *Pittsburgh Courier*, September 11, 1926.

8. World War I draft registration card for Charles Walker, accessed at https://www.Ancestry.com; Certificate of Death for Charles H. Walker, dated October 2, 1940, accessed at https://www.Ancestry.com; Charles E. Pendleton, "Snapshots of 'Big Shots' in the World of Sports," *Pittsburgh Courier*, March 7, 1931.

9. William G. Nunn, "WGN Broadcasts," *Pittsburgh Courier*, July 23, 1927; William G. Nunn, "WGN Broadcasts," *Pittsburgh Courier*, August 20, 1927; "The Sportive Realm," *Pittsburgh Courier*, April 14, 1928.

10. Certificate of Death for Charles H. Walker, dated October 2, 1940, accessed at https://www.Ancestry.com; Cum Posey, "Posey's Points," *Pittsburgh Courier*, October 12, 1940; 1930 United States Census for Homestead, PA, s.v. Charles Walker, accessed at https://www.Ancestry.com.

11. Fred P. Alger, "Independent Clubs Jolted by Industrial Conditions," *Pittsburgh Daily Post*, June 21, 1925.

12. Fred P. Alger, "Homestead Grays Drawing Only Big Crowds of Season," *Pittsburgh Daily Post*, July 20, 1926; Fred P. Alger "Periscoping the Independent Circuit," *Pittsburgh Daily Post*, June 20, 1926; "High-Class Colored Attraction to Furnish Opposition to Locals Saturday," *Warren (PA) Tribune*, August 23, 1926; "Game Tonight to be Played Unless Downpour Occurs," *Canonsburg (PA) Daily Notes*, June 21, 1928; "Heavy Rain Halts Game Last Night," *Canonsburg (PA) Daily Notes*, June 22, 1928.

13. Cum Posey, "Posey's Points," *Pittsburgh Courier*, June 5, 1937.

14. "Cum" Posey, "In the Sportive Realm," *Pittsburgh Courier*, February 27, 1926.

15. "Speedways Meet Newts Tomorrow," *Monongahela (PA) Daily Republican*, June 4, 1927; "Hard for the Grays to Beat These Hurlers," *Pittsburgh Press*, June 29, 1929.

16. "Colored Stars to Play Game Here Tonight," *New Castle (PA) News*, June 2, 1926; "Pittsburg Team at Dunbar Park Saturday, 4:30," *Connellsville (PA) Daily Courier*, June 3, 1926.

17. "To Muse and Amuse by Sports Editor," *Altoona (PA) Mirror*, June 14, 1929.

18. "Homestead Grays Will Show Great Comedian Here Sunday," *Akron Beacon Journal*, April 20, 1926.

19. "Sport Shots," *Warren (PA) Tribune*, August 10, 1926; "Current Comment," *Uniontown (PA) Evening Standard*, October 7, 1927.

20. Michael Gershman, *Diamonds, the Evolution of the Ballpark* (Boston: Houghton Mifflin, 1993), 88; "Keenan Answers Posey; Rates Lincolns 'Best Ever'; Will Meet Grays Halfway," *Pittsburgh Courier*, August 16, 1930.

21. "'Cum' Posey, Manager of Homestead Grays, and League Bosses, Agree to Disagree as Sequel to Hard Fought Battle of Wits," *Pittsburgh Courier*, January 16, 1926.

22. *Ibid.*

23. J.M. Howe, "Sport Sidelights," *Philadelphia Tribune*, August 11, 1927.

24. "Posey Forfeits Game to Lincolns," *Chicago Defender*, July 7, 1928; W. Rollo Wilson, "Grays Walk Off Field in Manhattan," *Pittsburgh Courier*, July 7, 1928; W. Rollo Wilson, "Eastern Snapshots," *Pittsburgh Courier*, August 8, 1925.

25. Posey, "The Sportive Realm," *Pittsburgh Courier*, March 3, 1928.

26. Cum Posey, "In the Sportive Realm," *Pittsburgh Courier*, March 31, 1928; William G. Nunn, "WGN Broadcasts," *Pittsburgh Courier*, August 6, 1927.

27. Posey, "The Sportive Realm," *Pittsburgh Courier*, January 8, 1927.

28. "Posey Forfeits Game to Lincolns," *Chicago Defender*, July 7, 1928; W. Rollo Wilson, "Grays Walk Off Field in Manhattan," *Pittsburgh Courier*, July 7, 1928; W. Rollo Wilson, "Eastern Snapshots," *Pittsburgh Courier*, August 8, 1925; "Lincoln Giants Whip Grays," *New York Amsterdam News*, July 4, 1928.

29. Posey, "The Sportive Realm," *Pittsburgh Courier*, January 29, 1927.

30. Posey, "The Sportive Realm," *Pittsburgh Courier*, January 21, 1928.

31. "Lloyd Believes That New Eastern League Would Be a Success," *Pittsburgh Courier*, August 20, 1927; "Eastern League Goes on Rocks; New Body Nam'd," *Baltimore Afro-American*, April 21, 1928.

32. Posey, "The Sportive Realm," *Pittsburgh Courier*, March 9, 1929; Ira F. Lewis, "The Passing Review," *Pittsburgh Courier*, January 26, 1929; W. Rollo Wilson, "Sport Shots, Press Box & Ring Side," *Pittsburgh Courier*, January 26, 1929.

33. W. Rollo Wilson, "All-Star Eastern Baseball Team Selected," *Pittsburgh Courier*, September 28, 1929.

34. John Holway, *Voices from the Great Black Baseball Leagues* (New York: DaCapo Press, 1992), 79.

35. Posey, "The Sportive Realm," *Pittsburgh Courier*, March 9, 1929.

36. James A. Riley, *Biographical Encyclopedia*, 741.

37. "Hilldale Suspends Stevens Again," *Pittsburgh Courier*, August 10, 1929.

38. "Joseph H. Rainey, "Seven Baseball Players En-Route Here Injured When Machine Overturns," *Philadelphia Tribune*, June 27, 1929.

39. W. Rollo Wilson, "Grays and Hilldale Figure in Big Trade," *Pittsburgh Courier*, March 9, 1929; "Hilldale Suspends Stevens Again," *Pittsburgh Courier*, August 10, 1929.

40. "Baseball War Looms as East Raids Western Clubs," *Chicago Defender*, July 13, 1929.

41. "Homestead Grays Represent Cleveland," *Philadelphia Tribune*, March 7, 1929; S. B. Wilkins, "An East-West World Series?" *Pittsburgh Courier*, August 31, 1929; Bill Gibson, "The Passing Review," *Baltimore Afro-American*, October 19, 1929.

42. "Clan Held to Stalemate in First Encounter Comes Back to Take Final Game," *Philadelphia Tribune*, May 23, 1929; "Charleston Deposed as Hilldale Leader," *Baltimore Afro-American*, May 25, 1929.

43. Bill Gibson, "The Passing Review," *Baltimore Afro-American*, October 19, 1929.

Chapter Five

1. "Cooper Signed by Homestead Grays, *Pittsburgh Post-Gazette*, April 23, 1930; W. Rollo Wilson, "Sports Shots, Press Box and Ring Side," *Pittsburgh Courier*, September 9, 1931.

2. Robert L. Tiemann, "Major League Attendance," in *Total Baseball, Seventh Edition*, ed. John Thorn, Pete Palmer, and Michael Gershman (Kingston, NY: Total Sports Publishing, 2001), 76; Bob Hoie, "The Minor Leagues, in *Total Baseball*, 497.

3. W. Rollo Wilson, "Sports Shots, Press Box and Ring Side," *Pittsburgh Courier*, August 22, 1931.

4. James E. Overmyer, *Black Ball and the Boardwalk: The Bacharach Giants of Atlantic City, 1916–1929* (Jefferson, NC: McFarland, 2014), 247.

5. "Grays Rounding into Fine Form at Springs," *Pittsburgh Courier*, March 22, 1930.

6. William A. Young, *J. L. Wilkinson and the Kansas City Monarchs: Trailblazers in Black Baseball* (Jefferson, NC: McFarland, 2016), 70–74.

7. Havey J. Boyle, "Mirrors of Sport," *Pittsburgh Post-Gazette*, May 6, 1930.

8. Havey J. Boyle, "Mirrors of Sport," *Pittsburgh Post-Gazette*, July 11, 1930; William A. Young, *J. L. Wilkinson and the Kansas City Monarchs*, 74.

9. "Real Test," *Akron Beacon Journal*, July 12, 1930.

10. Paul A. R. Kurtz, "Grays Cop Thriller," *Pittsburgh Press*, July 19, 1930.

11. Ralph Davis, "Night Baseball Here Success," *Pittsburgh Press*, July 19, 1930.

12. Havey J. Boyle, "Mirrors of Sport," *Pittsburgh Post-Gazette*, July 21, 1930.

13. "Smoky Joe Scores 27 Strikeouts," *Pittsburgh Courier*, August 9, 1930.

14. "Cum Posey Reminisces:—," *Pittsburgh Courier*, April 25, 1936.

15. "Grays-Lincolns Series May Materialize; Posey Breaks Silence; States Terms," *Pittsburgh Courier*, August 9, 1930.

16. "Keenan Answers Posey; Rates Lincolns 'Best Ever'; Will Meet Grays Halfway," *Pittsburgh Courier*, August 16, 1930.

17. "Jim Keenan's Final Stab," *New York Amsterdam News*, August 27, 1930; "'Posey Giving Fans the Run-Around'—Keenan; Big Series Hangs Fire," *Pittsburgh Courier*, August 30, 1930.

18. American League Baseball Club of New York records, National Baseball Hall of Fame and Library, Cooperstown, NY.

19. James A. Riley, *Biographical Encyclopedia of the Negro Baseball Leagues*, 870; Cum Posey, "Posey's Points," *Pittsburgh Courier*, June 17, 1939.

20. James A. Riley, *Biographical Encyclopedia*, 292.

21. "Eastern League Must Have Strong Teams, Says Posey," *Chicago Defender*, October 31, 1931; "Cum" Posey, "Grays Undisputed Champs; Team Play Won–League Looms," *Pittsburgh Courier*, October 10, 1931.

22. John Holway, *Voices from the Great Black Baseball Leagues*, 195.

23. Cum Posey, "Looking Over the Baseball Horizon," *Pittsburgh Courier*, March 21, 1931.

24. "Cum" Posey, "Grays Undisputed Champs; Team Play Won–League Looms," *Pittsburgh Courier*, October 10, 1931; "Cum Posey to Head New East and West Baseball League, Reports State," *New York Age*, January 9, 1932.

25. W. Rollo Wilson, "Sports Shots, Press Box and Ring Side," *Pittsburgh Courier*, June 4, 1932.

26. "Syndicate Baseball" at Baseball-Reference.com, http://www.baseball-reference.com/bullpen/Syndicate_baseball.

27. Quincy Trouppe, *20 Years Too Soon*, 60.

28. John Holway, *Black Diamonds: Life in the Negro Leagues from the Men Who Lived It* (Westport, CT: Meckler Books, 1989), 64–65.

29. "Posey Answers Umpire's Charges; Depression Blamed for Troubles, *Pittsburgh Courier*,

July 16, 1932; "Support Needed; May Stop Salaries," *Pittsburgh Courier*, July 2, 1932.

30. Rob Ruck, *Sandlot Seasons*, 46–49.

31. *Ibid.*, 51, 59; W. Rollo Wilson, "Sports Shots, Press Box and Ring Side," *Pittsburgh Courier*, March 28, 1931; William G. Nunn, "WGN Broadcasts," *Pittsburgh Courier*, July 5, 1930.

32. Rob Ruck, *Sandlot Seasons*, 137; "Restaurateur Feeds 700 Homeless Men," *Pittsburgh Post-Gazette*, December 26, 1931; Chester L. Washington, "Deep Wylie," *Pittsburgh Courier*, May 18, 1929.

33. *The WPA History of the Negro in Pittsburgh*, 288–289.

34. "City Wide Open for Organized Depravity," *Pittsburgh Daily Post*, September 21, 1926; Rob Ruck, *Sandlot Seasons*, 145; Measuring Worth website, www.measuringworth.com/uscompare/relativevalue.php.

35. Ray Sprigle, "We've Got Your Number, Racket Has First Bout with Police, Staggers, Revives and Then Booms," *Pittsburgh Post-Gazette*, February 11, 1936.

36. Ray Sprigle, "We've Got Your Number, Splitting the Numbers 'Take' Proved Headache to Operators," *Pittsburgh Post-Gazette*, February 13, 1936.

37. Rob Ruck, *Sandlot Seasons*, 145.

38. *Ibid.*, 151.

39. *Ibid.*, 61; "Grays, Crawfords, to Meet Saturday," *Pittsburgh Post-Gazette*, August 18, 1930.

40. Rob Ruck, *Sandlot Seasons*, 154; Donald Spivey, *If You Were Only White: The Life of Leroy "Satchel" Paige* (Columbia: University of Missouri Press, 2012), 73.

41. "Crawfords, Grays Claim Gibson for '32 Season," *Pittsburgh Courier*, February 6, 1932; "'Cum' Posey's Pointed Paragraphs," *Pittsburgh Courier*, February 13, 1932; Floyd G. Snelson, "Broadway Bound," *Pittsburgh Courier*, November 19, 1932.

42. James A. Riley, *Biographical Encyclopedia*, 124.

43. Buck Leonard, with James A. Riley, *Buck Leonard, The Black Lou Gehrig* (New York: Carroll & Graf, 1995), 58–59.

44. *Ibid.*; John Holway, *Black Giants*, 106.

45. John L. Clark, "The Rise and Fall of Greenlee Field," *Pittsburgh Courier*, December 10, 1938; Roberta J. Newman and Joel Nathan Rosen, *Black Baseball, Black Business: Race Enterprise and the Fate of the Segregated Dollar* (Jackson: University Press of Mississippi, 2014), 68; Geri Strecker, "The Rise and Fall of Greenlee Field: Biography of a Ballpark," *Black Ball, a Negro Leagues Journal* 2, no. 2 (Fall 2009): 39.

46. Strecker, *ibid.*; Lewis Dial, "The Sport Dial," *New York Age*, June 18, 1932.

47. Evan Posey Baker, Jr., interview; *The WPA History of the Negro in Pittsburgh*, 48.

48. "Mrs. Myrtle Page Dies After a Lingering Illness," *Pittsburgh Courier*, August 16, 1912; "The Death Roll, Mrs. C. W. Posey," *Pittsburgh Post-Gazette*, August 21, 1917; "W. N. Page, Manager of Negro Paper, Dies," *Pittsburgh Daily Post*, January 5, 1916.

49. "Mrs. Bessie P. Posey, *Pittsburgh Post-Gazette*, January 26, 1928; "Mrs. Posey's Death Shock to Many: Deceased Was Well Known in East and South," *Pittsburgh Courier*, February 4, 1928.

50. Measuring Worth website, https://www.measuringworth.com/uscompare/relativevalue.php; Will of C. W. Posey, with associated documents, filed in Allegheny County Register's Office July 15, 1925, at Allegheny County Department of Court Records, Pittsburgh, PA; "$29,000 Posey Estate Goes to Minor Son," *Baltimore Afro-American*, March 17, 1928; Legal notices, *Pittsburgh Press*, September 14, 1935.

51. "Pittsburgh Crawfords to Meet Jamestown Spiders in Double Bill Sunday; Art Might Start," *Warren (PA) Times Mirror*, August 5, 1932; W. Rollo Wilson, "Sports Shots, Press Box and Ring Side," *Pittsburgh Courier*, September 17, 1932.

52. "League Heads Veto Proposal," *New York Amsterdam News*, October 21, 1931; "Crawfords' Owner Makes First Statement About the Team, New Park and Plans," *Pittsburgh Courier*, February 27, 1932.

53. "Veteran Courier Writer Dead," *Pittsburgh Courier*, July 1, 1961.

54. John L. Clark, "Grays-Crawfords Clash Over League," *New York Amsterdam News*, January 6, 1932; John L. Clark, "Writer Sees League as Means for Cutting Players' Salary," *Chicago Defender*, January 23, 1932.

55. Cum Posey, "Cum Posey Abandons Modesty and Backfires at Crawfords," *Chicago Defender*, March 13, 1932.

56. John L. Clark, "Wylie Avenue," *Pittsburgh Courier*, January 4, 1941; "Religious Activities in Pittsburgh District," *Pittsburgh Courier*, October 14, 1933.

57. Lewis E. Dial, "The Sport Dial," *New York Age*, March 19, 1932.

Chapter Six

1. W. Rollo Wilson, "Sports Shots, Press Box and Ring Side," *Pittsburgh Courier*, May 20, 1933.

2. Cum Posey, "Independent Ball Only Hope for Survival," *Pittsburgh Courier*, July 8, 1933.

3. Lewis E. Dial, "The Sport Dial," *New York Age*, July 29, 1933.

4. "Cum Posey's Pointed Paragraphs," *Pittsburgh Courier*, July 15, 1933.

5. "Cum Posey's Pointed Paragraphs," *Pittsburgh Courier*, August 12, 1933.

6. Cum Posey, "Picks All-Star Teams; Cites Virtues, Flaws," *Pittsburgh Courier*, September 30, 1933; "Cum Posey's Pointed Paragraphs," *Pittsburgh Courier*, August 5, 1933; "Stars of Yesteryears Eclipse Present Day Stars," *Pittsburgh Courier*, July 22, 1933.

7. Randy Dixon, "Baseball Owners En route to Philly Pow Wow," *Pittsburgh Courier*, February 10, 1934; "Rollo Wilson Elected Potentate; Grays In; Schedule Drafted," *Pittsburgh Courier*, March 17, 1934.

8. W. Rollo Wilson, "National Game in Big Start," *New York Amsterdam News*, May 12, 1934.

9. "Boosters to Honor Grays at Big Fete," *Pittsburgh Courier*, April 8, 1933; "Grays Lose Morney and Harris," *Pittsburgh Courier*, March 31, 1934.

10. "Cum Posey's Pointed Paragraphs," *Pittsburgh Courier*, May 26, 1934.

11. Lewis E. Dial, "The Sports Dial," *New York Age*, July 28, 1934.

12. "Cum Posey Also Raps East-West Classic," *Atlanta Daily World*, July 26, 1934; Frank Young, "The East vs. West Game is No All-Star Contest," *New York Amsterdam News*, July 21, 1934; Lewis E. Dial, "The Sport Dial," *New York Age*, August 4, 1934.

13. "Craws–Grays Series Off, Says," *Pittsburgh Courier*, August 18, 1934.

14. "The Answer—," *Pittsburgh Courier*, August 25, 1934.

15. John L. Clark, "Clark Hits Back at Famed Club Owner," *New York Amsterdam News*, July 26, 1933.

16. Cum Posey, "Posey Answers Clark on League and Grays," *Pittsburgh Courier*, July 29, 1933.

17. *Ibid.*

18. Cum Posey, "Cum Posey 'Strikes Back' at Clark in League Feud, Scores Secretary's Tactics," *Pittsburgh Courier*, June 16, 1934; "Clark Answers Posey's Charges," *Pittsburgh Courier*, June 2, 1934; John L. Clark, "Clark Claims Posey May Quit League; Answers Charges," *Pittsburgh Courier*, June 9, 1934.

19. James A. Riley, *Biographical Encyclopedia*, 83, 135, 271, 308, 499.

20. Ralph Berger, "Buck Leonard," Society

for American Baseball Research Bioproject, http://sabr.org/bioproj/person/231446fd; Interview with Buck Leonard by Robert Peterson, September 15, 1967, National Baseball Hall of Fame and Library, Cooperstown, NY; John Holway, *Voices from the Great Black Baseball Leagues*, 257.

21. Evan P. Baker, Jr., interview.

22. Certificate of Incorporation for Homestead Grays Base Ball Club, Commonwealth of Pennsylvania, Department of State, Charter Book 337, Page 89, recorded June 22, 1934; "Cum Posey's Pointed Paragraphs," *Pittsburgh Courier*, April 28, 1934; John L. Clark, "Wylie Avenue," *Pittsburgh Courier*, May 5, 1934.

23. *Homestead City Directory (1927)*, R. L. Polk & Co., 321; Interview with Helen Jackson by Rob Ruck, Archives and Manuscript Collections, University of Pittsburgh Library, Pittsburgh, PA; Curtis Miner, *Homestead: The Story of a Steel Town* (Pittsburgh: Historical Society of Western Pennsylvania, 1989), 56.

24. Miner, *Ibid.*; Helen Jackson interview; Display advertisement, "New and Used Records," *Pittsburgh Courier*, June 1, 1940; "Talk O' Town," *Pittsburgh Courier*, January 20, 1934; 1940 United States Census for Homestead, PA, s.v. Rufus Jackson, accessed at https://www.Ancestry.com.

25. Helen Jackson interview; "Numbers Baron Held for Court," *Pittsburgh Press*, March 5, 1934.

26. "City Officials Sent to Prison in Conspiracy," *Pittsburgh Press*, September 15, 1927; James Jackson, "Sidewalks of Pittsburgh," *Baltimore Afro-American*, September 16, 1933.

27. Helen Jackson interview; "Rufus Jackson Dies," *Pittsburgh Press*, March 7, 1949; "Law's Niceties 'Save' Inn Serving Drinks to Minors," *Pittsburgh Press*, March 21, 1940.

28. "Grays' Co-Owner Defies Gangland Death Threat," *Pittsburgh Courier*, April 6, 1935.

29. Helen Jackson interview.

30. "Rosner Effects Combine With Negro Teams," *New York Amsterdam News*, June 8, 1935.

31. Cum Posey, "Posey's Points," *Pittsburgh Courier*, July 4, 1936.

32. Adrian Burgos, Jr., *Cuban Star: How One Negro-League Owner Changed the Face of Baseball* (New York: Hill and Wang, 2011), 14, 86; "70 Seized in Raids by Dewey to Break Huge Policy Ring," *New York Times*, January 15, 1937.

33. Neil Lanctot, *Negro League Baseball: The Rise and Ruin of a Black Institution* (Philadelphia: University of Pennsylvania Press, 2004), 46; "Owners Ask for Harmony," *Pittsburgh Courier*, October 3, 1936.

34. "American Giants Fired by League," *New York Amsterdam News*, May 23, 1936.

35. "Cum Posey's Pointed Paragraphs," *Pittsburgh Courier*, March 2, 1935.

36. "American Giants Fired by League," *New York Amsterdam News*, May 23, 1936.

37. Romeo L. Dougherty, "Sports," *New York Amsterdam News*, January 26, 1935; Neil Lanctot, *Rise and Ruin*, 44.

38. James A. Riley, *Biographical Encyclopedia*, 808; Interview with Edsall Walker by the author, July 11, 1990.

39. Riley, *ibid.*, 252; Cum Posey, "Satchell, Matlock and Leonard Make Posey's All-American Team," *Pittsburgh Courier*, October 17, 1936.

40. "Cum Posey's Pointed Paragraphs," *Pittsburgh Courier*, March 23, 1935; "Cum Posey's Pointed Paragraphs," *Pittsburgh Courier*, March 14, 1936.

41. "Cum Posey's Pointed Paragraphs," *Pittsburgh Courier*, February 9, 1935; "Cum Posey's Pointed Paragraphs," *Pittsburgh Courier*, February 8, 1936.

42. Cum Posey, "Posey's Points," *Pittsburgh Courier*, November 7, 1936.

43. "Cum Posey's Pointed Paragraphs," *Pittsburgh Courier*, March 28, 1936; Baseball War Over League Grounds in Pittsburgh Gets Hot; Greenlee Makes Charges," *New York Age*, April 25, 1936.

44. "Cum Posey's Pointed Paragraphs," *Pittsburgh Courier*, March 7, 1936; Neil Lanctot, *Rise and Ruin*, 49.

45. William Brashler, *Josh Gibson*, 101; "Greenlee Freed on $2,500 Bond," *Pittsburgh Press*, April 20, 1936.

46. "Grays Get Gibson; Greenlee League Prexy," *Pittsburgh Courier*, March 27, 1937; Measuring Worth website, https://www.measuring worth.com/uscompare/relativevalue.php.

47. "Homestead Grays Cinch Nat'l League Pennant," *Pittsburgh Courier*, September 11, 1937.

48. Richard J. Lamb, "Gus 'Whereas-es' Diplomats into Action over Foreign 'Raid' on Negro Ball Team," *Pittsburgh Press*, June 20, 1937.

49. "Dominican Republic: The Trujillo Regime," Encyclopedia Britannica online, www.britannica.com/place/Dominican-Republic/Caudillos#ref726640.

50. Donald Spivey, *If You Were Only White*, 123–124.

51. William Brashler, *Josh Gibson*, 107; Buck Leonard, *Buck Leonard, The Black Lou Gehrig*, 80.

52. "Two Jailed in Baseball War," *Pittsburgh Courier*, May 15, 1937; Rob Ruck, *The Tropic of Baseball: Baseball in the Dominican Republic* (Lincoln: University of Nebraska Press, 1999), 38.

53. Cum Posey, "Posey's Points," *Pittsburgh Courier*, September 18, 1937.

54. John L. Clark, "Greenlee Aid Takes Slap at World Series," *Pittsburgh Courier*, September 25, 1937; "Greenlee Claims Proposed 'World Series' is Unsanctioned by League," *Pittsburgh Courier*, September 18, 1937.

55. Neil Lanctot, *Rise and Ruin*, 79.

56. John L. Clark, "Wylie Avenue," *Pittsburgh Courier*, October 4, 1941; John L. Clark, "Wylie Avenue," *Pittsburgh Courier*, April 6, 1946.

Chapter Seven

1. "Kinney, Posey School Directors," *Homestead Daily Messenger*, November 4, 1931; Naomi Bright, "Homestead High School," *Pittsburgh Courier*, December 19, 1931.

2. Curtis Miner, *Homestead: The Story of a Steel Town*, 29.

3. *Ibid.*, 29, 45.

4. *Ibid.*, 46.

5. William Serrin, *Homestead: The Glory and Tragedy of an American Steel Town*, 23.

6. Curtis Miner, *Homestead: The Story of a Steel Town*, 45; "Murder Mars Homestead Primary; Election Riots Keep Courts Busy," *Pittsburgh Daily Post*, September 16, 1925, 2; "J.J. Cavanaugh, Long GOP Homestead Leader, Dies," *Pittsburgh Post-Gazette*, February 18, 1949.

7. *Fifteenth Census of the United States: 1930, Population, Volume III, Part 2* (Washington, DC: Department of Commerce), 1932, 688; "Testimonial," *Pittsburgh Post-Gazette*, August 26, 1927.

8. Bruce M. Stave, *The New Deal and the Last Hurrah: Pittsburgh Machine Politics* (Pittsburgh: University of Pittsburgh Press, 1970), 53; William Serrin, *Homestead: The Glory and Tragedy of an American Steel Town*, 179.

9. "Miss Perkins Parlay Barred by Cavanaugh," *Pittsburgh Post-Gazette*, August 1, 1933; "Gigantic 'Red' Plot Bared, Curbed by Cavanaugh Alone," *Pittsburgh Post-Gazette*, August 2, 1933.

10. "McLean Slaps Organization, Charges Bootleggers, Gamblers Dominate Politics in Borough," *Homestead Daily Messenger*, March 12, 1934.

11. "Burgess of Homestead 'Buried' in Mock Funeral," *Pittsburgh Post-Gazette*, November 4, 1937.

12. James E. Johnson, "Sidewalks of Pittsburgh," *Baltimore Afro-American,* March 31, 1934; "Homestead 'Cracks Down' on 'Nervous Burgess,'" *Pittsburgh Courier*, November 2, 1935.

13. James E. Johnson, "Sidewalks of Pittsburgh," *Baltimore Afro-American*, March 31, 1934.

14. "School Director Arrested by Albiez after Raid on Third Avenue Club Rooms," *Homestead Daily Messenger*, April 3, 1934; "Burgess Scores Police Tactics on High Forfeits; No Decision in Case," *Homestead Daily Messenger*, April 4, 1934; "Cavanaugh Scathingly Denounces 'Malicious Liar' but Frees Posey, *Homestead Daily Messenger*, April 7, 1934; "Homestead 'Grays' Owner Arrested," *Pittsburgh Post-Gazette*, April 4, 1934.

15. James E. Johnson, "Sidewalks of Pittsburgh," *Baltimore Afro-American*, April 14, 1934; "'Cum' Posey Framed; Jailed," *Pittsburgh Courier*, April 7, 1934.

16. "Posey Slashes at G.O.P. Activities," *Homestead Daily Messenger*, September 5, 1934.

17. "'Cum' Posey in Political Row," *Pittsburgh Courier*, September 14, 1935.

18. "Man Held for Quiz in 'Terror' Cases," *Pittsburgh Post-Gazette*, August 16, 1934.

19. "Judge Praises Jury's Verdict," *Pittsburgh Courier*, February 2, 1935.

20. *Ibid.*

21. "Uncle of Chapman Scores 'Cup' Jenkins' Ruthlessness," *Pittsburgh Courier*, February 2, 1935.

22. "Cum Posey's Pointed Paragraphs," *Pittsburgh Courier*, February 2, 1935.

23. Robert Hughey, "Homestead School Board Weighs Appeal to Open Gym to Race," *Pittsburgh Courier*, January 25, 1941; "Powell Fails to Appear; Shepard Lauds Truman," *Pittsburgh Courier*, October 27, 1945.

24. Cum Posey, "Posey's Points," *Pittsburgh Courier*, January 8, 1938.

25. Robert Hughey, "Homestead Citizens Plan Eviction Fight; Will Have to Give Up Homes if Mill Purchases Land," *Pittsburgh Courier*, May 10, 1941.

26. *Ibid.*; Charles H. Brown, "New Defense Plant Will Force 8,000 to Move in Homestead," *Pittsburgh Post-Gazette*, July 2, 1941.

27. Measuring Worth website, www.measuringworth.com/uscompare/relativevalue.php; Evan P. Baker, Jr., interview.

28. "Loendi Cue Aces Beat Y.M.C.A.," *Pittsburgh Courier*, February 28, 1931.

29. "Elks Plan National Court Tournament," *Pittsburgh Courier*, December 13, 1941.

30. Beatrice Lee interview.

31. "Ethel T. Posey, wife of founder of Grays team," *Pittsburgh Post-Gazette*, November 27, 1986.

32. Beatrice Lee interview.

33. Jerry Vondas, "Jazz Was King of the Hill," *Pittsburgh Press*, June 17, 1982.

34. Marriage license, Oliver C. Palmer and Mary E. Posey, Pittsburgh, PA, September 14, 1940, accessed at https://www.Ancestry.com; "Vital Statistics, Divorce Libels Filed," *Pittsburgh Press*, March 28, 1941; Marriage license, Lewis Sparkman Flagg III and Mary Elizabeth Posey Palmer, Pittsburgh, PA, December 8, 1947, accessed at https://www.Ancestry.com; Manifest of Crew Members, SS *Fitzhugh Lee*, January 27, 1946, accessed at https://www.Ancestry.com.

35. Marriage license, Lewis Sparkman Flagg III and Mary Elizabeth Posey Palmer, Pittsburgh, PA, December 8, 1947, accessed at https://www.Ancestry.com; Barbara Winslow, *Shirley Chisholm, Catalyst for Change, 1926–2005* (Boulder, CO: Westview Press, 2014), 31–32.

36. "Beatrice Posey Lee, Daughter of Homestead Grays Founder," *Pittsburgh Post-Gazette*, December 2, 1998; Sadie Feddoes, "Please Be Seated," *New York Amsterdam News*, February 11, 1978; Juli B. Jones, "Talk O'Town," *Pittsburgh Courier*, September 20, 1941; "Thousands Mourn Death of Rev. John W. Johnson," *New York Age*, May 24, 1930, 1; Photo of Beatrice Kathleen Posey, *Pittsburgh Courier*, September 28, 1946; Marriage of John H. Boxill and Beatrice K. Posey, August 9, 1946, New York City Marriage Indexes, 1907–1995, accessed at https://www.Ancestry.com.

37. Juli B. Jones, "Talk O'Town," *Pittsburgh Courier*, December 6, 1941; "Homestead Matron Buried Wednesday," *Pittsburgh Courier*, January 27, 1945; Certificate of Death for Ann Posey Harper, January 21, 1945, Commonwealth of Pennsylvania, Department of Health, accessed at https://www.Ancestry.com.

38. John L. Clark, "Wylie Avenue," *Pittsburgh Courier*, April 6, 1946.

Chapter Eight

1. Wendell Smith, "Smitty's Sports Spurts," *Pittsburgh Courier*, June 11, 1938; Cum Posey, "Posey's Points," *Pittsburgh Courier*, June 18, 1938.

2. Robert L. Tiemann, "Major League Attendance," in *Total Baseball*, 76; Bob Hoie, "The Minor Leagues, in *Total Baseball*, 497.

3. John T. Cunningham, *Newark* (Newark, NJ: New Jersey Historical Society, 1966), 293–296.

4. Neil Lanctot, *Rise and Ruin*, 147.

5. James A. Riley, *Biographical Encyclopedia of the Negro Baseball Leagues*, 476.

6. Cumberland "Cum" Posey, "Posey Picks Immortals," *Negro Baseball Pictorial Yearbook*

(Washington, DC: Sepia Sports Publications, 1945), 8.

7. James E. Overmyer, *Queen of the Negro Leagues: Effa Manley and the Newark Eagles* (Lanham, MD: Scarecrow Press, 1998), 153.

8. Wendell Smith, "Smitty's Sports Spurts," *Pittsburgh Courier*, April 5, 1941.

9. William Brashler, *Josh Gibson*, 122–124.

10. *Ibid.*, 76; Cum Posey, "Posey's Points," *Pittsburgh Courier*, October 14, 1939.

11. Cum Posey, "Posey's Points," *Pittsburgh Courier*, May 20, 1939.

12. Cum Posey, "Posey Tells His Side of the Story," *Pittsburgh Courier*, June 12, 1939; Wendell Smith, "Smitty's Sports Spurts," *Pittsburgh Courier*, June 19, 1939.

13. Cum Posey, "Posey's Points," *Pittsburgh Courier*, April 19, 1941.

14. James A. Riley, *Biographical Encyclopedia*, 262.

15. *Ibid.*, 52; 1940 United States Census for Homestead, PA, s.v. Sam Bankhead, accessed at https://www.Ancestry.com.

16. Edsall Walker interview.

17. Chester L. Washington, "Sez Ches," *Pittsburgh Courier*, July 12, 1941.

18. John Holway, *Black Diamonds*, 123.

19. Wendell Smith, "Smitty's Sports Spurts," *Pittsburgh Courier*, September 15, 1945; "Homestead Grays Application Blank," *Pittsburgh Courier*, March 25, 1944.

20. "Bolden Says Phila. Stars Should be Playing World Series, Not Grays," *New York Amsterdam News*, September 16, 1944.

21. Butts Brown, "In the Groove," *New Jersey Herald News*, September 16, 1944.

22. "Grays Win, 4 to 1; Monarchs Protest," *Pittsburgh Courier*, September 26, 1942.

23. Wendell Smith, "Smitty's Sports Spurts," *Pittsburgh Courier*, October 16, 1943; Fay Young, "Through the Years," *Chicago Defender*, October 23, 1943; "Dan Burley's 'Confidentially Yours,'" *New York Amsterdam News*, October 30, 1943.

24. "'Agreement' to Rule Series," *Pittsburgh Courier*, September 9, 1944.

25. Havey Boyle, "Mirrors of Sport," *Pittsburgh Post-Gazette*, June 16, 1938.

26. Chester L. Washington, "Sez Ches," *Pittsburgh Courier*, August 6, 1938.

27. "Grays Celebrate Birthday; Beat Newark, 8–4," *Pittsburgh Courier*, August 13, 1938.

28. Dan Park, "Sports Sparks," *Olean (NY) Times Herald*, August 12, 1941.

29. Edsall Walker interview.

30. Brad Snyder, *Beyond the Shadow of the Senators* (New York: McGraw-Hill, 2003), 53.

31. "Grays May Shift Home Park to D.C.," *Pittsburgh Courier*, July 8, 1939.

32. "Clark Griffith's 50 Golden Years in the American League," *The Sporting News*, July 30, 1952; Michael Beschloss, "The Washington Senators: A Monument to Bad Management," *New York Times*, May 1, 2015.

33. Brad Snyder, *Beyond the Shadow of the Senators*, 12.

34. *Ibid.*, 101.

35. Eddie Gant, "I Cover the Eastern Front," *Chicago Defender*, February 28, 1942; Snyder, 104–106.

36. Jack Munhall, "Paige, Grays Beat Stars, 8–1, Before 22,000," *Washington Post*, June 1, 1942.

37. Brad Snyder, *Beyond the Shadow of the Senators*, 136.

38. Art Carter, "From the Bench," *Baltimore Afro-American*, September 5, 1942; "Dan Burley's 'Confidentially Yours,'" *New York Amsterdam News*, February 27, 1943.

39. Brad Snyder, *Beyond the Shadow of the Senators*, 168–169.

40. *Ibid.*, 75.

41. *Ibid.*, 74; Joanne Hulbert, "Bobby Estalella," SABR Bio Project, Society for American Baseball Research, http://sabr.org/bioproj/person/488f6 ebd.

Chapter Nine

1. Letter, Cumberland Posey to Effa Manley, dated June 11, 1941, Newark Eagles business papers, Newark Public Library, Newark, NJ.

2. Letter, Cumberland Posey to Effa Manley, dated January 11, 1943, Newark Eagles papers.

3. Cum Posey, "Posey's Points," *Pittsburgh Courier*, January 22, 1938; *Ibid.*, June 25, 1938.

4. Cum Posey, "American League Votes to Have 6-Club Circuit," *Pittsburgh Courier*, February 26, 1938.

5. Chester L. Washington, Jr., "Sez Ches," *Pittsburgh Courier*, May 6, 1938.

6. Fay Young, "The Stuff is Here: Past-Present-Future," *Chicago Defender*, May 20, 1939.

7. C.W. Posey, "Posey Says 'American League Broke Agreement,'" *Pittsburgh Courier*, May 8, 1943.

8. "Tom Wilson Acts With J. B. Martin to End Disputes," *New York Amsterdam News*, June 12, 1943.

9. Daniel, "Baseball Magnates Try to Hold Players," *New York Amsterdam News*, March 2, 1940.

10. Letter, Cumberland Posey to Abraham Manley, dated December 26, 1940, Newark Eagles papers.

11. Wendell Smith, "Smitty's Sports Spurts," *Pittsburgh Courier*, April 5, 1941.

12. James E. Overmyer, *Queen of the Negro Leagues*, 189–190; Wendell Smith, "Smitty's Sports Spurts," *Pittsburgh Courier*, February 20, 1943.

13. Wendell Smith, "Diplomat, Grays' Owner in Rift Over Players," *Pittsburgh Courier*, July 17, 1943; Wendell Smith, "Grays' Owner a Happy Man; Has Won Fight for Players," *Pittsburgh Courier*, July 31, 1943.

14. Duke Goldman, "1933–1962, The Business Meetings of Negro League Baseball," *Baseball's Business, The Winter Meetings, Volume 2*, Steve Weingarden and Bill Nowlin, eds. (Phoenix: Society for American Baseball Research, 2017).

15. "NNL Turns Down Commissioner Plan for Circuits," *New York Amsterdam News*, July 1, 1939; Letter, Cumberland Posey to Abraham and Effa Manley, dated December 4, 1941, Newark Eagles papers.

16. Fay Young, "The Stuff is Here: Past-Present-Future," *Chicago Defender*, October 25, 1941.

17. Letter, Cumberland Posey to Effa Manley, dated November 22, 1942, Newark Eagles papers.

18. Cum Posey, "Posey's Points," *Pittsburgh Courier*, October 30, 1941; Butts Brown, "In the Groove," *New Jersey Herald News*, 9.

19. William E. Clark, "The Sports Parade," *New York Age*, July 22, 1939.

20. Cum Posey, "Posey's Points," *Pittsburgh Courier*, March 27, 1943; Cum Posey, "Posey Points," *Pittsburgh Courier*, November 12, 1938.

21. "Jackson Rejects National League Plan," *Chicago Defender*, January 14, 1939; Cum Posey, "Posey's Points," *Pittsburgh Courier*, December 26, 1942.

22. Cum Posey, "Posey's Points," *Pittsburgh Courier*, January 2, 1943; *Ibid.*, November 21, 1942.

23. Neil Lanctot, *Rise and Ruin*, 111.

24. James E. Overmyer, "Black Baseball at Yankee Stadium," *Black Ball, a Negro Leagues Journal* 7 (2014), 12.

25. Art Carter, "Metro Clubs Try to Oust Tom Wilson," *Baltimore Afro-American*, February 10, 1940; James E. Overmyer, *Queen of the Negro Leagues*, 92, 271.

26. Dan Burley, "National League Moguls Deadlock on Dr. C.B. Powell as Prexy," *New York Amsterdam News*, February 10, 1940; "Vote for President Ends in Deadlock," *Chicago Defender*, February 10, 1940; "Row May Split National League," *Chicago Defender*, February 24, 1940.

27. "Vote for President Ends in Deadlock," *Chicago Defender*, February 10, 1940.

28. Dan Burley, "National League Moguls Deadlock on Dr. C.B. Powell as Prexy," *New York Amsterdam News*, February 10, 1940; "Vote for President Ends in Deadlock," *Chicago Defender*, February 10, 1940.

29. Effa Manley and Leon Herbert Hardwick, *Negro Baseball ... Before Integration* (Haworth, NJ: St. Johann Press, 2006), 40–41.

30. Interview of Effa Manley by William Marshall, 1977, Albert B. Chandler Papers, University of Kentucky, Lexington, KY; Randy Dixon, "The Sports Bugle," *Pittsburgh Courier*, May 11, 1940.

31. Cum Posey, "Posey's Points," *Pittsburgh Courier*, February 17, 1940.

32. *Ibid.*; Letter, Effa Manley to Cumberland Posey, dated February 14, 1940, Newark Eagles papers.

33. Letter, Cumberland Posey to Effa Manley, dated February 17, 1940, Newark Eagles papers.

34. Dan Burley, "NNL Owners Go to Chi. To Elect C.B. Powell," *New York Amsterdam News*, February 24, 1940; Cartoon, Charlie, "Baseball Dinner," *New York Amsterdam News*, February 24, 1940.

35. Letter, Cumberland Posey to Effa Manley, February 17, 1940, Newark Eagles papers; "N.N.L. Retains Wilson as President," *Pittsburgh Courier*, March 2, 1940; Duke Goldman, "1933–1962, The Business Meetings of Negro League Baseball," 411.

36. Letter, Effa Manley to Cumberland Posey, dated October 13, 1941, Newark Eagles papers.

37. Letter, Cumberland Posey to Effa Manley, dated November 17, 1941, Newark Eagles papers.

38. *Ibid.*

39. "Posey Points," *Pittsburgh Courier*, October 11, 1941; "Posey Points," *Pittsburgh Courier*, November 22, 1941.

40. Robert Obojski, *Bush League: A History of Minor League Baseball* (New York: Macmillan, 1975), 23.

41. "N.N.L. Owners to Study Player Shortage," *Pittsburgh Courier*, January 23, 1943.

42. "'Boom Towns Will Save Negro Baseball'—Clark," *Pittsburgh Courier*, March 6, 1943.

43. "Special Buses Out for Baseball Clubs," *Newark Evening News*, March 31, 1943.

44. Jim Schlemmer, "Negro Nines Suffer from Travel Ban," *Akron Beacon*, April 1, 1943.

45. Cum Posey, "Posey's Points," *Pittsburgh Courier*, June 5 1943; Buck Leonard with James A. Riley, *Buck Leonard*, 163.

46. "Clark Griffith to Join League Heads in Appeal to ODT," *Pittsburgh Courier*, March 13, 1943.

47. Negro National League memo to Office of Defense Transportation, dated March 13, 1943, Newark Eagles papers.

48. Neil Lanctot, *Rise and Ruin*, 129–134.

Chapter Ten

1. Wendell Smith, "'No Need for Color Ban in Big Leagues'—Pie Traynor," *Pittsburgh Courier*, September 2, 1939.

2. Wendell Smith, "Publishers Place Case of Negro Players Before Big League Owners," *Pittsburgh Courier*, December 11, 1943; "Dan Burley's 'Confidentially Yours,'" *New York Amsterdam News*, December 11, 1943.

3. Effa Manley and Leon Herbert Hardwick, *Negro Baseball ... Before Integration*, 74; Brad Snyder, *Beyond the Shadow of the Senators*, 224.

4. Neil Lanctot, *Rise and Ruin*, 255.

5. Lee Lowenfish, *Branch Rickey, Baseball's Ferocious Gentleman* (Lincoln: University of Nebraska Press, 2007), 367.

6. Draft letter to Albert B. Chandler from C.W. Posey, dated November 1, 1945; Letter to Albert B. Chandler from Dr. J. B. Martin, Thomas T. Wilson, and C.W. Posey, dated November 9, 1945, both from Newark Eagles papers.

7. Letter to C. W. Posey from Clark Griffith, dated November 5, 1945, Newark Eagles papers.

8. Letter from Cumberland Posey to Effa Manley, dated January 10, 1946, Newark Eagles papers.

9. Wendell Smith, "'American League Owners Just Want a Fair Deal'—Martin," *Pittsburgh Courier*, December 25, 1943; Nat Low, "Would Negroes in the Majors Hurt Negro Baseball? Certainly Not, it Would Help, Says Negro Club Owner," *Daily Worker* August 13, 1942; Cum Posey, "Posey's Points," *Pittsburgh Courier*, February 19, 1938; *Ibid.*, March 4, 1939.

10. Nat Low, "Would Negroes in the Majors Hurt Negro Baseball? Certainly Not, it Would Help, Says Negro Club Owner," *Daily Worker*, August 13, 1942; Wendell Smith, "'American League Owners Just Want a Fair Deal'—Martin," *Pittsburgh Courier*, December 25, 1943.

11. Cum Posey, "Posey's Points," *Pittsburgh Courier*, June 27, 1942; Neil Lanctot, *Rise and Ruin*, 257.

12. Cum Posey, "Posey's Points," *Pittsburgh Courier*, August 1, 1942.

13. "Dan Burley's 'Confidentially Yours,'" *New York Amsterdam News*, April 1, 1944.

14. Wendell Smith, "The Sports Beat," *Pittsburgh Courier*, May 26, 1945.

15. Wendell Smith, "The Sports Beat," *Pittsburgh Courier*, February 2, 1946.

16. Letter, Cumberland Posey to Effa Manley, dated January 10, 1946, Newark Eagles papers; Paul Kurtz, "Sports Stew—Served Hot," *Pittsburgh Press*, January 14, 1946; Beatrice Lee interview; Letter, Effa Manley to Cumberland Posey, dated January 12, 1946.

17. Duke Goldman, *1933–1962, The Business Meetings of Negro League Baseball*, 430; "Cum Posey Has Relapse in N.Y., Returns Home," *Pittsburgh Courier*, March 2, 1946; Harry Keck, "Sports," *Pittsburgh Sun-Telegraph*, March 29, 1946; "Mrs. Posey Part Owner of Homestead Grays," *Pittsburgh Post-Gazette*, April 12, 1946.

18. "Homestead Honors Posey at Last Rites," *Pittsburgh Courier*, April 6, 1946.

19. "What They Said About Cum Posey," *Pittsburgh Courier*; Ches Washington, "Sports World Pays Final Tribute to Cum Posey," *Pittsburgh Courier*, both dated April 6, 1946.

20. Wendell Smith, "The Sports Beat," *Pittsburgh Courier*, April 13, 1946.

21. Beatrice Lee interview; "Cum Posey's Death Bring Many Sports Testimonials," *New York Amsterdam News*, April 6, 1946.

22. Neil Lanctot, *Rise and Ruin*, 386.

23. Chris Rainey, "Raymond Brown," Society for American Baseball Research Bioproject, http://sabr.org/bioproj/person/014355d1.

24. William Brashler, *Josh Gibson*, 146–147; Certificate of Death for Josh Gibson, January 20, 1947.

25. "Rufus Jackson, Grays' Owner, Dies," *New Jersey Afro-American*, March 12, 1949; Certificate of Death for Rufus Jackson, March 4, 1949; "Seward H. Posey, Homestead Grays Last Owner, Dies," *Pittsburgh Courier*, September 1, 1951; John L. Clark, "Wylie Avenue," *Pittsburgh Courier*, September 1, 1951; Certificate of Death for Seward Hays Posey, August 25, 1951.

26. Larry Lester, "Mine Eyes Have Seen the Glory of 'Only the Ball Was White' by Robert Peterson," The National Pastime Museum, https://www.thenationalpastimemuseum.com/article/mine-eyes-have-seen-glory-only-ball-was-white-robert-peterson.

27. "Guidelines for Nomination and Election into the Naismith Memorial Basketball Hall of Fame," Naismith Memorial Basketball Hall of Fame, http://www.hoophall.com/events/en shrinement/election-process.

28. John L. Clark, "Wylie Avenue," *Pittsburgh Courier*, April 6, 1946.

Bibliography

Books

Ashe, Arthur R., Jr. *A Hard Road to Glory: A History of the African-American Athlete 1919–1945, Vol. 2.* New York: Amistad, 1993.

Bankes, James. *The Pittsburgh Crawfords: The Lives & Times of Black Baseball's Most Exciting Team!* Dubuque, IA: William C. Brown, 1991.

Bodnar, John, Roger Simon, and Michael P. Weber. *Lives of Their Own: Blacks, Italians, and Poles in Pittsburgh, 1900–1960.* Urbana: University of Illinois Press, 1983.

Brashler, William. *Josh Gibson, a Life in the Negro Leagues.* Chicago: Ivan R. Dee, 2000.

Burgos, Adrian, Jr. *Cuban Star: How One Negro-League Owner Changed the Face of Baseball.* New York: Hill and Wang, 2011.

Cunningham, John T. *Newark.* Newark, NJ: New Jersey Historical Society, 1966.

Epstein, Abraham. *The Negro Migrant in Pittsburgh.* Pittsburgh: University of Pittsburgh School of Economics, 1918.

Fifteenth Census of the United States: 1930, Population, Volume III, Part 2. Washington, D.C.: Department of Commerce, 1932.

First Annual Edition—1890, Directory of Homestead, Munhall, Six Mile Ferry, and Adjacent Parts of Mifflin Township, Allegheny County, Pa. Pittsburgh: M.P. and J.R. Schooley, 1890.

Gershman, Michael. *Diamonds, the Evolution of the Ballpark.* Boston: Houghton Mifflin, 1993.

Glasco, Laurence A. "The Black Experience." In *City at the Point,* edited by Samuel P. Hays, 70. Pittsburgh: University of Pittsburgh Press, 1991.

_____. *The WPA History of the Negro in Pittsburgh.* Pittsburgh: University of Pittsburgh Press, 2004.

Goldman, Duke. "1933–1962, the Business Meetings of Negro League Baseball." In *Baseball's Business, the Winter Meetings, Volume 2,* edited by Steve Weingarden and Bill Nowlin.

Phoenix: Society for American Baseball Research, 2017.

Hoie, Bob. "The Minor Leagues." In *Total Baseball, Seventh Edition,* edited by John Thorn, Pete Palmer, and Michael Gershman, 497. Kingston, NY: Total Sports, 2001.

Holway, John. *Black Diamonds: Life in the Negro Leagues from the Men Who Lived It.* Westport, CT: Meckler, 1989.

_____. *Black Giants.* Springfield, VA: Lord Fairfax, 2010.

_____. *Voices from the Great Black Baseball Leagues.* New York: Da Capo, 1992.

Kuksa, Bob. *Hot Potato: How Washington and New York Gave Birth to Black Basketball and Changed America's Game Forever.* Charlottesville: University of Virginia Press, 2004.

Lanctot, Neil. *Negro League Baseball: The Rise and Ruin of a Black Institution.* Philadelphia: University of Pennsylvania Press, 2004.

Leonard, Buck, with James A. Riley. *Buck Leonard, the Black Lou Gehrig.* New York: Carroll & Graf, 1995.

Lowenfish, Lee. *Branch Rickey, Baseball's Ferocious Gentleman.* Lincoln: University of Nebraska Press, 2007.

Manley, Effa, and Leon Herbert Hardwick. *Negro Baseball ... Before Integration.* Haworth, NJ: St. Johann, 2006.

Miner, Curtis. *Homestead: The Story of a Steel Town.* Pittsburgh: Historical Society of Western Pennsylvania, 1989.

Newman, Roberta J., and Joel Nathan Rosen. *Black Baseball, Black Business: Race Enterprise and the Fate of the Segregated Dollar.* Jackson: University Press of Mississippi, 2014.

Ogden, David C. "Black Baseball at Forbes Field." In *Forbes Field: Essays and Memories of the Pirates' Historic Ballpark, 1909–1971,* edited by David Cicotello and Angelo J. Louisa, 62. Jefferson, NC: McFarland, 2007.

Ojobski, Robert. *Bush League: A History of*

Minor League Baseball. New York: Macmillan, 1975.

Overmyer, James E. *Black Ball and the Boardwalk: The Bacharach Giants of Atlantic City, 1916–1929.* Jefferson, NC: McFarland, 2014.

_____. *Queen of the Negro Leagues: Effa Manley and the Newark Eagles.* Lanham, MD: Scarecrow, 1998.

Pennsylvania Negro Business Directory. Harrisburg, PA: James H.W. Howard & Son, 1910.

Peterson, Robert W. *Cages to Jumpshots: Pro Basketball's Early Years.* New York: Oxford University Press, 1990.

Polk's Homestead City Directory, 1925. Pittsburgh: R. L. Polk, 1925.

Report on the Population of the United States at the Eleventh Census: 1890, Part I. Washington, D.C.: Department of the Interior, 1895.

Riley, James A. *Biographical Encyclopedia of the Negro Baseball Leagues.* New York: Carroll & Graf, 1994.

Ruck, Rob. *Raceball: How the Major Leagues Colonized the Black and Latin Game.* Boston: Beacon, 2011.

_____. *Sandlot Seasons: Sport in Black Pittsburgh.* Urbana: University of Illinois Press, 1987.

_____. *The Tropic of Baseball: Baseball in the Dominican Republic.* Lincoln: University of Nebraska Press, 1999.

Ruck, Rob, Maggie Jones Patterson, and Michael P. Weber. *Rooney: A Sporting Life.* Lincoln: University of Nebraska Press, 2010.

Serrin, William. *Homestead: The Glory and Tragedy of an American Steel Town.* New York: Random House, 1992.

Snyder, Brad. *Beyond the Shadow of the Senators.* New York: McGraw-Hill, 2003.

Spivey, Donald. *If You Were Only White: The Life of Leroy "Satchel" Paige.* Columbia: University of Missouri Press, 2012.

Stave, Bruce M. *The New Deal and the Last Hurrah: Pittsburgh Machine Politics.* Pittsburgh: University of Pittsburgh Press, 1970.

Tiemann, Robert L. "Major League Attendance." In *Total Baseball, Seventh Edition,* edited by John Thorn, Pete Palmer, and Michael Gershman, 76. Kingston, NY: Total Sports, 2001.

Trouppe, Quincy. *20 Years Too Soon.* Los Angeles: S&S Enterprises, 1977.

Winslow, Barbara. *Shirley Chisholm, Catalyst for Change, 1926–2005.* Boulder, CO: Westview, 2014.

Young, William A. *J. L. Wilkinson and the Kansas City Monarchs: Trailblazers in Black Baseball.* Jefferson, NC: McFarland, 2016.

Periodicals

Duquesne Monthly 23, no. 6 (March 1916).

Duquesne University Magazine 12, no. 2 (Winter 2014).

Ewell, Thomas C. "The Smoky City." *The Colored American,* December 1901.

Glasco, Laurence A. "Taking Care of Business: The Black Entrepreneurial Elite in Turn-of-the-Century Pittsburgh." *Pittsburgh History* 78, no. 4 (Winter 1995–96).

LaVie. University Park, PA, Pennsylvania State College (1911 and 1912).

NIKH, Howard University Yearbooks (1914).

Overmyer, James E. "Black Baseball at Yankee Stadium." *Black Ball: A Negro Leagues Journal* 7 (2014): 5–32.

"Pittsburg, Pa." *The Black Diamond* 24, no. 22 (June 2, 1900).

Posey, Cumberland. "Posey Picks Immortals." *Negro Baseball Pictorial Yearbook,* 1945.

Strecker, Geri. "The Rise and Fall of Greenlee Field: Biography of a Ballpark." *Black Ball: A Negro Leagues Journal* 2, no. 2 (Fall 2009): 37–67.

Web Content

Berger, Ralph. "Buck Leonard," Society for American Baseball Research Bioproject, http://sabr.org/bioproj/person/231446fd.

"Colored Basketball's World Champions, 1907–1925," Black Fives Foundation, https://www.blackfives.org/champions.

"Dominican Republic: The Trujillo Regime," Encyclopedia Britannica online, https://www.britannica.com/place/Dominican-Republic/Caudillos#ref726640.

"Guidelines for Nomination and Election into the Naismith Memorial Basketball Hall of Fame." Naismith Memorial Basketball Hall of Fame, http://www.hoophall.com/events/enshrinement/election-process.

"History of Ambridge," http://ambridgepa.gov office2.com/index.asp?Type=B_BASIC&SEC={BCB0E638-3DBD-4220-B2AC-F93A7A934590}.

Hulbert, Joanne. "Bobby Estalella." SABR Biography Project, Society for American Baseball Research, http://sabr.org/bioproj/person/488f6ebd.

Lester, Larry. "Mine Eyes Have Seen the Glory of 'Only the Ball Was White' by Robert Peterson." The National Pastime Museum. https://www.thenationalpastimemuseum.com/article/

mine-eyes-have-seen-glory-only-ball-was-white-robert-peterson.

Madarasz, Anne, "Sports History, the Early Days of Pittsburgh Basketball," Pittsburgh Sports Report (February 2006), http://www.pittsburgh sportsreport.com/2006-Issues/psr06020110.html.

Measuring Worth, https://measuringworth.com.

Negro Leagues Database. Seamheads.com, http://www.seamheads.com/NegroLgs/index.php.

Rainey, Chris. "Raymond Brown." SABR Biography Project, Society for American Baseball Research, http://sabr.org/bioproj/person/014355d1.

"Sellers McKee Hall," *Pittsburgh Music History,* https:// sites.google.com/site/pittsburghmusic history/Pittsburgh-music-story/managers-and-promoters/sellers-mckee-hall.

"Syndicate Baseball," Baseball-Reference.com, http://www.baseball-reference.com/bullpen/Syndicate_baseball.

Thorn, John. "The Color of Baseball." Our Game (blog), May 4, 2011, https://ourgame.mlblogs.com/the-color-of-baseball-2ebd78ffed0b.

Tucker, Helen A. "The Pittsburgh Survey: The Negroes of Pittsburgh, 1909." *Information Renaissance,* www.info-ren.org/projects/btul/exhibit/afamsur.html

Newspapers

Akron Beacon Journal
Altoona (PA) Mirror
Atlanta Daily World
Baltimore Afro-American
Canonsburg (PA) Daily Notes
Chicago Defender
Daily Worker
Homestead Daily Messenger
Monongahela (PA) Daily Republican
New Castle (PA) Herald
New Jersey Afro-American
New Jersey Herald News
New York Age
New York Amsterdam News
New York Times
Newark Evening News
Olean (NY) Times Herald
Philadelphia Tribune
Pittsburgh Courier
Pittsburgh Daily Post
Pittsburgh Post-Gazette
Pittsburgh Press
Pittsburgh Sun-Telegraph
Pittsburgh Weekly Gazette
The Sporting News
Uniontown (PA) Evening Standard
Warren (PA) Tribune

Archival Material

Allegheny County Department of Court Records, Pittsburgh, PA. Application for Marriage License:
    Lewis Sparkman Flagg III and Mary Elizabeth Posey Palmer, Pittsburgh, PA, December 8, 1947, accessed at https://Ancestry.com.
    Oliver C. Palmer and Mary E. Posey, Pittsburgh, PA, September 14, 1940, accessed at https://Ancestry.com.

Allegheny County Department of Court Records, Pittsburgh, PA. Will of C.W. Posey, with associated documents, filed in Allegheny County Register's Office July 15, 1925.

American League Baseball Club of New York records. National Baseball Hall of Fame and Library, Cooperstown, NY.

Commonwealth of Pennsylvania, Department of Health, death certificates:
    Ann Posey Harper, January 21, 1945, accessed at https://www.Ancestry.com.
    Rufus Jackson, March 4, 1949, accessed at https://www.Ancestry.com.
    Seward Hays Posey, August 25, 1951, accessed at https://www.Ancestry.com.
    Charles H. Walker, dated October 2, 1940, accessed at https://www.Ancestry.com.

Commonwealth of Pennsylvania, Department of State, Certificate of Incorporation for Homestead Grays Base Ball Club.

Commonwealth of Pennsylvania Veteran's Compensation applications:
    William Oscar Owens, accessed at https://www.Ancestry.com.
    Jasper Washington, accessed at https://www.Ancestry.com.

Hancock, Carole Wylie. Hancock, "Honorable Soldiers Too: An Historical Case Study of Post-Reconstruction African American Female Teachers of the Upper Ohio River Valley." PhD diss. Ohio University, 2008. https://etd.ohiolink.edu/rws_etd/document/get/ohiou1205717826/inline.

Manifest of Crew Members, SS *Fitzhugh Lee,* January 27, 1946, accessed at https://Ancestry.com.

Newark Eagles business papers. Newark Public Library, Newark, NJ.

New York City Marriage Indexes, 1907–1995. Marriage of John H. Boxill and Beatrice K. Posey, August 9, 1946, accessed at https://Ancestry.com.

"Twentieth Anniversary" booklet of the Loendi Club. 1917, Detre Library and Archives, Senator John Heinz History Center, Pittsburgh, PA.

United States Census:

1870 United States Census, for Winchester, VA, accessed at https://www.Ancestry.com.

1900 United States Census for Homestead, PA, accessed at https://www.Ancestry.com.

1930 United States Census for Homestead, PA, accessed at https://www.Ancestry.com.

1940 United States Census for Homestead, PA, accessed at https://www.Ancestry.com.

World War I draft registration cards:

Cumberland W. Posey, Jr., accessed at https://www.Ancestry.com.

Charles Walker, accessed at https://www.Ancestry.com.

Charles Henry Williams, accessed at https://www.Ancestry.com.

Interviews

Baker, Evan Posey, Jr., by author, June 15, 1995, Pittsburgh, PA.

Hoeritz, Dr. Kimberley J., University Registrar, Duquesne University, e-mail exchange with author, May 11 and July 21, 2016.

Jackson, Helen, by Rob Ruck, Archives and Manuscript Collections, University of Pittsburgh Library, Pittsburgh, PA.

Lee, Beatrice, by author, November 27, 1995, by telephone.

Leonard, Buck, by Robert Peterson, September 15, 1967, National Baseball Hall of Fame and Library, Cooperstown.

Manley, Effa, by William Marshall, 1977, Albert B. Chandler Papers, University of Kentucky, Lexington, KY.

Miller, Carol, supervisor, Transcripts & Certification, Office of the University Registrar, University of Pittsburgh, e-mail exchange with author, May 23, 2016.

Moody, Willis, by Rob Ruck, Archives and Manuscript Collections, University of Pittsburgh Library, Pittsburgh, PA.

Walker, Edsall, by author, July 11, 1990, Albany, NY.

Zyglowicz, Daniel, California University of Pennsylvania Archives & Special Collections, e-mail exchange with author, March 16, 2018.

Index